MACHADO DE ASSIS

G. Reginald Daniel

MACHADO DE ASSIS

Multiracial Identity and the
Brazilian Novelist

THE PENNSYLVANIA STATE UNIVERSITY PRESS
UNIVERSITY PARK, PENNSYLVANIA

Library of Congress Cataloging-in-Publication Data

Daniel, G. Reginald, 1949–
    Machado de Assis : multiracial identity and the Brazilian novelist / G. Reginald Daniel.
        p.   cm.
    Includes bibliographical references and index.
    Summary: "Examines how racial identity and race relations are expressed in the writings of Joaquim Maria Machado de Assis (1839–1908), Brazil's foremost author of the late nineteenth and early twentieth centuries"—Provided by publisher.
    ISBN 978-0-271-05246-5 (cloth : alk. paper)
    ISBN 978-0-271-05247-2 (pbk. : alk. paper)
    1. Machado de Assis, 1839–1908—Criticism and interpretation.
    2. Race in literature.
    3. Identity (Philosophical concept) in literature.
    I. Title.

PQ9697.M18Z594   2012
869.3'3—dc23
2011045316

Copyright © 2012
The Pennsylvania State University
All rights reserved
Printed in the United States of America
Published by
The Pennsylvania State University Press,
University Park, PA 16802–1003

The Pennsylvania State University Press
is a member of the Association of
American University Presses.

It is the policy of
The Pennsylvania State University Press
to use acid-free paper. Publications on uncoated
stock satisfy the minimum requirements of
American National Standard for Information
Sciences—Permanence of Paper for Printed
Library Material, ANSI Z39.48–1992.

For MY MOTHER

And he said...

"These are obsidian mirrors. Always look at yourself in an obsidian mirror because it is made of a single material. Don't look at yourself in ordinary mirrors because behind the glass there's a sheet of mercury. It's a duality."

And I said to him,

"The fundamental quality of a mirror is not to reflect but to be broken."

—ALEXANDRO JODOROSKY, *EL TOPO*

CONTENTS

Acknowledgments xi

Introduction: Machado de Assis: The Critical Legacy 1

ONE   Neither Black nor White: The Brazilian Racial Order 10

TWO   The Mulatto Author:
      The Literary Canon and the Racial Contract 34

THREE Black into White:
      Racial Identity and the Life of Machado de Assis 62

FOUR The Public Racial Text:
      Racial Identity and the Writings of the Unknown Machado 77

FIVE The Meta-Mulatto:
      Racial Identity and the Writings of Machado de Assis 101

SIX   The Hidden Racial Text:
      Racial Identity and the Writings of Machado de Assis 135

SEVEN Toward Literary Independence:
      National Identity and the Writings of Machado de Assis 153

EIGHT The Transformative Vision: Seeing with the Third Eye 190

NINE Machado de Assis: From Romantic Realism to Impressionism 211

      Epilogue: Machado de Assis: An Alternative Interpretation 238
      G. Reginald Daniel with Gary L. Haddow

Notes 255

References 267

Index 303

ACKNOWLEDGMENTS

Neither time nor space allows me to acknowledge the many individuals who helped bring this book to fruition. Nevertheless, I would like to express my deepest appreciation to Heitor Martins, Jon M. Tolman, Claude L. Hulet, Eduardo M. Dias, Maria P. P. Root, Teresa K. Williams-León, Paul R. Spickard, Ludwig (Larry) and Francis Lauerhass, E. Bradford Burns, Charles R. Boxer, and Emma Simonson for their guidance, interest, and above all, moral support. Jennie Marlow and Spotted Eagle always helped me maintain faith in the manuscript.

This manuscript would not have been possible without the stellar editorial assistance provided by Josef Castañeda-Liles, Christopher Bickel, Gary L. Haddow, and Brianne Dávila. Paulo de Luz Moreira and José Garcia are outstanding research assistants, who helped track down material in the United States and Brazil. David Foster provided most constructive and supportive feedback. I owe special thanks to Jeffrey H. Lockridge for his painstaking and nuanced copyediting. As always, David Estrin helped me tighten the manuscript without sacrificing my ideas. Jennifer Burton of Columbia Indexing Group is a miracle worker when it comes to compiling an index. I would also like to express my appreciation for the assistance provided by Vera de Araujo-Shellard and Sandra Soares of Susan Bach Books from Brazil, the directors and staffs of the Biblioteca Nacional, Academia Brasileira de Letras, Universidade Federal, and Pontifícia Universidade Católica, all in Rio de Janeiro, and the Lily Library at Indiana University in Bloomington. Miki Goral and Norma Corral, who were the backbone of the University of California, Los Angeles (UCLA), Research Library Reference Department when I conducted preliminary research for *Machado de Assis*, helped me acquire several critical sources. I am also indebted to Grafikart Copy Shop, particularly Sean Kim and David Miller, for technical support, as well as Kelly Johnson for her patience in helping to complete this project.

My thanks to the Fulbright-Hays Commission for a grant to do research in Brazil, and the University of California, Santa Barbara (UCSB), for awarding me an Academic Senate grant and an Institute for Social, Behavioral, and Economic Research Humanistic Social Science Research Grant to do archival research in the United States, as well as a Faculty Career Development Award for release time from teaching to devote time to completing the manuscript. However, completion of this project would not have been possible without a generous grant from the K&F Baxter Family Foundation.

Finally, I owe a special debt to my colleagues and the staff in the Center for African American Studies and the Latin American Center at UCLA, as well as the Center for Black Studies Research and Department of Sociology at UCSB. A special thanks to Paulette Haban, Jeremy Busacca, Kum-Kum Bhavnani, John Foran, and Roger Friedland, who provided me with shelter and transportation during my "migrant faculty" days. Others contributed directly or indirectly to this project. I think of Thomas E. Skidmore, F. James Davis, Francis (Frank) A. Dutra, Gary B. Nash, Connie McNeely, Sheila Gardette, Afrânio Coutinho, Carlos Quicoli, Emil Snyder, Miguel Enguídanos, Francisco de Assis Barbosa, Edilberto Coutinho, Antonio Torres, Helen Caldwell, Moacir C. and Edgarda Lopes, Dirce Côrtes Riedel, Antonio Callado, Affonso Romano de Sant'anna, Alencar Guimarães, Russell G. Hamilton, Stanley R. Bailey, Luiz Costa Lima, Ilza Viegas, Richard A. Preto-Rodas, Ioni de Andrade, Luis Dávila, John Dyson, Jeffrey D. Needell, Thales de Azevedo, Andetrie Smith, Allan Englekirk, David N. Sadowitz, Pieter David Miller, Marisa Williams, Deborah Forczek, Kip Fulbeck, William (Bill) P. Rougles, William (Bill) Perry, Lucinda Newsome, Manuel Ferreira, Ricardo M. and Judy Paiva, Socorro Castañeda-Liles, Gladys and Ivan Garcia-Lopez, Xuan Santos, Nicki Lisa Cole, Nicholas (Nick) Hall, Zackary and Sarah Markwith, Rebecca Romo, Anthony and Jennie Francoso, Victoria Bearden, Patrick Lopez-Aguado, Melissa Guzman, Cheryl Whitmore, Tara Atherly, Jan R. Weisman, Nancy and Roosevelt Brown, Ramona Douglass, Nina Gordon, Trica Keaton, Jeri Williams and Patrick Polk, Marzia Milazzo, Jessie Turner, Kendra R. Wallace, Michael and René Dennis, Carroll B. Johnson, Linda Hall, Shirley L. Arora, Patrick B. Miller, Lorena Garcia, Lisa Torres, Julio Cesar Monteiro Martins, Pilar O'Cadiz, Rebecca Lachter, José Maria and Maria Luisa de Almeida, Elisabeth Schäfer-Wünsche, Phyllis R. Klotman, Laurie Alper, Jennifer Creed, Kelly Bond, Wallace Pate, Tyler Fryerson, Michelle Martinez, Clay and Sujata Landon, Eudora Loh, George O. Feldman, William (Bill) Wood, Neda Maghbouleh, Clayton Childress, Bryce and Leanne Little, Eamon Buehning, Jennifer Gong, Nina Moss, Victor Pereira da Rosa, Beatrice, Gida, Dirce, Gracinha, and Severa, the Hubers (Dona Maria, Valburga, and Teresa), Abdias do Nascimento, Lélia González, Katie E. Ostrander, Gerardo Luzuriaga, Randal Johnson, Teresinha Castilhos, James N. Green, David Brunsma, Kerry Ann Rockquemore, Lori Pierce, Phyllis

Sladick, Hettie V. Williams, Ingrid Dineen-Wimberly, Jeannie and Daniel Palmer, Carlos A. Torres, Thomas Lopez, Laura (Laurie) Lewis, John Burdick, Shepard Forman, George E. Brooks, J. Michael Turner, Steven and Julia Riley, Fanshen Cox, Heidi Durrow, Aurelia Brooks, Edward E. Telles, Geoffrey Blum, Norris C. Hundley, David E. Lopez, Tracy Grayson, Laura Kina, Wei Ming Dariotis, Johanna Workman, Nicole Asong Nfonoyim, John (Jack) Loehr, Martin Jacinto, Alyssa Newman, Carolyn Piñedo-Turnovsky and Geoffrey Turnovsky, Bianca Brigidi, Hani Jalil, Anil Mukerjee, Blayke Barker, Jorge Dominguez, Miguel Becerra, César (Ché) Rodríguez, Levonne Gaddy, Lyman Johnson, Nancy Brown, Jorge González, Marina Pianca, Maria N. Villaseñor, Daniel L. Bennett, Charles (Charley) Driskell, Carmen Lopez, Mary Britton and Christopher Karczmar, Andrew Michael Lee, Jerry Flores, Phillip Handy, Nicole Pérez, Jennifer Nobles, Farzana Nayani, Joyce Higa, Donna Perkins, Paula Moore, Greg Tanaka, Lily Y. Welty, Angel Valdivia, Rafael Julio Corvera Hernández, and Victoria (Vika) Stansky.

I am eternally grateful to Nadia Kim, Julie Silvers, Shadi Alai, and the many other students in my classes who have had faith in my vision and me when others have not.

Sandy Thatcher, former director, and Kendra Boileau, current editor-in-chief, of Pennsylvania State University Press are exemplary editors. I am grateful to them and the readers recruited by the Press. In addition, there are many unnamed friends, colleagues, and relatives whose support contributed to making this a better book.

Finally, for decades, the life and writings of Machado de Assis have been a source of inspiration that has made the conceivable become achievable.

Santa Barbara, California
February 2011

Introduction

MACHADO DE ASSIS: THE CRITICAL LEGACY

On December 2, 1955, my first-grade teacher began class by saying, "Yesterday, in Montgomery, Alabama, a colored woman, Mrs. Rosa Parks, was arrested for refusing to let a white passenger have her seat on the bus. It's time we colored people stood up for our rights!" The question of "rights" went over my head, and I was especially confused by the phrase "we colored people." I knew that everyone was "colored." Some people were brown. Others were pink (which I knew to be a blend of red and white), beige, or tan (which were blends of varying degrees of brown and white). I remember how excited I was that year when Crayola came out with a box of crayons that included pink, beige, tan, and so on, although I was somewhat perplexed by the flesh crayon. It was similar to tan, but I knew that everyone was not "flesh"-colored. Nevertheless, I was happy to see my own tan color among the crayons. Up to that time, crayon boxes included only the basic colors. I could not get pink, beige, or tan, except when I did watercolors and had access to white paint to blend with red or brown. Just to get a clarification, I raised my hand and asked who "colored" people were. "Everyone in this school!" she said, startled. "What color are they?" I asked. "We're brown! We're Negroes!" I had seen brown people. (In fact, there were many at my school.) I also knew that my own tan-colored skin tone was part brown. However, I had never heard of the color

"Negro" before, much less come across it among my crayons or paints. This whole discussion left me confused.

At the end of class, my teacher gave me a note to take home to my mother instructing her to have a long talk with me about being Negro and about segregation. (Many years later, my mother told me that she had avoided this topic because she did not want me to develop a sense of inferiority. She now tried to explain the absurdity of segregated schools, water fountains, public parks, theaters, restaurants, hospitals, funeral homes, cemeteries, and so on.) She agreed that our family was "tan," rather than "brown." (There were some pink and beige family members, however, who I later discovered were not pink or beige at all but looked "white." I had never seen anyone the color of the white crayon, or blackboard chalk.) My mother went on to explain how we came to be "tan" Negroes, throwing in details about African slavery, about our European, Native American, and Asian Indian ancestry. She concluded by saying that although we were a blend of many things and, thus, only part Negro, we were still members of the Negro race, in other words, "colored people." This struck me as being somewhat illogical, so I said, "But Mommy, when you mix brown and white, you don't get brown or white, you get tan." She told me it was not the same with people. Outwardly, I acquiesced but could not understand how I could have African, Asian Indian, Native American, and European ancestry and still be only Negro. How could you take one part of my whole background, the African part, and then get rid of all the rest? "That's stupid," I thought. "That doesn't make any sense. One plus one equals two, not one."

I shelved this issue until 1965, when I stumbled upon Era Bell Thompson's *Ebony* magazine article "Does Amalgamation Work in Brazil?" I learned that Brazil had earned the reputation as a racial democracy by virtue of its absence of legalized barriers to equality in both the public and private spheres. What caught my attention was a passage that spoke of mysterious creatures called "mulattoes."[1] They were a racial blend of Africans, Europeans—primarily Portuguese—and Native Americans and were intermediate to these groups. "Just like me!" I thought. "Just like Tabitha on *Bewitched* . . . Like Mr. Spock on *Star Trek*!"

From that point on, the classroom became not merely an academic arena but also a platform for self-discovery, transformation, and personal liberation, albeit most often under the mocking and disapproving scrutiny of my peers and superiors. I wanted to understand why multiracial individuals of partial African descent were able to identify with their other backgrounds in Brazil but were prohibited from doing this in the United States. I discovered part of an answer in a social code called the "one-drop rule of hypodescent," which held that the offspring of interracial unions were defined as "African American," regardless of the racial background of their other parent. In addition, not only the children of interracial unions but, in fact, anyone who had any traceable African descent, anyone with "one drop of African blood," was designated as "black." Thus the one-drop rule supported a binary racial order that rendered racial identification as either black or white.

The dominant European Americans used the one-drop rule to justify legal prohibitions against interracial intimacy, and especially against interracial marriage, in order to preserve white racial and cultural "purity." The rule also conveniently exempted white landowners (particularly slaveholders) from the legal obligation of passing on inheritance and other benefits of paternity to their multiracial offspring. Moreover, the rule helped maintain white racial privilege by supporting legal and informal barriers to equality in most aspects of public and private life. At the turn of the twentieth century, these restrictions reached drastic proportions with the institutionalization of Jim Crow segregation. The one-drop rule did not become a normative part of the legal apparatus in the United States until the early twentieth century (circa 1915). However, it gained currency as the informal or "racial commonsense" (Omi and Winant 1994, 60) definition of "blackness" over the course of the seventeenth and eighteenth centuries. This was increasingly the case during the nineteenth century and definitively so by the 1920s.

The one-drop rule is such a normative part of Anglo–North America that most individuals are unaware that it is unique to the United States. Rules of hypodescent have been applied to the first-generation offspring of European Americans and Americans of color (e.g., Native Americans, Asian Americans, Latinas/os, and so on). Successive generations of individuals whose lineage includes a background of color, along with European ancestry, however, have been treated with greater flexibility. These individuals have not always been designated exclusively, or even partially, as members of that group of color. Furthermore, self-identification with that background has been more a matter of choice. This flexibility has not been extended to individuals of African American and European American descent. The one-drop rule has not only precluded any choice in self-identification but also ensured that African American ancestry is passed on in perpetuity. All future offspring are designated as "black." Most individuals in the United States never question the rule's logic, and thus reinforce, if only unwittingly, blackness and whiteness as dichotomous, if not hierarchical, categories of experience.[2]

Through my research in Brazil and the United States, I found that racial formation in both nations evolved as part of European colonial expansion and domination in the sixteenth century. Thus blackness and whiteness came to represent the negative and positive designations, respectively, in a hierarchy originating in African and European racial and cultural differences. Yet race relations in Brazil and the rest of Latin America display a more attenuated dichotomization of blackness and whiteness and more fluid racial markers compared to the U.S. binary racial order. This is reflected in the region's history of pervasive miscegenation and the validation of this blending by the implementation of a ternary racial order, which differentiates the population into whites (*brancos*), multiracials (*pardos* in official contexts; *mulatos* in everyday parlance), and blacks (*pretos*). Moreover, blackness and whiteness are merely extremes on a continuum where physical appearance (*marca*), in conjunction with class and culture, rather than ancestry (*origem*; Nogueira 1954/1985, 78–79), determine one's racial status and identity in the social hierarchy. This in turn has given rise to the belief that Brazil is a racial democracy.

I also found Joaquim Maria Machado de Assis (1839–1908)—Brazil's foremost author of the late nineteenth and the early twentieth centuries—to be an exemplary case study of Brazilian race relations. Indeed, there is no more fertile topic of controversy in Brazilian letters than the life and writings of Machado de Assis; and perhaps no subject has been as controversial as the question of race. Historically, Brazilians who have supported their country's more fluid racial order, as well as a more inclusive definition of whiteness, have considered Machado branco. Many individuals have referred to Machado as "mulato"; others have regarded him as *mestiço* (multiracial), which they consider a less pejorative term. Still others have emphasized that Machado was *negro* (i.e., African Brazilian) or, more recently, *afro-descendente* (African-descended). Their goal is to challenge Brazil's ternary racial dynamics, which they consider an obstacle to mobilizing blacks and mulattoes in the antiracist struggle. And, for all that, some have ceased to refer to Machado's racial status and identity altogether.

Early criticism nurtured the belief that Machado's life and writings betray his racial self-negation, his indifference to the plight of African Brazilians and the cause of abolition. During the first half of the twentieth century, critics were influenced by, and in no small part helped nurture, this tradition of "socially determined" criticism. Critics searched for biographical details in Machado's writings and, conversely, used the limited existing biographical material as a means of explaining his writings. Yet the negligible autobiographical information complicates any discussion of Machado's feelings about his racial identity, views, or both on the topics of slavery and race relations (see Romero 1897; Santos 1908; Pujol 1934; Pontes 1939; Pereira 1936; Meyer 1935; Grieco 1960).

By the 1950s, a new generation of critics challenged the findings of these earlier studies. Through the discovery of previously unknown biographical data, they disputed the belief that both of Machado's parents were mulattoes. This research proved that it was only Machado's father who was mulatto; his mother was Portuguese and from the Azores. They also put to rest the notion that Machado abandoned his mulatto stepmother (his father's second wife) when he gained literary and social prominence (see Fonseca 1968; Massa 1969, vol. 1). Through a more thorough examination of Machado's writings, other scholars found that he did explore the question of slavery and racism. Unfortunately, some of these studies make Machado appear more comfortable with his racial background and more politically active in the African Brazilian struggle than actually seems to be the case (see Coutinho 1940; Sayers 1958; Broca 1957; Magalhães Júnior 1955, 1958a, 1958b; Oliveira 1958; Pereira 1959). Other analyses in the 1970s examined social stratification in Machado's writings, as well as the economic basis and social consequences of liberalism and paternalism in late nineteenth-century Brazil as reflected in social relationships in the earlier novels (see Chaves 1974; Schwarz 1977, 1990; Faoro 1976).

Beginning in the 1940s, many critics turned their attention to the long-overdue analysis of Machado's literary aesthetic, including his relationship with European literature, particularly nineteenth-century literary currents (specifically Romanticism and Realism-Naturalism). The critics also examined Machado's pessimism, irony, and skepticism, as well as the "two phases" of his writing, in which the earlier novels are classified as "Romantic" and the later novels as "Realist" (see Barreto Filho 1947; Gomes 1958, 1967, 1979; Coutinho 1966; Corção 1965; Castello 1969; Riedel 1959; Caldwell 1960, 1970). These studies include several linguistic analyses (see Câmara 1962; Soares 1968; Monteiro and Estrella 1973). This "aesthetically determined" criticism was consolidated in the 1970s and expanded rapidly in the 1980s and 1990s with nuanced analyses of narratology and characterization in Machado's writings, particularly his later novels (*Posthumous Memoirs of Brás Cubas, Quincas Borba, Dom Casmurro, Esau and Jacob,* and *Ayres's Memorial*).[3]

Alongside this aesthetically determined criticism, scholars have continued to provide socially inflected analyses of Machado's writings. These include examinations of the relationships between patrons and their *agregados* (free clients or dependents) and *afilhados* (adopted kin) within the contemporary social order.

There have been analyses of gender relations as well as the impact that literacy rates had on the composition of Machado's reading public and literary aesthetic (see Stein 1984; Xavier 1986; Lisboa 1996, 1997; Pietrani 2000). The topic of race has been the subject of several separate studies and part of larger discussions on slavery.[4]

In the chapters that follow, building on the socially and aesthetically determined traditions of Machadian criticism, I analyze Machado's writings—particularly his novels—as they relate to the cultural processes of race relations. I examine these phenomena as part of racial formation as outlined by Michael Omi and Howard Winant (1994). Racial formation theory considers race a social construct while acknowledging that the construct is based on biological characteristics. Yet the selection of particular human features for purposes of racial signification has changed over time and is necessarily a sociohistorical process. Racial formation theory makes it possible to analyze how a society determines racial meanings and assigns racial identities in the racial order—the combination of ideological beliefs, institutions, and social practices that establishes a given society's racial categories, group boundaries, and membership.

More important, the state plays a crucial role in maintaining the racial order. It has exercised power not only in enforcing racial definition, classification, and, ultimately, identification but also in the politics of both racial exclusion and inclusion. The racial order thus has a significant impact on the distribution of resources, wealth, power, privilege, and prestige, which in turn determines groups' social location and status in relation to one another. That said, at any given spatiotemporal juncture, many interpretations of race exist in the form of "racial projects." Every racial project is a discursive or cultural initiative that seeks to represent or explain racial dynamics by means of identity politics. At the same time, each racial project is a political initiative that seeks to organize and redistribute resources, a process in which the state is often called upon to play a role (Omi and Winant 1994, 55–60).

My analysis draws from scholarship in Latin American Cultural Studies, which interrogates the distinction between culture, political economy, and history, as well as reevaluates forms of culture often deemed unworthy of academic investigation. Although informed by British and U.S. Cultural Studies that emerged in the 1970s, Latin American Cultural Studies as consolidated in the 1980s and 1990s has formulated a perspective originating in developing nations. It not only builds on cultural analyses informed by Latin American intellectuals but also frames Latin America's complex interactions with the West. This provides the context for reexamining Cultural Studies analyses, particularly the concepts of hegemony, postcoloniality, and hybridity (García Canclini 2003, 12–23; Hart and Young 2003, 1–11; Lund 2006, ix–64; Santiago 2000, 9–26; Trigo 2004, 1–14).

Chapter 1 analyzes racial formation and nation making as these relate to questions of multiraciality and the social location of mulattoes in colonial and nineteenth-century Brazil. Chapters 2, 3, and 4 situate Machado's life and writings within the mulatto experience and African Brazilian literary culture by examining biographical data and reviewing various sociological considerations relevant to the cultural processes of race relations and the literary trajectories that have emerged among mulatto authors.

Chapter 5 reconsiders the argument that Machado's literary works are a meticulously veiled documentation of his experiences as a mulatto, which he might otherwise have discussed openly in his writings had the historical and social circumstances been different (e.g., Gledson 1984; Haberly 1983). By veiling his observations, so the argument goes, Machado could avoid tarnishing the career that served as a vehicle for escaping blackness; this literary tactic helped touch up his "real" racial status as a mulatto by furthering his situational status as white.

However, an examination of statements made by Machado and an analysis of his writings give rise to the following questions. To what extent does the apparent lack of racial consciousness in Machado's life and writings actually reflect a *denial* of being a mulatto? To what extent might this phenomenon reflect a desire to *transcend* racial ascription altogether and achieve a sense of "racelessness"? Is it possible that Machado was seeking to go beyond the physical limitations of being mulatto and embrace an identity and a literary aesthetic based on a more inclusive or universal self, beyond questions of racial, cultural, or any other specificity? As a mulatto who was both black and white, yet neither, was Machado seeking to grapple with universal questions of duality and ambiguity of human existence—miscegenation in a higher sense?

In 1981, I sought to answer some of these questions and coined the term "meta-mulatto" to frame my analysis in a paper I presented at the Fourth Symposium on Portuguese Traditions, University of California, Los Angeles.[5] David Haberly made similar arguments in his insightful *Three Sad Races: Racial Identity and National Consciousness in Brazilian Literature* (Haberly 1983, 74–77; see also Daniel 1981, 10, 11–13). However, my interpretation differs somewhat from Haberly's. I contend that Machado veiled his mulatto experience in metaphor not simply as a type of camouflage and evasion because of any discomfort he might have felt about expressing that experience in his writings, but in an effort to *unveil* the basis of societal dis-ease, which he attributed to humanity's own metaphorically mulatto nature—particularly the dual and ambiguous relationship between the subjective and objective dimensions of human experience.

On the other hand, I concur with Haberly's argument that a key site where Machado examines societal dis-ease is the conflict between individual morality (or conscience) and the dictates of public success premised on egoism, ambition, and acquisitive, property-based individualism—a conflict perpetuated by Western consciousness and behavior due to the materialist rationalism that became preeminent with modernity. Indeed, material considerations have more often than not overpowered the desire for and ability to achieve loving relationships.

That said, considering the racial ecology of his time, it would not be surprising if Machado felt sensitive about his racial background and projecting his experience as a mulatto in his writings. Indeed, in chapter 6, I maintain that Machado's use of irony, parody, and the grotesque, which reflects his humor, is part of a hidden racial text (or subtext). One of the sources of this subtext is Machado's confrontation with racist pressure and with Eurocentric standards that rewarded whiteness and restricted, if not negated, blackness in literature as well as in society. The hidden racial humor in this subtext had two functions. Psychologically speaking, it allowed Machado to distance himself from the traumas of living in a racist society. Sociologically speaking, it allowed him to launch an oblique attack on a supposedly virtuous society that depended on slavery and racial oppression for its survival. I maintain that elucidating the relationship between Machado's critique and the African Brazilian struggle is at least as important as recognizing Africanisms, linguistic signs, thematic indicators, and the subaltern tone in more politically engaged Brazilian literature.

In fact, Machado cautioned against writing polemical and politically engaged literature, which risked falling prey both to the myopia and tendentiousness of propaganda in literary disguise and to the dangers of literary mortality, unless authors brought greater universality to the particularistic social or historical context of their writings. I assert that, apart from concerns he might have had about his racial background or jeopardizing his social and professional standing, this aesthetic prompted Machado to avoid explicit discussions of race (except in some of his short stories, chronicles, and a few passages in his novels). And when he did explore racial and other social issues, his understanding was farsighted and universal enough to convey more than their immediate implications (Nunes 1983, x).

Chapter 7 discusses race, nation, and the formation of Brazilian literary identity. In it, I maintain that Machado's same search for the universal explains the lack of national consciousness or Brazilianness (*brasilidade*) in his writings, a consciousness expressed through racial types, external descriptions of local flora and fauna, and certain idioms in the writings of some of his contemporaries and successors. Machado went beneath the Brazilian epidermis to capture what he considered the "national instinct" that linked the Brazilian psyche with all humanity—a psychological world emerging from the geography and mores of Rio de Janeiro and Brazil but existing outside space and time.

In chapters 8 and 9, I reevaluate the tendency to classify Machado's earlier novels as "Romantic" and his later novels as "Realist." Instead, in light of Machado's own statements, I argue that his novels represent a growing sophistication and daring in maintaining a dialogue between the aesthetic subjectivism of Romanticism (and its offshoots) and the aesthetic objectivism of Realism-Naturalism. Accordingly, Machado's earlier novels have more in common with a hybrid mid-nineteenth-century current often referred to as "Romantic Realism." In addition, his later novels have more in common with another late nineteenth-century and early twentieth-century hybrid: literary Impressionism.

Providing a cultural analysis of Romantic Realism and Impressionism, I examine specific aspects of Machado's novels—narrative structure, narrative point of view, characterization—that demonstrate his affinity with these currents. Without constituting a formal or well-defined school, and apart from whether they directly influenced the writings of Machado, Romantic Realist and Impressionist authors were kindred spirits who sought to bridge the subjectivist aesthetics of Romanticism (and similar trends) with the objectivist aesthetics of Realism-Naturalism. In their historically and stylistically different trajectories, Romantic Realist and Impressionist authors nevertheless metaphorically shared in the mulatto phenomenon.

In sum, I believe that Machado's experience of being *both* black and white, yet *neither*, provided him with a keen sensitivity to the liminal space that shapes that experience. In the epilogue, I maintain that his experience of liminality enhanced Machado's ability to convey shades of meaning when discussing issues ranging from slavery to national literature, literary aesthetics, and modernity. Given Machado's location in the late nineteenth and the early twentieth centuries, I maintain that this "both/neither" perspective displays an affinity with the "postmodern sensibility."

ONE

NEITHER BLACK NOR WHITE: THE BRAZILIAN RACIAL ORDER

Racial Formation in Colonial Brazil: Multiraciality and the Ternary Racial Order

Brazil's allegedly more equitable ternary racial order, popularized by Gilberto Freyre in *The Masters and the Slaves* (1933), *The Mansions and the Shanties* (1936), and *Order and Progress* (1959), was attributed to exceptional racial altruism on the part of the Portuguese colonizers. In reality, attitudes toward miscegenation and the social differentiation of multiracial individuals from whites and blacks were primarily motivated by self-interest. They were influenced less by the national and cultural origins of the colonizing Europeans than by social conditions that prevailed in the Americas, particularly the ratios of European men to women and whites to blacks (Cox 1970, 351–76; Degler 1971, 213–38; Harris 1964, 54–64, 79–94).

In Brazil, particularly in the slaveholding coastal lowlands, the early colonizing Europeans were mostly single adult males, whether bachelors, widowers, or married men who arrived without their wives (Cox 1970, 351–76; Degler 1971, 213–38). Exceptions to this pattern were Brazil's southern provinces of Santa Catarina and Rio Grande do Sul, to which the Portuguese Crown organized the immigration of families, and where family enterprises based on small holdings and involved in food production prevailed over slave labor and plantation agriculture for the export market (Degler 1971, 230; Prado Júnior 1969, 95–96). The shortage of single European women in Brazil at the time of colonization in the early 1500s was exacerbated by two factors: the few settlers Portugal was able to send (e.g., only 400 in 1531; Coon 1965, 70–72) included virtually no unmarried women; and the Crown restricted immigration from other parts of Europe. Brazil's intractable tropical environment and the hostility of its Native Americans to Portuguese settlement held scant appeal for immigrants, especially when compared to the riches of "civilized" India. Thus, even after making some 200 crimes punishable by exile to Brazil, the Crown found it difficult to get anyone to settle there (Coon 1965, 70–72; Schwartz 1987a, 21).

Although there are no reliable national data on Brazil's racial composition prior to 1872, the number of whites remained small throughout the colonial period. As late as the seventeenth century, whites, predominantly European by birth, represented about one-third of the population. In 1798, estimates indicate that whites numbered 1 million, slaves 1.5 million, free coloreds 225,000, and "pacified" Native Americans 250,000 out of a population of almost 3 million (Alden 1963, 173–205; Burns 1970, 103; Marcílio 1984, 37–63). African slaves were the primary source of labor and constituted a large portion, if not a majority, of the population in the coastal lowlands. In some areas, slaves outnumbered Europeans by 15 to 1. In many urban centers, almost half of the colonial population had some degree of African ancestry (Burdick 1992, 37, 40–42).

Africans supplemented or replaced the Native American labor force, slave or otherwise, which dwindled due to overwork, physical abuse, Old World diseases, and the cloistered life of the missions. Being less familiar with the terrain than Native Americans, Africans found it harder to escape from slavery into the interior; with their greater immunity to European diseases, they were thus a more reliable source of labor.

Miscegenation and the Foundation of the Racial Order

The preponderance of Africans in Brazil's slaveholding coastal lowlands, in conjunction with the shortage of European women, gave rise to permissive attitudes toward miscegenation between white men and women of African descent, as it had with attitudes toward liaisons with Native American women. Yet this phenomenon historically originated in relationships that were largely consummated more through coercion and violence, as in rape, fleeting extramarital relations, and extended concubinage, than through mutual consent and peaceful means. Whether interracial intimacy involved coercion or mutual consent, Portuguese civil and ecclesiastical authorities condemned miscegenation during most of the colonial period (Furtado 2008, 65–68; Russell-Wood 1982, 30).

Marriage codes mandated by the Church insisted on the racial and class equality of marriage partners. Relationships between social unequals were necessarily restricted to concubinage or consensual unions. The Church frowned upon concubinage but required supporting evidence, typically through the testimony of witnesses, before pressing charges. Many accusations of concubinage were unsubstantiated. Moreover, some argue that the Church only prosecuted cases in which the relationship was so open that it was viewed as scandalous. Yet, once such accusations were proven, the ecclesiastical judge admonished the guilty partners. According to Muriel Nazzari, they were given absolution when they repented, promised not to repeat the sin, and performed a penance or paid a fine. If, after three admonitions, the couple continued in sin, the ecclesiastical prosecutor could sentence them to an even greater fine or to prison, exile, or excommunication. Given the pervasiveness of these relationships, as compared to extant records of involving accusations, prosecutions, or convictions, one can conclude that the Church turned a blind eye to the majority of individuals actually involved in concubinage. Consequently, miscegenation continued unabated (Furtado 2008, 65–68; Nazzari 1996, 108–24; Russell-Wood 1982, 173).

In 1726, the Crown attempted to halt interracial intimacy by ruling that only whites—husbands or widowers of white women—should be eligible to hold posts on Municipal Councils in Brazil. The implicit rationale was to encourage white men to marry only white women and to have children by them rather than by black or mulatto concubines (Nazzari 1996, 109; Russell-Wood 1982, 31, 71, 173). Yet, whereas interracial marriages in the southern and some northern colonies in Anglo–North America were socially proscribed and highly stigmatized where they were not legally prohibited, in colonial Brazil, the interracial family was informally legitimized, notwithstanding the legal barriers to interracial marriage. This was due to the fact that few Portuguese women immigrated to Brazil, which limited opportunities for the perpetuation of the European Brazilian. In practice, common-law unions of some duration involving European men and women of color produced "legitimate" offspring alongside more widespread clandestine and fleeting liaisons involving births out of wedlock. These common-law unions became the norm and were more or less approved, if not encouraged, by the unwritten moral code (Degler 1971, 213–38; Harris 1964, 54–64, 79–94). Moreover, the considerable financial expenditure involved in contracting legal marriages was a significant disincentive for individuals across the racial spectrum (Nazzari 1996, 110).[1] Consequently, seventeenth-century Portuguese law recognized "common law" marriage and this was just one of the "virtually every kind of union" approved in order to increase the population (Pierson 1942/1967, 113).

In fact, legislation was implemented from 1755 to 1758 during the reign of Dom José I (1750–77) and masterminded by Portugal's Prime Minister Sebastião José de Carvalho e Melo (1699–1782), the first Marquês de Pombal, both to increase the frontier population and to assimilate the indigenous inhabitants. These laws emancipated the indigenous population from slavery and encouraged marriages of whites with Native Americans and *mamelucos* (multiracial individuals of European and Native American descent);[2] they also sought to eliminate the stigma attached to offspring of such interracial marriages, promising them preferential treatment in the allocation of royal favors and social equality in their eligibility for "any employment, honor or dignity" (Hemming 1987, 1–2). Whites had historically been willing to circumvent laws and define less rigorously the interstices distinguishing mamelucos from free mulattoes where it served their interests. Yet there were probably few whites in colonial Brazil who were not themselves actually mamelucos. Official policy and social convention more often than not treated mamelucos as whites, whereas all African Brazilians were considered inferior beings (Mattoso 1986, 193, 195, 203–4; Morse 1974, 10; Poppino 1961, 55–58; Russell-Wood 1972, 93).

Consequently, the Pombaline reforms were not matched by royal decrees favoring emancipation of African Brazilian slaves.[3] More important, marriages between whites and individuals of African descent were excluded from these provisions (Russell-Wood 1972, 93, 109). These unfavorable circumstances in terms of African Brazilians were in decline by the early nineteenth century, and had ended by the time of Brazil's independence from Portugal in 1822 (Degler 1971, 213–38). Although interracial marriages continued to be stigmatized (Degler 1971, 213, 214, 226–38; Karasch 1975, 375), informal relationships between European Brazilian males of all social classes and women of color were widespread. Whereas more than a few European Brazilians from the petty bourgeoisie and proletarian sectors (particularly recent European immigrants) married individuals of color, intermarriages between European Brazilians of the capitalist class—the bourgeoisie proper—and African Brazilians were far less common. There was also formidable social prejudice against even informal unions between white women and African Brazilian men, whether black or mulatto (Degler 1971, 213, 214, 226–38; Karasch 1975, 375).

During the colonial period, most multiracial individuals were mamelucos. When Native Americans began to die by the thousands, colonists increasingly imported African slaves. And when, after 1600, the transition to African labor was complete in most regions, there was a significant increase in the numbers of multiracial individuals of African and European, or African, European, and Native American descent (*mulatos*)—and to a lesser extent, individuals of African and Native American descent (*cafusos*) whose parents' racial groups had limited intimate and lasting contact after the early phase of colonization and slavery. Exceptions to this trend were the *quilombo* settlements of runaway slaves scattered throughout the interior, where unions (especially in the Northeast) between African men and Native American women were facilitated by the shortage of African women (Lockhart and Schwartz 1987, 197–200; Prado Júnior 1969, 121–22).

As slaves, multiracial individuals worked in the sugar and coffee plantations, the gold mines, and urban centers alongside enslaved blacks. But the artisans and domestics among them were often assigned prestigious and exacting tasks that were less physically demanding, required greater skill, and symbolized greater personal worth. Some of these tasks also gave them more intimate exposure to, and greater knowledge of, the sociocultural values of the dominant whites. Mulatto offspring of white masters and slave concubines were frequently reared in the master's house, where many learned to read and write. Some concubines thus benefited from these relationships, as did their children, notwithstanding the fact that these liaisons were inherently coercive, even taking into consideration any genuine affection that may have existed between the two parties involved. The scarcity of white women limited not only any collective outcry against these relationships but also opposition to them from the legal wives. This enhanced the likelihood that mulatto offspring would receive socially tolerated demonstrations of affection, as well as economic and educational protection. Some were provided with a formal education, either locally through public institutions or by private tutors, or in Europe, if their white fathers had ample financial means. In exceptional cases, they were bequeathed large inheritances (Hoetink 1973, 23).

Escape Hatch or Trap Door?

When the numbers of slaves in Brazil and elsewhere in the Americas were large and the numbers of free coloreds and whites small, free coloreds filled interstitial economic roles, providing many mulattoes, who were a majority of free coloreds, with opportunities to become plantation overseers or farmers who worked parcels of land that supplied nearby sugar plantations with food. Still, free colored subsistence farmers depended on large white landowners for land rights, credit, and protection (Burdick 1992, 40–42). Other free coloreds migrated to Salvador, São Luís, and Rio de Janeiro, where they became self-employed artisans and merchants. Throughout the Americas, free coloreds frequently competed with cheaper slave labor in many of these capacities. Yet, in Brazil, they dominated most of the skilled crafts and trades. Moreover, by the eve of Abolition in 1888, mulattoes outnumbered blacks by a ratio as high as four to one in these areas of employment (Cohen and Greene 1972, 1–2; Harris 1964, 54–64, 79–94; Klein 1986, 227–28, 230; Klein 1972, 318; Russell-Wood 1972, 84–133, 309–34). Burdick states that some free colored urban artisans advanced from the artisanal and skilled trades into the arts, letters, and liberal professions (including medicine, engineering, law, and the civil service; Burdick 1992, 40–42).

Because of the shortage of whites, free coloreds also performed a critical role in the civilian militia. Throughout the colonial period, the European monarchs in Portugal often viewed the free colored militia as a means of expanding the frontier. They also secured Portugal's territorial borders in that region against foreign interlopers and attacks by Native Americans, while also providing a military brake on the ambitions of independence-minded whites. Given the large number of mulattoes among free coloreds, whites also viewed them as natural allies against the black slave majority. So reliable were free coloreds that Brazilian slaveholders used the free colored militias to suppress slave uprisings, as well as to catch and return fugitive slaves. The incorporation of free coloreds into the security apparatus of the colonial state, however, contributed as much to their own circumscribed status as to the superordinate position of whites. Free colored militia could hardly have hoped to overthrow whites and simultaneously hold slaves in their place. Any attempt at revolt would have brought them into opposition to the Crown as well as the colonial government, resulting in severe reprisals in the event of defeat (Klein 1972, 309–34; Russell-Wood 1972, 84–133).

During the colonial era, free coloreds were often allowed to serve as notaries and clerks, and engage in service occupations. Yet they were generally barred from public office and high-status occupations in the clergy and governmental bureaucracy, and their access to education was also limited. All important privileges, titles, or positions in the Portuguese Empire were bestowed only on those who could prove they were Old Christians, which conflated religion with ancestral definitions of race (Russell-Wood 1982, 69–71). Eventually, this came to mean genealogical proof of one's "pureza de sangue" (purity of blood), that is, evidence that one's ancestry was not tainted with that of "infected races" (Nazzari 1996, 109).

According to Charles Boxer, Anthony Russell-Wood, and Maria Luiza Tucci Carneiro the purity of blood statutes in the fifteenth century, the Ordenações Afonsinas (Afonsine Ordinances; 1446–47), were initially directed only against Iberians of Jewish, New Christian (Jewish individuals who had been forced to accept Christianity), and Moorish ancestry. This provided a legal framework that was later broadened to encompass other groups of "unclean blood." The Ordenações Manuelinas (Manueline Ordinances; 1514–21) extended these restrictions to gypsies and individuals of Native American descent. The Ordenações Filipinas (Filipine Ordinances; 1603) added blacks and mulattoes to the list.[4] Over the course of the seventeenth and eighteenth centuries, individuals of African descent were legally and specifically discriminated against by virtue of the close association between African ancestry and chattel slavery (Boxer 1969, 266; Carneiro 2005, 49–52; Russell-Wood 1982, 73, 79–80).[5] Pombal's 1774 reforms revoked the restrictions on the descendants of Jews, Moors, and Native Americans, but restrictions on the descendants of Africans remained in force and were only revoked with Brazil's 1824 constitution (Carneiro 2005, 49–52; Marmignon 2002, 26; Souza 2008, 93).

Nevertheless, civil and religious authorities could circumvent obtrusive regulations when necessary (Mattoso 1986, 191–92). In Salvador, for example, where African ancestry permeated all levels of society, there was the long-standing tradition of ensuring that multiracial individuals would be considered white in official documents (e.g., those recording appointment to high government office; Mattoso 1986, 191–92). Admittance to the *misericordias* and other brotherhoods as well as to the priesthood or a monastic order required proof of the purity of ancestry (Dutra 2006, 113; Russell-Wood 1982, 79–80). Yet being a mulatto was not inherently an impediment to an ecclesiastical vocation (Furtado 2008, 48–49). For example, the Company of Jesus, which ostensibly barred African Brazilians, included among its members Father António Vieira (1608–97; Mattoso 1986, 191–92; Russell-Wood 1982, 73, 79–80).

Vieira was born in Lisbon to Maria de Azevedo and Cristóvão Vieira Ravasco, the son of a mulatto servant woman in the household of the Conde de Unhão in Portugal. As a child, he accompanied his family to Salvador, Bahia, where his father had been appointed as secretary of the high court. Vieira was educated in the Jesuit College in Salvador, entered the Society of Jesus as a novice in 1623, and was ordained in 1635 (Boxer 1957, 5; Dutra 2003, 25–29; Russell-Wood 1982,

75). Despite the fact that his paternal grandmother was a servant (though not a slave) and a mulatto, Vieira's father's prominence and his own Portuguese birth were likely mitigating factors in his ordination, which took place after adoption of the Filipine Ordinances (1603), when blacks and mulattoes were added to the list of "infected races" (Carneiro 2005, 49–52; Russell-Wood 1982, 79; Souza 2008, 87n3).

Vieira became a prolific writer and a religious leader who had immense influence in seventeenth-century Portugal as well as Brazil. As evidence that he did not share the view common at the time that whites were innately superior to blacks, Boxer cites Vieira's famous "Sermão da Epiphania" (Epiphany Day Sermon; 1662), preached to Dona Luisa and Dom Afonso VI. For Vieira, religion rather than race was the hallmark of a civilized individual. An ardent defender of both New Christians and Native Americans, he passionately condemned the inhuman treatment of African slaves, comparing their sufferings on sugar plantations to those of Christ on the Cross. Yet he accepted, and indeed condoned, the importation of even more Africans as the best way to protect Native Americans from enslavement in Brazil (Alden 1996, 487–90, 511; Boxer 1957, 22–23, 1963, 102–3; Russell-Wood 1982, 4, 76, 102, 201). Vieira's rise to social prominence was an exception to the norm for individuals of African descent. Yet he is an excellent case study of the considerable social acceptance whites in Spanish and Portuguese America extended to light mulattoes. Emilia da Costa maintains that most did so not through competition in the open market but through the support of patrons in the white elite (Costa 1985, 239–43; Russell-Wood 1982, 76–77).

This window of opportunity, which Carl Degler calls the "mulatto escape hatch" (Degler 1971, 140), does not imply, however, that mulattoes gained carte blanche access to the ranks of whites by virtue of being mulatto as opposed to black. Rather, Degler argues, the escape hatch was an informal social mechanism by which select individuals with visibly African phenotypical traits or of known African ancestry were, for reasons of talent, culture, or education, allowed entry into the more privileged sectors of society in accordance with their approximation to European phenotypical norms (Degler 1971, 140, 196–99). In its broadest sense, however, the escape hatch made it possible over time for millions of individuals whose ancestry included African forebears, but who were phenotypically white, or near white, to be socially designated as "white." The social construction of whiteness—as well as the extension of white racial privilege—is thus more inclusive in Brazil than in the United States, where the one-drop rule can transform into black an individual who otherwise appears to be white (Daniel 2006, x).

By granting multiracial individuals an intermediate status somewhat superior to that of blacks, but significantly inferior to that of whites, European Brazilians held the resentment of these individuals in check and won their loyalty, without undermining white domination. This in turn helped prevent the formation of any alliance between the free coloreds and the black slave masses (Burdick 1992, 40–42; Cohen and Greene 1972, 1–23; Klein 1972, 309–34; Russell-Wood 1972, 84–133). Most of the free colored elite studiously avoided taking a public stand against slavery before abolition became a popular cause between the 1870s and 1880s. Others such as the Baron de Contegipe (João Maurício Wanderley; 1815–89), a Bahian mulatto and mill owner who became minister of foreign affairs during the last years of the Empire (1885–88), were strongly antiabolitionist (Borges 1992, 25; Burdick 1992, 40–42).

Nevertheless, African Brazilian resistance and antislavery protests intensified during the Paraguayan War (1864–70),[6] when the state combined appeals to patriotism with the use of violence to recruit soldiers, many of them slaves and free coloreds. Dale Graden argues that this unrest led, to a large extent, to the passing of the Lei do Ventre Livre (Law of the Free Womb) of 1871 (Graden 2006, 228), which stipulated that all children henceforth born to slaves and all slaves belonging to the state were to be free. Graden attributes increasing abolitionist sentiment not only to the Paraguayan War but also to an intense interprovincial slave trade prompted by the Northeast's declining sugar economy and the Southeast's coffee boom. This led to the forced migration of slaves from the Northeast to the plantations of Rio de Janeiro, Minas Gerais, Espirito Santo, and São Paulo in the Southeast. The resulting breakup of slave families was a contributing factor to revolts, street protests, and slave flights, which reinforced one another in both regions (Graden 2006, 71, 115, 131, 133, 140; Conrad 1972, 33). Moreover, free coloreds became involved in the mass movement inciting the wholesale flight of slaves from the plantations in the 1880s (Graden 2006, 146, 200, 214, 228). And a younger generation of mulatto intellectuals and lawyers also generated considerable antislavery ferment (Graden 2006, 146–52, 162–71).

Yet, prior to the 1870s, free coloreds risked public condemnation and serious reprisals, including interrogation by police and imprisonment, if they were even suspected of harboring antislavery sentiment. For their part, few whites voiced opposition to slavery, and those who did had a limited impact and often went unheard (Conrad 1972, 8–9; Graden 2006, 32, 42, 48–49). That said, by the 1870s, abolitionist societies increased their influence in politics, newspapers, and literary works (Graden 2006, 146–52, 162–71). By the 1880s, when the abolitionist campaign gained full momentum, the politics and economics of slavery superseded humanitarian concerns or issues of racial solidarity. Blacks, whites, and mulattoes fought together for and against the institution (Flory 1977, 205, 208, 210, 220).

Moreover, free colored attitudes toward abolition were influenced by the fact that from the 1820s through the 1840s slave ownership in places like Rio de Janeiro and other parts of the Southeast translated into considerable upward mobility. Indeed, Zephyr Frank contends that slave ownership was the most widespread and common means of wealth accumulation among free wealth holders (Frank 2004, 3, 42, 44–45, 50, 63, 75, 96; 2005, 248, 253; 2005, 232; Karasch 1987, 71, 343; Luna and Klein 2003, 3–4, 20–22, 120–21).[7] This was most evident in the cities, particularly large cities like Rio, which provided conditions for hired slaves (*escravos de ganho*; Frank 2004, 3, 27, 47–48; Harding 2006, 6–7; Martins and Abreu 2001, 546–47; Nishida 2003, 20–21). Urban slave owners hired out their slaves daily to search the streets for paid labor. These slaves could sometimes save enough from the fees charged for their services after the slave owners' share in the profits to purchase their freedom (Algranti 1988, 52; Frank 2004, xii, 18, 61–63; Karasch 1987, 59; Martins and Abreu 2001, 546–47).

Many wealth holders of modest means, or "middling" wealth holders, as Zephyr Frank calls them, bought, sold, or hired out slaves for profit due to the unavailability of other forms of wealth—including real estate.[8] This was enhanced by the dramatic increase in slave imports during the first half of the nineteenth century and the hoarding of slaves in the face of British pressure to end the Atlantic slave trade, which made prices affordable prior to 1850, when the trade was indeed ended (Frank 2004, 50–69, 70; Martins and Abreu 2001, 545). These middling wealth holders were numerous and came to control nearly half (44.9 percent) of Rio de Janeiro's wealth in slaves (Frank 2004, 42). They ranged from members of the upper echelons of society to day laborers at the bottom; cutting across racial lines, they included many *libertos* (former slaves; Frank 2004, 4, 8, 17–18, 50, 114, 142, 148; Naro 1996, 61–62).

This window of opportunity closed abruptly with the abolition of the Atlantic slave trade. The subsequent increased cost of slaveholding, along with growing European immigration and labor competition, and the Southeast's developing export economy, left middling groups with few income-generating (and wealth-generating) assets. Their turn away from slave labor was due less to progressive ideals than economic imperatives. Frank argues that the maintenance of slavery cannot simply be attributed to ideological support for the institution or even to the economic interests of the powerful slave-owning planters in parliament. Indeed, in large urban centers such as Rio de Janeiro, middling wealth holders' proportion of wealth in slaves peaked in the 1850s, which slowed the spread of abolitionist sentiment (Frank 2004, 3, 68–69, 71, 93, 165). Yet, by dint of the changing circumstances, the heirs of many free coloreds, who managed to build small fortunes in the 1830s and 1840s through wealth held in slaves, experienced significant downward mobility during the second half of the nineteenth century. With the increasing concentration of wealth among the predominantly white elite, the gap between white haves and the nonwhite have-nots grew ever wider (Frank 2004, 8, 77, 85–87, 167).

That said, rural and urban free coloreds alike enjoyed considerable upward mobility in both socioeconomic and geographic terms throughout Brazil prior to 1888. In rural Rio de Janeiro, along with neighboring parts of Minas Gerais and São Paulo, which relied on coffee and sugar cultivation and on the production of foodstuffs for local markets, free coloreds could be found in most of the occupational and household categories that were once the preserve of whites (Castro 1995, 31–35; Klein and Luna 2000, 938–41). Hebe Maria Castro argues that these circumstances led to increased flexibility in definitions of racial categories and to a noticeable absence of racial designators in legal and other records in these rural areas over the course of the nineteenth century (Castro 1995, 31–35, 104–10). Increasingly, "pardo" referred to freeborn nonwhites, and "preto" and "negro" to slaves or former slaves who had acquired their freedom, whether these individuals were black or multiracial. Arguing that these changes cannot be reduced to simple racial whitening, Castro suggests that they indicated both a decreased racial differentiation between working-class brancos and free pardos and the formation of a class consciousness (Castro 1995, 104–10). By comparison, race or color had less salience as a social signifier (Castro 1995, 104–10; Klein and Luna 2000, 938–41).

Despite shifting definitions of racial categories, however, mulattoes had social advantages over blacks, which increased their chances of upward mobility (Costa 1985, 186; Klein and Luna 2000, 940–41; 2004, 1–28). This also helps explain their silence on the question of racism, which kept them in a position of second-class citizenship during slavery. And it would keep the African Brazilian masses at the bottom of the social hierarchy for generations (Degler 1971, 167–70; Klein 1972, 332–33; 1986, 268). Collectively speaking, mulattoes tended not to opt for drastic social change but sought improvements in their own individual status. This is evident in the colored militia during the eighteenth century, the mulatto press of the early 1830s, and the colored brotherhoods. Even the mulatto press largely framed its protests in terms of partisan politics, rather than race (Bernd 1987, 17–18; Flory 1977, 209). More common individual responses to the racial status quo appear to have involved avoiding situations that might reinforce second-class status or refusing to recognize or even discuss racial issues; many mulattoes boasted of Native American rather than African ancestry. Many severed connections with their African Brazilian friends, neighbors, and families to avoid drawing attention to their African ancestry, especially when that ancestry was masked by a European phenotype (Degler 1971, 167–70; Klein 1972, 332–33; 1986, 268).

Abolition sealed this "racial contract" (Mills 1997, 4–7, 9–40).[9] European Brazilians continued to rely on mulatto support long after slavery ended. Burdick argues that as long as blacks were retained in the least remunerative sectors of the secondary labor force, mulattoes settled for token integration into the skilled trades, the petty bourgeoisie, intelligentsia, and the primary labor force (Burdick 1992, 37, 40–42; Cohen and Greene 1972, 12, 17; Klein 1972, 328; 1986, 232–33; Moura 1983, 3; Russell-Wood 1972, 123, 125). Although some mulattoes were among the first to protest social injustices, overall, their tendency to shun alliances with slaves and their silence on racial inequality say as much about their anomalous position as they do about their corruptibility or their commitment to and acquiescence in the racial order. With one wrong step, the escape hatch could easily become a trap door (Cohen and Greene 1972, 1–23; Hoetink 1973, 108; Klein 1972, 84–133; 1986, 232; Pierson 1942/1967, 165–76; Russell-Wood 1972, 309–34).

The Nineteenth-Century Racial Order: Europeanization, "Cryptomelanism," and the Whitening Ideology

Some of these attitudes toward race originated in the early colonial period. The "questionable" social origins (Schwartz 1987a, 28) of many Portuguese immigrants and the frequency of sexual liaisons or marriages between European settlers and Native Americans or Africans among even the wealthiest Brazilian families led to the suspicion that all colonial-born whites were of multiracial descent. These factors nurtured a sense of insecurity among the Brazilian elite and increased their sensitivity to color hierarchies and their desire for the grants of nobility, knighthoods, and pensions. As late as the 1790s, when concepts of nobility were being challenged in Portugal, the Brazilian elite increasingly sought to obtain noble status. Yet the Portuguese Crown did not create a titled Brazilian nobility until the arrival of the Portuguese Court in March 1808.

Because the colonists lacked the traditional credentials of noble status, they sought to demonstrate their nobility in other ways: by maintaining an aristocratic life style on landed estates with numerous slaves, displaying liberal and patriarchal attitudes, and exercising a penchant for personal justice. Eventually, commissions in the militia and similar honors served as substitutes for noble status (Haring 1968, 8, 67; Schwartz 1987a, 28–30). Stuart Schwartz maintains that, in the eighteenth century, the elite created genealogical histories to further their aspirations to nobility. The longer the planter families had been in Brazil, the easier it was to overlook the humble birth of their progenitors. These families became "noble by antiquity" (Schwartz 1987a, 29). Any connection with a noble house in Portugal was used to imply nobility. As a last resort, families could be considered at least "honorable" or "free of stain" (Schwartz 1987a, 29). If Native American ancestry could not be ignored, it was pointed out that "alliances of the soil" (Schwartz 1987a, 29) between Portuguese men and Native American women were common among Brazil's most prominent families and did not diminish the respect these families commanded. Moreover, nobility could be conferred on the family lineage by designating these indigenous women as "princesses" (Schwartz 1987a, 29).

Because the ravages of colonization and disease had neutralized the Native American threat to Brazilian territorial expansion, many elite Brazilians felt comfortable acknowledging, and even romanticizing, their remote indigenous ancestors. In stark contrast, African ancestry was stigmatized, the stigma exacerbated in pre-Abolition times by the presence of millions of black slaves (Brookshaw 1989, 1–11; Haberly 1983, 10–14; Hemming 1987, 466–81). Moreover, blacks constituted a distinct majority of the total population; they included a large number of *boçal* (African-born) slaves well into the nineteenth century. After the official abolition of the slave trade in 1850, *crioulos* (creoles or Brazilian-born blacks) became the sole source for replenishing the slave and free African Brazilian population. Yet the presence of considerable numbers of African-born slaves meant that first- and secondhand accounts of Africa continued to hold significance for new generations of African Brazilians. African Brazilian culture remained strongly African—particularly in areas with large concentrations of slaves—even after several centuries of enslavement (Butler 1998, 52–58; Costa 1985, 4–5, 143; Needell 2006, 18–20). African culture helped shape the contours of an African Brazilian culture and also influenced the European core culture (Costigan and Hamilton 2007, 7; Freyre 1963b, 278–476; Hemming 1987, 468–81; Mendonça 1973, 42–94).

From Colonial State to Republic

Indeed, by the eve of political independence from Portugal in 1822, the memories of European life were already losing their meaning for new generations of Portuguese in the Americas. Even with the transfer of the Portuguese Court to Rio de Janeiro, individuals of European descent were coming to view themselves less as Europeans and more as Brazilians. Although European Brazilians may have been unaware of their transformation in this process in the early colonial period, by the first decades of the nineteenth century, they became increasingly and painfully aware of this fact. The arrival of the Portuguese Court exacerbated these sentiments. It also intensified the existing insecurity about and obsession with phenotype and ancestry.

At the urging of Britain and flanked by a small British escort squadron, Dom João VI (1767–1826), the royal family, and the Portuguese Court fled to Brazil after Napoleon's invasion of Portugal in November 1807 (Martins and Abreu 2001, 533–34; Wilcken 2005, 249). Luciana Martins and Mauricio Abreu point out that the arrival of the royal family and continuous influx of Portuguese vessels carrying an entourage of the Portuguese elite augmented the population of Rio by as much as 30 percent (Martins and Abreu 2001, 533–34). Patrick Wilcken adds that members of this entourage ranged from nobles, courtiers, and religious leaders to government ministers, military advisors, and lawyers—along with their families and cadres of servants and attendants (some 10,000 to 15,000 individuals crammed into thirty ships; Wilcken 2005, 249). Moreover, the arrival of the Portuguese Court and the opening of the city's port to foreign trade and merchants, created an economic boom in Rio de Janeiro in the early nineteenth century, later fueled by the expanding coffee economy after the 1830s. Rio de Janeiro's increased economic and political prominence and rapid growth soon made the city a magnet for Portuguese immigrants (Nunes 2000, 38–41).

After relocating to Brazil, the Portuguese elite imported the "old order" (ancien régime) from Europe, with its pretentious and extravagant nobles who continually sought privileges, preferences, and public posts. Although the Portuguese Crown finally created a titled Brazilian nobility, Portuguese nobles claimed superior status over the local Brazilian elite by virtue of their noble birth, European phenotype, and European ancestry. In fact, many Portuguese, regardless of their social standing, treated the Brazilian elite as people of color and discriminated against them (Haring 1968, 9; Karasch 1987, 143; Martins and Abreu 2001, 542). Yet the Brazilian elite relished their titles of nobility, which separated them from the general populace, and particularly from individuals of color. When the Portuguese nobles returned to Portugal after Brazil's independence in 1822, the Brazilian elite immediately took their place at the top of the social hierarchy (Karasch 1987, 143; Martins and Abreu 2001, 542).

The Portuguese elite had transferred to Brazil their prerogatives of "high culture" and "refined" tastes, that is, the codified set of beliefs, values, customs, and artifacts held in the highest, official esteem, as opposed to the "low culture" associated with the "subculture" or "popular" culture of the masses. Of course, the boundary between "high" and "low" culture is never absolute; there is an ongoing interplay between them (Bakhtin 1981, 4; Bourdieu 1979/1984, 41; Gellner and Smith 1996, 367–68). Nevertheless, prior to the arrival of the Court, the only "high culture" in Brazil was that provided by the Church (which had been undermined by the expulsion of the Jesuits in 1759) and that which came from Portugal (Needell 1999, 2). Accompanying the Court was all the equipment necessary for the installation of the imperial bureaucracy, including a printing press, previously forbidden in the colony (Beattie 2001, 27; Martins and Abreu 2001, 533–34; Wilcken 2005, 249).

According to Luciana Martins and Mauricio Abreu, what transpired in Brazil did not reflect the pure, rational, and enlightened model bequeathed by European liberalism. Far from it. British liberalism supported Portuguese absolutism: the colonial regime based on slavery and land ownership existed alongside the new phenomenon of industrial capitalism and a market economy, most closely connected to Britain's efforts to expand consumption in overseas markets (Martins and Abreu 2001, 538–39, 534, 547). The juxtaposition of colonial absolutism and industrial capitalism was especially apparent in Rio de Janeiro when Dom João raised Brazil from its rank as an *estado* (state) to that of a *reino* (kingdom). According to Jeffrey Needell and Kirsten Schultz, the positions of colony and metropolis were inverted. Rio de Janeiro, a colonial city, was transformed into a metropolitan capital (Needell 1999, 2; Schultz 2001, 1–2). These developments were not simply a product of the diffusion of "modern" metropolitan values to a "traditional" society. Martins and Abreu contend that they imbued Rio de Janeiro with a palpable hybridity that was integral to the city's modernity (Costa 1985, 23; Martins and Abreu 2001, 358–39, 547).

Shortly after the arrival of the Portuguese Court, Dom João brought about changes that gradually reorganized Rio de Janeiro's urban spaces to fit a modern (European) model and European aesthetic sensibility (Schultz 2001, 104). This linkage between state and culture became explicit when he commissioned the

French Artistic Mission in 1816 to establish an Escola das Belas Artes (School of Fine Arts) in Brazil under his patronage. In keeping with European Romanticism, which proposed the centrality of national specificity and historical tradition in cultural origins and expression, French artists were charged with not only formulating a picturesque and historical Brazil but also awakening "the disposition of the Brazilians for the arts" (Spix and Martius 1824, 155). The French style was also applied to the design of new buildings, which provided a marked contrast with the older Baroque colonial architecture (Martins and Abreu 2001, 544–45; Süssekind 1990, 39). Needell argues that the seeming contradiction of looking to France for cultural training can be explained by the fact that Europeans such as the prince and his Court, as well as the Brazilian elite trained in Europe, deemed French culture to be the most advanced and universal (Needell 1999, 2; Benchimol 1990, 36–38).

That said, the first attempt by the Brazilian state to impose a national culture on the country took place during the reign of Dom Pedro I (1798–1834). In 1822, he became the first monarch of an independent Brazilian nation state, the Empire of Brazil. His policy of cultural imposition was sustained by the three Regency governments (1831–40) that succeeded him upon his abdication and ruled in the name of his son, Pedro II (1825–91), and by the young emperor when he was crowned in 1841 (Needell 1999, 2, 3). In addition, the Brazilian Crown founded a central high school named Imperial Colégio de Pedro II (the Imperial College of Dom Pedro II) in 1837, modeled on the lycées of Restorationist France, and, in 1838, organized the Instituto Histórico e Geográfico Brasileiro (Brazilian Historical and Geographical Institute), fashioned after France's Institut Historique (Needell 1999, 3). Dom Pedro II supported cultural and intellectual endeavors that went well beyond those of artists employed in the Escola das Belas Artes; they encompassed individuals who sought to provide Brazil with cultivated, literate, and artistic expressions that were consciously Brazilian. Many of these painters, scholars, and poets received pensions, sinecures, and titles from Dom Pedro II (Needell 1999, 3). This tradition continued until Dom Pedro II was overthrown by a military coup on November 15, 1889, when Marshal Deodoro da Fonseca proclaimed Brazil a republic.

Needell argues that the dissonance between European Romanticism's sense of the centrality of history and Brazilians' sense that they had no national history but were a new nation was resolved through a suspension of disbelief. In terms of literature, Brazilian Romantics either "discovered" a national past by recovering the writings of colonials whom they defined as "Brazilian" or they invented one, by writing the historical epics that the past, in fact, denied them. The linkage between the state and what was regarded as "Brazilian" or national culture was defined, produced, and effectively imposed by the sovereign and his devotees. It stood in stark contrast to the regional and hybrid (read "inferior") vernacular culture in which all Brazilians participated, and in which African, Native American, and Portuguese elements commingled (Needell 1999, 3–4).

Brazil and Rio de Janeiro's Belle Époque

Eventually, the elite sought to reckon with the embarrassing gulf between themselves and the masses by imposing their Europeanizing and modernizing culture upon them (Needell 1999, 4–5). The intensification of this process became the hallmark of Rio de Janeiro in the late nineteenth century; it came to full fruition in the city's Belle Époque (1880–1914), particularly during the presidency (1902–06) of Francisco de Paula Rodrigues Alves (1848–1919; Needell 1999, 6). City planning, architecture, elite education, social clubs and institutions, the salon, the family and its relationships, consumer fetishism, and literature were marked by a pervasive culture of European origin. The elite fostered this as part of their effort to elevate Rio de Janeiro to the status of a modern capital in the image of a European metropolis (Jaguaribe 2001, 295–302; Meade 1996, 18–19, 23; Needell 1987b, 31–51, 161–71).

Yet Rio de Janeiro was still characterized by a social order where slavery was an integral part of capitalist modernity. This was borne out in census data (Hall and Schwarz 1998, 23; Martins and Abreu 2001, 538–39, 547). In 1872, Minas Gerais was the largest slave province, with 370,459 slaves. However, a population of 341,576 slaves still existed in Rio de Janeiro (city and province), with approximately 48,939 residing in the capital (37.4 percent of its population; Klein 1971, 580n21; Oliveira 2000, 200). Moreover, as one of the most populous regions, with 782,724 inhabitants or almost 8 percent of the national population, the province of Rio de Janeiro served as Brazil's economic, administrative, and political center. Whites constituted 38.7 percent of the province's population, blacks 34.6 percent, and mulattoes 25.7 percent, whereas caboclos constituted only 1 percent (Directoria Geral de Estatística 1872; Oliveira 2000, 200–201).

In addition, the city of Rio de Janeiro's European exterior was tinted (or tainted according to many European and European American observers) by the sheer visibility of blacks and mulattoes (Martins and Abreu 2001, 545; Needell 2006, 18–20). Although, of the capital's 274,972 inhabitants in 1872, whites were a majority

(55.2 percent), mulattoes and blacks represented a sizable plurality (44.5 percent). Moreover, free coloreds made up 59 percent of the city's total African Brazilian population of 122,250 (Directoria Geral de Estatística 1872). According to the 1890 census, the city's population had almost doubled, to 522,651. Whites were now a larger majority (62.7 percent), having increased considerably in numbers due to European immigration, with mulattoes and blacks constituting more than one-third (34.4 percent) of the city's inhabitants (Martins and Abreu 2001, 538–39; Needell 1987b, 22).[10]

Thomas Skidmore points out that, although Brazil was not without its own social ills, racially disparaging attitudes on the part of Europeans and European Americans intensified—and frequently catalyzed—the formation of local sentiments and racial anxieties (Skidmore 1974, 48–69). During the nineteenth and the early twentieth centuries, Brazil was saturated with the racist ideas of European and Anglo–North American thinkers such as Georges Vacher de Lapouge (1854–1936), Arthur de Gobineau (1816–82), Josiah Nott (1804–73), George Gliddon (1809–57), and Samuel George Morton (1799–1851). These individuals expounded upon the genetic, psychological, and cultural superiority of Europeans, the inferiority of individuals of color (particularly individuals of African descent), and the evils of miscegenation (Knight 1974, 84–93; Skidmore 1974, 48–69; Torres 1969, 87–89, 317).

An examination of the second national census conducted in 1890 helps explain Brazil's racial anxieties. The data indicate that just over half (56 percent) of the country's approximately 14 million inhabitants were African Brazilians. There had been a decrease in the proportion of pardos (called "mestiços" on the 1890 census) since the 1872 census, from 44 percent to 41 percent, and pretos, from 20 to 15 percent, and an increase in the proportion of brancos, from 38 to 44 percent. Yet African Brazilians (mulattoes and blacks) still outnumbered whites by 12 to 10 (6.7 million to 5.5 million; Directoria Geral de Estatística 1898; Conselho Nacional de Estatística 1961, 201; Skidmore 1974, 44–45).[11]

Moreover, not even the most phenotypically and culturally European individuals of the elite could be certain their genealogy was free of African ancestors. By the second half of the nineteenth century, the majority of Brazilians, in the words of Afrânio Coutinho, were de facto "mulato claro" (clear [light]-skinned mulatto) or "claramente mulato" (clearly mulatto) in terms of culture, ancestry, or phenotype (Coutinho 1989, 8–12). This gave rise to a pervasive paranoia about "invisible blackness," which Renzo Sereno and Thomas Mathews refer to as "cryptomelanism" (Sereno 1947, 261; Mathews 1974, 318). According to Freyre, in portraits of the period, "the retoucher's art was taxed to the utmost to transform the least Caucasian features into perfectly Aryan ones . . . and to provide rosy complexions for those . . . whose pigmentation was suspiciously suggestive of the tar brush" (Freyre 1970, 201).

If, according to scientific racism, "darkening" through miscegenation and cultural blending was the disease, whitening through miscegenation and the Europeanization of Brazilian culture was the elite's prescription for a cure. To achieve this goal, the state actively encouraged and indeed subsidized the immigration of Europeans (Klein 1995, 208), especially those of Germanic origin. Moreover, parliament passed legislation automatically granting naturalization to all European immigrants residing in Brazil prior to November 15, 1889, "unless they declared a desire to keep their original nationality within six months" (Pastore 2001, 96–97).[12] Jean-Baptiste Lamarck (1744–1829) had contended that individuals adapted and perfected traits during their lifetime and transmitted these genetic improvements to their offspring and future generations. By the early twentieth century, the neo-Lamarckian movement, which theorized that traits, and thus culture, were acquired via local human and climatic environments, lent its support to the call for racial whitening. Unlike Mendelian genetics (which was rediscovered in 1900), with its accompanying notions about "the fixity of race" (Dávila 2003, 25) and its racially deterministic suppositions about people of color, neo-Lamarckism offered Brazil the hope of "progress" (Borges 1993, 249; Dávila 2003, 24–25; Lange 2008, 23; Stepan 1991, 69, 154–56).

In keeping with this quest for progress, modernity, and international acceptance, many Brazilian thinkers considered the idea of permanent improvement through human intervention to be a favorable resolution to their social ills. The corresponding eugenic proposition that a single "national race" was biologically possible provided a convenient ideological framework for support of policies that furthered the whitening of the nation through the state-sponsored immigration of "desirables." Indeed, the growth in the white population was due more to European immigration than to whitening through miscegenation (Borges 1995, 60–61; Meade 1996, 31; Skidmore 1974, 44–46). Moreover, as Burdick points out, the state passed waves of legislation restricting the immigration of blacks. In the early twentieth century, many Brazilians, according to Skidmore, expressed alarm at efforts by U.S. organizers working with local developers to persuade African Americans to immigrate to Brazil (Skidmore 1974, 193–97). Such immigration, wrote one journalist, would undermine the numerical disappearance of blacks in

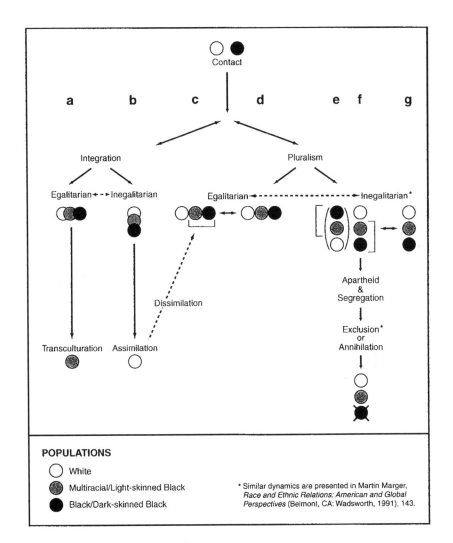

Fig. 1   Pluralist and integrationist dynamics

Brazil (Burdick 1992, 41; Lesser 1991, 115–37; Meade 1996, 31; Meade and Pirio 1988, 85–110).

According to Skidmore, the nineteenth-century ideology of Europeanization or whitening (*embranquecimento*) became central to the twentieth-century evolution of Brazil's racial democracy ideology. And, indeed, centuries of commingling among Africans, Europeans, and Native Americans had resulted in an omnipresent racial and cultural blending (Nascimento 1979, 78; Ortiz 1947, ix–xi; Skidmore 1974, 44–46). Yet Abdias do Nascimento maintains that, despite its *rhetoric*, which called for transracial/transcultural (or egalitarian) integration (fig. 1, dynamic a), the *goal* of racial democracy was premised on inegalitarian integration (i.e., *assimilation* in disguise). It was an unnatural contest between unequal participants manipulated in order to purge the Brazilian pedigree and culture of its "inferior" African and Native American traits with the goal of perpetuating only European traits (Nascimento 1979, 72; fig. 1, dynamic b).

Due to these racial attitudes, blacks and mulattoes in post-Abolition Brazil were pushed to the margins of society. Regional variations notwithstanding, they were sharply differentiated from whites in terms of color and occupation. Social progress was slow and subject to reversals. In a sense, the plight of African Brazilians worsened. When slavery disappeared, and with it slaveholders, who, if for no other than practical reasons, provided slaves with food and shelter, there was no attempt to grant the recently freed African Brazilians (libertos) land or to consider their educational needs. Many of the libertos remained on rural estates in the service of their former masters earning meager wages as domestics and servants. In the areas of slowest economic growth, where labor was scarce, manumitted slaves continued to work on plantations with few changes.

Moreover, the libertos were ill prepared, if at all, for entering the new wage-earning economy. This made the promise of urbanization and the emerging industrial order difficult, if not impossible, to fulfill (Andrews 1991, 51–52; Butler 1998, 45, 69; Fernandes 1969, 17; Taylor 1978, 26–27; Toplin 1981, 45–50). As rural and urban workers, the former slaves were forced to compete with European immigrants, brought in from the late 1880s to the 1910s, to replace them in the labor force, particularly in southern Brazil. Whereas impoverished but light-skinned European immigrants and their descendants experienced considerable upward mobility, African Brazilians were concentrated in the most underpaid and intermittent types of employment, as domestics and other service workers and as low-wage day laborers, or they were relegated to the informal or underground economy. Many became vagrants, beggars, prostitutes, or thieves (Andrews 1991, 60–85; Butler 1998, 74–78; Taylor 1978, 28). This legacy of informal, inegalitarian pluralism (fig. 1, dynamic f) was envisioned as the "final solution" that eventually would eliminate the "black peril" through "laissez-faire genocide" (Haberly 1972, 46) of sharply lower levels of education and higher rates of poverty, malnutrition, disease, and infant mortality (Domingues 2004, 270; Meade 1996, 30–31).

Such practices were prevalent during the Old Republic (1889–1930), whose governments sought to adapt European and European American models of international relations, public health, and city planning to their ends (Needell 1987b, 31, 51, 161–71; 1999, 6–8). Accordingly, Rodrigues Alves's distinguised minister of foreign affairs, the Baron do Rio Branco (José Maria da Silva Paranhos Júnior; 1845–1912), concluded international negotiations that enhanced Brazil's prestige in Europe and the United States. The baron advanced a European image abroad by recruiting men from Brazil's elite, whom he selected for their European and aristocratic appearance, style, and cultivation to fill the most important diplomatic posts. Rio Branco also promoted visits by influential foreign opinion makers—writers, actresses, statesmen—who were treated to the Europeanized drawing rooms, theaters, and boulevards of which Brazilians were so assiduously proud (Needell 1987b, 31–51; 161–71; 1999, 6–8).

In the area of disease control, Rodrigues Alves authorized the eradication of the contagious diseases that had tarnished Rio de Janeiro's reputation abroad. Osvaldo Gonçalves Cruz (1872–1917), a public health officer trained at the Institut Pasteur in France, was given carte blanche to stamp out Rio's infamous smallpox, plague, and yellow fever. Although Cruz achieved notable successes in eradicating plague and yellow fever, his attempts at mandatory vaccination against smallpox galvanized popular antagonism to the point of an urban insurrection, the Vaccine Revolt of 1904, during which the opposing oligarchs nearly succeeded in overthrowing the Rodrigues Alves government in a November 1904 coup (Bello 1966, 181–83; Carvalho 1989, 90–138, 145–46; Meade 1986, 301–22; 1996, 89–101; Needell 1987a, 33, 233–69; 1999, 6–8). Narrowly surviving, however, the government went on to other achievements. Republican leaders confronted head-on what they considered to be the inadequacies of Brazil's urban infrastructure. Their efforts resulted in substantial modifications in the appearance of the large cities, particularly the state capitals. As the principal and most explicit testament of the state's imposition of a national cultural identity, the federal capital of Rio de Janeiro was also subjected to dramatic reforms (Jaguaribe 2001, 295–302; Lemos 1995, 219–20).

It was under Rodrigues Alves, his transportation and public works minister, Lauro Severiano Müller (1863–1925), and Francisco Pereira Passos (1836–1913), mayor of Rio de Janeiro between 1903 and 1906, that municipal and federal governments collaborated to rebuild Rio de Janeiro's port along the most modern European lines and to make over the capital's thoroughfares, official buildings, and premier boulevards using Haussmann's Paris as the blueprint (Azevedo 2003, 39–79; Benchimol 1990, 192–203; Carvalho 1989, 95; Jaguaribe 2001, 328–29; Needell 1983, 83–103; 1987b, 31–51; 1999, 6–8; Philippou 2005, 248; Sevcenko 1983, 25–44; Skidmore 1974, 95–96).[13] These developments made clear the conflation of European models of city planning and the aspirations of Brazilian policy makers to "civilization" and "progress." Yet Needell states that the meaning of European elements in Brazil's elite culture was, at least in part, reinterpreted with a specifically Brazilian inflection (Needell 1987b, 31–51, 161–71; 1999, 6–8; Green 1999, 17–19; Sevcenko 1983, 25–77).

The elite sought to express a modernizing ideology by identifying itself with France, Britain, and other "civilized" European nation-states in order to raise Brazil above itself as a nation of color, shackled to colonial "backwardness" (Green 1999, 17–19; Meade 1996, 18–19, 23). Needell argues that, to this end, not only was a selective, state-imposed notion of European civilization affirmed, but vernacular Brazilian culture, and specifically African Brazilian culture, was also actively repressed as shameful (Needell 1987b, 31–51, 161–71; 1999, 6–8).

The sprawling and overcrowded *cortiços* (tenements) and winding streets of the Old City, long identified with African Brazilian life and culture, were often destroyed to create Parisian boulevards and grand buildings with Beaux Arts–style façades (Bello 1966, 183–84; Green 1999, 17–19; Needell 1987b, 31–51, 161–71; 1999, 6–8). Originally occupied almost entirely by blacks and mulattoes, the cortiços had gradually become home to poor whites as well, particularly many European immigrants who arrived in the late nineteenth century (Frank 2004, 80–81; Oliveira 1996, 74–75). Although socioeconomic status was a key factor in residential patterns, to some extent, racial discrimination also played a role (Frank 2004, 31–33).[14] Despite the more fluid racial orders in the states from Rio de Janeiro northward as compared to the states from São Paulo southward, color differences and socioeconomic status set African Brazilians apart from and subordinated them to their white counterparts, particularly European immigrants, who were more readily integrated as equals. This was especially true in the city of

São Paulo, which had its own sprawling, high-density, and even more racialized enclaves (Butler 1998, 57, 70, 74–77; Domingues 2004, 132–83).

Even more squalid, disease-ridden, and unfit for habitation than cortiços were the favelas (shantytowns), which originated as densely populated squatter settlements built (often precariously) on empty, unclaimed, or unprotected urban land by people (often the displaced) who generally had nowhere else to live. According to the authorities, the shantytowns and tenements were not simply eyesores but a blight to be obliterated from Rio de Janeiro's landscape (O'Hare and Barke 2002, 1).

On the cultural front, a campaign was mounted to expunge African Brazilian religious expressions such as *candomblé* and *macumba*, in which Africans worshipped African deities disguised as equivalent Catholic saints.[15] African Brazilian religion had not merely been ritual and tradition but also the site of resistance and solidarity against racial oppression. As such, it posed a threat to national progress as defined by the nation's elites. In response to these concerns, African Brazilian religion was criminalized in the Penal Code of 1890, which gave police license to raid candomblé *terreiros* (houses of worship; Johnson 2001, 19).[16] That threat also mirrored the weakness of the Catholic Church and its religious orders, which were often overwhelmed by the vigor of the African Brazilian religious expression (Graden 2006, 113–14, 129–31).[17]

The state's ethnocultural pogroms also sought to eradicate *capoeira*, a martial art developed by African slaves, as well as the African-derived musical and dance forms of *batuque* and the samba (Meade 1996, 77–79; Needell 1999, 9–10).[18] These grassroots countercultural expressions celebrated African Brazilian solidarity—particularly during carnival—in response to the elite culture of the largely European Brazilian bourgeoisie (Borges 1995, 60–61; Butler 1998, 167, 187–88, 201–7). That said, now refurbished for *flanerie* (public strolling) by the privileged classes, the central streets of Brazil's major cities were explicitly forbidden to the scantily clad poor and their boisterous carnival rituals and frivolity (Green 1999, 52; Needell 1999, 9). And even though Brazil's turn-of-the-century elites participated in the vernacular African Brazilian culture that surrounded them, Needell is quick to point out that they never lost sight of the "low" ranking of that culture vis-à-vis the official, "high" Eurocentric culture the state sought to impose on the nation. They used Europe's nation-state model, progress, and civilization to explain and justify not only European superiority but also their own (Needell 1999, 8–10).

THE MULATTO AUTHOR: THE LITERARY CANON AND THE RACIAL CONTRACT

The Mulatto Author: Literary Blackness and the White Aesthetic

From the introduction of slavery in the mid-1500s to the final decades of the nineteenth century, the planter aristocracy controlled national life in Brazil. With the abolition of African slavery (1888), however, and with the overthrow of the monarchy (1889) and the establishment of the Republic (1890), Brazil's sugar-coffee economy shifted from slave to paid labor, paving the way for urban expansion and industrialization; the white urban bourgeoisie replaced the white landowning and slaveholding elite as the dominant sector of society. And even though the highest strata continued to be overwhelmingly European Brazilian and the lowest overwhelmingly African Brazilian and disproportionately black, the urban elite brought with them the promise of change. As new specialists and professionals—merchants, politicians, journalists, lawyers, artists, and intellectuals—they replaced hereditary values with meritocratic ones, where ambition, education, talent, and intellect were the criteria for personal worth and advancement. This new social order provided some African Brazilians, particularly mulattoes, with increased opportunities for upward mobility into the petty bourgeoisie and intelligentsia. This was especially true of the arts, letters, and liberal professions (including engineering, law, medicine, and the civil service; Burdick 1992, 40–42; Costa 1985, 239–43).

Color, Culture, Class, and the Racial Divide

Post-Abolition Brazil thus shifted away from white domination, which characterized the colonial racial order. Pervasive exclusion and coercion (or inegalitarian pluralism; fig. 1, dynamic g) was increasingly juxtaposed with patterns of selective inclusion (or inegalitarian integration), through the racial alchemy of the mulatto escape hatch (fig. 1, dynamic b), and with considerably less pervasive patterns of integration based on equality (fig. 1, dynamic a). However, given that the larger social order was still underpinned by racial hierarchy, it follows that integration would be deeply marked by inegalitarian dynamics. Michael Omi, Howard Winant, and James Scott, drawing from the work of Antonio Gramsci, encapsulate this form of inegalitarian integration (or assimilation) with the term "hegemony" (Omi and Winant 1994, 66–69, 84, 115, 148; Scott 1990, 70–96). The shift from white domination to white hegemony thus created the illusion of equality while effectively allowing European Brazilians to maintain power, control, and hierarchy.

Indeed, in the minds of European Brazilians, the concept of blackness was so irreconcilable with social advancement that virtually any degree of achievement or prominence could confer white status on an African Brazilian (Butler 1998, 53–54; Degler 1971, 103, 140, 196–99; Mattoso 1986, 191; Pierson 1942/1967, 139). There have historically been individuals of known African Brazilian ancestry in high public office, including one president—Nilo Peçanha (Thompson 1965, 32).[1] Yet they never referred to themselves as "negro" or even as "mulato," nor did others (Butler 1998, 51; Fernandes 1969, 1–13; Toplin 1981, 45–50). Still, mulattoes remained closer to blacks in status than to whites. Nevertheless, the hierarchy that clearly favored European Brazilians over African Brazilians ensured that those few African Brazilians who benefited from the meritocracy were largely mulattoes rather than blacks (Andrews 1991, 249–54; Prado Júnior 1969, 116; Russell-Wood 1972, 93).

In addition, the mulatto escape hatch brought with it the expectation, if not the actual achievement, of social advantages for multiracial individuals. This supposedly benevolent gesture, which became a key component of Brazil's racial democracy ideology, actually retarded, if not prevented, political mobilization along racial lines. It achieved this by encouraging mulattoes to view blacks as a separate class of social outcasts with whom they had little common cause. This, in turn, guaranteed that many individuals most likely to possess the sociocultural capital to serve as mouthpieces in the African Brazilian struggle were neutralized, or co-opted, into silence.

Literary scholars argue that this "silence" is reflected in the lack of race-specific consciousness in literature by African Brazilians (Bastide 1943, 17). Besides the few references to social inequalities and even rarer nostalgic allusions to a preslavery past, African Brazilians in colonial and nineteenth-century Brazil produced literature that is hardly distinguishable from that of European Brazilians. It was not until the beginning of the twentieth century that the African Brazilian intelligentsia expressed an interest in projects explicitly aimed at racial affirmation. As a result, black and mulatto authors forged an aesthetic that differentiated them not only from their European Brazilian contemporaries but also from their counterparts in colonial and nineteenth-century Brazil (Alberto 2011, 4–5, 10, 20–21; Gomes 2007, 153–62; Preto-Rodas 1970, 14–15; Rabassa 1967, 20–34).

This thinking among African Brazilian intellectuals and artists paralleled a larger international trend that interrogated Eurocentric discourse in the post–World War I era. More specifically, it reflected a national ethos in which some Brazilian thinkers sought a more "authentic" national identity, believing they could devise a workable social order reflecting Brazil's uniqueness (Brookshaw 1986, 85–88; Franco 1970, 117–47). Thomas Skidmore maintains that, between 1889 and 1914, though some German immigrants in the southern states sought to segregate themselves from native Brazilians, most elite European Brazilians fully supported whitening through miscegenation. That said, a new confidence emerged among Brazil's intelligentsia, in part because European and European American thinkers no longer considered race prima facie the most important determinant of historical development. Indeed, far from precluding its future as a great nation, Brazil's racial (and cultural) liabilities, particularly those rooted in its African and Native American origins, could now be transformed into assets (Skidmore 1974, 64–77, 78, 98, 176–79, 207–8; Borges 1995, 70–71).

This is not to deny the existence of a vibrant African Brazilian literary life prior to that time. Indeed, African Brazilians, more specifically mulattoes, founded journals to champion the abolitionist cause in publications such as *O Brasileiro Pardo* (*The Brown Brazilian*), *O Mulato* (*The Mulatto*), *O Homem de Côr* (*The People of Color*), *O Cabrito* (*The Little Goat*), and *O Crioulo* (*The Creole*). They also constituted the bulk of the editorial staffs and subscribers' lists of the African Brazilian press. Thus, when we speak of literature written by colonial and nineteenth-century African Brazilians, we are generally referring to literature written by mulattoes rather than by blacks (Preto-Rodas 1970, 14–15; Sayers 1958, 132–34). Yet with the exception of the mulatto press of the early 1830s, one looks in vain for explicit signs of racial awareness in this literature (Gomes 2007, 153–62).

Evasion, Erasure, and Exclusion

Although some may contend that the lack of race-specific consciousness in the literature by African Brazilians reflected the integrative aspect of Brazilian race relations, critics argue that such integration was assimilationist rather than egalitarian. And, in point of fact, African Brazilian authors went to great lengths to erase or conceal their race. Their writings reveal as much about the inegalitarian dimension of pluralism as the writings of authors seeking to counter both exclusion and assimilation do about its egalitarian dimension (Brookshaw 1986, 176). Given the disproportionate rates of illiteracy among African Brazilians, black and mulatto authors wrote largely for white audiences and were beholden to the European Brazilian literary establishment for publication (Cândido 1995, 122; Guimarães 2004, 65–66; Havighurst and Moreira 1965, 71–76; Oliveira 2007, 66–67, 74; Rego 1997, xviii).

That said, official data indicate that illiteracy was endemic in late-nineteenth and early twentieth-century Brazil, ranging from some 82 percent in 1872 to 67 percent in 1900 (Directoria Geral de Estatística 1872; Conselho Nacional de Estatística 1961, 201; Fischer 1994, 181–214; Neto 1973, 253). In other words, only between 18 and 33 percent of Brazilians were literate, most of whom were white (Guimarães 2004, 65–66; Havighurst and Moreira 1965, 71; Neto 1973, 253).[2] In 1877, it was estimated that only 20 percent of free inhabitants (including immigrants) were able to read and write, whereas 80 percent could not (Graham 1972, 17). Machado de Assis expressed alarm at this state of affairs by quoting similar literacy statistics: "The nation is totally illiterate. Only 30% of residents are able to read ... 70% remain in profound ignorance" (*Crônicas, História de 15 dias*, Oc, 3:345).[3] At least half of the literate population included magazine readers, who were typically women (a fact reflected in Machado's constant references to the "lady reader"). Yet, even if a wider audience of women read serialized novels in magazines, the data indicate that literary production occurred in a highly unfavorable climate. For example, in 1892, Rio de Janeiro, the nation's center of cultural activity, had only six bookstores (Fischer 1994, 181–214). On the other hand, the 1872 census indicates that of Rio's 235,381 inhabitants 2,806, or slightly more than 1 percent, were professionally engaged in literary pursuits—writers, journalists, secretarial staff, and scribes (Guimarães 2004, 74–75; Directoria Geral de Estatística 1986, 197).

In the first detailed examination of the relationship between Machado and his readership, Hélio de Seixas Guimarães notes that, even in the best-case scenario involving a first-run printing of 1,500 copies, it took years for a book to sell out.

Guimarães believes that not even individuals in the literary professions purchased one another's books in large numbers and that there may in fact have been fewer readers than writers of books (Guimarães 2004, 74–75; Neto 1973, 84). Arguing that Machado vigorously sought to tackle these deficits and to cultivate more urbane readers, Guimarães contends that, to these ends, Machado placed increasing intellectual demands on readers over time. Whereas his earlier novels are more straightforward and conventional narratives requiring attentive but largely passive readers, the later novels are more provocative narratives, effecting a certain ambiguity, disorientation, and uneasiness and requiring more engaged readers, who are expected to participate as both spectators and performers in the unfolding of the novels' meaning (Guimarães 2004, 34, 36, 82, 149, 175–77). With these later novels, Machado was indeed challenging his readers, given the literacy rates and the fact that most readers were steeped in the straightforward and entertaining Romantic literature of the period (Guimarães 2004, 39).

Writers of Machado's time were concerned not only about the size and quality of their readership but also about the absence of "impartiality" in Brazil's literary culture to protect them from "the caprice and protectionism of personal taste and allegiance" (Fischer 1994, 194). Machado addressed such concerns in an early essay "O ideal do crítico" (The Ideal of the Critic [1865]; Fischer 1994, 181–214). He criticized the professional readers in Rio de Janeiro's literary public sphere, which he found dominated by "hate, cronyism, and indifference" (Crítica, Oc, 3:798), for their distorted perspective and aesthetic judgment. He presented a list of qualities necessary for the professional critic: sincerity, justice, independence, impartiality, tolerance, urbanity, moderation, and perseverance (Crítica, Oc, 3:799–800).

Unlike Europe, however, Rio de Janeiro—and by extension, Brazil as a whole—lacked the cultural framework and liberal values necessary to support these literary qualities, in part because of Brazil's limited educational system (Fischer 1994, 191–214). Until the late eighteenth century, elementary instruction was largely provided by private schools or monasteries (Haring 1968, 108–10; Massa 1969, 1:45). The few extant public schools in larger urban centers taught little more than rudimentary reading, writing, and mathematics, with some Latin and Greek. Established after 1776, these schools were understaffed and their teachers underpaid (Prado Júnior 1969, 160–61). During the Empire (1822–89), efforts to create a substantive educational system were hampered by the absence of the necessary infrastructure, with the result that public education consisted of a few, poorly attended "ABC schools" and fewer still, inefficiently operated secondary schools (Havighurst and Moreira 1965, 74; Haring 1968, 108–10).

By 1876, the number of public schools had increased to 6,000 and the number of students, to 200,000 (Graham 1972, 17; Havighurst and Moreira 1965, 76). And, by the end of the Empire and the beginning of the Republic, public and private schools numbered 7,500 and students almost 300,000 (approximately 2.1 percent of the population); there were some 300 secondary schools with a total enrollment of almost 10,500. In 1899, fewer than 3 percent of Brazil's population of 14 million attended schools at all levels (Havighurst and Moreira 1965, 76). Education and its benefits remained largely the preserve of those "entitled by birth or social position" (Graham 1972, 17). In addition, higher education consisted of a few professional schools devoted to training doctors, lawyers, and engineers. There were two schools of medicine (Rio de Janeiro and Salvador) with 800 students, two higher schools of law (São Paulo and Olinda), with 1,329 students, and one engineering or polytechnic school (Rio de Janeiro), with 161 students. There was no similar training in the pure sciences, social sciences, or humanities (Fischer 1994, 191–214; Haring 1968, 108–9; Havighurst and Moreira 1965, 75–78; Peard 2000, 15–16).

Writers and intellectuals had few universities or other institutions to support their endeavors, financially or otherwise. Most were self-taught, with few professional opportunities apart from the rare teaching positions in those universities and in secondary schools. Many, like Machado de Assis, pursued careers in journalism, eking out their meager income by also working as somewhat better paid public functionaries. Also, one should not underestimate the constraints placed on literary culture by a clientele system, which dominated the public sphere and in which powerful families headed by patriarchs maintained agregados (dependents) in exchange for absolute loyalty in elections and local feuds (Caldwell 1970, 17; Fischer 1994, 191–184; Miskolci 2006, 367–68). Moreover, the "contradictory" (Bourdieu 1996, 60) social location of artists, writers, and intellectuals engendered a sense of marginality. On the one hand, writers developed unique worldviews and techniques; on the other, they depended for their livelihoods on the very social order they often criticized in their writings. This dependency constantly threatened to reduce their accountability to the larger public and worked to narrow writers' worldview to that of the ruling class and powerful special interests embodied in the public sphere (Bourdieu 1996, 60; Mannheim 1956, 121–65; Miskolci 2006, 367–68).

The anomalous location of artists, writers, and intellectuals was exacerbated by the fact that black and mulatto authors operated within a political economy and ideological environment deeply influenced and indeed dominated by a white literary establishment and readership. European Brazilian literary critics, book reviewers, formulators of public opinion, and readers alike significantly shaped African Brazilian literary culture (Desan, Ferguson, and Griswold 1989, 1–10; Guimarães 2004, 46–56; Oliveira 2007, 66–67, 74; Washington 2001, 1–8).[4] As Wendy Griswold states, literature "is shared meaning embodied in form," where authors, critics, reviewers, opinion makers, and readers all serve as "agents who interact with texts, working to encode meanings" (Griswold 1993, 465). Joining these in determining writers' access to the public sphere were the gatekeepers—the mentors, patrons, publishers, and editors.

An examination of African Brazilian literary texts thus provides insights into the relationship between the racial order and the internal organization of ideologies as normative messages and symbolic systems in those writings (Desan, Ferguson, and Griswold 1989, 1–10; Egejuru 1978, 15; Guimarães 2004, 65–66; Washington 2001, 1–8).[5] Although African Brazilians' location in the racialized social structure subjected them to particular experiences that influenced their conception of reality, which in turn informed their writings, their perspectives and writings were refracted through ideological perspectives emanating from the European Brazilian establishment. African Brazilian authors therefore essentially granted legitimacy to the dominant European Brazilian discourse, which made its preeminence appear natural rather than imposed. (Daniel 2006, 34–39; Washington 2001, 1–8; Omi and Winant 1994, 66–69, 84, 115, 148; Young 2006, 4–5, 7, 17).[6]

European Brazilians thus played an important role, albeit often hidden, in distorting or marginalizing any oppositional ideology and the power to frame alternatives. Their influence was critical both to the formation of ideological meanings projected by African Brazilian literary figures and to the prominence of certain of these figures in the public sphere (Desan, Ferguson, and Griswold 1989, 1–10; Lajolo and Zilberman 2005, 250, 258, 261; Oliveira 2007, 66–67, 74; Washington 2001, 1–8; Young 2006, 4–5, 7, 17).[7] African Brazilian writers' efforts to avoid or minimize the topic of race in order to appeal to a larger white constituency played a decisive role in deracinating an explicit African Brazilian literary consciousness; they account in large part for why so few examined the racism experienced by blacks and mulattoes in their writings (Brookshaw 1986, 178; Egejuru 1978, 14; Jackson 1979, 10–12; Oliveira 2007; 66–67, 74; Preto-Rodas 1970, 14–22; Washington 2001, 1–8; Young 2006, 4–5).

Authenticity, Authorship, and the Authority of Experience

Richard Preto-Rodas contends that colonial and nineteenth-century African Brazilian writers made a conscious attempt to appear European in their cultural orientation; they often stood apart from their European Brazilian counterparts by reflecting the latest European literary and philosophical currents (Preto-Rodas 1970, 14–15). Yet, even as African Brazilians chose to write within the European canon, white writers chose to use African Brazilian vernacular forms as well as themes, including the topics of slavery and racism, in their writings (Brookshaw 1986, 10; Pereira 1995, 875). This in turn has led scholars to debate, on the one hand, whether African Brazilians are the only authentic interpreters of their collective experience and, on the other, whether African diasporic literature in general expresses racial consciousness through its content or its form (Brookshaw 1986, 10–14; Jackson 1979, 1–14; Williams 1987, 245–46).

Critics who support a more pluralist perspective of the Brazilian racial order, typified by the writings of Abdias do Nascimento, regard African Brazilian literature as culturally autonomous, with a style and themes forged in exile and derived largely from the history of racial oppression. Some contend that authors' affirmation of their African Brazilian identity is more important than mere technique. Others contend that African Brazilian literature contains thematic constants, such as the portrayal of characters in conflict with the dominant white society. And still others contend that there is a distinctively "black" style of writing, and that African Brazilian authors' identification with "blackness" and their encounters with the black experience influences their choice of words, images, and symbols (Jackson 1979, 1–14; Williams 1987, 250). Most holding this pluralist perspective would agree, however, that only African Brazilians have the requisite experience, insight, and mastery of techniques to depict their situation accurately (Gomes 2007, 153–62; Williams 1987, 245–46).

Critics who support the traditionally more integrative (or racially democratizing) perspective on Brazilian race relations have argued that artistic expression should not—and indeed cannot—be equated with racial ancestry or experience. This perspective, which draws its inspiration from the works of Gilberto Freyre, contends that many white authors have been able to bridge the gap between white and African Brazilian subjects and have created credible African Brazilian subject matter and characters. Likewise, it does not consider the stylistic devices used by some African Brazilian writers to be racially specific because black, white, and mulatto writers share the same cultural context and, given comparable talent, are equally capable of interpreting the African Brazilian experience authentically and sensitively (Isfahani-Hammond 2008, 46–74; Williams 1987, 245–46).[8]

That said, the affirmation of a black aesthetic through the use of African Brazilian vernacular forms or the literature of racial vindication by African Brazilian authors involves subjects who are themselves also the objects of their focus

(Gomes 2007, 153–62). This sets African Brazilian writings apart from those of white authors, at least in terms of impetus and authority of experience, no matter how authentic and sensitive white authors' presentation of the subject matter or articulation of African Brazilian cultural forms may be. The response to the writings of Jorge Amado (1912–2001) sheds light on this debate. Although Amado was one of Brazil's most prestigious and widely known white exponents and defenders of African Brazilian culture, some have questioned the authenticity of his portrayals of black and mulatto characters. There is disagreement as to whether his work achieved the depth of characterization displayed in the writings of African Brazilians (Brookshaw 1986, 153–74; Jackson 1988, xvi, 21).

Moreover, one cannot ignore the power dynamics of the larger social context. White authors may borrow and interpret vernacular forms or themes relating to African Brazilians (including the topic of racism) in the form of what Alexandra Isfahani-Hammond refers to as "White Negritude" (Isfahani-Hammond 2008, 5). Yet this engagement in no way alters their racial privilege or social location. In fact, this borrowing and interpreting can easily be seen as "appropriation" or "cultural theft" (Cruz 1999, 25), given their membership in the dominant racial group (Brookshaw 1986, 118–19; Butler 1998, 42–45; Cruz 1999, 23–26). Unlike their white counterparts, African Brazilian authors have risked reprisals for affirming a race-specific black consciousness. Indeed, seeking to unmask the social forces that maintain their subordinate status has had destructive consequences for African Brazilian writers (Brookshaw 1986, 192). Thus most African Brazilian authors have historically displayed at least public conformity to, if not complete private acceptance of, the dominant European Brazilian literary canon (to include avoiding the topic of racism) as a means of gaining access to the few opportunities available to them.

The Mulatto Author: Literary Whiteness and the Black Aesthetic

That said, the existence of what some critics refer to as "white" literature (i.e., literature reflecting the dominant European Brazilian canon), written by African Brazilians requires careful consideration of the available literary possibilities. Catherine Innes, who examined colonized intellectuals, particularly writers in Ireland and Africa, and David Brookshaw, who applied Innes's theoretical framework to Brazil, note three principal literary trajectories that have emerged among African Brazilians (Brookshaw 1986, 176, 179–204; Innes 1978, 10–24). I refer to these as the "cultivated tradition," the "vernacular tradition," and the "tradition of opposition," although individual authors may display aspects of more than one trajectory (Bernd 1987, 63–65; Preto-Rodas 1970, 14–31; Proença Filho 2004, 161–87).

Those who write in the cultivated tradition typically reflect the "high culture" of the official literary canon. They may seek to conceal their identity and take pride in their ability to write so skillfully in the dominant style that no one can guess their racial origin. Those who write in the vernacular tradition employ techniques and themes associated with the African Brazilian popular or "low" culture beneath the racial comportment line, that is, the demarcation of beliefs, values, and customs deemed acceptable by the dominant whites. And those who write in the tradition of opposition or open protest against racial oppression may use the language and forms of the vernacular tradition, the cultivated tradition, or both.

The Cultivated Tradition: Silva Alvarenga

Most literature by mulatto authors in colonial and nineteenth-century Brazil is in the official style of the cultivated tradition. This required them to present African Brazilian themes or characters, if contemporary literary style called for them, in race-neutral settings that could convey universal concerns. Yet their use of the dominant literary cultural norms and even their avoidance of African Brazilian characters and themes need not be interpreted as assimilation to the white-dominated status quo. Rather, they may have sought to prove they could perform literary conventions as well as, if not better than, whites themselves. By besting racial oppression at its own game, these authors could "thus counterbalance their subordinate status through overcompensation and exaggerated display and performance of what has been termed as 'literary whiteness'" (Jackson 1979, 10–11).

Manuel Inácio da Silva Alvarenga (1749–1814) is the earliest and one of the most frequently mentioned mulatto authors of the cultivated tradition. Born out of wedlock to an African mother and an indigent white musician, Silva Alvarenga overcame social and financial obstacles to earn a degree at the University of Coimbra in Portugal in 1776. It is likely that without the patronage of his father's powerful friends he would never have developed his talents as a poet and musician. Staunchly adhering to the constrained elegance of the Arcadian movement of the Mineira School in Minas Gerais (i.e., the Brazilian adaptation of eighteenth-century European neoclassical aesthetics), Silva Alvarenga's writings lack any allusions to his African ancestry.[9]

Indeed, Alvarenga makes only one reference to African Brazilians in his poem "O desertor das letras" (The Deserter of Letters), where he satirizes the educational methods and theories that prevailed at Coimbra before the reforms implemented by Portugal's premier the Marquês de Pombal (Pereira 1995, 876; Sayers 1958, 115–17). Alvarenga relates how, after a riot, the hero, Gonçalo, is taken with a group of friends to a prison in the same way that the defeated inhabitants of a quilombo (a runaway slave settlement) might be led into captivity by the Native Americans employed by the Portuguese to help capture them. The poet's sympathies, however, lie with the Native American victors rather than the vanquished African Brazilians (Brookshaw 1986, 7–16, 205, 240–286; Preto-Rodas 1970, 21–31; Sayers 1958, 115–17).

Alvarenga's madrigals reflect the prevalent taste for the lovesick suitor who languishes for his rural beauty Glaura, as they wander through the lush countryside populated with crystal fountains. Raymond Sayers and Roger Bastide argue that Alvarenga chose to make Glaura a mythical nymph rather than a real maiden because he may have feared public ridicule, if not censure, as a mulatto lover of a white woman. Sayers also points out that Alvarenga could not dedicate his poetry to a black or mulatto woman because there was no precedent for this in the Portuguese poetic canon. More specifically, Alvarenga's education at Coimbra and the protection he received from Pombal may have prompted his identification with the privileged classes despite his humble origins (Sayers 1958, 115–17; Bastide 1943, 30–36; Preto-Rodas 1970, 15–16).

What is remarkable about Silva Alvarenga, Preto-Rodas points out, is his engagement with the civic values of the French Enlightenment and the literary and scientific trends emanating from England at the end of the eighteenth century. Almost alone among his contemporaries, Alvarenga sought to disseminate the ideals of intellectual inquiry and independence in a society that was still characterized by cultural obscurantism. He was enthusiastic about Pombal's educational reforms and dedicated odes praising the discoveries in the natural sciences. Keenly aware of the increasing importance of a natural setting for poetic inspiration in European literary circles, Alvarenga, alone among Brazil's poets of the time, often provided a Brazilian forest as a setting for his ardent shepherds, who were otherwise indistinguishable from the shepherds of his Portuguese and European Brazilian contemporaries (Preto-Rodas 1970, 15–16).

The Vernacular Tradition: Caldas Barbosa

A prominent, if somewhat problematic, trend within the African Brazilian vernacular tradition featured authors articulating their racial identity in a minstrel-like fashion (which often earned them a sizable amount of money in the process; Epp

2003, 17–35). This typically involved projecting images whites considered acceptable for African Brazilians (e.g., folk figures, natural entertainers, jesters, clowns), including African Brazilian dialect, and "the two main stops, humour and pathos" (Brookshaw 1986, 179). Nevertheless, given the limitations of the racial order, those writing in the vernacular tradition also may be viewed as nonconformists who subverted (consciously or unconsciously) the dominant aesthetic canon.

The most commonly cited mulatto author of the vernacular tradition is eighteenth-century poet and composer of popular songs Domingos Caldas Barbosa (1740–1800). Born in Rio de Janeiro in 1740, Caldas Barbosa was the son of a Portuguese merchant named António de Caldas Barbosa and an African Brazilian woman named Antónia de Jesus. It is believed that Caldas Barbosa's mother was a slave owned by his father and brought with him from Angola to Brazil, but that, when Antónia became pregnant, António purchased her freedom to prevent their child from being born a slave (Costigan 2007, 172–80; Marques 2011, 49; Tinhorão 2004, 11–26).

After receiving his education from the Jesuits in Rio de Janeiro and joining the military of Colony of Sacramento in Uruguay, Caldas Barbosa was sent to study at the University of Coimbra in Portugal (circa 1775). Due to the sudden death of his father, he was unable to pursue his education and faced myriad difficulties, including illness, poverty, and homelessness. To survive, Caldas Barbosa became a minstrel and secured the patronage of the Conde de Pombeiro (José de Vasconcellos e Sousa) and brother of Luís de Vasconcellos, who lived in Rio de Janeiro (Costigan 2007, 172–80; Marques 2011, 50–51).[10] Caldas Barbosa joined the Nova Arcadia literary society, which met in the palace of his patron. Elected as the society's first president, he wrote many compositions praising his patrons and other members of the Court who bestowed favors upon him (Costigan 2007, 172–80; Tinhorão 2004, 27–66).

Besides neoclassical verses, Caldas Barbosa is best known for his *modinhas* (sentimental ballads) and *lundus* (flirtatious couples' dances usually accompanied by a guitar), which displayed a lighthearted sensuality. He sang these verses while accompanying himself on the viola; he blended stylistic devices of the vernacular and cultivated traditions in their composition. Unequivocally evocative of the exotic tropics, his verses bluntly equated his Africanness with social and financial inferiority (Béhague 1968, 46–47; Brookshaw 1986, 188–92; Budasz 2007, 18–19; Costigan 2007, 172–80; Pereira 1995, 876; Sayers 1958, 117–20; Tinhorão 2004, 67–124).

Early in his career Caldas Barbosa was called "Caldas de Cobre" (Copper Caldas) to distinguish him from his white contemporary Father António Pereira de

Souza Caldas (1772–1814), who was called "Silver Caldas" (Caldas de Prata). In a poem addressed to Pereira de Souza Caldas, Caldas Barbosa cleverly blends color and social status with metaphors involving coins of different value. Copper symbolizes his color and subdominant status, whereas silver represents his namesake's light skin and more affluent status (Preto-Rodas 1970, 18; Tinhorão 2004, 151–52).

> You are Caldas, I am Caldas;
> You are rich, and I am poor;
> You are silver Caldas;
> I am copper Caldas. (Barbosa 1958, 23)

In the poem "Lereno melancólico" (Melancholy Lereno), Caldas Barbosa attributes Lereno's melancholy to his "unfortunate color" (*triste côr*; Barbosa 1944, 1:101–4; Rennó 1999, 151) and appeals to the sympathies of the white women in the audience by asking for their understanding. In another selection, "Retrato de Lucinda" (Portrait of Lucinda), he praises the darker complexion of a mulatto woman compared to the paler rosy-cheeked countenance of her white counterparts.

> Your cheeks are not
> Of jasmine and rose,
> But your complexion
> Is imbued with much more grace.
> Your complexion is indeed the envy of all
> In addition, there are some whose deepest wish is
> To be dark and comely like you. (Barbosa 1944, 2:10–12)

This sentiment pandered to attitudes among the dominant white males whose predilection for sexual liaisons with African Brazilian women (Brookshaw 1986, 191) was attributed to the supposed greater sexual ardor and appeal of these embodiments of the "dusky Venus" (Bastide 1961, 10). Caldas Barbosa also expressed racial concerns by combining modesty with humor and pathos, which he often directed at himself. This indulged the dominant European sentimentality, humor, and interest in the slightly risqué, providing it was voiced by an African Brazilian (Brookshaw 1986, 189–92; Epp 2003, 17–35). Indeed, Flora Süssekind characterizes Caldas Barbosa as a perfect example of the picturesque poet or clown whose identity was configured by the interests of the white elite (Süssekind 1982, 13). Caldas Barbosa conformed to stereotypical (and servile) images whites held of

African Brazilians. This, apart from his poetic talents, undoubtedly helps explain his notoriety among European audiences (especially considering that blacks and mulattoes were "in vogue" at the Portuguese Court; Brookshaw 1986, 189–192; Porter 1951, 266; Süssekind 1982, 195; Tinhorão 2004, 67–124).

Caldas Barbosa was not without his detractors, however. The same racially inflected style that brought him fame at the Court also attracted disparaging remarks from more erudite poets such as Manuel Maria Barbosa du Bocage, who wrote two sonnets attacking him (Porter 1951, 267). Bocage, also a member of the Nova Arcadia literary society, called Caldas Barbosa a "poor little orangutan," whose facial expression was like that of a witch doctor, and, in a second sonnet, "a foul-smelling monkey that a Brazilian sorceress had dressed up as a human" (Bocage in Sayers 1958, 117–118). Another poet, Filinto Elísio, described Caldas Barbosa as "Queen Ginga's grandson," referring to the celebrated black Angolan potentate (Brookshaw 1986, 189).

Caldas Barbosa's modinhas were popular in Brazil, although literary mandarins disparaged his writings as being "low culture" (Süssekind 1982, 12–13; Veríssimo 1916/1963, 132). It was not until the 1920s that he received broader appreciation from the literary establishment. At that time, poets searching for nativistic forms with which to forge a literary nationalism began to draw inspiration from African Brazilian vernacular culture. Despite various negative characterizations of Caldas Barbosa and his poetry, poet Manuel Bandeira (1886–1968) described him as the first individual in whom the nation could find an authentically Brazilian sensibility (Brookshaw 1986, 188–192; Porter 1951, 269). More recently, Lúcia Costigan, Jane Malinoff, and Heitor Martins have argued that Caldas Barbosa's writings are the earliest articulations of a genuine Brazilian sensibility in a colonial literature largely characterized by uninspired imitations of Portuguese models. They further argue that Caldas Barbosa, as the first Brazilian composer to translate African Brazilian speech patterns and rhythms into lyrics, created a separate African Brazilian poetry that held great appeal for contemporary audiences. They consider Caldas Barbosa one of the most important precursors of African Brazilian literature and Brazilian popular music (Costigan 2007, 173–74; Malinoff 1981, 195; Marques 2011, 53–54; Martins 1983, 119–26; Araújo 1963, 11).

Caldas Barbosa's use of vernacular forms directly challenged the legitimacy of forms imported from Europe as well as their dominance in the colonial periphery (Brookshaw 1986, 190; Malinoff 1981, 195; Porter 1951, 269; Rennó 2001, 13–28, 127–130). Not someone who simply accepted or functioned beneath the racial compartment line, he succeeded in negotiating a contact zone between the high culture above the comportment line and the low culture beneath it. Though this zone did not deconstruct the dichotomous and hierarchical ranking of African and European racial and cultural differences, and indeed emphasized those differences to its advantage, it did use the permeable nature of the comportment line to create a space for popular African Brazilian culture within the white elite culture of Portugal and Brazil, a culture generally hostile to its existence (Budasz 2007, 18–19; Costigan 2007, 178–79; Peres 1998, 210; Rennó 1999, 24, 100; Süssekind 1982, 12).

The Tradition of Opposition: From Luís Gama to Lima Barreto

In this third, potentially dangerous, and thus historically less common African Brazilian literary tradition, authors speak out against racial oppression. Many fought for African Brazilian rights and sought to bridge the divide between pretos and mulatos by identifying as "negros." Although they openly criticize the dominant European Brazilians and the subordinate positioning of African Brazilians, they typically do so in the language of the dominant culture or cultivated tradition, but they may also make use of vernacular forms and humor to convey their message. The lighthearted banter of authors in the vernacular tradition, who set themselves up as objects of laughter, becomes the bitter, mocking, and caustic satire of authors in the tradition of opposition, who make whites the objects of this laughter and whose goal, whatever technique they may use, is to articulate racial protest.

LUÍS GAMA   One of the most cited authors of the tradition of opposition is the poet, journalist, and lawyer Luís Gonzaga de Pinto da Gama (1830–82). An anomaly among mulatto writers, Gama spoke out on the topic of racism and suffered reprisals for doing so (he was fired from his job as clerk at the police department and imprisoned several times; the authorities closed down several of the radical newspapers in which he published). Gama was born in Salvador, Bahia. His mother, Luisa Mahin, was African-born and a member of one of the Yoruba-speaking peoples of West Africa. Luisa eventually gained her freedom and was reportedly involved in the slave rebellions that shook Bahia in the early part of the nineteenth century (Azevedo 1999, 24, 35). Although Mahin's fate is uncertain, Dale Graden states that she joined the exodus of African Brazilians to Rio de Janeiro in the wake of the 1835 Malês Revolt (Graden 2006, 73).[11] Gama's father, whose name is shrouded in mystery, was apparently a Bahian aristocrat of Portuguese lineage given to excessive drinking and gambling. Indeed, two years after Luisa Mahin's disappearance, Gama's father sold his son into slavery to pay off a gambling debt (Azevedo 1999, 35; Brookshaw 1986, 192–94; Campos 2011, 127; Kennedy 1974, 255–60; Sayers 1958, 105–7; Silva 1989, 59–69).

Gama gained his freedom by running away after secretly obtaining documents that proved the illegality of his enslavement. He eventually secured employment as a clerk in the police department, which allowed him to devote his free time to writing poems for newspapers. In 1859, Gama's first and only book, *Primeiras trovas burlescas* (*First Burlesque Ballads*), satirical poems ridiculing the Brazilian aristocracy, avarice, women's fashions, and the emperor's generosity in granting titles of nobility, catapulted him into prominence in São Paulo. The most widely read are Gama's witty and biting verses against the social snobbery of nineteenth-century Brazil, with its Eurocentrism and whitening ideology (Azevedo 1999, 17, 27).

In his most renowned poem, entitled "Quem sou eu?" (Who Am I?), sometimes called "A Bodarrada" (The Goat Herd), Gama employs the term *bode* (goat)—an epithet whites used when referring to a mulatto—to remind everyone that, because of centuries of miscegenation, all Brazilians, no matter how European in appearance, are bodes despite claims to the contrary (Azevedo 1999, 49). Moreover, in another poem "Pacotilha" (Poorly Made Product), Gama jests that even those mulattoes with the most delicately formed noses could not avoid smelling of *catinga*, a body odor traditionally associated with African Brazilians (Gama 1904, 78). And, in yet another poem, "Sortimento de gorras para a gente do grande tom" (An Assortment of Hats of the People of Great Tone), he also ridicules the barons that Dom Pedro II created, who also have relatives buried in distant Africa (Gama 1904, 23). All of them, from the most opulent noble to the most humble plebeian, are braying "billies" of the goat herd—all are mulattoes.

> Who Am I?
> . . . .
> Am I goat, or a man whose skin is black?
> For practical purposes, what matters the fact?
> There are billy goats in every caste,
> And my friends indeed the species is vast.
> . . . .
> Rich billies, poor billies, some stupid, some wise
> Nonetheless, all billies, and should any we despise?
> Billy merchants and opportunists of value and worth
> All billies with horns, bellowing upon God's good earth.
> (Gama 1904, 110–14)

After having won acclaim as a poet, Gama dedicated his life to abolishing slavery; indeed, his campaign against slavery and racial hypocrisy was the spark that kindled the abolitionist movement. Gama participated in underground organizations that worked to organize the massive flight of slaves from the plantations. Moreover, he continued to wage his abolitionist campaign in the radical press (writing under various pseudonyms) and in the courtroom. Yet Gama had no formal legal training. Rather, he received instruction while a clerk in the law office of Francisco Maria de Sousa Furtado de Mendonça, who taught Gama the rudiments of law and provided him with law books. Gama's knowledge of jurisprudence, keen rhetoric, and sarcastic wit, as well as clever and eloquent defenses—which he often used to ridicule his opponents—along with his repeated successes in litigation, earned him esteem both among radicals of the elite and in legal circles. In the courts, he gained freedom for hundreds of slaves and dared to say: "According to the Law, any crime committed by a slave against his master is justifiable.... Any slave who kills his master does so in self-defense" (Gama in Kennedy 1974, 257, 262).

The Lei do Ventre Livre (Law of the Free Womb) of 1871, which stipulated that children henceforth born to slaves and all slaves belonging to the state were to be free, merely intensified Gama's desire for total abolition. Yet the law's provisions proved to be less effective than advocates had hoped. Slave owners who refused to accept the state's indemnity payment for slave children at age 8 still had the option of retaining the "freeborn" children as de facto slaves until they reached the age of 21. Notwithstanding the 1871 legislation, one faction in the abolitionist movement, represented by Gama and his followers, wanted more radical change. They envisaged African Brazilian participation not only in the struggle for abolition but also in efforts to replace the monarchy with a democratic government. Another faction, representing the aristocracy and led by Joaquim Nabuco, wanted to prevent direct African Brazilian participation in the abolitionist campaign and to maintain the monarchy and the status quo. He feared that African Brazilians would imbue the campaign with a revolutionary spirit that would lead to the downfall of the regime and to deposing the aristocracy from positions of national leadership (Kennedy 1974, 263–67; Silva 1989, 59–69).

Gama's position on these issues, along with his courtroom successes, made him intensely unpopular among slaveholders and high-ranking government officials and even led to threats on his life. When, over his objections, the Brazilian Republican Party, which he had helped found, adopted a manifesto in 1873 calling for gradual emancipation of slaves with indemnification to slave owners, a disillusioned Gama withdrew his support. He had believed that, as an advocate of democracy, the party would favor the immediate and unconditional abolition of slavery, but many Republicans were themselves large plantation owners whose livelihoods depended on slavery.

By the late 1880s, however, the abolitionist movement gained momentum across the nation. Abolitionist propaganda dominated the press; clandestine organizations and grassroots organizing among African Brazilians helped slaves escape from plantations and prevented their recapture, dealing slavery the final blow. As the army became more sympathetic to the cause and refused to pursue runaway slaves, slaveholders found themselves helpless in face of a general slave exodus from the plantations.

The struggle to end slavery reached a climax when slave owners themselves rushed to free their slaves and take some credit for the "great humanitarian act" of emancipation (Trochim 1988, 285). Yet it was African Brazilians who proposed significant social and economic reforms in the post-Abolition period (Trochim 1988, 285). Mulatto engineer André Rebouças (1838–98), for example, played a key role in formulating a program for "rural democracy" and the distribution of land among the libertos, a program adopted by many abolitionist organizations. Another mulatto, newspaper editor and activist José do Patrocínio, publicized Rebouças's ideas in his popular daily *A Cidade do Rio* (*The City of Rio*) and in public meetings.

Gama did not live to see the realization of his dream (Andrews 1991, 3–42; Kennedy 1974, 265–66). He died on August 24, 1882, of complications stemming from diabetes. Yet the campaign launched by him and others, along with growing public antislavery sentiment, and the strong abolitionist stance of Princess Isabel, finally prompted the government to enact legislation ending slavery. On May 13, 1888, six years after Gama's death, under the leadership of Prime Minister João Alfredo Correio de Oliveira (1835–1915), parliament passed Law no. 3353, known as the "Lei Áurea" (Golden Law) abolishing slavery. Princess Isabel, acting as regent while Emperor Dom Pedro II was in Europe, signed this legislation (Conrad 1972, 157; Trochim 1988, 286).

JOSÉ DO PATROCÍNIO   It is not surprising that few upwardly mobile mulattoes in late nineteenth-century Brazil followed Gama's lead (Flory 1977, 199–224; Kennedy 1974, 255–67). Exceptions include orator, journalist, poet, and novelist José Carlos do Patrocínio (1853–1905; Sayers 1958, 371–79), the out-of-wedlock son of Father João Carlos Monteiro, parish priest and owner of an estate near Lagoa de Cima in Campos, Rio de Janeiro, and Justina Maria do Espírito Santo, one of his father's young slaves. That Monteiro was indeed Patrocínio's father might never have been known had not another parish priest, Father Luís Ferreira Nobre Pelinca, revealed this information. In no small part because he was a priest and a socially prominent white patriarch, Monteiro never legitimated his son. José was given the last name "Patrocínio" because his baptism coincided with the second Saturday in November, which was traditionally called the "Patrocínio da Virgem Santíssima" (Holy Day of the Patron Blessed Virgin) in Brazil (Magalhães Júnior 1969, 10; Orico 1953, 33).

Reared as the privileged son of a doting father, Patrocínio once felt justified in whipping a slave across the face for not opening the estate gate quickly enough on his return from a horseback ride. As he matured and under the guidance of his father, however, his attitude toward slaves changed radically. Indeed, he later became so upset at the spectacle of his father's overseer punishing a slave, he threw himself down a flight of stairs—which fractured his skull—to stop the lashings. Patrocínio also helped several slaves escape from his father's estate (Magalhães Júnior 1969, 10–12; Orico 1952, 52–54; Santos 2011, 205).

Patrocínio's father helped find him employment in Campos as a teenage apprentice in a commercial firm. Soon dismissed when several white customers expressed discomfort at seeing an individual of color working in the establishment, Patrocínio left Campos for Rio de Janeiro, where he served as an apprentice in the Santa Casa de Misericórdia (Holy House of Mercy). Years later, he enrolled in the School of Medicine as a pharmacy student, graduating in 1874 (Magalhães Júnior 1969, 16–17, 25–28; Orico 1952, 57–62; Patrocínio 1877/2003, 336–37).

In 1875, however, Patrocínio discovered his true vocation when he began writing for the satirical journal *Os Ferrões* (*The Bee's Stingers*). He then joined the *Gazeta de Notícias* (*News Gazette*), a leading newspaper in Rio de Janeiro, in 1877 and soon became one of the most celebrated journalists of that time (Magalhães Júnior 1969, 28–36). By 1879, Patrocínio had also become actively involved in the abolitionist movement. In 1881, he went to write for the *Gazeta da Tarde* (*Evening Gazette*; Carvalho 1996, 1–5; Patrocínio 1877/2003, 336–37; Porter 1952, 66–77). During this period, Patrocínio founded the Confederação Abolicionista (Abolitionist Confederation). In September 1887, he left the *Gazeta da Tarde* to found and manage his own newspaper, *A Cidade do Rio* (*The City of Rio*), which counted among its contributors some of Brazil's finest journalists, most notably Olavo Bilac (1865–1918) and Coelho Neto (1864–1934; Carvalho 1996, 1–5; Magalhães Júnior 1969, 47; Patrocínio 2003, 336–37; Porter 1952, 73–79).

Shortly after Princess Isabel signed the Lei Áurea abolishing slavery in 1888, Patrocínio masterminded the creation of the Guarda Negra (Black Guard), a secret society that sought to advance social and economic reform in post-Abolition Brazil and to overcome the divide between blacks and mulattoes, which had prevented traditional organizations from promoting African Brazilian solidarity. Patrocínio's strategy was to unite all abolitionist groups with the larger reform movement to counter efforts by reactionary planters and Republicans to control the libertos by imposing "forced labor, harsh vagrancy laws, and forced military recruitment" on them (Andrews 1991, 44–45; Magalhães Júnior 1969, 273; Trochim 1988, 286–90). The Republicans feared that the monarchy, having capitulated to the abolitionist movement, would support further reforms.

For its part, the Black Guard supported the monarchist cause and, in particular, the Conservative administration that came to power in 1888 under the leadership of João Alfredo Correio de Oliveira and that seemed prepared to implement progressive social and economic reforms (Andrews 1991, 44–45; Trochim 1988, 289–91). It drew most of its members from the ranks of ordinary libertos but also attracted less reputable elements, including some local *capoeiristas* (Trochim 1988, 288–93), who were not averse to violence when expressing their frustration over the lack of opportunity for economic and social advancement.[12] Thus, between December 1888 and July 1889, the Black Guard was involved in violent public disruptions of Republican gatherings in Rio de Janeiro, disruptions Patrocínio and others of his organization called attempts by African Brazilians to defend their rights against the assaults of racist Republicans.

But, as Michael Trochim contends, the Black Guard's use of violence undermined its legitimacy even among sympathetic whites and left a legacy of antipathy toward the formation of explicitly political African Brazilian organizations (Trochim 1988, 298–300). Indeed, judging from the less partisan press, many Brazilians rejected the very notion that African Brazilians could mobilize politically on their own. They viewed the Black Guard as no more than a group of simpleminded African Brazilians manipulated by the João Alfredo government and Princess Isabel to destroy the planter class for their own political purposes (Andrews 1991, 44–45; Trochim 1988, 294–98). When the Republic was declared in November 1889 and the Republicans and army took control of the government, the public activities of the Black Guard immediately diminished and soon ceased altogether; the reforms advocated by abolitionists were shelved.

In 1891, Patrocínio openly opposed Floriano Vieira Peixoto (1839–95), the new president of the Republic, for which he was exiled to Cucuí in Amazônia. Peixoto was an army marshal when elected vice president in 1891 and later became president following the resignation of Marshal Deodoro da Fonseca (1827–92), the first president of Brazil, in November 1891. Because Article 42 of the Constitution stipulated that, in the case of resignation of the president, the vice president could only assume the presidency if at least half of the president's term of office was completed, Peixoto's ascendancy to the presidency was deemed unconstitutional, a finding Peixoto chose to disregard by proclaiming a state of emergency (Burns 1993, 238–44; Orico 1952, 249–54, 264–70). Although Patrocínio quietly returned to Rio de Janeiro in 1893, the state of emergency was still in effect, and publication of *Cidade do Rio* remained suspended. Patrocínio's political participation in subsequent years was minimal. He dedicated himself to building the "Santa Cruz," a dirigible forty-five meters in length, which never left the ground. On January 29, 1905, at 51 years of age, Patrocínio died, mired in debts and relegated to relative obscurity (Carvalho 1996, 1–5; Magalhães Júnior 1969, 47, 396–416).

Given Patrocínio's prominence in the abolitionist campaign, his political activities and articles on slavery, which are considered to be among the finest abolitionist essays published in Brazil, have overshadowed his works as a novelist and orator and the hundreds of articles he wrote as a political journalist about the imperial Court and about the first years of the Republic, among many other topics (Motta 2008, 9–10). One of Patrocínio's most important contributions was his coverage of the great drought in Ceará (1877–80) and its impact on the impoverished communities in the Northeast (Magalhães Júnior 1969, 60–70, 80–81). Patrocínio included photographs along with his extraordinary written reports— the first time a Brazilian journalist used photographs to document events (Motta 2008, 94–97, 137–44). His treatment of the drought was published as a serialized novel, *Os retirantes* (*Refugees of the Drought*; 1879), in the *Gazeta de Notícias*. Besides *Os retirantes*, Patrocínio wrote two other novels, *Pedro Espanhol* (*Peter Spain*; 1884) and *Motta Coqueiro ou a pena de morte* (*Motta Coqueiro or the Death Penalty*; 1887). Unlike *Os retirantes*, the other novels contain African Brazilian characters, although overall racial questions and the African Brazilian experience are not their primary focus.

In *Motta Coqueiro*, the only Patrocínio novel to discuss slavery, the primary target is capital punishment. Protagonist Motta Coqueiro is a wealthy white slave owner, who lives in the small coastal town of Macaé in Rio de Janeiro province, more than half of whose inhabitants are nonwhite and enslaved. Considered a threat to the aspirations of local political rivals, Motta Coqueiro is framed for a murder and condemned to death. *Motta Coqueiro* is based on an account of actual historical events in 1854–55 pieced together from Patrocínio's careful examination of the evidence (Bruzzi 1959, 41; Magalhães Júnior 1969, 48–55; Naro 1996, 59, 65–66; Patrocínio 1877/2003, 17, 22; Santos 2011, 213–15).

Patrocínio suggests that the real Motta Coqueiro paid for the crimes of a society that had brutalized untold numbers of slaves. Indeed, in an ironic inversion of the social order, the false testimony of Motta Coqueiro's household slaves, which was motivated by revenge and hatred of whites, was given more credence than his own claims of innocence. Although information obtained from slaves during interrogation was not admissible in court except to clarify details, their statements became the mainstay of the prosecution. For Patrocínio, the Motta Coqueiro case signaled a world turned upside down, in which a white plantation and slave owner became a captive of public sentiment. The testimony of slaves, endorsed by poor local free citizens and low-ranking civil servants, became the basis for sentencing a wealthy planter to death (Naro 1996, 1, 66, 71).

Silviano Santiago classifies *Motta Coqueiro* as a "romance de tese" (thesis or didactic novel). Patrocínio fashions the novel around the physical and psychological description of the characters and links together the sequences of dramatic scenes with the purpose of persuading readers to consider the injustice involved (Santiago 1982, 135–39). Despite the novel's Romantic plot and language, as well as Patrocínio's tendency to moralize, *Motta Coqueiro* displays the influence of Naturalism that was beginning to sweep in to Brazil from France: it reports the facts with scientific and clinical objectivity and indeed is impressively faithful to the actual unfolding of events.

The novel also provides detailed descriptions of life on a large mid-nineteenth-century plantation and the impotence of virtue in a world of evil. Patrocínio was among the first writers to deal with slavery in his works. He does not, however, appear to question African Brazilian stereotypes commonly applied to slavery at the time. Indeed, Patrocínio was instrumental in helping create two stereotypical and recurring characters in Romantic abolitionist literature. These were the "bad slave," who does not accept slavery and who is generally a sorcerer (in *Motta Coqueiro* the character is a woman; Patrocínio 1877/2003, 67–69); and the "good slave," who does accept slavery and who cooperates with the white master. Furthermore, Patrocínio makes no attempt to conceal any of the sexual aspects of slaves' lives. Indeed, he emphasizes African Brazilian sexuality, particularly that of mulattoes, and its link with racial makeup in obedience to the literary conventions of Naturalism.

Many white writers who were self-proclaimed abolitionists also used these images (Marotti 1982, 66, 116–21). Naturalism held that the products of generations of abused and malnourished slaves were inferior and dangerous. The message of

Naturalist novels is that, because blacks and mulattoes have no control over their animal instincts and no morality of their own, they could have disastrous effects on those who do (i.e, whites). By declaring that the crimes of slavery were simply the result of uncontrollable natural forces, Naturalism abolished white guilt. But it also advised those outside that environment and free of its inferior genes to avoid possible contagion through contact with those forever damaged by their enslaved condition and impaired by their heredity (Branche 2006, 160–61; Haberly 1972, 30–46; Marotti 1982, 116–21).

Given other aspects of Patrocínio's views and writing, not to mention his own racial background, it is hard to believe that he actually subscribed to this line of thinking. But Eduardo Duarte argues that, despite being a leader in the abolitionist movement, Patrocínio "left etched in his writings the characteristic discourse of racial hegemony" (Duarte 2007b, 138). That said, some of Patrocínio's African Brazilian characters may reflect a common opposition among Naturalist writers toward the *idea* of a nation associated with the Republican regime, which threatened to neutralize regional, gender, sexual, racial, and class differences through the projection of a unitary and centralized white, male, heterosexual, and bourgeois subject. According to Eva Bueno, this opposition manifested itself, in part, by appropriating the very alignments of race, gender, sexuality, and class that were problematized and challenged in Naturalist novels (Bueno 1995, ix–iv, xxii; Foster 1991, 9–22).

LIMA BARRETO   Although Mario de Andrade (1893–1945) continued Luís Gama's criticism of the Eurocentric bias of Brazil's national psyche and sought to forge a "multiracial aesthetic" (Haberly 1983, 136–60), there were few early twentieth-century successors to Gama's tradition of aggressive racial protest. Of these, the most important was mulatto author Afonso Henriques de Lima Barreto (1881–1922). Born into the petty bourgeoisie of suburban Rio de Janeiro, Lima Barreto struggled financially most of his life and suffered a tragedy at an early age. His mother, Amália Augusta, died of tuberculosis when he was six years old; with the advent of the Republic in 1889, his father, João Henriques, lost his job as a typographer at the monarchist press *A Tribuna Liberal* (*Liberal Tribune*). That said, João Henriques's close association with the Visconde de Ouro Prêto (Afonso Celso de Assis Figueiredo Júnior; 1860–1938), with whom he worked at the *Tribune*, and who became godfather to his son, proved to be invaluable. Although imprisoned and briefly exiled after the closing of the *Tribune*, Celso continued to wield considerable influence. This influence, along with the intervention of

Minister of the Interior Cesário Alvim, who had worked with João Henriques and Celso at another newspaper, *A Reforma* (*Reform*), helped João Henriques secure a job as warden at a mental institution on the Ilha do Governador, where Lima Barreto would spend most of his childhood (Barbosa 1959, 3–72; Duggan 1976, 14, 20; Fantinati 1978, 25, 43, 39, 40; Herron 1968, 1–24; Machado 2002, 55–90; Marotti 1982, 211–251; Rabassa 1965, 363–402).

Having completed his secondary education at the elite Colégio de Dom Pedro II (Dom Pedro II Academy), in 1897, with the encouragement and financial support of his father, Lima Barreto enrolled at the Escola Politécnica (School of Engineering; Barbosa 1959, 73–102), where he would repeatedly fail at rational mathematics and devote an inordinate amount of time to reading philosophy rather than studying engineering and attending class. When João Henriques's declining mental health forced him to resign from his position on the Ilha do Governador, Lima Barreto abandoned his engineering studies and, in 1903, began working as a clerk in the Ministry of War in order to assume financial responsibility for his family (Duggan 1976, 18–24; Barbosa 1959, 77–78; Herron 1968, 7).

Lima Barreto's civil service employment (1903–19), which was his main source of income for the greater part of his adult life, along with the small income he earned as a budding journalist, provided him with a modicum of financial stability (Barbosa 1959, 103–248). Yet the tedium of the ministry's bureaucratic environment and the burden of caring for his father took its toll psychologically. Lima Barreto descended into depression and alcoholism, adopting a bohemian life style punctuated by drinking binges. Adding to his woes, his brutally honest portrayal of society was coldly received by the literary establishment.

Although the small pension he received upon retiring from the ministry in 1919 freed him to pursue his writing, Lima Barreto's most productive years took place during his tenure there. Nevertheless, despite his mental illness, he continued to write after 1919, producing a flurry of chronicles, articles, essays, and short stories dedicated primarily to political and social concerns. Weakened by alcoholism, Lima Barreto died of influenza and a heart attack at the age of 41 on November 1, 1922—just two days before his father's own demise (Barbosa 1959, 295–349; Duggan 1976, 14, 20–30; Figueiredo 1995, 7–27, 95–97; Herron 1968, 19).

Like many writers of the time, Lima Barreto began his career as a journalist but sought to establish himself as a fiction writer. He spoke out openly and caustically on controversial issues. Among his primary targets were the bureaucracy, the world of journalism, and the Republican oligarchy. Ahead of his time in his awareness of and willingness to speak out against racism, he vehemently condemned

Brazilians' addiction to soccer. He felt that the sport, imported from England, privileged white or more European-looking players over plainly African Brazilian players in international competitions—with the goal of making Brazil appear more European than it was in reality. Jim Crow segregation and U.S. imperialism in Latin America were also objects of his wrath (Aiex 1990, 24–25; Daniel 1996, 389–99; Duggan 1976, 15–31; Herron 1968, 1–31; Marotti 1982, 211–51; Nunes 1979, ix–x, 1–9).

The first African Brazilian fiction writer to refuse to toe the racial comportment line, Lima Barreto openly discussed the topic of racism from an African Brazilian point of view, specifically the lives of the largely black and mulatto inhabitants of suburban Rio de Janeiro. Lima directed his harshest criticism at Brazil's ruling elite, who were obsessed with the pursuit of material wealth and whiteness while discriminating against African Brazilians. Yet he seems to have remained ambivalent toward African Brazilian vernacular culture. Recognizing that culture as the authentic culture of Rio de Janeiro—and, by extension, of Brazil—compared to the pretentious and Europeanized culture of Rio de Janeiro's Belle Époque elite, he nevertheless situated it among the "intangible degenerating influences of Rio" and thought it might benefit from being "filtered and civilized" (Borges 1995, 68). Indeed, for the most part, he found it difficult to incorporate African Brazilian vernacular culture into his own work (Borges 1995, 66–68).

Lima Barreto was also not immune to the effects of internalized racism. Although he articulated a militant African Brazilian consciousness in his novels and short stories, a large body of diary entries and personal correspondence document his passage from a prideful (and perhaps overly self-confident) mulatto to someone plagued by deep self-doubt (Daniel 1996, 389–99). His growing sense of inadequacy and physical unattractiveness spilled over into his relationship with society as a whole and had disastrous consequences for his personal and professional life (Daniel 1996, 389–99).

As a young man, Lima Barreto believed that mulattoes might well be superior to both blacks and whites. Because they were objects of confrontations and challenges, mulattoes developed an internal character and will to succeed, which made them capable of overcoming adverse circumstances and surviving in a hostile society. Moreover, Lima felt a sense of personal superiority in this regard, compared to other African Brazilians (Barreto 1956, 44). Over the course of his life, however, he became a frustrated and fearful individual; though his esteem for African Brazilians as a whole never wavered, it diminished significantly with regard to himself (Daniel 1996, 389–99). Admiring the physical attractiveness of varying degrees of blackness in others, Lima found himself physically unattractive (especially to white women), due, in large part, to his own internalization of Eurocentric norms (Daniel 1996, 389–99; Silva 1976, 57–58).

Lima Barreto's discussion of racial concerns is most evident in his novels *Recordações do escrivão Isaías Caminha* (*Memoirs of the Notary Public Isaías Caminha*; 1909), *Vida e morte de M. J. Gonzaga de Sá* (*The Life and Death of M. J. Gonzaga de Sá*; 1919), and *Clara dos anjos* (*Clara of the Angels*, completed in 1922 but not published until 1948). His explicit treatment of racial questions made it difficult for him to secure patrons among the white elite, who were essential for his social advancement. His first novel, *Isaías Caminha*, was a merciless roman à clef attacking powerful contemporary figures in Carioca journalism.[13] Consequently, Lima had to have the book published in Portugal, although he was more successful in securing Brazilian publishers for subsequent novels and collections of short stories (Brookshaw 1986, 193–99; Coelho 2011, 296–300; Daniel 1996, 389–99; Duggan 1976, 15–31; Figueiredo 1995, 7–22, 95–97; Herron 1968, 1–24; Lins 1976, 24–27; Marotti 1982, 211–51).

Although the Academia Brasileira de Letras (Brazilian Academy of Letters) repeatedly refused to admit Lima Barreto, it did give honorable mention to his more restrained and refined "Machadian" novel, *The Life and Death M. J. Gonzaga de Sá*, in 1920 (Figueiredo 1995, 69; Herron 1968, 18). Lima Barreto always denied any influence of Machado and bristled at any comparison with him (Marins 2004, 13; Wasserman 2008, 85), yet the protagonist in this second novel bears striking similarities to Machado, and the narrator actually bears his name. Atypical of Lima Barreto's generally caustic style, the novel recounts the fictional life of the white Gonzaga de Sá from the perspective of the mulatto narrator, Augusto Machado. It juxtaposes the racial and cultural contradictions and complexities of Brazil's Eurocentric colonial past, represented by Gonzaga de Sá, with the recognition of Brazil's need to embrace its truly multiracial and multicultural past, represented by Augusto Machado, if it is to meet the challenges of the future, represented by the young mulatto Aleixo Manuel, to whom Gonzaga de Sá becomes a guardian when Aleixo's father dies. In his more typical first novel, *Isaías Caminha*, Lima directs his harshest criticism at the world of journalism, although racial inequality figures prominently in this critique. Its narrator-protagonist, the mulatto journalist Isaías Caminha, relates his travails, racial and otherwise, with the chicanery, nepotism, and mediocrity that pervade the literary establishment and world of journalism (Barbosa 1959, 239–44, 277; Coutinho 1974, 13–32). As a person, Lima Barreto sought comfort in his own multiraciality, which he considered the foundation of

Brazil's past, present, and future, but, as an author, he symbolized this blend in other ways (Aiex 1990, 32–36; Duggan 1976, 15–31; Herron 1968, 1–24; Marotti 1982, 211–51; Sevcenko 1983, 124–25); indeed, he is considered the most important writer of the transitional period between Realism-Naturalism and Modernism in Brazilian literature, namely, "Premodernism" (Bosi 1970, 339–426).

However interconnected questions of Latin American aesthetic and cultural Modernism may be with the structural and social aspects of modernization and development, they by no means coincide (Moehn 2008, 166). Sociologists typically designate modernity as the period beginning in the Renaissance, which was accompanied by the rise of European nation-states to global dominion along with the ascent of materialist rationalism, secularism, capitalism, and individualism over other kinds of mentation. This was accompanied by a shift from traditional or premodern societies based on small, homogeneous, kin-based communities (typically rural), where religious and sacred traditions guided human existence, to more heterogeneous societies, where individualistic and secular concerns increasingly eclipsed communal and sacred ones. Latin American Modernism of the late nineteenth and the early twentieth centuries (in the form of cultural nationalism) reflected a desire to rearticulate and rehabilitate the traditional worldview associated with Native Americans and Africans in support of the concept of hybridity. However much it borrowed from or was inspired by contemporary Western European forms, Latin American cultural Modernism actually rejected the worldview associated with modernity as defined by sociologists.

For his part, Lima Barreto rejected what he considered the sterile Parnassian classicism of Realism-Naturalism, which was supported by purist Portuguese-oriented grammarians. The school of Parnassian poets, who stressed "correct form," dominated the Brazilian Academy of Letters in Rio de Janeiro during the late nineteenth and the early twentieth centuries when revolutionary aesthetic movements that rejected formalistic literature were gaining momentum in Europe (Skidmore 1974, 176–78). Before World War I, Filippo Marinetti and other writers spearheaded an attack on prevailing European grammatical and literary canons. Symbolizing their rupture with the past, these iconoclasts called themselves "Futurists." Among others things, they glorified and sought to give artistic expression to the fast pace of twentieth-century life and the fluidity of contemporary technology. Yet most of Brazil remained unaffected by the Futurists' concerns. The exception was Brazil's most vibrant economic hub, São Paulo, where a booming coffee economy helped finance the modernization of commercial agriculture and the beginnings of industrialization. Though less cosmopolitan than Rio de

Janeiro, São Paulo was home to an expanding urban middle class whose artistic intelligentsia first absorbed Modernist ideas from Europe and ultimately toppled the rigid standards of their Rio de Janeiro counterparts (Brookshaw 1986, 85–116; Skidmore 1974, 176–78). In keeping with this new trend, Lima Barreto sought to forge a language more closely reflecting Brazilian speech patterns, which in many ways prefigured one of the objectives the Modernists in São Paulo of the 1920s. In addition, he attained a level of social consciousness that qualifies him as a precursor of the Social Realist novelists of the 1930s, particularly in the Northeast (Brookshaw 1986, 194–99; Coutinho 1974, 54–56; Daniel 1996, 389–99; Franco 1970, 115; Marotti 1982, 211–51; Nunes 1979, ix–x, 1–9; Prado 1976, 11–13; Silva 1976, 31, 34).

BLACK INTO WHITE: RACIAL IDENTITY AND THE LIFE OF MACHADO DE ASSIS

From Livramento to Laranjeiras: A Biographical Sketch

The most frequently cited example of the cultivated tradition is Machado de Assis. Some critics have argued that his literary works, far from concerning themselves with questions of race, much less slavery, focus on the upper echelons of society. In addition, Machado is considered a classic case study of a mulatto who devoted his life to being accepted above the racial comportment line. He broke through the wall of second-class citizenship and studiously avoided any reference to his racial origins (Brookshaw 1986, 179–81; Sayers 1958, 385–400). That said, despite the more fluid race and cultural relations in nineteenth- and early twentieth-century Brazil—particularly in the state of Rio de Janeiro, where Machado was born and spent his life—mulattoes were subject to both covert and overt forms of discrimination (Klein 1972, 309–34; Russell-Wood 1972, 84–133; Spitzer 1989, 102). Although Machado was not a slave, he could not psychologically escape the fact that he was descended from African slaves (Azevedo 1955, 84–85, 97–101; Bicudo 1947, 205–7; Coutinho 1940, 22–24; Degler 1971, 213–16, 223–32; Hoetink 1973, 21–45; 165–76).

Machado's reticence regarding racial concerns, Raymond Sayers tells us, was most likely influenced both by his marriage into a European Brazilian family of Portuguese descent and by his rise in the bureaucracy and increasing literary prominence, which culminated in his election as the first president of the Brazilian Academy of Letters. Machado's epileptic illness may also have been a contributing factor (Sayers 1958, 388–89). Machado probably had epilepsy his entire life but experienced more frequent and more severe seizures during his adult years, particularly after his marriage in 1869 (Lopes 1981, 14). Only in his correspondence with Mario de Alencar between 1898 and 1908 and nowhere else in his writing did Machado discuss his illness (Chapman and Chapman-Santana 2000, 1154; Yacubian 2002). And, even there, he was careful to describe it with euphemisms such as "original sin" (*pecado origina*; *Epistolário, Oc*, 3:1086) or "nervous phenomena" (*fenômenos nervosos*; *Epistolário, Oc*, 3:1081) or by allusion. Thus, in his final letter to Alencar, on August 29, 1908, one month before Alencar's death, Machado wrote: "My dear friend, I read a few pages of the biography of Flaubert. I found the same solitude and sadness that I have, and even the same sickness, as you know, the other" (*Epistolário, Oc*, 3:1094).[1]

It is believed that Machado had "right temporal lobe epilepsy" that included "complex partial seizures, with secondary generalization" (Guerreiro 1992, 378–82). The embarrassment of having a seizure in public was doubtless a constant source of anxiety for him and must have prompted Machado to avoid, whenever possible, situations he felt might trigger a seizure. This anxiety was not unwarranted, given that he did have a seizure in public, which was photographed in September 1907 at Cais Pharoux (Pharoux Wharf) in Rio de Janeiro at the disembarkation of Paul Doumer, a future president of France (1931–32; Pérez 1962, 88; Viana Filho 1974, 263).

Machado's sensitivity about his illness was also intensified by the fact that epilepsy was so little understood in his day and was a source of social stigma.[2] Epileptics were often shunned by society. Treatment was poor and often worse than the illness. Although some believed that epilepsy imbued individuals with genius and unusual mental abilities, many others, including some psychiatrists, considered epilepsy a form of progressive mental illness, moral insanity, or criminality and violence. Indeed, physicians and criminologists associated epilepsy with violence; when they wrote about epilepsy and crime, they meant violent crime. In the public imagination, the illness was frequently thought to be contagious (Fernandes et al. 2004, 213–18; *Epilepsia* 2003; Friedlander 2001, 1–13, 210–11, 239–76; Schneider and Conrad 1980, 34; Sun 2007, 107–109; Temkin 1971, 262, 298, 364–82).

Apart from the difficulties posed by his epilepsy, Machado's racial origins, combined with his humble socioeconomic background, meant that he received little formal education and was mostly self-taught (Caldwell 1970, 24; Massa 1969, 1:45; Viana Filho 1974, 13).³ That said, he learned to read and write, and he also learned French, which at the time was essential for social and intellectual acceptance among the elite (Haberly 1983, 72). Machado furthered his education by immersing himself in Rio's celebrated Real Gabinete Português de Leitura (Royal Portuguese Library; Viana Filho 1974, 16). His personal library consisted of some 600 books, 400 brochures, and 400 pamphlets and fascicles, many of them in foreign languages. In addition, his writings contain many quotations from and allusions to foreign literature (Bagby Júnior 1975b, 225–33; Grupo de Estudos da Historia do Brasil 2006).

After analyzing Machado's literary quotations, borrowings from English literature, and use of English translations of Greek literature, Helen Caldwell concluded that he was proficient at reading and translating English. Indeed, he was proficient enough to translate Dickens's *Oliver Twist* into Portuguese, which was printed in serial form in the *Jornal da Tarde* (*Evening Journal*) in 1870.⁴ Jean-Michel Massa points to Machado's collection of classical and contemporary English literature, including nine books by Macaulay, twenty-four by Shakespeare, and some thirty by Dickens, to mention some of the most representative works. In addition, as a reflection of his interest in Longfellow and Poe, Machado owned at least a dozen books of U.S. literature. Clearly, an understanding of the tone, feeling, and nuances of these works demanded a sophisticated understanding of English (Bagby Júnior 1975b, 229).

Alberto Bagby Júnior concludes that Machado knew French, English, Spanish, Italian, and German (Bagby Júnior 1975b, 225–33; Massa 2001, 30–46, 59–60, 62–67, 70–71). He appears to have been almost bilingual in Portuguese and French, exhibited conversational skills in English and Spanish, and was able to read, write, and translate from each of these languages.⁵ The data indicate that he could read and write but not speak Italian and had limited knowledge of German. Massa believes that Machado had reading, writing, and good conversational ability in French and English; reading and writing ability with lesser conversational ability in Italian; and reading ability in German and Spanish (Massa 2001, 30–46, 59–60, 62–67, 70–71). Judging from the contents of a notebook containing written exercises in Greek, he apparently had a rudimentary knowledge of that language as well, and he aspired to master it, as he had Latin.⁶ Massa believes that Machado gave up these aspirations around the age of 44, perhaps after realizing that many of the books he wished to read in Greek had been translated into French (Massa 1961, 195–238; Bagby Júnior 1975a, 225–33).

Machado's accomplishments are even more impressive considering his parents' backgrounds. His birth mother, Maria Leopoldina Machado da Câmara (born 1812), was a Portuguese washerwoman and seamstress from Ponta Delgada, São Miguel, in the Azores (Caldwell 1970, 13–14: Magalhães Júnior 1981, 1:8; Massa 1969, 1:38). His father, Francisco José de Assis (born 1806?), was a mulatto housepainter (Caldwell 1970, 14–15; Massa 1969, 1: 33–34; Viana Filho 1974, 12–14). Machado's parents' marriage was atypical for the era, although some whites in the working class (particularly recent European immigrants) married people of color, in part because of the large percentage of blacks and mulattoes in that class (Karasch 1975, 291, 375; Klein 1972, 322–23, 325). As noted in chapter 1, significant numbers of Portuguese immigrated to Rio de Janeiro prior to 1850, especially young and mostly single males, seeking job opportunities as clerks and merchants in the city's retail sector (Menezes 2000, 164–65; Nunes 2000, 37–61).

The disproportionate number of single males among Portuguese immigrants created a gender imbalance within Rio de Janeiro's white population. Statistics indicate that, throughout the 1830s and 1840s, there were more free male inhabitants than free women and a scarcity of white women, a state of affairs that continued well into the nineteenth century. In 1838, Rio had 27,606 free women and 32,419 free male inhabitants; in 1849, these numbers had grown to 47,744 and 68,581, respectively (Nunes 2000, 37–61). By virtue of the abundance of free male immigrants and the scarcity of white women, free white men often took African Brazilian women, slave and free, as their concubines, mistresses, or common-law wives (Karasch 1975, 294). Yet throughout society, there was a strong social prejudice against marriages between white women and African Brazilian men, which not only made available white women even scarcer and threatened the perpetuation of the white population, but also placed subdominant men in a role that was the exclusive preserve of dominant males.

Although scattered references to interracial marriages existed before the abolition of slavery, one of the first systematic and detailed surveys, which involved over 40,000 married couples, was not conducted in the city of Rio de Janeiro until two years after abolition. The study revealed that, far from being the norm, interracial marriages represented only 6 percent (5,000) of the total marriages recorded (80,000). There were six times as many marriages between white men and mulatto women as there were between mulatto men and white women—and ninety times as many as there were between black men and white women. However, these data indicate that prevailing social attitudes permitted a significant minority of interracial unions, some 15 percent of which had white female partners (Klein

1969, 44–45; 1972, 322–23, 325). Moreover, though betrothed several times, Maria Leopoldina did not marry until 1838, when she was twenty-six years old. Because this was considered an advanced age for a woman, she may have viewed marriage to Francisco as attractive for practical reasons—apart from whatever affection she may have felt for him and despite the social taboo involved (Fonseca 1968, 35; Trípoli 2006, 85–86).

After Machado's mother died of tuberculosis on January 18, 1849 (Caldwell 1970, 13–14; Magalhães Júnior 1981, 1:8; Massa 1969, 1:38), his father remarried in 1854 to a mulatto woman named Maria Inês da Silva (born 1821; Caldwell 1970, 14–15; Viana Filho 1974, 12–14). By this time, working as a clerk, bookkeeper, typesetter, or proofreader, Machado was already becoming financially self-supporting (Haberly 1983, 72). During the late 1850s, under the patronage of Paula Brito, an influential mulatto printer and publisher in Rio de Janeiro, Machado gained entrée to the literary world and began publishing his first works (Haberly 1983, 72; Viana Filho 1974, 14–17). From that point on, Machado's ambition, social skills, and literary talents moved him slowly upward. In 1873, he was named to the first of a series of civil service posts—which allowed him to consolidate his reputation as a writer by giving him economic security. By 1897, with volumes of poems, short stories, chronicles, essays, literary criticism, and novels to his credit, Machado was elected the first president of the newly organized Brazilian Academy of Letters, of which he was a co-founder.

Accompanying Machado in his rise to social and literary prominence, and serving as both his critic-proofreader and companion, was his devoted wife, Carolina. However, Machado and Carolina Augusta Xavier de Novais (born 1834), a woman from a Portuguese family and sister of émigré poet Faustino Xavier de Novais, married over the serious objections of her family, as reported in two extant letters Machado wrote to Carolina (Caldwell 1970, 29–31, 205). Apparently, two of Carolina's siblings, Miguel and Adelaide, felt that Machado's mulatto background would bring disgrace upon the family even though he had achieved some recognition as a writer and public functionary and was one of Faustino's esteemed friends (Viana Filho 1974, 82).

Rumors of Machado's epilepsy and knowledge of his meager earnings may also explain the family's opposition to the marriage, particularly considering Carolina's own financial situation since the death of her parents. Though her father, Antonio Luís Pimental de Novais, had once been a jeweler of some distinction in Oporto (Porto), Portugal, Carolina and her five siblings found themselves in dire financial straits, despite assistance from friends and associates, when he and their mother, Custódia Emília Xavier de Novais, died in close succession. Concerns about the couple's finances were certainly borne out by the serious economic hardship Machado and Carolina endured as newlyweds (Caldwell 1970, 24, 205; Viana Filho 1974, 79–80).

Although Carolina came to Brazil to care for her ailing brother, Faustino (Caldwell 1970, 26, 32, 205), her immigration had the added benefit of providing her an opportunity to find a marriage partner (she had been unsuccessful in this endeavor in her native Portugal). Carolina's need to marry and her somewhat advanced age may explain in part the family's eventual, albeit begrudging acceptance of her marriage to Machado (Trípoli 2006, 85; Viana Filho 1974, 79). On November 12, 1869, three months after Faustino died, Machado and Carolina were married in Igreja de Santa Rita (Santa Rita Church). Carolina would serve as a force in her husband's life until her death on October 20, 1904 (Caldwell 1970, 25–33, 197; Fonseca 1968, 32; Pérez 1962, 89; Viana Filho 1974, 80–95). Along with his literary and bureaucratic careers, Machado's marriage to Carolina brought him a level of respectability that helped him put psychological and physical distance between his present life and humble social origins. It also helped erase—or mask—the stigma of race and secure for all posterity Machado's position in white-dominated elite circles. This elevated social status was publicly recognized on September 30, 1908, when Machado was buried alongside his wife in tomb no. 1359 in Rio de Janeiro's prestigious São João Batista cemetery (Magalhães Júnior 1981, 4:362, 367).

The Origin of the Controversy: Denial, Disassociation, and the "Black Legend"[7]

Despite his successes, however, Machado was not without his detractors. One of Machado's most outspoken critics during his lifetime was José do Patrocínio. Once, upon hearing someone mention Machado's name, Patrocínio is reported to have directed the most frenzied and vitriolic outburst against him: "Only one man inside and outside Brazil, remains indifferent to all the hosannas and infamy, clamor, tempest, fire, and flood of [abolitionist fervor that has engulfed the nation].—And that man is Mr. Machado de Assis. Hate him, because he is evil; hate him because he hates his race, his country, and his people" (Patrocínio in Murat 1926, 146–48).

Not long after Machado's death, Hermetério José dos Santos, a black elementary school teacher, published an article in the *Gazeta de Notícias* (*News Gazette*) that totally negated Machado as a man and as an author. Among other things, Santos accused Machado of being indifferent to the plight of slaves. He was, Santos charged, a fraud and a wretched mulatto who abandoned his stepmother, Maria Inês, to whom he owed everything, including the ability to read and write (Caldwell 1970, 8; Fonseca 1968, 265–66). Many people accepted Santos's accusations at face value, which spawned new accusations and fueled old ones, reproaching Machado for being a supporter of slavery, a man who sought to hide his racial origins and, worst of all, who disliked African Brazilians.

"Every night," Santos wrote, "Maria Inês would teach him a little bit of reading and writing.... I knew this wonderful, kind-hearted mulatto woman and saw her in her old age, living in obscurity, contented, but crying in the abandonment with which she had been left, never again to be acknowledged by the one who had abandoned her since he moved from São Cristovão, a working-class section of Rio, to the opulent and aristocratic Laranjeiras" (Santos in Fonseca 1968, 265–66; Magalhães Júnior 1958a, 106).

On the other hand, Raimundo Magalhães Júnior points out that Santos, in his attempt to accumulate "facts" against Machado, overlooked the fact that São Cristovão, where Machado's father and stepmother lived, was not only where many laborers lived but was also within view of the imperial palace and surrounded by the dwellings of many aristocrats. Moreover, although home to many affluent and prominent individuals, the Laranjeiras district of Rio de Janeiro was far from opulent (Magalhães Júnior 1958a, 106; Viana Filho 1974, 128).

In 1869, not long after they were married, Machado and Carolina lived in a modest dwelling at 119 Rua do Fogo (currently, Rua dos Andradas) in Rio de Janeiro's central city (Viana Filho 1974, 91). Subsequently, they moved to Rua da Lapa (1874), to the more upscale Rua das Laranjeiras (1875) in the Laranjeiras district, and to the Rua do Catete (1878) in the Bairro do Catete district. In 1884, they moved once again, to a chalet on 18 Rua Cosme Velho in the affluent Bairro do Cosme Velho district, where they would spend the remaining years of their lives (Fonseca 1968, 286; Viana Filho 1974, 128).

These residential moves paralleled increases in Machado's earnings with his promotions as a public functionary. He served in this capacity for almost thirty-five years, under thirty-six ministers (Caldwell 1970, 206). In 1873, just four years after Machado's marriage, Dom Pedro II named him to his first public service position as a scribe (*amanuense*), who took dictation or copied manuscripts, at the Ministry of Agriculture, Commerce, and Public Works (Pérez 1962, 79). In December of that year, Machado was promoted to first officer, with a salary of

4 million réis annually, or 333,333 réis per month (Fonseca 1968, 282; Magalhães Júnior 1958b, 123; Pérez 1962, 79; Revista de Historia 2008). In December 1876, Princess Isabel named Machado section head of the Secretariat of Agriculture (Fonseca 1968, 284; Pérez 1962, 80, 84; Viana Filho 1974, 109). With this appointment, Machado earned an annual salary of 5.4 million réis (Pérez 1962, 80; Secchin, Almeida, and Melo e Souza 1998, 24). By way of comparison, during the final years of the Empire, appellate judges earned 6 million réis (Secchin, Almeida, and Melo e Souza 1998, 24). In November 1902, after several other promotions, he was appointed director general of accounting for the Secretariat of Industry at the Ministry of Transportation, Industry, and Public Works. Machado held this position until June 1908, three months before his death, at which time he was earning 10 million réis annually, or 840,000 réis per month (Grupo de Estudos da Historia do Brasil 2006; Magalhães Júnior 1958b, 125; Pérez 1962, 84, 87).

Besides his salary as a civil service employee, Machado earned money by selling the rights to his literary works. In 1902, he sold the rights to *Várias histórias* (*Various Stories*) for 1 million réis (Grupo de Estudos da Historia do Brasil 2006); in 1905, the rights to his short story collection *Relíquias da casa velha* (*Relics of the Old House*) for 1.5 million réis. In 1906, he sold the rights to *A mão e a luva* (*The Hand and the Glove*) to the publisher Garnier for 500,000 réis; and in 1908, he received 1.5 million réis from Garnier for the rights to *Ayres's Memorial*, which was published in 1908, the year he died.

These resources, along with Machado's earnings from his work for newspapers and magazines, provided him with a standard of living far above the average Brazilian.[8] They made it possible for Carolina and him to rent their comfortable home in Cosme Velho, for which they paid 150,000 réis per month until July 1906, when the heirs of the original owner, Condessa de São Mamede, increased the rent to 200,000 réis. Machado's earnings also provided the resources to hire two domestic servants, Jovita Maria de Araújo and Carolina Pereira da Silva, who were paid a monthly salary of 55,000 réis (660,000 réis per year, plus room and board) until Machado's death (Magalhães Júnior 1981, 4:262, 378; Grupo de Estudos da Historia do Brasil 2006).

An inventory of Machado's holdings indicates that the total worth of his estate was approximately 23.5 million réis. This consisted of 12.2 million réis in government bonds and 11.3 million réis that included 4.9 million réis in a bank account, as well as stocks, cash, furniture, and books, plus Machado's salary of 840,000 réis for the month of September 1908. Less his accumulated debts and expenses, Machado's estate was worth approximately 21.1 million réis (Magalhães Júnior

1981, 4:343, 378; Grupo de Estudos da Historia do Brasil 2006). In the belief that his wife would survive him, and having no children, Machado had named Carolina his sole heir.[9] When she did not, he drafted a second will on October 12, 1905, almost a year after her death, naming Laura, the eleven-year-old daughter of his niece Sara Braga Gomes da Costa, his sole heir.[10] Laura's mother, Adelaide Xavier de Novais, was Carolina's sister; Machado named Sara's husband, Major Bonifácio Gomes da Costa, his first executor. Notarized on May 31, 1906, this second and final will asked that Machado be buried alongside his wife in São João Batista Cemetery (Magalhães Júnior 1981, 4:216, 258–59, 334–37, 342–43, 378; Pérez 1962, 89; Grupo de Estudos da Historia do Brasil 2006).

Exculpatory Evidence and Empirical Reprieve

Much of these data on Machado's personal holdings, which are now preserved in the National Archives, were only revealed in the late 1950s and early 1960s. Caldwell also indicates that it was not until 100 years after Machado's birth, and after decades of misinformation concerning his life and origins, that the record of his baptism was uncovered in the Santa Rita Church registry in the Senhora do Livramento (Our Lady of Livramento) parish of Rio de Janeiro, where he was born. It was learned from this that Machado' mother, Maria Leopoldina Machado da Câmara, was Portuguese, a native of the island of São Miguel, one of the Azores, white, and not of African ancestry, as had been stated in previous biographies. Machado's godparents were members of the elite: Chamberlain Joaquim Alberto de Sousa da Silveira was a twice-decorated chamberlain of the imperial palace; Dona Maria José de Mendonça Barroso, Portuguese by birth, was the widow of a brigadier general and senator of the Empire (Caldwell 1970, 13).

As had long been believed, Machado and his family did in fact live as dependents (agregados) on the widow's estate in Rio de Janeiro (Caldwell 1970, 13–15; Fonseca 1968, 31–32), which encompassed most of the Morro do Livramento (Livramento Hill), where he was born. But the evidence indicates that Machado's family surroundings, though "humble," were not "uncultured" (Caldwell 1970, 15), that he was at least two generations removed from slavery on his father's side, and that he was raised by his white Portuguese mother and supported by his mulatto father. At the time, the urban parishes of Rio de Janeiro had slightly more than 100,000 inhabitants—at least 40 percent of whom were slaves. Belying the beauty of its natural setting, Rio de Janeiro was a highly unsanitary city swept by epidemics of tuberculosis and other diseases, which contributed to high infant mortality and short life expectancy (Magalhães Júnior 1981, 1:5–12; Nunes 2000, 39, 41).

Between 1939 and 1959, Godín da Fonseca discovered other documents that cast further doubt on Santos's story that Maria Inês taught Machado to read when he was a child. As noted earlier, Machado's birth mother did not die until he was almost ten years old (1849; Fonseca 1968, 78) and his father did not remarry until Machado was fifteen years old and already out in the world earning a living (1854; Fonseca 1968, 113). Machado doubtless lived with his father and stepmother for some period after they moved from Morro do Livramento to São Cristovão (Massa 1969, 1:83; Fonseca 1968, 81). Although Maria Inês must have had some influence on Machado's personal and social development, Fonseca suggests that it is more probable that Machado learned to read and write from his mother. Indeed, Fonseca determined that Maria Leopoldina could read and could write at least her own name in a "firm, well-formed, flowing hand" (Caldwell 1970, 14) and that Machado's own handwriting resembled his mother's in a number of respects (Fonseca 1968, 39; Massa 1969, 1:45, 72). Moreover, Machado's father was able to read and write (Massa 1969, 1:36).

Fonseca discovered that Machado's father, Francisco, did not die until April 22, 1864, when Machado would have been nearly 25 (Caldwell 1970, 15; Fonseca 1968, 279). Citing notices for separate masses to be held for Machado's deceased father, one by Maria Inês, her mother, and brother, and another by Machado, Luiz Viana Filho notes that the announcements' wording and tone indicate that Machado, even before his father's death, was not on good terms with his stepmother and her family, although the reasons for the estrangement are unknown (Viana Filho 1974, 54–55; Caldwell 1970, 15). On the other hand, of equal interest is an account by one of Machado's close friends, the author Coelho Neto. According to this account, Machado, in a state of depression, asked Neto to accompany him to a burial in São Cristovão. There, within a coffin, was the body of an elderly woman. "It's my mother," Machado is said to have told Neto (Magalhães Júnior 1958a, 107). The woman was Maria Inês. Yet Machado attended her burial, which does not support the claim that he completely "abandoned" his stepmother.

Caldwell found that, in 1855, Machado dedicated the poem "Um anjo" (An Angel) to the memory of his only sister, Maria (who died of measles in 1846 when he was six years old; Caldwell 1970, 5, 14; Trípoli 2006, 81), and that he dedicated his first volume of verse, *Crysálidas* (*Chrysalids*; 1864), to the memory of his father and birth mother (Caldwell 1970, 5). Contrary to the belief that Machado avoided blacks and mulattoes, Magalhães Júnior shows that he included a number of African Brazilians among his associates and friends, most notably, the writers Antônio Gonçalves Teixeira e Sousa (1812–61), José Ferreira de Menezes (1845–81), and Laurindo Rabelo (1826–64), as well as Senators Francisco Otaviano de Almeida

Rosa (1825–89), the Visconde de Jequintinho (Francisco Gomes Brandão; 1794–1870), and Dom Manuel de Assis Mascarenhas (1805–67; Magalhães Júnior 1958a, 108–9). These facts, however, do not negate the possibility that Machado felt uneasy about his background. The dedications to family members are significant. Yet they were written early in Machado's career, before he had fully established himself in elite white circles, and, therefore, before his background could have become an issue in his social standing. In addition, the blacks and mulattoes Magalhães Júnior mentions as part of Machado's circle of friends and associates were also part of the largely white intellectual and social elite.

That said, Machado wrote nothing that could be considered racially autobiographical (Magalhães Júnior 1981, 1:1, 19–10; Massa 1969, 1:55–56, 64–69). Nor is there any record of Machado's feelings about the controversy surrounding his marriage to Carolina or their life together as an interracial couple (Caldwell 1970, 31, 33). Shortly before his death, Machado reportedly gave two friends a box containing letters between Carolina and him written before their marriage and requested that the box and the letters be burned. The friends appear to have complied with his request, although one letter and part of a second somehow escaped burning (Caldwell 1970, 27, 222; Pereira 1936, 112). It is not unreasonable to conclude that, by asking that these earlier letters be destroyed, Machado may have sought to avoid bringing attention to his background. His silence on this topic seems to speak for itself.

Many critics contend that, to further his rise to social and literary prominence, Machado disguised his mulatto facial features by wearing a thick moustache and a beard and that he also wore his hair closely cropped in his later years to enhance this camouflage (Dixon 1989, 1–3; Pérez 1962, 85). Machado displays traces of African ancestry in the fullness of his lower lip, extended jaw, skin color, and hair (Massa 1969, 1:47–49). This is apparent in some of his earlier photographs and in the plaster death mask molded by Rodolfo Bernadelli (Magalhães Júnior 1981, 4:360). Francisca de Basto Cordeiro, a woman of an aristocratic background and a writer on women's issues (Rachum 1977, 124), who was a close associate of Machado and his wife, described Machado as having "slightly wavy, shiny black hair . . . a tan complexion . . . accentuated prognathism in the lower jaw [and] dark eyes" (Cordeiro 1961, 13–14).

Although Machado was more European than African in terms of his ancestry, he did not display the phenotype one might expect from the child of a European woman and a half-European and half-African man. In other words, he did not appear to be someone who was three-fourths European and one-fourth African (i.e., a "quadroon" in the racial parlance of the era; Daniel 2002, xii–xiii; Day 1932,

10; Massa 1969, 1:49). Machado's mulatto (or pardo) father may have been more African than European in ancestry. Indeed, as Massa points out, it was not uncommon for pretos to be reclassified as "pardos" in civil registries once they were emancipated (Massa 1969, 1:49). Nevertheless, photographs of Machado indicate a more European appearance in his later years.[11] It is not implausible that Machado, proceeding silently, bringing as little attention to his origins as possible, may have chosen to "hide" the fullness of his lips and the waviness of his hair. On the other hand, he may have grown a beard because it was stylish at the time, and a moustache because it was indeed obligatory among men of the elite (Duarte 2007b, 135), and he may have simply chosen to wear his hair short, which coincidently gave him a more European appearance.

White by Definition[12]

In post-Abolition Brazil, those mulattoes who, along with a more European phenotype, also acquired the social, economic, intellectual, and cultural attainments characteristic of the privileged class, were able to integrate themselves more easily into the dominant European Brazilian society (Spitzer 1989, 102). Thus Machado's perceived race moved closer to the white end of the continuum once he acquired intellectual erudition, cultural "refinement," and a white spouse. It is also important to consider that Machado's mother was white. And, although he was only two generations or so removed from slavery, his mulatto father's antecedents had been established in the free classes for at least one generation.

Furthermore, since the beginning of the seventeenth century, Western civilization had come to view writing as the most visible sign of intellect. Individuals of African descent who could write and publish imaginative literature were said to have taken "a few giant steps up" (Gates 1986, 8–9) the ladder of evolution (Mazama 1998, 6, 9). A literary career was instrumental to the upward mobility of many mulattoes (Haberly 1983, 74; Needell 1987b, 185). This was especially true of the new profession of journalism (Costa 2005, 561), which attracted "those whose marginal status, due to race or class, effectively barred them from more traditional careers" (Flory 1977, 213). Christine Costa observes that Machado, like many of his contemporaries, necessarily entered "the great halls of literature through the service entrance of journalism" (Costa 2005, 561).

David Haberly suggests that a career in letters cosmetically touched up Machado's "real" racial status as a mulatto, by furthering the illusion of his situational status as white (Haberly 1983, 74). Massa indicates that some individuals considered Machado a mulatto; others considered him white (Massa 1969, 1:48). Thus it is interesting to note Joaquim Nabuco's (1849–1910) response to José Veríssimo (1857–1916) when the latter, some weeks after Machado's death, wrote an article about the deceased author.

> Your article was simply beautiful, but this following sentence caused chills to run up my neck: "A mulatto, he was indeed a Greek of the best epoch." I would have never called him a mulatto, and I think nothing would cause him greater pain than your having concluded this. I beg that you remove this epithet when your article is made part of permanent records: The word is not literary and is pejorative. To me, he was white, and I believe that is what he considered himself: whatever foreign blood he may have had in no way affected his perfect Caucasoid makeup. I, at least, saw only the Greek in him. (Nabuco in Massa 1969, 1:47)[13]

What is noteworthy about Nabuco's remarks is his assumption that Machado considered himself white despite the lack of oral statements or written records that would indicate how he identified racially. However, because Machado apparently never stated that he identified as mulatto, Nabuco assumed this lack of racial specificity meant by default that he must have identified as white (Fanon 1952/1967, 138n24; Young 2006, 22). Moreover, Nabuco's reaction should not seem unusual if we consider that, in popular thought, "mulato" was said to be derived from "mulo" (the Portuguese word for "mule"). Supposedly, it was an epithet referring to the belief that, like the sterile offspring of a donkey and a horse, the mulatto, as the offspring of a black and a white, was degenerate and low in fertility, if not actually sterile.[14] Considering that, on several occasions, Machado and Luís Gama use "mulatto" in their writings, it is doubtful that these two individuals, both mulattoes, would use this word with the pejorative meaning of "half-breed" in English. "Mulatto" could have a negative connotation, but was more often used simply to designate a multiracial individual of African and European descent.

If we examine a letter written to Machado by mulatto author Gonçalves Crespo (1846–83), a native Brazilian whose family had immigrated to Portugal, we can see that the problem was not so much in the word "mulatto," but elsewhere.

> Coimbra, June 6, 1871, Couraça de Lisboa, no. 93
> The Honorable Mr. Machado de Assis,
> Fifteen days ago, I sent you my first book, *Miniaturas* [*Miniatures*]. Not having written you then, I am writing you now. Locally, my book was well

received and immediately acclaimed, which gives me great satisfaction because I am not a Portuguese national and have kept myself apart from the chicanery and nepotism that abound here. There were three fellow Brazilian writers to whom I sent my book: The Honorable P. Guimarães, Alencar, and Macedo.... As far as yourself is concerned, I had heard of you by name for quite some time as well as by a secret sympathy that won me over when I was told you were . . . [sic] a man of color like myself. Is it true? Should this not be true, however, I should neither desist in pursuing my desire to make your acquaintance nor hesitate to sign my name here with all the exuberance of genuine sympathy and affectionate respect.

From your compatriot and humble admirer,

G. Crespo (in Magalhães Júnior 1958a, 109–10)

With his ellipsis, Crespo conveys a certain hesitation, even embarrassment, in alluding to Machado's racial background. This may suggest that Nabuco was implying that someone of Machado's stature should not be referred to as a "mulatto." His concern is all the more logical given the racist thinking of the time about the negative consequences of miscegenation and the diminished mental capabilities of mulattoes. For all practical purposes, Machado was not a mulatto because he was not treated as a second-class citizen situationally. From Nabuco's perspective, any reference to Machado as a mulatto not only devalued his social and literary prominence but also undermined his contribution to Brazilian culture. Regardless of his racial origins, Machado had to be white, a status that was formally and publicly acknowledged in his obituary, which appeared in the *Correio da Manhã* (*Morning Mail*): "I, Olympio da Silva Pereira, official of the civil registrar and senior notary of the sixth magistrate of the Federal District, on September 29, 1908—do hereby certify that on page 63 of the register of obituary under number 52 is recorded the obituary of Joaquim Maria Machado de Assis: age 69, widower, native of Rio de Janeiro, public functionary, white, death due to arterial sclerosis, at 3:20 a.m." (Pereira in Sousa 1958, 168).

Suffering from his ever-worsening eyesight problems, Machado had been seriously weakened by his bouts with epilepsy, as well as by chronic nausea, diarrhea, and loss of appetite and periodic vomiting (Magalhães Júnior 1981, 4:226, 278, 339, 347). The latter four are "typical early symptoms of any excessive intake of bromides" (Chapman and Chapman-Santana 2000, 1153). Although potassium bromide was regarded as the first and primary treatment for epilepsy, the major therapeutic problem was achieving a balance between suppressing seizures and the frequent negative side effects of the medication—deterioration of cognitive functions, general behavior, and health. There would not be a better drug for epilepsy until phenobarbital was marketed in 1912 (Pearce 2002, 412; Sun 2007, 108–9; Temkin 1971, 298–99; Yacubian 2002).

Machado apparently took bromide, at least during certain periods, for an indefinite amount of time, and was probably plagued with gastrointestinal difficulties due to the drug (Chapman and Chapman-Santana 2000, 1153–54; Pérez 1962, 81; Yacubian 2002). In addition, a few days before his death, Machado developed a cancerous ulcer on his tongue, attributed to the cumulative effect of the biting that often took place during his epileptic seizures. This ulcer caused Machado great discomfort and made it difficult for him to swallow solid foods (Magalhães Júnior 1981, 4:348; Pérez 1962, 81). Finally, one cannot underestimate the tremendous grief Machado felt on the death of Carolina, which no doubt exacerbated these physical ailments. Indeed, several observers wrote about Machado's "cult of Carolina" (placing flowers on her grave every Sunday, leaving the pair of head pillows on their bed, and having two sets of silverware placed at the table). Others reported a noticeable sadness in Machado's demeanor, although he maintained an active professional, social, and personal life until his death (Caldwell 1970, 10; Machado 1953, 214; Pérez 1962, 89; Viana Filho 1974, 239–88).

FOUR

THE PUBLIC RACIAL TEXT: RACIAL IDENTITY AND THE WRITINGS OF THE UNKNOWN MACHADO

Slavery and the African Brazilian Presence: Machado's Criticism, Poems, Chronicles, and Short Stories

Many critics have asserted that Machado's metamorphosis from an unlettered youth to the undisputed literary lion of late nineteenth- and early twentieth-century Brazil reflects at once his racial self-negation and his lack of interest in or silence on the plight of African Brazilians, the cause of abolition, and other critical social concerns. They point to the paucity of racial observations in his correspondence and literary writings and to the absence of African Brazilian characters, settings, and themes in his literary works. Machado's social comportment as witnessed by individuals who knew him, his supposed avoidance of the term "mulatto" in referring to himself and in his writings, and his profoundly erudite and elitist cultural formation are held to qualify him as an example of the cultivated tradition (Magalhães Júnior 1958b, 144–77; Proença Filho 2004, 161–93).

That said, Raimundo Magalhães Júnior was one of the first critics to discover unknown—or unexamined—facts about Machado's writings, which revealed that he was hardly insensitive to slavery and racism (Magalhães Júnior 1956, 144–77). For example, in 1860, Machado wrote two theatrical reviews in which he characterized *Demônio familiar* (*Familial Devil*; 1857) and *Mãe* (*Mother*; 1860), two plays by José de Alencar, as follows: "Without leaving the realms of artistry, these plays, through their own depiction of effects and feelings, are a protest against the institution of slavery" (*Diário do Rio de Janeiro*, "Revista dramática," March 29, 1860, *Oc*, 3:872). In that same year, Machado made a favorable reference to *Uncle Tom's Cabin* (*Oc*, 3:840) and, in 1862, made similar comments on *Haabás*, an antislavery drama (Assis 1957b, 22:138–40; Sayers 1958, 393).

On the other hand, Eugênio Gomes, Leonardo Pereira, Jean-Michel Massa, and João Faria contend that Machado, in one of his opinion pieces as a theatrical censor (1859–64) for the Conservatório Dramático Brasileiro (Brazilian Theater Conservatory), displayed a notable conservatism on the question of slavery reflecting the social prejudice and intolerance of the time.[1] They argue that this attitude was in direct contradiction to the liberal principles Machado then espoused in his journalistic writings (Faria 2008, 66–67, 274; Gomes 1958, 14–15; Massa 1969, 338; L. A. M. Pereira 1994, 28). The opinion piece in question, written in 1862, early in Machado's career, when he was only twenty-three years old, pertained to *Mistérios sociais* (*Social Mysteries*) by Portuguese playwright Cesar de Lacerda. The play's plot centers on the slave protagonist Lucena, who, along with his mother, was sold into Mexico by his father. Years later, after having gained his freedom, Lucena travels to Portugal in search of his father and former master. While there, he meets and falls in love with a baroness and then marries her.

Questioning the play's verisimilitude, Machado made the following observation: "Philosophical theory does not recognize any difference between two individuals such as these who possess virtues to the same degree; however, given the conditions of our contemporary society, this manner of concluding the play should be altered" (Faria 2008, 274). He suggested cutting out the marriage between the baroness and the former slave, which would mean eliminating entire scenes and would make the character of the baroness completely superfluous. He also suggested having Lucena's father, the viscount, sell his now freeborn mistress and their son into slavery in Mexico, which would render the viscount's actions even more despicable. Moreover, in the penultimate scene, after Lucena announces, "It is still not finished," Machado would have him say: "A letter from my mother informed me that we were, before the law, free, and that between her prostitution and slavery she chose to remain silent and submit to that slavery into whose chains my father had shackled her" (Faria 2008, 274).

Examining Machado's rulings, José Jobim and Mark Streeter determined that, generally speaking, his "role as a moral censor triumphed over that of aesthetic guide, even though his rulings were more 'liberal' than those of his colleagues"

(Jobim and Streeter 2004, 19). Rodrigo Godoi goes further, arguing that Machado's rulings on *Mistérios sociais* were an implied interrogation of the prejudice and intolerance of nineteenth-century Luso-Brazilian society, in light of which having a freed slave ascend socially to the point where he could win a baroness's hand in marriage simply lacked credibility. But Godoi is careful to point out that, to Machado, the issue here was not the politics of slavery or the essential equality of individuals but, rather, aesthetic integrity and dramatic verisimilitude (Godoi 2009, 109–24).

In 1864, in one of his chronicles (*crônicas*), Machado praised an individual who bought a pathetic slave at an auction with the intention of freeing her (Sayers 1958, 393). In *Americanas* (*American Verses*; 1865), a collection of Machado's poetry, the poem "Sabina" tells of a brief love episode between Sabina and Otávio, the master's handsome son, who, during his vacation from school, leaves the mulatto slave Sabina pregnant. After returning to school, Otávio falls in love with a white girl. Now a college graduate, he returns home married to this young woman, having forgotten his interlude with Sabina, who is now carrying his child. In desperation, Sabina decides to drown herself and the baby in the river at the place where Otávio had seduced her. But the call of motherhood wins out in the end. The poem ends with Sabina lying stoically on the river's edge but uncertain of the future (*Poesias completas, Americanas, Oc*, 3:140–45).

In 1876, Machado praised the United States for abolishing slavery. And in an October 1 chronicle of that same year, he satirized a man who lamented the passing of the "good old days" when slaves were handled with the whip.

> The Law of September 28 is now five years old. God giveth health and life! This law was a great step forward in our life. If it had come thirty years earlier, conditions would be different now.
>
> But thirty years ago, the law did not come; instead, slaves came, smuggled and sold openly at Valongo. Besides the sale, there was a public prison. An acquaintance of mine sighs, nostalgic for the bygone days of the whip.
>
> —"These days slaves have become arrogant," he says frequently. "If you give a beating to one there is always someone else who intervenes and even calls the authorities. Ah, the good old days! I still remember the time when people saw a black all bloody pass by and they would say: "Keep going, you devil, you deserve it!"—Nowadays . . .
>
> And the man sighs deeply from his heart . . . it is so touching. Ah, the poor fellow! (*Crônica, História de 15 dias, Oc*, 3:352)

In 1876, twelve years before Brazil abolished slavery, Machado understood that Brazilians should have prepared for the emancipation of their slaves—and the concomitant transformation of the social order—decades earlier. Although the eradication of slavery was laudable, he points out that, unless accompanied by broader social reforms, it would be an empty proposition (Marotti 1982, 156).[2] Brazil's gradualist approach to abolition included the Law of September 28, 1871, known as the "Lei do Ventre Livre" (Law of the Free Womb), which stipulated that, thenceforth, all children born to slave mothers and all slaves belonging to the state were to be free. Yet the law's provisions proved to be less effective than advocates had hoped. If slave owners refused to accept the state's indemnity payment for children at age 8, they still had the option of retaining "freeborn" children in a de facto slave status until they reached the age of 21. The Lei dos Sexagenários (Sexagenarian Law) followed in 1885. It unconditionally freed all slaves over 65 years of age (who were thus condemned to hunger after a life of work) and conditionally freed those between 60 and 65 (who had to render three more years of service to the masters; Butler 1998, 7; Skidmore 1974, 16–17).

During this period, Machado served at the Ministry of Agriculture, Commerce, and Public Works, which had among numerous other responsibilities jurisdiction over labor, including statutes governing slaves (Caldwell 1970, 207). Magalhães Júnior's *Machado de Assis, funcionário público* (*no Império e na República*; *Machado de Assis, Public Servant* [*During the Empire and the Republic*]; 1958) provided an early account of Machado's tenure at the ministry. However, Sidney Chalhoub's *Machado de Assis: Historiador* (*Machado de Assis: Historian*; 2003) is the most comprehensive analysis of this little-explored aspect of Machado's life. Chalhoub carried out a meticulous search of the National Archives of Rio de Janeiro for documents on the activities of the second section of the Board of Agriculture of the Ministry of Agriculture during the 1870s through the late 1880s. Machado headed the section during this period (Chalhoub 2003, 10, 13).

Chalhoub discovered that the section was specifically charged with monitoring implementation of the Lei do Ventre Livre. Consequently, Machado was called upon to make judgments on its enforcement. Both Magalhães Júnior and Chalhoub found that Machado consistently sought to interpret the law in favor of the slave's freedom. This was often a daunting task given the concerted efforts of the master class to circumvent procedures intended to achieve this objective. Chalhoub's analysis of speeches from parliamentary debates surrounding slavery provide insight into the hypocrisy of the elite that relied on slave labor at a time when Brazil was the last bastion of African servitude (Chalhoub 2003, 145–55, 166–92).

Nevertheless, Chalhoub and Magalhães Júnior conclude that, regardless of which party was in power, Machado defended the prerogatives of the public trust against the perennial wrath of the master class (Chalhoub 2003, 10, 13, 291; Magalhães Júnior 1958a, 62).

Chalhoub believes that Machado's experience as a civil servant shaped his consciousness, which in turn informed his literary persona. He argues that the political and social struggle surrounding the Lei do Ventre Livre—driven by the hypocrisy and economic interests of the master class—served as a focal point for Machado's conceptualization of his novels *Helena* (1876), *Iaiá Garcia* (1878), *Memórias póstumas de Brás Cubas* (*Posthumous Memoirs of Brás Cubas*; 1881) and *Dom Casmurro* (1899; Chalhoub 2003, 50–58, 64–90, 131–39; Magalhães Júnior 1958a, 5–8, 21–28). Chalhoub maintains that the social forces culminating in the Lei do Ventre Livre also served as the organizing principle for the short story "Mariana" (1864). However, Chalhoub notes that when Machado wrote the story, he could not have imagined that shortly afterward he would become deeply involved in the daily application of the law's provisions (Chalhoub 2003, 136–39).

In 1877, Machado, writing under the pseudonym "Malvólio," composed a poem in African Brazilian dialect satirizing the parliamentary debates concerning slavery:

> "A Holy Day I jess ain't got
> Not ev'n Sunday, and little ta eat:
> Saucers an' beans, an' coffee, jess a drop
> It be jess 'nough ta wet mah teeth.
> "'Cause uh dis, I be here ta tell
> Dis Institute, so great and brave:
> *You talked* it fine and *speaked* it well,
> But, *you be free*; I still be a slave."
> (*Gazeta de Noticias*, September 27, 1887)[3]

In a chronicle dated June 15, 1877, written under the pseudonym "Manassés," the narrator relates the story of an individual who is so inspired by an anonymous donation of a sizable sum of money to the orphans of the Santa Casa de Misericórdia (Holy House of Mercy) that he performs the noble and generous act of freeing Clarimunda, a sixty-year-old female slave, without compensation. Her former master brags about his benevolence to his friends after refraining from publicizing his gesture in the newspaper (*Crônica, Histórias de 15 dias, Oc,* 3:368).

Chalhoub and Giorgio Marotti point out the unmistakable irony of the situation. The master who had already profited from the slave's labor seven or eight times over the original purchase price now frees her without financial compensation so that she might die of starvation (Chalhoub 2003, 227–29; Marotti 1982, 156, 235–36). Machado, ever the detached chronicler, discerned the ideological underpinnings of the abolition of slavery and exposed its underlying societal deficiencies. It should be noted that this chronicle was written eight years before passage of the Lei dos Sexagenários of 1885. Marotti argues that this indicates that Machado was acutely aware of various social problems and even anticipated them (Marotti 1982, 156).

On May 11 and May 19, 1888, in a series of columns entitled "Bons Dias!" (Good Morning!), Machado published two chronicles under the pseudonym "Boas Noites" (Good Night) that called into question the supposed altruism behind the planters' mass manumissions in the face of the government's imminent emancipation of their slaves (*Oc*, 3:488–93). The narrator argues that the voluntary freeing of slaves was merely a means by which slave owners could free themselves of elderly and weak slaves they deemed unproductive. Likewise, Abolition has left the former slaves prey to starvation wages (Chalhoub 2003, 234–38; Faoro 1976, 322–25). The May 11 chronicle focuses on runaway slaves who have secured employment as paid laborers on plantations. The narrator ridicules the hope that a just republic might be established in the wake of Abolition. In the May 19 chronicle, published five days after the declaration abolishing slavery, the narrator tells the story of a typically ambitious man, who, perceiving the inevitability of the abolition of slavery, decides to free an eighteen-year-old slave named Pancrácio. In order to celebrate his benevolence, the man hosts a dinner to which he invites five guests (although the newspapers state that there were thirty-three guests in all, the number "33" being Christ's age when he died), with great speeches, toasts, and Pancrácio rushing in and hugging his master's knees. Later on, letters of congratulation arrive while the benefactor's friends are already considering immortalizing him in a portrait (*Crônica, Bons dias, Oc*, 3:490–91).

Ultimately, Pancrácio remains with his former master as a servant earning a meager monthly wage of 7,000 or 8,000 réis. Whereas elderly slaves like Clarimunda obtained their freedom only to die of hunger, Pancrácio is young, has shelter and employment that provides a source of income, however meager. Yet even after being granted his freedom, Pancrácio is abused by his former master for not performing his duties properly. In a chronicle dated June 26, 1888, the narrator recommends, in the manner of Nikolai Gogol's *Dead Souls*, a plan to purchase dead slaves and then backdate the bill of sale in order to secure governmental funds offered to slave owners for their loss of property (*Oc*, 3:494–95).

These and other chronicles provide abundant evidence of Machado's active engagement with some of the major issues of the period, and with slavery in particular (Gledson 1986, 114–60). However, given his use of pseudonyms, Machado's contemporaries were probably unaware that he was the author of these commentaries.[4] In the oppressive sociopolitical climate of the Empire, writing under a pseudonym was a prudent tactic, used by most prominent journalists of the era (Magalhães Júnior 1956, 5–18). Moreover, pseudonyms gave writers free rein for "shameless commentary" (Duarte 2007b, 136–38), which they could not indulge in under their own names (Magalhães Júnior 1956, 9–26).

When considering Machado as the chronicler, the novelist, the short story author, and as himself, along with his different narrative voices in different genres and periods of his life, one needs, above all, to avoid confusing the narrator's and the author's voice. That said, it is difficult to determine when the narrator is speaking and when Machado is speaking. Indeed, Machado's *ambiguity* is center stage whenever critics try to understand the deceptive narrative voice in his work. Nevertheless, Chalhoub maintains that Machado's chronicles reflect a shift between 1868 and 1888 not only in public attitudes toward slavery in Rio de Janeiro but also in his own views on private manumissions.

Chalhoub believes that three main arguments informed Machado's views on what motivated the process of abolition (Chalhoub in Borges 2007, 242–43; Chalhoub 1990, 99). First, as the May 11 chronicle indicates, respect for private property in the form of slaves was no longer a sacrosanct principle unifying the elite. Second, as both May chronicles show, gratuitous manumission had often become a way to turn ex-slaves into submissive free dependents (Chalhoub in Borges 2007, 242–43; Chalhoub 1990, 99). And third, as indicated in the May 19 chronicle, the slave population's power had grown between 1870 and 1888, which reflected an increasing resolve among slaves to secure their freedom—or at least an increasing awareness of that growing power by slave owners (Chalhoub in Borges 2007, 242–43; Chalhoub 1990, 101). The May 19 chronicle shows this indirectly, Chalhoub points out, when the narrator emphasizes the slave's towering size ("You grew immensely") despite the narrator-master's claim to be the individual deciding everything (*Crônica, Bons dias, Oc*, 3:490).

In addition, Chalhoub indicates that the narrators in these chronicles displayed the characteristically penetrating insight found in Machado's writings on the contradictions of abolition by having the slave master tell Pancrácio, "You are free, you may go anywhere you wish" (*Crônica, Bons dias, Oc*, 3:490). In fact, Chalhoub found that the freedom to live on one's own was a common demand among slaves and libertos alike in Rio de Janeiro (Chalhoub in Borges 2007, 242–43; Chalhoub 1990, 236, 238–48). Finally, Chalhoub argues, Machado believed not only that clientelistic relationships originating in the logistics of slavery undermined liberal ideals, but also that the demise of slavery was a negotiated process in response to pressure from slaves (Chalhoub in Borges 2007, 242–43; Chalhoub 1990, 151–52, 251–53).

That said, although African Brazilian characters are rare in Machado's novels and short stories and are never protagonists, they appear more frequently there than in the works of most other nineteenth-century Brazilian writers of urban fiction. Moreover, Machado develops some of these characters more fully than other writers of his own time and before do, and he presents all of them in consistently sympathetic and meaningful ways (Sayers 1958, 393). Thus, in the short story "Vidros quebrados" (Broken Panes; 1883), a young black domestic aids her young mistress in the mistress's love affair with a young man, only to be blamed and beaten once the affair is discovered (*Outros contos, Oc*, 2:948–61). Thus, too, in the short story, "Virginius" (1864), the slave farm worker Julião, a character based on an ancient Roman who kills his own daughter, Virginia, rather than see her submit to captivity, murders his mulatto daughter, Elisa, who has decided to commit suicide rather than submit to rape by the landowner's son, to spare her from having to take her own life.

Eduardo Duarte compiled an inventory of references to slavery and African Brazilians in Machado's writings. He points out that "Virginius" (*Outros contos, Oc*, 2:737–48) depicts the social and moral aspects of slavery and their degrading effects on everyone concerned, with special attention given to its impact on African Brazilian women (Duarte 2007a, 253). Moreover, based on these and other references in his texts, Machado displayed a commitment against slavery and racism, however obliquely he may have framed these issues. Machado's perspective, Duarte argues, was clearly shaped by his experience as someone physically marked as an individual of African descent (Duarte 2007a, 8).

In "Mariana" (1864), a beautiful mulatto domestic slave girl falls in love with her young master, Coutinho. After fleeing twice, and convinced of the impossibility of her love, she kills herself (*Outros contos, Oc*, 2:771–83). Coutinho relates the tale of Mariana's tragic death and comments that he has never been loved by anyone with such intensity. Yet hardly any time passes before Coutinho goes off with some male friends to ogle women descending from carriages as they stop on a local street. Duarte argues that this is one of Machado's signature narrative techniques: he masks his own position by giving voice to the racial "Other," who exposes and makes explicit white insensitivity to the plight of African Brazilians (Duarte 2007b, 140–41; Bim 2010, 115–21; Coutinho 2010, 96–98; Hapke 2010, 103–6).

In "Verba testamentária" (Testamentary Clause; 1882; *Papéis avulsos, Oc,* 2:357–64), young patriarch Nicolau breaks dishes over the slaves' heads and kicks the dogs before falling asleep, but when he wakes up, he is kind and affectionate to everyone, dogs and slaves. "And everyone, dogs and slaves, forgot the abuses from the previous day, and would hurry about obeying his orders, as if this were their true master rather than the one who meted out the beatings" (*Papéis avulsos, Oc,* 2:360).

According to Raymond Sayers, "O caso da vara" (The Case of the Whipping Stick; 1891; *Páginas recolhidas, Oc,* 2:577–82), is the only short story in Brazilian pre-Abolition literature to provide a revealing glimpse into the lives of urban slave children (Sayers 1958, 394–95). The plot centers around the white youth Damião, who, having run away from the seminary, takes refuge at the home of Sinhá Rita, a friend of his godfather who instructs young slave girls how to embroider and make lace, and who Damião hopes will assist him in leaving the seminary. Damião notices that one young slave girl, Lucrecia, is ill and unable to keep pace with the others in completing her tasks. When Sinhá Rita warns Lucrecia she will be beaten with the whipping stick (*vara*) unless she finishes in a timely manner, Damião takes pity on her. Sensing he may be her salvation but fearful of being beaten, the girl runs away screaming. The mistress catches her and, after dragging her back by her ears, asks Damião to hand her the stick. Though he had felt compassion for the girl just minutes before and even now, because he needs Sinhá Rita's assistance, Damião complies.

These short stories display Machado's fascination with the conflicts, paradoxes, and contradictions of human nature. Damião, the fugitive seminary student, is a kindhearted individual who feels compassion for the young slave unable to finish her tasks. Even Sinhá Rita, in whose home Damião takes refuge, is a sympathetic character, who expresses genuine concern for his predicament. Yet both become accomplices in punishing the slave. Damião participates in this punishment unwillingly. Yet he must choose between his own bondage in the seminary and that of the young slave girl. The woman, in contrast, displays neither doubts nor remorse; she simply enforces the laws of the social order of which she is a part (Marotti 1982, 160; Tauscher 2010, 142–44).

Machado's short story "Pai contra mãe" (Father Against Mother; 1906), written after Abolition, is a poignant account of fugitive slaves and clearly emphasizes the inhumane practices of slavery (*Relíquias de casa velha*, Oc, 2:659–67). Indeed, Maria Salgueiro asserts, though Machado was not one to write inflamed speeches from the pulpit, "we may find vigorous pages about the Brazilian mentality toward slaves at the time and about the not always veiled racism," which is particularly moving in often-overlooked short stories like "The Case of the Whipping Stick" and "Father Against Mother" (Salgueiro 2005, 288). The narration in "Father Against Mother" opens with a short introduction on the historical and social reality of slavery, neither supporting nor condemning the institution. The narrator takes readers inside this unquestioned reality, whose function is explained "objectively" from the perspective of a detached (and ironic) observer:

> Slavery brought with it offices and devices such as would most likely happen with other social institutions. I have chosen to mention the following devices simply by virtue of the fact that they were connected to some specific task. One of them was the neck ring and another was the foot ring; in addition, there was the tin mask. The tin mask certainly cured slaves of the vice of drinking by plugging up their mouth. It had only three holes, two to see through and one through which they could breath, and it was locked behind the head. Curing slaves of the habit of drinking had the added benefit of ridding them of the temptation to steal because it was generally the master's pilfered pocket money they spent in order to quench their thirst. Thus two sins were dispensed with at one fell swoop, whereas honesty and sobriety were ensured. The mask was grotesque, but human and social order cannot always be achieved without grotesqueness and sometimes cruelty. The blacksmiths kept the masks hanging on display, on the doors of their stores. However, let us not discuss masks right now.
>
> The neck ring was used on fugitive slaves. Imagine for a moment an enormous collar with a large handle, either on the right or on the left, coming over the head and locked from behind with a key. Of course, the neck ring was heavy, but the punishment was actually less serious than it might seem at first. Slaves who ran away in those conditions, wherever they went, indicated that they were old offenders who had been recaptured shortly afterward.
>
> Half a century ago, slaves would run away frequently. Runaways were numerous, and indeed not everyone adapted well to slavery. Occasionally,

slaves would be beaten and not everyone liked being beaten. The majority were simply scolded; there was always someone in the house who would come to the slave's defense and even masters were not particularly wicked; besides, the sense of ownership moderated their actions because, when all is said and done, even wealth can be the source of considerable pain. (*Reliquías de casa velha*, Oc, 2:659)

The detached yet ironical tone is typical of the prologues in Machado's writings (Marotti 1982, 161–64), which present the institution of African slavery is a normative part of the social order, as simply a matter of "racial common sense" (Omi and Winant 1994, 59, 106). The pain inflicted by the instruments of punishment is mitigated by the lighthearted and ironical tone, by the consideration of the positive results derived from the use of such devices, and by a generous description of the master's attitude. The universe that Machado's characters inhabit is a serene and logical one: individuals walk around with their heads enclosed inside instruments of punishment, others run away, and still others who capture these fugitives maintain a social order that requires grotesqueness and even cruelty to maintain itself. Human beings seem almost lacking in any sense of responsibility and are indeed "actors in a comedy whose meaning escapes them" (Marotti 1982, 162). Yet, Renata Wasserman explains, in its directness, the story reveals the indifference and detachment of the narrative voice as a cover and a deflection of pain. Moreover, "it functions as an aggressive stance against itself and the reader, whom Machado de Assis accuses, flatters, and disdains at the same time" (Wasserman 2008, 93).

At a textual level, the introduction to "Father Against Mother" seems to say that, if the slaves run away, there should be someone responsible for capturing and returning them: "To capture fugitive slaves was a job at the time. Mind you, seizing runaway slaves was by no means a noble task but considering that it was an instrument of force through which law and ownership are maintained it implied a nobility intrinsic to the vindicating actions" (*Reliquías de casa velha*, Oc, 2:659–60). Indeed, one of the protagonists employed to capture fugitive slaves, Cândido Neves, is a good fellow, who, unable to commit himself to a fixed routine of a normal job, finds the rather adventuresome task of slave catcher perfectly suited to his temperament.

One day, Cândido falls in love with a beautiful and good woman named Clara.[5] They marry and live with her aunt Mônica, a kind and affable woman; their family life is happy. Cândido goes to hunt fugitive slaves while Clara devotes her time to sewing clothes, assisted by Mônica. They have faith in God and the Virgin Mary, to whom they pray with serene and sincere devotion during hard times. They rejoice when Clara gives birth to a son, who will further strengthen the happy family. Yet this happiness is clouded by the fact the new baby is born at a most inauspicious time, when the number of fugitive slaves has diminished. Cândido's earnings decrease just when he needs greater financial resources to support his growing family. To make matters worse, the now penniless Neves family is evicted. And though Aunt Mônica manages to secure a room in the home of a charitable woman, she insists that Cândido and Clara leave their son on the doorsteps of an orphanage. There are scenes of heartbreaking despair in which the parents try by any means possible to postpone the inevitable. In the end, when all hope is lost, Cândido picks up the baby and leaves.

The narrative engages the reader emotionally in the desperate situation confronting Cândido and Clara, who are very much in love, only to inject another, altogether destabilizing character into the story: Arminda, a fugitive mulatto woman whom Cândido runs into by chance. Leaving his son at a pharmacy, he seizes Arminda, who screams, struggles, and asks God for assistance with the same ardor Clara displayed and who finally appeals for mercy by telling Cândido she is pregnant. Devoid of any compassion and bent on performing his duty, he responds: "You are the guilty one, who ever told you to run away and have children?" (*Reliquías de casa velha*, Oc, 2:666). After a lengthy struggle, Cândido manages to drag Arminda to her owner's house, where he immediately receives the large reward that had been promised. Meanwhile, Arminda, thrown to the floor, has a miscarriage: "The fruit of a certain time entered this world without life among the mother's moans and the master's gestures of despair. Cândido Neves was a witness to all this; he had totally lost track of time. Whatever time it was he had to run to Ajuda Street, which is what he did without even wanting to find out about the consequences of the disaster" (*Reliquías de casa velha*, Oc, 2:667).

Cândido dashes off, desperately looking for his own son. Of course, he finds him: "The father grabs his son with the same fury with which he had only a short while before seized the fugitive slave; of course it was a different fury, a fury of love" (*Reliquías de casa velha*, Oc, 2:667). The return is triumphant, and the tragedy concludes with a happy ending: "Once Aunt Mônica heard the explanation, she accepted the return of the child because [Cândido had] brought back [a reward of] 1,000 milréis. It is true that she had some harsh words for the fugitive slave because of [her] escape as well as the miscarriage. Cândido Neves, kissing his son, with tear-filled eyes, blessed that escape and did not display the slightest concern about the miscarriage:—'Not all children survive'" (*Reliquías de casa velha*, Oc, 2:667).

At the subtextual level, "Father Against Mother" goes beyond the question of Cândido's responsibilities and the thesis that someone should be responsible for capturing runaway slaves. In effect, the protagonist slave catcher is himself a slave in a world that has failed to instill in him the value of the work ethic, a world that has compelled him to play his own enslavement against the life of the newborn. He feels neither shame nor guilt because he has simply obeyed the laws of the contemporary social order (Bim 2010, 121–24; Coutinho 2010, 98–99; Lopes 2007, 85–102; Marotti 1982, 164; Moraes 2009, 1–12).

Slavery and the African Brazilian Presence: Machado's Novels

In Machado's first novel, *Ressurreição* (*Resurrection*; 1872), we get a brief glimpse of a slave, an insignificant figure, about whom the narrator observes: "The slave whose spirit was accustomed to obedience did not distinguish it from duty" (168).[6] Matching the normative expectations of the period, submission to the white master was the African Brazilian slave's only task. Thus, in *Helena* (1876), when the devoted young slave reveals the truth about his young mistress believing that she is in danger, Helena responds: "I thanked God . . . because He infused into the vile body of the slave such a noble spirit of devotion" (202). This is typical of Romantic fiction. The slave has no relevance, and Helena's reaction simply mirrors contemporary attitudes, particularly that of young women from prominent families.

Iaiá Garcia (1878) contains a more developed African Brazilian character, the freed slave Raimundo, whom the narrator describes in such a way as to call our attention to several important observations and debates:

> Raimundo seemed as if he were expressly made to serve Luís Garcia. He was a fifty-year-old black man, of medium stature, strong, despite his age, a type of African that was submissive and dedicated. He was still essentially a slave although a free man. When Luís Garcia inherited Raimundo from his father,—he did not want to accept him as part of the spoils,—and immediately gave him his freedom papers. Raimundo, who was nine years older than his master, had carried the latter in his arms and loved him as a son. Finding himself a free man, Raimundo felt his freedom was a way of expelling him from the household, which made him feel a daring yet generous

impulse. He actually made a gesture to tear apart the manumission papers but caught himself in time. Luís Garcia noticed only the generosity, not the boldness; he understood the affection of the slave, he felt his good heart. Between them then there was a bond that united them forever.

"You are free," said Luís Garcia; "you may live with me as long as you wish." From then on, Raimundo was like the external spirit of his master; he thought for him and reflected his most intimate thoughts in all his actions, always silent and punctual. Luís Garcia never gave Raimundo orders; he always had everything at the right moment and at the right place. Although Raimundo was the only servant in the house, he actually had time, in the evening, to converse with his former master, in the garden, as the night approached. There they talked of their small world, of the usual everyday domestic events, of what tomorrow's weather would be like, and this or that external event. (74–75)

Iaiá Garcia was written ten years before the abolition of slavery, when the freedom of manumitted slaves was recognized as long as the underlying social order remained essentially intact. Raymundo Faoro argues that Raimundo's disobedient yet generous impulse at the novel's end, which in fact originated in disappointment, encapsulates the dilemma brought on by the abolition of slavery: once free, slaves lost their food and shelter and were left to survive on their own, which most likely would mean a life of poverty. Luís Garcia, Raimundo's master, is oblivious to this reality. Indeed, granting Raimundo freedom while at the same time allowing him to remain a servant for as long as he wants seems to Luís Garcia like the utmost generosity. Yet, like so many white abolitionists, Luís Garcia was caught up in the liberal ideological fervor of abolitionism without having seriously considered the plight of former slaves in the aftermath of slavery. The harsh truth surfaces in the narrator's clear yet subtle allusions to the fact that a purely formal freedom, incorporated into the system of slavery, is meaningless (Faoro 1976, 326).

Raimundo plays a decisive role when Iaiá Garcia, Luís Garcia's daughter, sends an imprudent note to a man. Raimundo exercises a certain degree of agency by refusing to deliver the message:

> Iaiá remained motionless for a few moments. Raimundo removed the letter from his pocket and held it in his hands without daring to raise his eyes; finally, he raised them and said firmly:

—Raimundo did not think it was nice that Iaiá wrote to that man, who is neither your father nor your fiancé, so I came back to talk to Miss Estela. (233)

True to the essentially classic Romantic image of the faithful African Brazilian slave, devoted to his master: "Raimundo gave her the letter and shook his gray head, as if he wanted to push back the years that weighed upon him, and go back in time, to when Iaiá was a mere child—mischievous and nothing more" (233).

Posthumous Memoirs of Brás Cubas (1881), whose irony is often ferocious and whose tone is one of disillusionment, marks the start of what has been called Machado's "second phase." The narrator, Brás Cubas, begins by telling the reader about himself. The only son of wealthy parents, who spoiled him as a youngster, Brás is possessed by his absolute power over their slaves (Marotti 1982, 146–49):

> Since the age of five, I had earned the nickname "devil child"; and truthfully, I was just that; I was one of the most malevolent children of my time, malicious, indiscreet, sassy, and willful. For example, one day I split open the head of a slave because she denied me a spoonful of a coconut cake she was preparing, and still not content with that evil deed, I threw a fistful of ash in the dish, and still not satisfied with that mischief, I went to tell my mother that it had been the slave herself who ruined the cake out of spite; and I was only six years old. (117–18)

During these early years, Brás's favorite sport is to turn Prudêncio, his personal house servant, into a mount with saddle and whip.

> Prudêncio, a house *moleque*, was my everyday horse; he would get down on his hands and knees, take a rope in his mouth as a bridle. I mounted on his back with a whip in my hand, I whipped him, I made thousands of turns on each side and he obeyed,—sometimes moaning—but he obeyed without saying a word or just an "Oh, Massa"—to which I answered:—"Shut up, you animal!" (118)[7]

Through the personage of Brás Cubas, Machado, ever the detached chronicler, describes a scene from daily life in wealthy nineteenth-century households. Yet Roberto Schwarz contends that narrator Brás is an innovative device that

Machado employed to expose and criticize the elite class through the voice of an insider—to destabilize the social order and its power relations from within (Schwarz 1998, 47–64). Indeed, some years before, Marotti had argued that many readers of Machado's time probably recognized themselves in his narrator's descriptions but few realized they were the objects of Machado's irony (Marotti 1982, 146).

However, this irony is unmistakable when it comes to African Brazilian characters. By chance, Prudêncio and Brás meet again as adults. Brás notices a crowd staring at a black man whipping another black man. The individual with the whip is none other than Prudêncio, who, having been freed, has purchased a slave of his own. At every scream and invocation, Prudêncio responds with "Shut up, you animal," just as Brás Cubas did when they were children. Brás reflects that his own past behavior causes Prudêncio to whip his slave. The two recognize each other, and Prudêncio, thanks to Brás Cubas's intervention, forgives his slave:

> On the surface, the Valongo episode was depressing; but only on the surface. As soon as I dug the blade of reasoning deeper, I found it to have a mischievous, fine, and even deep core. It was a way that Prudêncio had to rid himself of the beatings he had received,—by transferring them to someone else. As a child, I used to ride him, put a bridle in his mouth and mistreat him without compassion; he moaned and suffered. Now that he was free, however, and could do what he wanted with himself, with his arms, his legs, now that he could work, rest, and sleep unfettered from his former status, now he vented himself: he purchased a slave and was paying him back with high interest on the amount he had received from me. Just look at the shrewdness of that rascal! (206)

Despite the playful and ironic tone, the passage is an indictment of the dehumanizing effects of slavery on masters *and* slaves. Prudêncio must lash out at his slave to free himself psychologically from his own previous bondage and mistreatment at the hands of his master.

In Brás's description of his brother-in-law, Cotrim, we see how virtues and vices are fused together:

> Cotrim's scruples might appear excessive to one who does not know he possessed a ferociously honorable character. I myself was unjust with him during the years following the execution of my father's will. I have come

to realize he was a model. They accused him of avarice and I think they were right; but avarice is merely the exaggeration of a virtue and virtues must be like budgets; oversupply is better than deficit. Because he had an abrupt manner he had many enemies who accused him of being a barbarian. The only fact alleged on this point is that he frequently sent his slaves to prison, from which they would emerge all covered in blood; but, aside from the fact that he only sent the recalcitrant and fugitive slaves to prison, it so happens that, for some time, he had been involved in smuggling slaves, and had become accustomed, in a certain sense, to manners that were somewhat harsher than that type of business required, and one cannot honestly attribute to the natural character of a man what is merely the result of social conditioning. The proof that Cotrim had pious feelings was conveyed in the love he had for his children and in the grief he suffered when Sarah died a few months later; this is, I think, irrefutable proof, and not all of it. He was the treasurer of a fraternity and a member in various brotherhoods. He was even a redeemed brother in one of them, which does not mesh well with his reputation for avarice; and, truth be told, that the benefit had not fallen on barren soil: the brotherhood (for which he was a judge) had his portrait painted in oil. He was not perfect, it is true; he had, for example, the mania of informing the newspapers of some good deed he had performed,—a reprehensible and unpraiseworthy habit, I agree; but he defended himself by saying that good works are contagious once they are made public; and one cannot deny that this reason has some weight. I do believe (and here I give him the highest praise) that he only practiced those occasional good deeds in order to arouse the philanthropy of others; and if that was his intent, I must confess that publicity is indeed indispensable. (268–69)

Marotti cites this passage as an example of the subtle irony and balancing act of which Machado is such a master (Marotti 1982, 148–49). He notes, for example, that "ferociously" (*ferozmante*) serves to reinforce the irony of "honorable" (*honrado*) for a man who used to have his slaves beaten until they were bloody. The accusation of Cotrim being a "barbarian" (*bárbaro*) is ironically mitigated by his sending only "the recalcitrant and fugitive slaves" (*os [escravos] perversos e os fujões*) to prison. His "hard manners" (*trato um pouco mais duro*) are considered a consequence of smuggling slaves, which was a crime although the statutes were imposed under pressure from Great Britain and not generally accepted in Brazil (Marotti 1982, 149). The accusation of being avaricious is canceled out by parsimony. Good deeds are contradicted by vanity, which in turn is mitigated by public philanthropy. Cotrim's love for his children is juxtaposed with that of selling the family members of other human beings. Narrator Brás depicts a gloomy Cotrim imprisoned in his concept of honor, a slave butcher, a smuggler of other human beings, attached possessively to his family, greedy, bigoted, bound by the interests of fraternities and brotherhoods, frugal and circumspect in good deeds, and vain (Marotti 1982, 149). Brás concludes with the final irony: "He may have owed in a few courtesies, but he did not owe a cent to anyone" (269).

In *Quincas Borba* (1891), the protagonist Rubião, a wealthy urbanized country bumpkin, arrives in Rio de Janeiro when the city is on the verge of a significant social transformation. The urban bourgeoisie is about to replace the landowning and slaveholding elite as the dominant sector of society; those with ambition, education, talent, and intellect will have increased opportunities for upward social mobility. Rubião directs all of his efforts toward taking on a guise suitable to the new social rules. One of the rules for those aspiring to high status was to have white servants, particularly European immigrants, who were part of the state's plan of displacing African Brazilians in even the most low-skilled jobs:

> The servant was waiting, tense and serious. He was Spanish; and it was not without resistance that Rubião accepted him from the hands of Cristiano; no matter how many times he told him that he was accustomed to his blacks from Minas, and did not want foreign languages in the house, his friend Palha insisted, pointing out the necessity of having white servants. Rubião yielded with reluctance. His good houseboy, whom he had wanted to put in the drawing room, as a sort of provincial piece, he had not been able to leave in the kitchen, where Jean, a Frenchman reigned; the houseboy was demoted to other jobs. (108)

In another, earlier passage, Rubião contemplates all the items, expensive and not necessarily in good taste, that he has been compelled to buy in order to present himself as a gentleman, leaving the reader with the impression that servants are merely objects and pieces of property, and not very precious ones at that, to be confined in the least conspicuous parts of the house. Later, Rubião encounters a procession involving African Brazilian men on their way to being sentenced.

> At the corner of Ourives Street, he was stopped by a crowd, and a rather odd procession. A man, in judicial attire, was reading aloud a paper, a

sentencing. Besides the judge, there was a priest, soldiers, and some curious onlookers. However, the principal figures were two African Brazilians. One of them, light-skinned, thin, of medium height, kept his eyes lowered. His hands were tied behind his back and around his neck was a rope, the ends of which were tied to the other individual, a dark-skinned man. He was looking straight ahead, bravely confronting the crowd's curiosity. After the paper had been read, the procession continued down Ourives Street; it had come from the prison and was on its way to Moura Square. (158)

Because readers are led to believe the men have committed a crime, the fact that they are African Brazilian does not in and of itself appear to be significant. Yet the matter-of-fact description of the reading of the sentencing and the procession actually heightens the dramatic impact of the scene and is intended to evoke pathos. The presence of the shackled men subtly raises questions about criminality and justice as these relate to the institution of slavery and the shackled freedom of African Brazilians, quite apart from whether they are guilty or innocent.

In *Dom Casmurro* (1899), a painfully insightful introspection into a past love relived and destroyed again through ruthless memory, background figures include an anonymous black slave who surprises Bentinho and Capitu in one phase of their romance. There is only a momentary focus on African Brazilians, when Bentinho shows his friend Escobar his slaves. Thanks to his friend's observation, Bentinho realizes that their names begin with all the letters of the alphabet. The slaves then recede into the background as exploitable goods and invested capital: some work at home, some are rented out, and others work at the country house. They all have purely economic functions, like the houses Bentinho owns and rents out (Marotti 1982, 150).

Esau e Jacó (*Esau and Jacob*; 1904) displays Machado's signature distancing, in which the narrator, Counselor Ayres, drifts through momentous political events of the era: the abolition of slavery, the proclamation of the Republic, and the exile of the emperor. Of these events, slavery does not figure directly in the plot; and the main characters are somewhat removed from the political events that have crystallized around the institution by virtue of their race and class (Wasserman 2008, 93). Yet, according to Wasserman, this is criticism by omission, reinforced by the fact that the main characters not only own slaves but also unquestioningly accept the institution as a normative part of the social fabric (Wasserman 2008, 93). In fact, the financier Santos, though he thinks abolition will destroy the Brazilian economy, profits substantially from the speculative frenzy (*encilhamento*) that occurred in the aftermath of Abolition. This frenzy, which destabilized the Empire's financial policy, was fueled in part by pressure from planters on the state for the extension of easy credit to lessen the impact of their loss of property (Schulz 2008, 7–8; Needell 1987b, 12–13; Wasserman 2008, 94).

In *Esau and Jacob* we encounter several interesting scenes relating to the novel's central characters, twin brothers Pedro and Paulo: "Paulo was the more aggressive, Pedro the more devious, and, because both ended up eating the fruit from the trees, it was a moleque who climbed up there to pick the fruit, either out of fear of the beatings [Paulo] gave him or because of the promises [Pedro] made. The promises were never kept; the beatings, which were always anticipated, were always given, and sometimes even repeated after the service was rendered" (98).

Marotti suggests that the beatings of the moleque, although another indictment of slavery's brutalities, are not in and of themselves significant. He considers this passage meaningful by virtue of what it conveys about the changes in Brazilian mores brought on by slavery (Marotti 1982, 150–51). According to these mores, the seven-year-old Pedro and Paulo are deprived of one of the basic and genuine pleasures of childhood—climbing a tree and picking fruit. This was typical of thousands of other affluent Brazilian households in which custom deprived children of direct encounters with life by delegating that contact with reality to slave intermediaries.

In another interesting scene, Santos tells his wife he has been nominated to become a baron. At his celebration festivities, the slaves are jubilant because their master's noble title has elevated their own social status, thus distinguishing them from the neighboring slaves. African Brazilians, like other characters in *Esau and Jacob*, are subject to the narrator's biting irony, where enslaved individuals at the bottom of the social hierarchy feel a sense of increased self-esteem compared to other slaves by virtue of the recent social elevation of their master. Slavery can only produce slavery as long as humans are still bound by their own hierarchical thinking (Marotti 1982, 151).

At odds over most everything, Pedro and Paulo are in complete accord in supporting abolition although, ironically, within their common ground there is an area of dispute:

> One must not forget that, in 1888, there was a serious and indeed serious question in which the two twins were in complete agreement, yet for different reasons. The date explains the fact: it was the emancipation of slaves. They were at opposite ends of the spectrum, but they were unified in their

support of abolition. The only difference that separated them had to do with the reform, which Pedro deemed an act of justice, and that Paulo considered the beginning of a revolution. Paulo himself expressed such an idea, when summing up a conversation that took place in São Paulo, on May 20:

"Abolition is the dawn of freedom; let's wait for the sun; now that the black is free, it remains for us to free the white." (130)

Paulo's statement is similar to one Machado made in *Gazeta de Notícias* (*News Gazette*) in 1884, concerning the freeing of slaves in Ceará. "Ceará is a star; yet, it is imperative that Brazil be the sun" (Assis in Magalhães Júnior 1955, 125). He praises the abolition of slavery in one province and proclaims it to be imperative throughout Brazil.

Ayres's Memorial (1908), Machado's final novel, brings the question of abolition into sharper focus. Protagonist Counselor Ayres is a retired diplomat, an elderly gentleman with reserved habits who, ever the chronicler, observes other people's stories and, to some extent, his own. The novel is set in 1888 and constructed as a diary, from the perspective not of the slaves but of the master class (Marotti 1982, 151–54). We have the case of the old-fashioned aristocrat Baron de Santa Pia, who, on the eve of the law abolishing slavery, frees all his slaves. His action is a form of rebellion against the law he considers unjust: "I want to make it perfectly clear that I judge the government's action an expropriation since it intervenes in the exercise of the right that belongs exclusively to the owner, and that I am going to assert at my own loss, because I want to and I can" (93).

Marotti argues that what is interesting here is that there is no emphasis on the protection of property as the most essential human right to support the claim that the masters' right to their human chattel took priority over the slaves' right to liberty (Marotti 1982, 151–52). Perfectly in keeping with the ruling class's conception, the baron's brother observes: "'My brother believes in the government's attempt, but not in its outcome, unless what one wants is the destruction of the plantations. The actions simply express the sincerity of his convictions and his violent genius. He is capable of urging all the owners to free their slaves and, the next day, proposing the fall of the very government that tried to achieve the same thing through legal means'" (93–94).

Santa Pia's position reflects fears about the destruction of agriculture and is in keeping with that of the master class (at least in the Rio de Janeiro region, which had not yet shifted from slave to wage labor, as it had in the São Paulo region, which changed over several years before the abolition of slavery). His conclusion concerning the slaves is also typically aristocratic: "I am certain that few of them will leave the plantation; the majority will stay with me earning the salary I shall determine, and some will work for nothing—just to have the pleasure of dying where they were born" (94). Even the conclusion of the novel is typically patriarchal: once the baron is dead, the beautiful young mistress and heroine, Fidélia, decides to leave and may even sell the plantation; all of her former slaves would like to follow her to town, where she intends to move: "It cost her considerably to make those poor people understand that they would have to work for wages, and that here there would no means of employing them right away. But she did promise not to forget them, and, in case she did not return to the countryside, to put in a good word for them with the new owner of the property" (126).

With Abolition, the master class is no longer bound by the financial responsibility of maintaining slaves; the masses of former slaves remain with their former masters as a last refuge against their new, potentially harsher conditions as free laborers. Between the two episodes, one with the Baron de Santa Pia as protagonist and the other with Fidélia as the protagonist, is the promulgation of the law abolishing slavery (Marotti 1982, 152–53). At this point, Counselor Ayres is inserted as a protagonist (in a scene Machado himself probably experienced) in a passage in which he refers directly to the events of May 13, 1888:

> Finally, it is law. I have never been, nor did my professional duty permit me to be, a propagandist for the cause of abolition, but I must confess that I felt the greatest pleasure when I learned of the Senate's final vote and the sanctioning of the vote by the Regency. At the time, I was on Ouvidor Street, where there was great commotion and general happiness.
>
> An acquaintance of mine, a gentleman from the press, seeing me there, offered me a seat in his carriage, which was on Nova Street, and was going to line up in the procession organized to parade around the Palace and acclaim the Regency. I almost, almost accepted, such was my state of excitement. Yet my quiet habits, my custom as a diplomat, my very nature and my age restrained me even more strongly than the coachman's reins of my friend's carriage held back his steeds, and I declined the invitation. And I declined with considerable regret I might add. I let them go, my acquaintance and the others, who joined them and departed Primeiro de Março Street. They told me later that the demonstrators stood up on their coaches, which were open, and made great acclamations, in front of the royal palace, where all

the ministers were with the Princess Regent. If I had been there, I probably would have done the same and even so would have not understood myself.... No, no, I would have done nothing; I would have put my face between my knees. (96)

Yet Machado's actual attitude on that day may have been somewhat different from that of Counselor Ayres, the detached diplomat. As the author-narrator recalled in a May 14, 1893, chronicle of *A semana*: "There was sunshine, bright sunshine, that Sunday in 1888, when the Senate voted in the law, which the Regency ratified, and everyone poured out onto the streets. Yes, I, the most introverted of introverts, also went out in the street, and entered the procession headed to the palace in an open coach, the guest of an absent great friend; we all breathed happiness, everything was complete delirium. It was truly the only day of public delirium I remember having witnessed" (*Oc*, 3:583).

In a passage from *Ayres's Memorial*, Counselor Ayres hints perceptively at the paradoxical nature of abolition. When Fidélia decides to turn over the family plantation to the libertos, a gesture that draws praise from her friends and relations, the counselor calls this a just act yet questions whether "the slaves will be able to work together on their own." Granted, "the freed slaves will probably respond with dancing and tears; but it also may be that this new or first responsibility ... [sic]" (207). The ellipsis speaks for itself: Abolition had not given slaves the necessary preparation to take responsibility for their own lives. Fidélia's generosity was no more an act of altruism than the slaves' appeal was an indication that they were content with their lot under slavery. Rather, the incident exposes the cruelty of emancipation as endorsed and disguised by talk of freedom (Wasserman 2008, 94). Machado was astute in observing that, more than anything, emancipation would free slaveholders from a tremendous financial burden and serve as the path to misery for the recently freed African Brazilian slaves (Faoro 1976, 327; Gledson 1986, 144–207).

Faoro, Gledson, and Wasserman emphasize that abolition is presented not as a gesture motivated by benevolence toward slaves but rather as an economic incentive that would benefit slave owners. Moreover, granting land to former slaves was a cynical transfer of assets that were declining in value. Furthermore, the libertos had neither the capital nor training to operate plantations, and certainly had no preparation to be incorporated into the newly emerging wage economy. Indeed, they were deliberately replaced by European immigrants. Slave owners were willing to abandon their newly freed slaves to fend for themselves in the new wage economy. The abolition of the *institution of slavery* was the preoccupation of the political-minded (Faoro 1976, 327; Trípoli 2006, 129–30). Machado, through the voice of the narrator—a former diplomat with a more universal perspective—directs our attention to the broader issue: *true emancipation*.

FIVE

THE META-MULATTO: RACIAL IDENTITY AND THE WRITINGS OF MACHADO DE ASSIS

Beyond Black and White: From "Tragic Mulatto" to Human Tragicomedy

To judge from the previous examples, Machado's political engagement in the fight against slavery and racism seems both qualitatively meek and quantitatively sparse, compared to that displayed by Luís Gama and José do Patrocínio. Although the plantation, on which Brazil's political economy depended, appears in its most developed form in *Brás Cubas*, *Esau and Jacob*, and *Ayres's Memorial*, even there it is not central. Indeed, references to either slavery or individuals of African descent, slave or free, appear infrequently in Machado's writings. Moreover, his social criticism, for all its pointed irony, never reaches the level of caustic, almost vicious, satire and mockery displayed by Lima Barreto (Gledson 1984, 5; Marins 2004, 36, 40, 45; Neto 1976, 5; Param 1973, 240–46; Wasserman 2008, 85, 97).

Beneath the Epidermis

It should be noted, however, that only a fraction of Machado's more than 900 characters are described in a way that would allow us to clearly infer their race (Daniel 1973, 119). It is true that those characters referred to as "black" or "mulatto," directly or indirectly, are few, as compared to those directly or indirectly referred to as "white." Nevertheless, the apparent dearth of discernibly African Brazilian characters can be explained in part by the lack of what Machado considered "epidermal descriptions" and "long digressions, which would fill the paper without helping the action of the story" (*Oc*, 2:27). Thus it is assumed that those characters lacking racial specificity are white due to the white's pervasive and universal status as the hegemonic "Other" against which all other "Otherness" is posited (Fanon 1952/1967, 138n24; Young 2006, 22).

This dearth of discernibly African Brazilian characters may also be explained by the fact that Machado's main characters are primarily drawn from that small segment of Brazilian society—the urban bourgeoisie—that was also his primary audience. Due to social stratification and racial demographics, these individuals would have been overwhelmingly white despite the demographic preponderance of blacks and mulattoes in the public sphere and their significant presence in the private sphere of most whites. Moreover, as Gizêldo Nascimento and Mailde Trípoli point out, an accurate portrayal of the private lives of the white urban bourgeoisie would, for the most part, require that African Brazilians be characterized as shadowy, if not invisible, figures, on the periphery of their social milieu (Nascimento 2002, 53–62; Trípoli 2006, 90–91).

But if Machado chose to depict the urban bourgeoisie in all its splendor, vanities, psychology, and manners, why did he not chronicle the experiences of an important element within that society: the upwardly mobile mulatto? Machado's few mulatto characters, all of them are female, do not actually portray the "mulatto experience," that is, the conflicts, strains, and ambiguities specifically originating in the status and identity of multiracial individuals of African and European descent in a society that prized whiteness and stigmatized blackness. To understand this void in Machado's works, we need only consider his own firsthand knowledge of the subject matter and another, highly controversial work of prose fiction, Aluísio Azevedo's *O mulato* (*The Mulatto*), written in 1879 and published in 1881. The novel is an attack on slavery and the racial bigotry of provincial society. Set in the state of Maranhão prior to the abolition of slavery, it involves a tragic love affair between the mulatto Raimundo, the main character, and his sexually unfulfilled wealthy white cousin, Ana Rosa.

That Machado deliberately chose to avoid such an approach can be seen in several journal articles he wrote in *O Espelho* (1859), *O Futuro* (1862), and *Diário do Rio* (1866), where he advises:

> Do not involve yourself in polemics, be they of a political, literary, or any other nature.... Our intentions are to see cultivated by Brazilian muses

the literary novel that unifies the state of human passions and feelings with the original and delicate touches of poetry. This is the only way to write a true work of fiction that will make a mockery of the passing of time, always remaining the same and pure, under the rigid judgment of posterity.... Art destined to march in the vanguard of the people as an instructor must be immortal and relevant to future societies. (*Crítica, Oc*, 3:793; Viana Filho 1974, 21, 42–43)

This does not mean, of course, that the oppression experienced by blacks and mulattoes in nineteenth-century Brazil could not serve as a source of artistic inspiration by virtue of its historical specificity (Jackson 1988, xv). Indeed, as we have seen, Machado explores such oppression in some of his works. Moreover, his understanding of this and other social issues of the time "was farsighted enough to convey more than their immediate implications" (Nunes 1983, x). Yet, in Machado's opinion, writers who examined the African Brazilian experience risked falling prey to the myopia and tendentiousness of political or social propaganda— regardless of the aesthetic or ethical merit of the content—unless they could also bring broader human significance and greater universality to their work (Booth 1961, 118). And, given the weight of racial oppression, African Brazilian writers would find it difficult to temper their subjectivity and speak to universal concerns when discussing the topic of race.

Because Machado's writings focused on familial relationships and love among the ruling class, where interracial marriage was socially frowned upon, it would have been impossible to introduce a mulatto (let alone a black) character into the main plot without forcing his novels to take on an explicitly sociological or political cast (Expilly 1935, 277–80). Machado's conspicuous avoidance of the topic of interracial intimacy in his writings, so sharply criticized by Gilberto Freyre (1962, 117–18), holds true for both the earlier novels (1872–78)—*Resurrection, The Hand and the Glove, Helena, Iaiá Garcia*—and the later ones (1881–1908)—*Posthumous Memoirs of Brás Cubas, Quincas Borba, Dom Casmurro, Esau and Jacob*, and *Ayres's Memorial*. But, by virtue of the intense intimacies in, for example, *The Hand and the Glove* and *Quincas Borba*, it would have been difficult to avoid introducing the issue of interracial romance and marriage unless their characters were all mulatto and black or all white, which they appear to be.

That said, the struggles for upward social mobility experienced by Helena in *Helena* and by Guiomar in *The Hand and the Glove* lend themselves to the "tragic mulatto" theme, wherein an archetypical mulatto individual, caught between the white and black worlds without fully belonging to or being accepted by either, becomes depressed, emotionally unstable, and even suicidal. The tragic mulatto characters, frequently females, are victims of a society divided by race (especially in the United States, where no intermediate ground is permitted), which often leaves them vulnerable. One purpose for creating this archetype in films and novels was in fact to pathologize miscegenation. The prevailing ideology focused on the "psychological dysfunctioning" of multiracial individuals as a justification for discouraging miscegenation, rather than on the social forces that made psychological functioning problematic (Berzon 1978, 99–111; Raimon 2004, 1–25; Zackodnik 2004, ix–xxxii, 42–74).

In the United States, this argument buttressed claims that any breakdown of the social divisions between blacks and whites would lead to pervasive racial hybridization (or "mongrelization"). This would cause European Americans to decline and eventually die out altogether, which in turn would lead to the ultimate decline of Anglo-American civilization (Young 1995, 160–65). Extensive miscegenation was already a fact in Brazil. Consequently, a slightly different, albeit equally racist, logic underpinned Brazil's ideology of whitening through miscegenation, as well as the rendering of the "tragic mulatto" figure in Brazilian literature (Brookshaw 1986, 21–68; Daniel 2006, 37–41, 47–64; Skidmore 1974, 48–69; Torres 1969, 87–89, 317). Thus, had the protagonists of *Helena* and *The Hand and the Glove* been mulatto, their social ambition would have included the extra burden of race; and the tone and plot of the novels would have suffered serious alterations.

A View from Olympus

Thus Machado refrained from explicit discussion of slavery, racial discrimination, African Brazilian themes in general, and the mulatto experience in particular not simply to sidestep controversy, but because he also wished to create enduring works of art that had broader and universal human significance. This was quite apart from any concerns about how being a mulatto and writing about racial matters might affect him personally or his ability to publish his work. Nevertheless, some would argue that Machado's posture reflects his internalization and support of the inherently Eurocentric assumption that universality is a necessary criterion for art, and, in particular, that the literature of the subaltern is worthy only to the extent that it overcomes parochialism. But Machado did not support universality simply because it was part of the European canon. He did so because it was also a guard against the danger of falling into the catacombs of literary history (*Oc*, 3:912–13).

Deeply engaged in probing universal psychological motivations (Machado 1953, 95), Machado limited explicit discussion of race to a few of his short stories, his more journalistically oriented chronicles and essays, and a few passages in his novels. And, even in these cases, one of his goals remained the exploration of the underlying impulses behind human behavior, which are a tragicomic blend of complex and often contradictory feelings, where "seriousness stimulates laughter, and pain pleasure," in the words of eighteenth-century German critic Gotthold Lessing (1968, 6:353; Carlson 1993, 170). Indeed, most of the main characters in Machado's writings experience a crisis of identity as they confront their incongruous and ambiguous natures. And they all experience a split between themselves and the outside world, between conscious desires and deeper motivations and the choices they make. Yet, instead of being defined by their moral goodness or badness, they are a complex blend of doubt coupled with hope, pride, egoism, and ambition, twinned with altruism, social responsibility, and self-sacrifice.

In the bulk of his prose fiction, especially his novels, Machado seeks to have his readers identify with what is universal about the particulars in the tragicomedy of the human experience (Bone 1958, 2–3, 5; Daniel 1973, 103–4, 115–18; Fitz 1989, 2, 5; Gayle 1976, ix; Machado 1953, 95). To achieve this, Machado does in his writings what Brás Cubas from *Posthumous Memoirs of Brás Cubas* did in his famous delirium:

> I climbed to the top of a mountain . . . and from there I saw everything compressed into one . . . a reduction of centuries into one, a parading of them all, every race, every passion and feeling . . . the war of avarice and hate, the reciprocal destruction of beings and things. . . . I saw everything . . . from what we call glory to what we call misery. . . . There came greed that devours, anger that kindles, envy that enslaves, and glory and grief, humid sweat, ambition, hunger, vanity, melancholy, wealth,—love—and all of them struggled within humanity. (112)

From this somewhat Olympian vantage point, Machado was concerned more with exploring the basis of societal problems—human nature—than with explicit sociological analyses of human behavior, as Luís Gama and Lima Barreto were. Alfredo Bosi believes Machado developed his own "tone of quiet resignation" rather than voicing an "expressionist anguish" in the "convulsive prose" of many other writers (Bosi 1999, 156, 157). On the other hand, critics such as Sílvio Romero and Gilberto Freyre have taken Machado to task for being profoundly disconnected from Brazilian social reality (Romero 1897, 122, 130, 307–8; Freyre 1962, 151–52). But Machado did not simply ignore social and economic realities. Far from it, claims Astrojildo Pereira in his pathbreaking essay "Machado de Assis: Romancista do Segundo Reinado" (Machado de Assis: Novelist of the Second Reign; 1944): there "exists an intimate and profound consonance between Machado de Assis's literary laboratory and the sense of Brazil's political and social evolution" (Pereira 1944, 15–16). Indeed, Pereira was the first to argue that Machado's literary themes, such as "the resistance of archaic institutions to modernization, were informed by the most relevant contemporary sociohistorical tensions in Brazil" (Kristal and Passos 2006, 22).

For their part, Roberto Schwarz and John Gledson see Machado's writings as subtle investigations into the social order of nineteenth-century Brazil (Schwarz 1977, 63–70; 1999, 224; Gledson 1984, 1–8; Sayers 1993, 3; Stein 1984, 132–33; Xavier 1994, 33–48). Bosi argues that, quite apart from faithfully portraying society in the state of Rio de Janeiro at the end of the nineteenth century, they are also elaborate constructions of characters that have universal relevance far beyond the Brazilian context (Bosi 1999, 12–13). And, referring back to arguments made by Roger Bastide (1940), José Merquior finds the oblique sophistication of Machado's writings to be emblematic of Brazilian post-Romanticism (Merquior 1998, 34–35).

Thus, beginning in the 1970s, many critics came to view Machado's writings as sources of important insights into the social order of imperial Brazil. Antônio Cândido's "Esquema de Machado de Assis" (An Outline of Machado de Assis; 1970) mapped out the groundwork, if not the details, of the argument Schwarz would flesh out in his masterful study *Ao vencedor as batatas: Forma literária e processo social nos inícios do romance brasileiro* (*To the Winner Go the Potatoes: Literary Form and Social Process in the Beginning of the Brazilian Novel*; 1977). Cândido calls attention to Machado's "profound sense, beyond the merely documentary, of social status ... and the power of money" in the social order of his time (Cândido 1970b, 31). In "Dialética da malandragem: Caracterização das *Memórias de um sargento de milícias*" (The Dialectic of Tricksterism: Characterization in *Memoirs of a Police Sergeant*; 1970), Cândido articulates an argument about the relationship between social milieu and narrative form that applies not only to Machado's writings but to literature more generally (Kristal and Passos 2006, 23; Schwarcz and Botelho 2008, 148–50).

That said, "The Dialectic of Tricksterism" was primarily a study of Manuel Antônio de Almeida's *Memoirs of a Police Sergeant* (1854),[1] which Cândido considers Brazil's first nationalist novel and which recounts the lively story of Leonardo, the son of two Portuguese immigrants. A problem child who grows up to be an immoral and shiftless young man, Leonardo is arrested by the police and given the chance of becoming an officer instead of going to prison. The novel provides a compelling and humorous chronicle of daily working-class life in Rio de Janeiro during the reign of Dom João VI.

After examining criticism that defined *Memoirs of a Police Sergeant* as a picaresque novel, a documentary novel, and so on, Cândido proposes instead that it be thought of as a novel of manners, in which tricksterism (*malandragem*; Cândido 1970a, 67–71, 74–75, 77) is metaphorically embodied in the dialectical movement between order and disorder, structure and antistructure, licit and illicit in the interstitial space occupied by the popular classes. In mediating between the novel and social reality, as well as between the universal and the particular, this dialectic captures a key aspect of the Brazilian national character (Cândido 1970a, 77, 79–84; Schwarcz and Botelho 2008, 148). Thus, on the one hand, *Memoirs of a Police Sergeant* represents a popular national version of the adventures of the trickster (the "malandro"), which is also an archetype common to folklore.[2] On the other hand, it portrays the social reality of early nineteenth-century Brazil (Cândido 1970a, 71; Schwarcz and Botelho 2008, 149).

One of Cândido's key arguments is that a literary work is not simply influenced by personal circumstances and concerns but is also grounded in sociohistorical ones that have national and global significance (Schwarcz and Botelho 2008, 148, 150). More important, and with regard to the relationship between social milieu and narrative form as this applies to Machado, Cândido states:

> Therefore, [*Memoirs*] is a profoundly social novel, not in the sense of being documentary, but rather, by being constructed according to the general rhythm of the society, seen through one of its sectors. And above all because it dissolves what is sociologically essential in the twists and turns of literary construction.
>
> In fact, it is not the representation of particular concrete data that produces the feeling of reality in fiction, but rather, the suggestion of a certain generality. (Cândido 1970a, 82)

Among analyses in the 1970s that emphasized Machado's penetrating insight into the social reality of his time was Raymundo Faoro's *Machado de Assis: A pirâmide e o trapézio* (*Machado de Assis: The Pyramid and the Trapezoid*; 1974).[3] Gathering characters and situations from across Machado's works, Faoro's study synthesized them into a collection of social types characteristic of the period. The general framework of its interpretation harks back to his earlier work *Os donos do poder: Formação do patronato político brasileiro* (*The Owners of Power: Formation of Brazilian Political Patronage*; 1958). Here, after criticizing previous interpretations of the development of Brazil's political economy, particularly orthodox Marxist analyses, Faoro sought to apply ideas more aligned with those of Max Weber (Faoro 1958/1975, 1:15–17, xi–xii, 133; Schwartzman 2003, 208). Yet Faoro's contribution went beyond mere Weberian analyses of Brazil's political economy. It called attention to the necessity of examining the political system itself, and not simply as a manifestation of class interests, as had been the case in Marxist interpretations (Schwartzman 2003, 207–9).

Whereas some Marxists theorists, in particular Caio Prado Júnior, stressed the capitalist origins of Brazil's economy and society, most argued that Brazil originated in a rural, semifeudal society that had not succeeded in producing a modern working class and a national bourgeoisie capable of developing the nation's economy and eventually giving rise to socialism (Schwartzman 2003, 208; Schwarz 1992, 23). Faoro questioned this conventional Marxist interpretation on two fundamental grounds. First, notwithstanding the largely dispersed and rural character of colonial Brazil, what had always predominated, Faoro maintained, was the force of centralized power. This situation evolved from the beginning of colonization through the hereditary captaincies and continued through the Empire, with a strong presence in urban centers, where the power of the state was installed, and on whose consent and authority the power of landowners depended (Faoro 1958/1975, 1:133; Schwartzman 2003, 207–9).

And second, political power in Brazil was exercised not to address the interests of the landed gentry, bourgeoisie, or agrarian classes but rather as a means unto itself by a social group that sought to dominate the political and administrative machinery of the state, through which it derived its benefits of wealth, power, privilege, and prestige. It was, in Weberian terms, a "bureaucratic estate." Faoro argued that it originated with the formation of the Portuguese state upon, if not before, the discovery of Brazil and would be reincarnated as Brazilian political patronage (Faoro 1958/1975, 1:18–20, 84–85).

The bureaucratic estate had its origin in what Max Weber referred to as "patrimonialism" (Weber 1947, 347–58), a form of political domination typical of centralized systems. For Weber, patrimonial monarchies and similar forms of government were projections of patriarchy onto a broader set of social relationships, based on the rulers' family households. The ruler's authority is personal-familial, and the workings of the household were the model for political administration. Weber contrasted patrimonial with rational-legal bureaucracies, in which impersonal rulers regulated and actors were substitutable, in which spheres of competence were clearly defined, hierarchies of personnel and procedures ordered, and the "private" and the "official" institutionally separated (Weber in Adams 2005, 238–39; Weber 1968, 2:1028–32).

Weber's overarching argument was that, with modernity, patrimonial forms of government gave way to bureaucratic rationalism as the abiding logic of governance. The bureaucratic estate commanded both the civil and the military branches of the public administration, seizing and leading the economic, financial, and political spheres. In the economic field, it assumed direct management of enterprises and went well beyond the regulative function accorded to it by the ideology of liberalism, surpassing even the system of regulated concessions (Faoro 1958/1975, 2:738–39). In the absence of a counterbalancing political decentralization, this would evolve into modern forms of bureaucratic-authoritarian patrimonialism, in contrast to the forms of rational-legal domination that predominated in capitalist nation-states of Western Europe (Faoro 1958/1975, 1:133, 2:743; Schwartzman 2003, 207–9).

Faoro drew from *The Owners of Power* to provide the main structure for *Machado de Assis: The Pyramid and the Trapezoid*. Leopoldo Waizbort points out that the nucleus linking the two books is Faoro's analysis of the estate structure in nineteenth-century Brazil, which in Machado's case, was complicated by the transition to a social order based on social classes (Waizbort 2007, 30). Faoro utilized two geometric configurations, the pyramid and the trapezoid, to illustrate the structures of social classes and estates, respectively, as they represented characters throughout Machado's writings that were typical of certain social locations during the Empire. Faoro argued that social classes (the pyramid) were constructed by a minority of hereditary estates composed of bureaucrats, political leaders, public officials, and diplomats (the trapezoid), who organized and governed Brazil from the colonial era into the twentieth century (Faoro 1976, 3–40; 1958/1975, 1:88–89).

The vertical structure of the social classes—the pyramid—was directly related to production and commerce. Its primary activity was the accumulation of wealth or high consumption at the apex of the pyramid, which was composed of the propertied classes, for example, plantation owners, senior officials, commissioners, and bankers. The merchant class was located in the middle of the pyramid and ranked in proportion to its accumulation of assets and capital. The wide base of the pyramid was composed of manual laborers, primarily slaves and secondarily paid laborers, including agregados (socially and economically dependent free clients) and former slaves (Bosi 2004, 362–64; Faoro 1976, 3–40).

The horizontal structure of the estates—the trapezoid—was superimposed on and had a mutual relationship with the economy's agricultural-export sector by means of bureaucrats, magistrates, imperial and provincial functionaries, the clergy, and the armed forces, which incorporated power and depended on the legislative bodies and the emperor. Membership in the estates changed periodically according to shifts in the political economy. Yet this social stratum always sought to use the power and wealth of the state for its own benefit. Correspondingly, this prevented the masses from actually ruling the country for the benefit of the majority. The estates were thus organs of the state and tended to be closed groups. Individuals generally entered these realms by reason of birth, unlike classes, which were defined by economic interests (Bosi 2004, 362–64; Faoro 1976, 3–40). Summarizing Weber's argument, Faoro maintained that "estates govern, classes negotiate. Estates are organs of the state, classes are social categories" (Faoro 1958/1975, 1:47).

Yet the estates were never absolutely closed in Brazil because there was always the possibility of upward mobility by reason of merit or wealth (e.g., titles of nobility awarded by the emperor for military service or through purchase) or by marriage. Indeed, titles of nobility sold and granted to rural landowners maintained the social and political power firmly centered on the emperor (Bosi 2004, 363; Faoro 1976, 4–7, 10; Lima 1988, 195–96; Wasserman 2008, 88). Luiz Costa Lima and Fernando Uricoechea claim that Brazil's political economy was not purely class or estate based but a blend of both. Because the state could not forgo the revenue generated from export agriculture, the only substantial economic activity of the era, it co-opted rural landowners; in the absence of a market, this gave rise to clientelistic politics (Lima 1988, 196; Uricoechea 1978, 112). José Carvalho adds that a surplus of college graduates generated a desperate search for public employment, which reinforced the clientelistic character of the imperial bureaucracy (Carvalho in Lima 1988, 196; Carvalho 1980, 71).

One of Faoro's central arguments is that Machado captured the gradual collapse of the traditional social order. The hereditary values, which were primarily based on honor and service, were in irreversible decline. They were being replaced by those of a modern class-oriented social order that drew its lifeblood from an acquisitive property-based individualism based on ambition, competition, and achievement (Faoro 1976, 5, 8, 23). Thus Faoro's analysis, according to Dain Borges, Renata Wasserman, and José Merquior, maps the transfer of power over Brazil's political economy from the rural and agrarian slave-owning aristocracy to the urban bourgeoisie (Borges 2007, 238; Wasserman 2008, 88; Merquior 1998, 43; Faoro 1976, 4, 23). Faoro believes that Machado's writings, though not presenting the historical totality of Brazil during this period, provide deep insight into its shifting values with all their resulting clashes, confusions, and contradictions (Faoro 1976, 8, 504).

Despite Faoro's important contribution to this topic, Gledson, Kristal, and Passos point out that this line of reasoning was not fully developed until Roberto Schwarz's *To the Winner Go the Potatoes* (1977; Gledson 1986, 24; Kristal and Passos 2006, 23), which analyzes the development of the Brazilian novel and consists of one study on José de Alencar and another on Machado. Its title is derived from Machado's *Quincas Borba*, which satirizes Social Darwinist thinking embodied in the philosophy of Humanitism.

Unlike Faoro's argument against Marxist theories of the ruling class, Schwarz's analysis draws heavily from both Marxist literary theory and the work of Cândido (Borges 2007, 238). One of Schwarz's main objectives is to challenge the long-standing notion of Machado's "absenteeism" in addressing social concerns of the time. Schwarz argues that Machado's novels may display subtle, indirect, and hidden assertions but are hardly disengaged from his surroundings. On the contrary, Schwarz maintains, Machado was actively engaged in a probing investigation of the social order. This is apparent in his portrayal of the contradictions that arose from Brazil's slave-owning economy and its aspirations to participate in a global culture and political economy (Schwarcz and Botelho 2008, 147–53; Wasserman 2008, 87).

Economic and political power in the dominant Western nation-states was shifting to a class of bourgeois entrepreneurs who prized economic activity (Schwarz 1977, 12–13). According to Wasserman (2008, 95), this development was contingent on a market of labor and products, invoked the liberal philosophy of Adam Smith and John Stuart Mill, and "endorsed democratic governments and a compact of civil rights and civic obligations (excepting women, racial, religious, or ethnic minorities as a matter of course)." Contrary to this trend, the premodern or traditional practices associated with a system of clientelism and favor were never eliminated in Brazil (Avelar 2005, 163), where leisure continued to function as a requisite status symbol. A high premium continued to be placed on living off interest or slave labor, which in turn devalued all labor because of its association with slavery (Schwarz 1977, 13–14; Wasserman 2008, 88). Borges adds that liberalism, which posits autonomous actors, was an even more inaccurate description of the social order in Brazil than in Europe due to the institution of slavery (Borges 2007, 239; Schwarz 1977, 12). Modernization in Brazil did not substitute or eliminate the social structures inherited from the colonial experience but, rather, reflected a precarious mix of old and new. Accordingly, Schwarz considers liberalism a "misplaced idea" (*uma idéia fora do lugar*) in Brazil.[4]

Whereas Brazil's most prominent nationalist novelist of the time (and Machado's immediate predecessor), José de Alencar, failed to examine the unsettling distortions that liberal ideology underwent as it was manifested in Brazil, Machado was able in his earlier novels to exploit the opportunity that eluded Alencar (Schwarz 1977, 39–46, 83, 86; Schwarcz and Botelho 2008, 150–51). Indeed, through the dialogical nature of his narratives, Machado unveils the *transition* in the Brazilian social order arising from a fracture in the monolithic and authoritarian edifice constructed by the landed or seigniorial elite (Reis 1992, 47, 52).

As noted before, Schwarz and Faoro argue that this transition involves the shift of an estate-based or seigniorial (traditional) social structure toward a more mercantile and bourgeois (modern) social order, with all the attendant contradictions. The seignorial class is at once mercantile and modernizing, the amenities of the liberal façade rest on the foundations of compulsory and semicompulsory labor, and law is accommodated to patronage (Reis 1992, 14). However, the key here is Roberto Reis's concept of "transition," which conveys the notion of ambiguity and contradiction. Indeed, this historical period, particularly the "twilight of the Second Reign," was a "mixed" political economy that embodied what had ceased to exist and that which had not yet come into existence (Reis 1992, 58, 18).

Though not insensitive to the cruelties of slavery, Machado does not present his criticism in explicitly racial terms, which would necessarily focus on the more obvious and politically controversial topic of the master-slave relationship or race relations in the larger society (Nunes 1983, 140; Sayers 1958, 392–93). Drawing from Avery Gordon's analyses in *"Ghostly Matters": Haunting and the Sociological Imagination* (Gordon 1997, 8), however, one can argue that slavery provides an important and seething backdrop in Machado's writings, however shadowy its presence (Gledson 1984, 6). Gledson and Schwarz argue that Machado examined the more ambiguous and volatile relations between the oligarchic patriarchal family and its agregados (Gledson 1984, 6; Schwarz 1996, 167–68; Borges 1995, 61), who were not slaves (although many were African Brazilian and mulattoes in particular). Yet they lived in precarious circumstances resulting from a slave-owning society that was at odds with its professed liberal ideology. These free clients found it necessary to seek out the patronage of slave-owning masters. Given the universal power and authority of the oligarchic European Brazilian family, their civil status as free individuals was contingent—and indeed somewhat constrained (Sayers 1993, 6–7; Schwarz 1977, 16–17; 1996, 167–68; Xavier 1994, 33–48).

Bosi, Kristal, and Passos point out that Machado's purpose was to expose the highly asymmetrical power relations that arose from clientelistic ties of patronage and dependency, which sustained a social order based on pervasive exploitation (Bosi 1999, II, 58; Kristal and Passos 2006, 23–24). The tensions perpetuated by these social dynamics provided Machado with the perfect terrain to investigate the real operation of power at the nexus of freedom and servitude. The European Brazilian family imposed its will on individuals who were not "blood relations" or related by marriage, even though, to some extent, they may have been "adopted" into the family (Gledson 1984, 6–7; Xavier 1994, 33–48). In the process, Machado brings into sharp focus the mechanism of paternalism, which was the official rationale behind not only oligarchic control but also the existence of slavery itself (Chalhoub 2001, 172–73; Gledson 1984, 6; Xavier 1994, 33–48).

In his earlier novels, where love, money, and ambition come into play, Machado examines the ambiguous social location of free clients through the *agregada* who falls in love with the son and heir of the family. Machado scrutinizes the attitudes and behavior of these young women who ruthlessly exploit patronage to achieve upward mobility by seeking to marry well and thus enhance their social standing. This situation creates serious difficulties and, with the exception of Guiomar in *The Hand and the Glove* (Gledson 1984, 6; Xavier 1994, 35–36), almost never culminates in marriage. The aspiring lovers in Machado's earlier novels overcome obstacles to their marriage but only through manipulation of their patrons. By contrast, in the later novels such as *Dom Casmurro* and *Brás Cubas*, Machado presents the urban environment as more complex and the careers through which an intermediate class can achieve some real economic independence as more numerous. Yet the basic slavocratic structure, although attenuated or disguised, is still powerful. Machado portrays this conservative and archaic social order in the throes of a painful and, to some extent, futile and self-destructive attempt to retain its power and self-confidence (Gledson 1984, 9). A rarity among his contemporaries, Machado displayed the insight that the institution of slavery was a symptom of a larger social order and not the underlying pathology of that order. He also emphasized that, even with the abolition of slavery, the social structures that supported a slave society remained intact (Marotti 1982, 142–43).

Schwarz's second book, *Um mestre na periferia do capitalismo* (*A Master on the Periphery of Capitalism*; 1990), is a study of *The Posthumous Memoirs of Brás*

Cubas. He examines the aesthetics of Machado's second phase with the goal of locating his writings in the contemporary Brazil social order using his concept of "misplaced ideas" as the framework. As was the case in *To the Winner Go the Potatoes*, Schwarz argues that the importation of European forms had contradictory outcomes in Brazil when combined with slavery and paternalism (Schwarcz and Botelho 2008, 150). The liberal ideas derived from European models were deeply in conflict with an economy based on slavery, which forced the elite to define themselves "simultaneously as supporters of slavery and as enlightened individuals" (Schwarz 1990, 41).

Machado drew considerable attention to the contradictions between public appearances and private feelings, to a society that, for all its virtuous pretenses, was in fact cynical, dishonest, motivated by egoism, and sustained by slavery (Borges 1995, 61; Brookshaw 1986, 179–81; Gledson 1984, 6–7; Sayers 1993, 389–90). Machado gives aesthetic expression to this historical clash, Schwarz argues, with his narrators' characteristic tone of ironic detachment, particularly in his later works (Schwarz 1990, 41, 40–43), a detachment that figures prominently in the massive shift from his rather unremarkable and conventional earlier novels to the five extraordinary later ones. In particular, Schwarz traces this shift through the manner in which narrators evolve from the first to the second phase of Machado's writings.

Whereas the narrators in the novels of the first phase are restrained and deferential, those in the second are transgressive and intrude themselves into the narration (Schwarz 1990, 213–16). To achieve this shift, Machado makes use of narrative "volubility" (*volubilidade*; Schwarz 1990, 30, 45–46, 209), in which the unpredictable and unreliable narrative voice functions as a critique of the entire Brazilian upper class (Schwarz 1990, 18, 35–36, 83, 163, 21, 213, 218). In *Posthumous Memoirs of Brás Cubas* (1881), the first novel of Machado's second phase, the narrator Brás Cubas is a self-serving, vain, opinionated idler. Schwarz maintains that Brás's strategic and unexpected shifts in tone, sentiment, and opinion were Machado's way of stylizing the paternalism, clientelism, and patronage that the Brazilian upper class used to maintain its social and political power and control (Schwarz 1990, 20, 35–36). More important, Machado employs this narrative device to establish a dialogue of complicity between the narrator and the reader (Schwarz 1990, 23), which serves as a hegemonic sanctioning or reaffirmation of the inequality engendered by those dynamics.

In Schwarz's view, Machado uses Brás Cubas as a representative of Brazil's entire nineteenth-century elite, to criticize its volatility and abusiveness (Schwarz 1990, 18, 21, 83, 163, 213–16, 218). More generally, Machado uses this whimsical and impulsive narrative voice in his later novels to reflect the contradictions and capriciousness embedded in the nineteenth-century Brazilian social order. Schwarz maintains that the similarity between Machado's narrative and social structures is what defines his innovative brasilidade and that, to fully understand Machado's later novels, one must understand the parallels between his aesthetic form and the social structure of nineteenth-century Brazil.

Like Schwarz, Gledson has examined Machado's writings extensively for their historical and sociological referents. Taking Schwarz's *To the Winner Go the Potatoes* as a key point of departure, Gledson agrees that the agregado is central to understanding Machado's perspective on the complex system of clientelistic social relationships based on patronage and favor (Gledson 1984, 12). He notes that the tensions and ambiguities in this situation were the perfect terrain for Machado's ruthless irony, informed by the fact that Machado and his family were themselves agregados on a large estate in Rio de Janeiro. This experience served as a catalyst for Machado's carefully disguised contempt for the oligarchy and penetrating insight into its ideals and motives (Gledson 1984, 14).

Moreover, Gledson argues, Machado viewed the European Brazilian family as the ruling class in a microcosm (Gledson 1984, 9). Although agregados often had considerable, albeit precarious, standing within the family—as in the case of José Dias in *Dom Casmurro*—their freedom of movement could be restricted (Xavier 1994, 40–48), and they were dependent upon the favor of the patriarch or his representative. According to Gledson, this subject matter allowed Machado to examine the question of freedom and servitude, which, though different in degree and kind, could be extended to the slaves' situation as well as the "racialized agregado" experience of some free blacks and mulattoes (Gledson 1984, 6; Xavier 1994, 33–48).

Gledson's first book, *The Deceptive Realism of Machado de Assis: A Dissenting Interpretation of "Dom Casmurro"* (1984), though devoted to a study of *Dom Casmurro* (1899), also includes analyses of Machado's other novels and some of his shorter fiction. In his second book, *Machado de Assis: Ficção e historia* (*Machado de Assis: Fiction and History*; 1986), Gledson examines works published by Machado between 1885 and 1908: *Relics of the Old House, Quincas Borba, Esau and Jacob, Ayres's Memorial*, and a series of chronicles published between April 1888 and August 1889. This was a period of decisive events, including the abolition of slavery and the declaration of the Republic. Indeed, the fictional time frame of these works (1840s–1890s) almost entirely coincides with the reign of Dom Pedro II (1831–89).

Gledson disagrees with theorists who simply study Machado's formal innovations or his before-its-time Freudian precision in anatomizing the human psyche (Dennis 1990, 76; Freitas 2001, 22, 157–58; Gledson 1984, 2–3, 12–13, 90). Rather, he sees in Machado's "notoriously unreliable" first- and third-person narrators, who speculate about the texts they are writing and the problems they encounter as narrators, "an immensely sophisticated and skeptical awareness of novelistic structure, a tendency to indulge in digressions of doubtful relevance to the plot, a concern with time and memory, and a thoroughgoing relativism" (Gledson 1999, 2).

Machado's narrative technique has been praised as a precursor of the modern novel and, specifically, of the modern Latin American novel (Dennis 1990, 77). Though not dismissing Machado's "modernity," Gledson emphasizes that Machado was deeply influenced by his time and place—nineteenth-century Brazil—and that, like other Realists, he used the novel as a means of portraying the social order of his time (Gledson 1984, 3–4, 11; 1986, 16; 1999, 1; Baptista 2003b, 14–15). Machado proposed an incisive but masked critique of the contradictions, compromises, and impasses of the Second Empire and first years of the Republic, a critique, that informs all of Machado's later novels (Gledson 1986, 20–22).

Gledson's iconoclastic—"dissenting"—interpretation of Machado's writings emphasizes the writer's attention to sociological rather than psychological considerations. Gledson concludes that Machado's *primary* objective was to provide a critical portrait of the oligarchic, patriarchal, and clientelistic social structure of his time (Gledson 1984, 12). Moreover, he intended *Dom Casmurro* in particular to be a profoundly unsympathetic representation of the oligarchy (Gledson 1984, 5, 14)—an oligarchy that, like the novel's protagonist, Bento Santiago, continuously sought to justify its existence by transforming reality into a "seamless web" (Gledson 1984, 209).

Gledson believes that the key to understanding *Dom Casmurro* lies in analyzing the social location of its characters and their responses to their circumstances: "The plot and the portrayal of the characters are determined in the first instance by social factors" (Gledson 1984, 9). The novel's message is to be gleaned from the fortunes of Bento Santiago and his family vis-à-vis those of the oligarchy during the middle years of Dom Pedro II's reign (Gledson1984, 2, 4, 93). Only through scrutiny of the text and interpretation of its allegories and metaphors can one elucidate Machado's subtly concealed real—that is, sociological—intention (Gledson 1984, 9, 14, 94).

One of Gledson's strategies for deciphering Machado's allusions includes searching for historical allusions in characters' names and in specific dates or events within the novels, which in turn yield Machado's "real" intention. Yet critics have faulted Gledson's allegorical analyses for at times relying too heavily on a one-to-one correspondence between Machado's texts and historical circumstances, events, and individuals (Haberly 1985, 80; Oakley 1986, 1029; Woodridge 1986, 239). Perhaps the most cited example of this tendency is Gledson's interpretation of the episode in *Dom Casmurro* involving Manduca and Bento, which he considers a veiled critique of Brazil's participation in the Paraguayan War. For Gledson, Bento symbolizes Brazil, Manduca symbolizes Paraguay, and their perspectives on the Crimean War convey differing views on the Paraguayan War from the standpoint of the respective victorious and defeated forces (Gledson 1984, 140–46). Questionable interpretations aside, critics generally agree that Gledson is superbly methodical in his search for political and social allegories and provides compelling evidence that *Dom Casmurro* is a powerful critique of the contemporary social order.

On the other hand, many disagree with Gledson that Machado's primary aim was to render an authentic portrait of society (see especially Baptista 1994, 159). Indeed, it is possible that Machado's objective was neither to truly characterize Brazil's social order, as Gledson argues, nor to provide sophisticated and nuanced psychological analyses and highly ambiguous and deceptive narratives, as other critics have suggested. Rather, in conveying his insights into Brazilian society through literary structures of masterful deception and ambiguity, Machado may have been calling upon readers to see through these structures to the universal dimensions of the human psyche and experience.

Drawing from the pioneering work of Schwarz and Gledson, Sidney Chalhoub, in his book *Machado de Assis: Historian* (2003), argues that Machado's novels portray a society based on slavery and the concomitant production of dependency and everyday social inequalities as the basis of its organization. Indeed, slavery was the ultimate form of dependency that served as the foundation for all other types of exploitation (Chalhoub 2003, 18, 48–49, 57). In particular, Chalhoub believes that Machado's writings map out the ideological framework of the master class and the historical changes it underwent because of the social forces leading up to and culminating in the Law of the Free Womb (Chalhoub 2003, 17–20).

Thus, Chalhoub asserts, in *Helena*, which unfolds during the 1840s and 1850s, the omnipresent and indisputable hold the master class maintained over the social order is central to the sequence of events surrounding the novel's two main characters, who represent the opposing social forces of the master class (Estácio) and free clients (Helena). Whereas Estácio is unaware of the tension between these forces because the paternalism, clientelism, and patronage underpinning the master class ideology have, for the most part, remained unchallenged, Helena is quite conscious of it and of her social and economic dependency as an agregada. Consequently, she attempts to manipulate Estácio to achieve her goals. Because, however, the crisis in the master class ideology had not yet manifested itself, this tension could not be resolved in Helena's favor and, instead, results in her death (Chalhoub 2003, 44–47).

Chalhoub considers *Helena* to reflect the historical period marked by the consolidation of the Empire, the Conservative Party (or Party of Order), and conservative ideology (Chalhoub 2003, 18). Some argue that the Conservatives sought to expand the master class's power by neutralizing progressive social and political movements and suppressing popular unrest. Indeed, the period following the abdication of the Dom Pedro I in 1831 and the installation of the Regency, which served as governing body until Dom Pedro's son and successor, Pedro II, came of age, was plagued by social turmoil and uprisings. This period concluded with a challenge to the power of Conservative forces in 1860, initiating a crisis that would, decades later, bring about the end of the Empire (Mattos 1987, 2–7; Ricupero 2004, 179–204).[5]

Jeffrey Needell contends, however, that the primary goal of the Conservatives was to establish a representative, constitutional monarchy, which, though dominated by the ruling class, welcomed widespread participation by their "social inferiors," especially slaveholders, who included poor as well as rich Brazilians of all racial ancestries. They viewed their political adversaries as lending strength to popular unrest, decentralization, and a weak state, all of which they thought would perpetuate the destructive tendencies of the Regency. Much of the Conservatives' ideology was liberal in origin: although they sought to reestablish the social order, their goal was to "civilize" Brazil along European lines.[6]

The crisis in the master class (slaveholding) ideology figures prominently in *Iaiá Garcia*, *The Posthumous Memoirs of Brás Cubas*, and *Dom Casmurro*, as demonstrated by the growing antagonism between the masters and their dependents in these novels (Chalhoub 2003, 91, 96). In *Iaiá Garcia*, which unfolds between 1866 and 1871, around the time of passage of the Law of the Free Womb, the master class's ideology has clearly begun to lose its unquestioned status (Chalhoub 2003, 67, 69, 71). But even though Valéria is aware of this change, she refuses to accept and act on this awareness. In *The Posthumous Memoirs of Brás Cubas*, the narrator, writing between 1870 and 1871 (but who is now dead), relates events of his life that took place between 1840 and 1869 (Chalhoub 2003, 73). *Dom Casmurro* unfolds between 1857 and 1900 and is narrated in the latter year. In these last two novels, Machado demonstrates that the authority of the master class has already been challenged. This is reflected in the novels' pessimistic and nostalgic tone relating to a world of lost illusions, as represented by the protagonists Brás Cubas and Bento Santiago (Chalhoub 2003, 83–84, 106–7). To Chalhoub, Machado is a consummate craftsman at capturing momentous historical changes in Brazil that have broader and universal significance.

Race, Multiraciality, and Metarace: Miscegenation in a Higher Sense

By striving toward universality—and perhaps what Joaquim Nabuco meant when he said he saw in Machado only the Greek—Machado de Assis may have appeared to be masquerading as white. Indeed, no doubt feeling "betwixt and between," he may have found it expedient to be silent on the issue of race and to subdue one racial component to the other in his public life to ensure his social survival (Daniel 1981, 6; Moniz 1984, 173–74). That said, based on examination of his statements and analysis of his writings, I submit that Machado's apparent lack of racial consciousness reflects his desire not to deny being a mulatto but to become "raceless."

Blackness, Whiteness, and Racelessness

The ability to experience racelessness—a humanity unfettered by racial oppression—is a natural corollary of the ability to claim whiteness. Consequently, seeking to become raceless and seeking to "masquerade" as white both involve the absence of attitudinal and behavioral markers that specifically affirm an affinity with racialized "Otherness." Although both reflect integrationist dynamics, they diverge significantly in terms of motivation and operationalization.

"Masquerading" as white is an assimilationist identity based on inegalitarian integration, which leads to the denial or dilution of something deemed inferior or undesirable, which, according to Irving Goffman, has a socially discrediting impact because it is stigmatized. Stigma, he argues, is a specific discrepancy between one's "virtual" social identity, which reflects the assumed demands and character imputed to individuals, and one's "actual" social identity, which reflects the category and attributes that individuals can in fact be proven to possess (Goffman 1963, 2–3). Kenji Yoshino, borrowing from Goffman, examines the assimilationist response to stigma as part of the phenomenon of "covering," in which individuals seek to downplay stigmatized traits in order to blend into the larger society. Given that all individuals may possess stigmatized attributes of some kind, he argues that covering in varying degrees may be a normative part of social life (Yoshino 2006, 18).

In the extreme this phenomenon may involve "passing," which, for example, has been associated with the adoption of a "virtual" white racial identity by individuals whose "actual" identity is that of African Americans according to the legal definition of blackness based on rules of hypodescent (Daniel 1992, 92–94; 2002, 49–55; Goffman 1963, 48–51).[7] They have pirated an identity that allows them to escape racial subordination and gain privileges and status that are not "rightfully" theirs (Ginsberg 1996, 3–5). As compared to dramatic frontline battles waged against racial inequality by individuals of African descent, passing may appear on the surface to be a form of opportunism, selling out, or full acceptance of the racial status quo. And passing certainly can exact a heavy emotional toll.[8] If viewed as part of a spectrum of tactics, however, it is clear that passing is an underground tactic, a conspiracy of silence that seeks to best oppression at its own game. Passing exposes not only the political motivations behind racial categories (Daniel 1992, 92–94; 2002, 49–55) but also racial difference as a continually emerging distinction devoid of any essential content. It attests to the fact that whiteness can be donned by someone who has mastered the art of racial cross-dressing and disguise (Ginsberg 1996, 3–5).[9]

The absence of racial/cultural specificity (or deracination) that emerges in this process, whether in the form of covering or passing, where the goal is the dilution, denial, or erasure of something that is stigmatized and deemed undesirable, should not be confused with "racelessness," which is based on egalitarian or transracial/transcultural integration. The objective of racelessness is to embrace a metaracial philosophy of life, one that seeks a more inclusive identity transcending racial ascription altogether (Daniel 2002, 106–11; Renn 2004, 91–92; Rockquemore and Brunsma 2002, 71–72). Nonetheless, the fact that these two phenomena are mutually exclusive does not preclude them from existing sequentially or simultaneously over the course of an individual's psychological development (Daniel 2002, 106–11; Poston 1990, 52–55).

Notwithstanding the long-held belief that Machado sought at best to camouflage and at worst to deny being a mulatto, I contend that his primary motivation was to achieve a sense of racelessness. He endeavored to go beyond the physical limitations of being a mulatto to become a "meta-mulatto," that is, a mulatto whose writing grappled with the universal questions of duality and ambiguity in all human existence—miscegenation in a higher sense. He displayed what has been termed "mestizo consciousness," "radical mestizaje," and "critical hybridity" (Anzaldúa 1987, 77; Ramirez 1983, 6; Sandoval 2000, 72; Daniel 2005, 264; Lund 2006, 55) by affirming a mulatto identity grounded in a more inclusive or universal self, beyond questions of racial, cultural, or any other specificity. As a multiracial individual of African and European descent in a society that prized whiteness and stigmatized blackness, Machado viewed the challenge of achieving upward mobility and public success without also compromising his personal integrity as merely one of the myriad epiphenomena of universal duality and ambiguity.

Thus, contrary to David Haberly, I contend that Machado's manner of operating has little to do with feelings of discomfort that sociological theorists have traditionally associated with the condition of racial marginality, held to be necessarily pathological and the source of lifelong personal conflict, divided loyalties, ambivalence, and hypersensitivity. Based largely upon misinterpretations of the work of sociologist Robert E. Park, this "pathological" view of marginality characterized social science frameworks prior to the 1970s and supported the prevailing ideology, which opposed miscegenation and ignored the sociological forces that put multiracial individuals at risk psychologically. This "negative" view of marginality, especially as articulated by Everett Stonequist (1937, 44–48, 139–58, 201–9), distorted or ignored the nuances of Park's actual theory of marginality and overshadowed arguments that marginality could give individuals a broader vision and wider range of sympathies.

Indeed, Park argued that marginal individuals were likely to be alert, critical, intelligent leaders. He believed that whatever alienation marginal individuals might experience could be counterbalanced by the role they might play in facilitating mutual understanding between groups and between individuals from different groups. This "positive" view of marginality in turn would assist social scientists in gaining deeper insights into the dynamics of race and ethnic relations and perhaps eventually into how to improve them (Park 1928, 881–93).[10]

Machado undoubtedly experienced the ambiguities, strains, and conflicts that come "naturally" with marginality in a society that viewed white identities as dominant and black identities as subdominant, and thus both as mutually exclusive categories of experience. That said, these identities coexisted with another, and possibly overriding, desire to transcend all racial ascriptions and embrace a more universal humanity. Far from espousing a naive egalitarianism that deflects attention away from—or even denies the existence of—racial inequities, Machado calls into question the notion that the most important thing about one's personhood is one's "community of descent" (Hollinger 2008, 1034). In doing so, his behavior is consistent with the identity paradigms captured by Peter Adler, Manuel Ramirez, and others. Indeed, the identity Machado claims is indicative of an individual who

> has an orientation and view of the world [that] profoundly transcends ... his indigenous culture.... He is ... the timeless "universal" person described ... by philosophers through the ages. He [is] the classical ideal of a person whose lifestyle is one of knowledge and wisdom, integrity and direction, principle and fulfillment, balance and proportion.... [His] identity ... is based, not on a "belongingness" which implies either owning or being owned by culture, but on a style of self consciousness that is capable of negotiating ever new formations of reality.... He is neither totally a part of nor totally apart from his culture; he lives, instead, on the boundary. (Adler 1974, 24–25)

As an individual living on the boundary of a society where white was an absolute good and black an absolute evil, Machado was surely aware that his mulatto appearance and racially blended ancestry (or "actual" racial identity; Goffman 1963, 2–3) made him "inferior" to the members of the elite European Brazilian circles in which he moved. At the same time, he realized that these same physical characteristics, in conjunction with his cultural "refinement" and intellectual accomplishments, made him "superior" to the African Brazilian masses and succeeded in moving his perceived racial identity (or "virtual" racial identity; Goffman 1963, 2–3) closer to the white end of the social spectrum (Brookshaw 1986, 11, 57, 180; Daniel 1981, 6; Haberly 1983, 74). Nevertheless, because his somatic identity was always apparent, Machado remained fundamentally vulnerable in his European Brazilian sociocultural milieu (Daniel 1981, 6; Haberly 1983, 74; Reis 1987, 80–83; Spitzer 1989, 12).

Given the prevailing attitudes among the white elite, Machado was no doubt privy to their racist attitudes and comments. Indeed, one of Machado's closest associates and the most respected leader of the abolitionist movement, Joaquim Nabuco, made racist statements publicly (Murat 1926, 146–48; Santos 2002, 66). In his speeches as federal deputy during 1879, he expressed openly what he only implied in his books (Santos 2002, 66): his belief that Europeans were superior and Africans and Asians inferior and his fear that Brazil would remain a nation with an African Brazilian majority (Nabuco 1983, 180–83, 188–91). Nabuco was also explicit about his desire for the eventual racial whitening of Brazil, believing that, because of their natural inferiority, African Brazilians would vanish either through miscegenation or attrition. "Considering that blacks and whites have lived together in the same society for centuries, the blacks' blood will naturally tend to be absorbed into that of the whites', or blacks will all together vanish, as the one race gives up the field to the other that is better prepared for the struggle of life" (Nabuco 1983, 182). At the beginning of his book *O abolicionismo* (*Abolition*), Nabuco proclaims, "In the future only an operation can save us—at the cost of our national identity—that is, the transfusion of the pure and oxygenated blood of a free race" (Nabuco 1938, 6).

Statements like this would heighten Machado's awareness of his vulnerability even if they were not directed at him. He no doubt had to become adept at what Edwina Barvosa refers to as "selfcraft," a style of self-consciousness in which individuals continuously incorporate here and discard there in response to each situation (Barvosa 2008, 175–92, 207–29). Essentially, Machado was an insider who remained to some extent a detached observer—an outsider. He was keenly aware of, and sensitive to, the vast territory between fact and fiction, the liminality of experience.

Liminality (from the Latin *limen*, "boundary or threshold") is typically associated with the initiation rites of adolescent males from boyhood into manhood among traditional peoples. In Victor Turner's work on rituals, ceremonial performances, and social change, *liminality*, a term introduced by Charles-Arnold Kurr van Gennep (1873–1957)—or *communitas*, to use Turner's term—refers to marginal social spaces outside everyday constraints. These spaces liberate participants from routine activity and come out of social rupture or discontinuity (pilgrimages, carnivals, religious conversions, life transitions, holidays) that is both transformative and generative. Turner conceived of communitas as an intense community spirit, a feeling of great social equality, solidarity, and togetherness in which individuals experience liminality together. In this transitional state between two phases, individuals are "betwixt and between"—they do not belong to the society of which they were previously members, and they are not yet reintegrated into that society (Turner 1969, 94–130; Whalen 2004, 1).

A similar dynamic can be observed in individuals who are members of two or more racially or culturally distinct groups (multiracial individuals; second-generation immigrants or recent migrants from country to city; and women in nontraditional female roles) and can be applied to practices, cultures, frameworks for knowing the world, and modes of communication between the divine and secular, the private and public, the linguistic and nonlinguistic. These categories follow a similar path from "either/or" to "both/neither" (Whalen 2004, 1). In this "twilight zone," the absolute truth about any pair of opposites is their inherent ambiguity as relative extremes on a continuum of grays (Hansen 1997, 250–51).

The Dual and Ambiguous Self

Although Machado's novels are not empirically autobiographical, neither are they, as Brookshaw and others have suggested, divorced from his racial origins. To the contrary, from his own experience of being a racial blend of *both* black and white and yet *neither*, Machado developed an acute sensitivity to even more pervasive dualities and ambiguities experienced by all humanity. He not only challenged the whole notion of exclusive (or dichotomous) categories of difference, racial and otherwise, but also called into question the hierarchical ranking upon which these differences are constructed. As Haberly and, to some extent, Gledson see it, Machado's novels are a "camouflaged" or metaphorical documentation of his own experiences with racial duality and ambiguity, which he might have discussed openly had the historical and social circumstances been different. Indeed, Haberly (1983) and I (Daniel 1981) argue that the dualism experienced by Machado (between himself and the dominant European Brazilian culture) was a source of his intense concern with subject-object duality and ambiguity as they relate to human identity. One can argue that the shadowy racial forces Gordon speaks of in her study of Toni Morrison's *Ghostly Matters* (Gordon 1997, 8) influenced the formation of Machado's aesthetic sensibility in more intricate ways than is often presumed.

That said, Machado went beyond dealing explicitly with the mulatto experience—and the theme of racial oppression in general—in order to uncover the universal basis of societal dis-ease: the conflict within humanity's own metaphorically mulatto nature originating in the dichotomous and hierarchical relationship between the subjective and objective aspects of human identity and experience. To do so, Machado's writings focus on the conflict between individual morality or conscience and the image reflected in the mirror through social interactions, which is motivated by egoism and the dictates of public success (Daniel 1981, 10, 11–13; Haberly 1983, 74–77). Machado considered the dominance of materialist rationalism to be the source of the extremity to which the schism between the internal and external self had progressed in Western consciousness and behavior. This mode of thinking was based not simply on delineating the subjective and objective aspects of human identity and experience into mutually exclusive, antagonistic, and hierarchical categories of experience. Rather, under the dictates of egoism, ambition, and greed, it also precluded a sense of mutuality between the two (Boyd 1975, 45; Brookshaw 1986, 179; Caldwell 1970, 125; Daniel 1981, 11; Haberly 1983, 74–75; Nunes 1983, 12, 82–84, 140, 142–43).

Nowhere is Machado's sensitivity to these questions more explicit than in the short story "O espelho" (The Mirror), where the narrator puts forth the notion that humanity possesses two souls: the subjective self (*alma interior*) and the objective self (*alma exterior*; *Oc*, 2:345–52). The importance of this dual essence is symbolized by Jacobina, a former military officer who needs to parade in front of a mirror in his decorated uniform—alma exterior—in order to reaffirm his existence. Ideally, the internal and external identities, the individual conscience and the dictates of public success should work together. Machado's characters, under the exigencies of Western European materialist rationalist thinking, are, however, a composite of aberrations in a vicious and amoral world dominated by greed and egoism. More often than not, the ambition for public success is at odds with the promptings of the individual conscience and morality, thus impeding—or precluding—a sense of mutuality between the two identities (Daniel 1981, 12; Haberly 1983, 76).

Alfredo Bosi's *Machado de Assis: O enigma do olhar* (*Machado de Assis: The Enigma of Perspective*; 1999) and José Luiz Passos's *Machado de Assis: O romance com pessoas* (*Machado de Assis: The Novel with People*; 2007) examine the significance of these internal and external identities. Bosi considers Machado to be a master analyst of the complicated and often murky relationship between the two identities, which he refers to as "first nature" (*primeira natureza*) and "second nature" (*segunda natureza*). First nature, which consists of individual inclinations, desires, and drives, is more often than not veiled by second nature, which is composed of conventions, habits, customs, and norms imposed by society. The strategic interplay between essences and appearances results in a host of vices that come masked as virtues through skillful calculation, hypocrisy, arrogance, lying, and other strategies (Bosi 1999, 81; 2004, 366–69).

Passos argues that Machado's protagonists display the tension between these two identities, between their desires and social norms, in the face of factual occurrences and that the effects of memory play a crucial role in this process by allowing a certain distancing between the actual facts and the consciousness operationalized in the narration. More than simply relating the facts, Machado is interested in exposing the conflict between the subjectivity of the characters and their respective objective social personae. This involves a process in which protagonists seek to fashion the public presentation of their selves by imagining alternatives to their actual origins, desires, and social predicaments (Passos 2009, 57). Machado's novels are not "stories." Rather, they are intricate reflections on how his characters make decisions and how they often seek to camouflage— or mask, according to Bosi—their underlying motivations from themselves and others (Bosi 1994, 79–81; Passos 2007, 44, 52, 68, 73, 79, 104–5, 108–10).

Passos maintains that the dialectic between these two identities is what provides the basis for the disconcerting, albeit humorous, ambivalence that emerges with Machado's novels, beginning with *The Posthumous Memoirs of Brás Cubas*. As an observer who can distance himself in time, narrator Brás feels free to speculate—and take the reader along as an accomplice—about the subtle game of intentions he exposes in the events he relates (Passos 2007, 58, 110–14, 123–30, 153–58). Yet, like Brás, most if not all of Machado's main characters are ambivalent, ambiguous, elusive, and contradictory. They straddle the fine margin between conscious thoughts and unconscious desires, between reason and sentiment, public appearances and private feelings, and between the objective reality of the senses and the subjective reality of the mind. All this occurs while they desperately attempt to preserve their egoistic lives from the ever-present threat of being consumed by the entropy of social responsibility, disillusionment, and death (Passos 2007, 52, 58; Moreci 2009).

Machado relentlessly investigates the manner in which his protagonists steer their lives and succeed or fail to exercise agency, achieve autonomy, and control over others (Passos 2007, 52). Passos maintains that Machado's novels focus on the moral formation of individuals, their motivations, and choices. Machado's protagonists are free to choose from complex ethical alternatives and not only respond to their environment but also change as they interact with it. Passos sees their psychological depth as a function of their "moral imagination" (Passos 2009, 57). This, in turn, makes them appear to be people drawn from real life, who lead independent lives of their own (Passos 2007, 12, 24, 38, 44–45, 59, 68, 104–5), rather than simply fictional characters or "mere symbols of abstract qualities" (Passos 2007, 103).

Notwithstanding their propensity for evildoing, Machado's characters are not defined by their moral goodness or badness. Rather, they are made from a complex blending of doubt with hope; of pride, egoism, and ambition with altruism, social responsibility, and self-sacrifice. Yet through their inability to achieve a balance between selfless love and self-love, most of Machado's characters become victims of themselves and of others. Selfless love typically sacrifices individuality so that the concern for others is inevitably eclipsed by slavish commitment to loyalty and duty; self-love manifests itself as egoistic narcissism rather than genuine self-respect and self-esteem (Borges 1995, 60–61; Daniel 1981, 12; Nunes 1983, 12, 82–84, 140, 142–43; Passos 2007, 42–47; Virgillo 1966, 778–86).

THE EARLIER NOVELS   *Resurrection* focuses on the psychological intricacies of individual morality rather than on its conflicts with the dictates of public success and social ambition (Nunes 1983, 27). Félix's unhappiness is essentially determined by his own inner weakness, his "complex, capricious and incoherent nature" with its "opposing, exclusive, and irreconcilable qualities" (64). Félix's failure to exercise his free will over his own nature is his tragedy (Caldwell 1970, 41; Nunes 1983, 28). In *Resurrection*, Machado is more concerned with individual morality itself, whereas in *The Hand and the Glove*, *Helena*, and *Iaiá Garcia* he pays more attention to the individual conscience or psychology and its response to the often constricting demands for success in society (Caldwell 1970, 67; Nunes 1983, 28). In *The Hand and the Glove*, intelligent and high-minded Guiomar, at times affectionate and at times aloof, is calculating (though not without scruples) in her desire for upward mobility to nullify, or at least compensate for, her humble past. On the one hand, as an agregada, she feels compelled to repay the baroness's kindness, no matter what the cost, by acquiescing to her desire that she marry her nephew Jorge. On the other hand, she is ambitious and attracted to Luís Alves, a successful lawyer who would further her ambitions. Inevitably, Guiomar's desire for upward mobility wins out and she marries Luís Alves with a clear conscience.

In *Helena*, the title character falsely presents herself as the natural daughter of socially prominent and wealthy Counselor Valle (now deceased) and represses her love for Estácio, his son and thus ostensibly her brother. At the same time, she is plagued by a guilty conscience for having assumed this false identity. She is further tormented by her pride for having accepted an inheritance from Valle based on these false pretenses. In her desperate struggle to balance these various emotions, Helena dies of a broken heart. Ultimately, the pride and conscience of her inner self prevent her from marrying Estácio, overruling the desire for upward social mobility of her external self (Caldwell 1970, 52).

In *Iaiá Garcia*, the focus is again on individual moral choices as they relate to the dictates of public success, particularly among the female characters (Caldwell 1970, 63). Estela's personal pride forces her to smother her passion for Valéria's son, Jorge, to avoid entering a marriage in which society would look upon her as a social inferior. Class-conscious Valéria is obsessed with having her son marry someone who is his social equal. So great is her social ambition that she ignores her conscience and interferes with the natural attraction between her son and Estela. She risks losing him by sending him off to war, in hopes that time and space will put an end to his passion for Estela, while also engaging in a devious scheme to match up Estela with Luís Garcia (Caldwell 1970, 64–65). Though Estela may appear to be the nobler of the two women, her sacrifice smacks of a reverse class pride that is as false and as deleterious as Valéria's because it is achieved at the expense of her integrity and conscience (Caldwell 1970, 64–65).

In sum, in Machado's earlier novels, the ambition for public success is in conflict with individual conscience and morality. Yet, as their characters navigate the social order, the inescapable conflict between their internal and external selves, and between their conscience and the dictates for public success, requires a series of compromises. These compromises typically prevent a balanced synthesis and lead, instead, to a sea of shipwrecked lives.

THE LATER NOVELS   The conflict between subjective and objective selves is still present in *The Posthumous Memoirs of Brás Cubas*, *Dom Casmurro*, and *Ayres's Memorial*, but it is primarily the complexity of their characters' internal reality that differentiates these novels from the earlier ones. So that, even though the restrictions accompanying his family's elite social status first appear to determine Brás Cubas's existence, for the most part, he is freed from the more mundane concerns of the external self by virtue of his social and financial security. These concerns are far more pressing for characters such as Eugênia, Marcela, and Virgília, with whom Brás becomes romantically involved (Haberly 1983, 84; Nunes 1983, 141). Paradoxically, the restrictions that come with his family's social status facilitate Brás's own freedom by allowing him certain advantages of education, career, and marriage (Nunes 1983, 141). His dilemma is that, because of the weak moral fiber of his internal self, this freedom from the constraints of the external self never moves him to make the right choices in life. One desire of his external self is to defeat time by accomplishing something of lasting importance. But he fails to achieve this goal during his lifetime; his only real accomplishment is his posthumous, "savagely ironic re-creation of that failure" (Haberly 1983, 84).

Brás's love affair with the courtesan Marcela and his career as a student at Coimbra make it abundantly clear that he is an irresponsible playboy, lacking moral strength and intellectual integrity (Nunes 1983, 119). This is exemplified during a crisis in his adulterous affair with Virgília. Her husband, Lobo Neves, is to become provincial president, bringing Virgília increased social prestige but also requiring her to leave Brás and depart with her husband. Brás is torn between the egoistic desires of his external self to maintain his affair with Virgília and the conscience of his internal self, which prompts him to give her moral support as the dutiful wife. Although he demands that Virgília sacrifice and make a firm commitment to him, he risks nothing. Subsequently, Brás reaches an equivocal compromise—to let Vigília reach a resolution on her own, a decision he first views as motivated by both the egoistic desires of his external self and the dictates of his internal self but later finds to be motivated by his egoism alone.

Brás's parody of the egoistic philosophy of Humanitism—a farcical blend of Comtian positivism and the Social Darwinism introduced in *Quincas Borba*—is also reflected in his characterization of himself (Chalhoub 2001, 185; Nunes 1983, 120). He constantly rationalizes or justifies the egoistic inclination of his external self and avoids taking responsibility for his actions (Nunes 1983, 120). An excellent example of this is his thinking about Eugênia, a beautiful young woman whose lameness and dignity force Brás to treat her with respect and to spare her from his sexually predatory advances. He compares the pain, preoccupation, and discomfort he feels in "resisting" Eugênia to the relief felt when one removes a pair of tight boots (163). Brás also constructs laws to assist him in his rationalizing, such as the "law of the equivalence of windows," according to which, when he has done something unprincipled, he assuages his ego and compensates for the action by opening another window, as it were, in order to air out his conscience (182). To rationalize his having made Dona Plácida, Virgília's elderly live-in companion and confidante, an accomplice in his affair with Virgília, Brás suggests that, had she not compromised her pride and conscience (her internal self) for a price (her external self), she would have come to a miserable end. He concludes with yet another law: "Vice is often the fertilizing manure of virtue" (214).

Self-centered and unloving as well as hypocritical and vain, Virgília is completely absorbed with her external self and proves to be a perfect match for Brás. Not only does her external self enjoy provoking Brás's jealousy through her vanity, but her weak internal self also prevents her from giving up her public considerations of marriage and running away with Brás. Virgília's primary concern is with social status and her external identity. Although she denies it, she demonstrates her lack of sincerity and commitment to Brás through her gestures and eventual marriage to Lobo Neves, who promises her a title as marchioness (Nunes 1983, 121).

Lucid, simple, and charming, Eugênia has a moral character as attractive as her physical aspect. When Brás comments on her slight limp, she reveals that she was born lame, which only highlights her assets. To Brás, physical and moral beauty juxtaposed with lameness seems a cruel and inexplicable prank of nature. In her dialogue with Brás, Eugênia reveals that she is the one wholesome character in the novel and the only one with apparently untainted motives (Nunes 1983, 121). This is best exemplified after their encounter in Tijuca and when Brás leaves to become a deputy through his marriage to Virgília and thus fulfill his father's dream. He has made the correct choice, Eugênia tells him, sensing his insincerity. Dignified and proud to the end, Eugênia refuses Brás's offer of financial assistance when he encounters her impoverished at the novel's end; she shakes his hand and goes about the business of living (299).

When compared to the novel's other characters, most of whom are consummate amoral egoists, Eugênia stands out as an oddity. Thanks, however, to Brás's satire, their social egoism seems more comical than destructive. The personification of vanity, Brás's father, Bento Cubas, is nevertheless simple and unaffected. Though tragically destroyed by her own greed, Marcela appears rather comical as she parades her flamboyant lifestyle in the streets of Rio in flagrant disregard of the city's vice code (Caldwell 1970, 85). Dona Plácida's lifelong struggle to transcend her birth out of wedlock and become a socially respectable woman and her setbacks in this struggle evoke laughter more than pity. Equally amusing is her embarrassment at having been forced by her poverty into working as an accomplice in concealing Brás's affair with Virgília (Caldwell 1970, 86). If Eugênia stands out as the only genuinely "good" and unegoistical character at whom we do not laugh, the sadism, avarice, and hypocritical scheming of Brás Cubas's greedy, slave-trafficking brother-in-law, Cotrim, make him perhaps the most completely amoral or evil character. Yet the tug-of-war between Cotrim's three principal vices for possession of his soul is humorous, at least as related by narrator Brás (Caldwell 1970, 85).

In *Dom Casmurro*, the superficial story is that of Bento Santiago himself, the author-narrator, born wealthy and secure and without ambition. The only evidence that he is indeed a lawyer is the narrative itself, which is cleverly organized to plead his case against Capitu, his adulterous wife. Dom Casmurro states that his internal self is still that of Bento Santiago at the age 16, whose innocence and overly trusting nature blind him to other people's ulterior motives and social ambition, thus making him easily manipulated. He either insinuates or makes clear that he is unaware, uncertain, and insecure because his own external self has no ambition. Consequently, it is easy for his ambitious wife to betray his trust with his best friend, Escobar (Haberly 1983, 85). Dom Casmurro assures us that, though he has not changed, he is uncertain about Capitu. Was she inherently self-aware and self-assured, with the potential to be manipulative and unfaithful? Or, as he asks himself and the reader, did Capitu's original innocence turn to infidelity because marrying him raised her to his social level and thus transformed her external self? (Haberly 1983, 85).

Capitu's story is considerably different. Though she is indeed self-aware and self-assured, her poverty and dependency deny her the luxury of an external identity like that of Bento. And though her marriage to Bento and its accompanying wealth do indeed transform her external identity, her internal self remains the same: she continues to think of herself as poor. Capitu's "eyes like the tide," Haberly (1983, 85) tells us, symbolize "this combination of external social mobility and mutability and internal stability and regularity." Escobar dies in the actual tide, but, as Haberly points out, the tide within Capitu's eyes is equally destructive. It is a constant reminder of evidence that Bento, in pleading his case, considers inadmissible: his own internal self has undergone a radical transformation. As his name changes from Bento to Dom Casmurro, he moves from "innocence to insane suspicion" (Haberly 1983, 86).

In *Quincas Borba*, the demands of the external self are pronounced. All the characters are propelled by the dictates of public success to ignore their conscience, thus betraying themselves and others (Chaves 1974, 46–53). Palha enjoys exhibiting his wife, Sofia, as his prized possession and the symbol of his social success and external self. At first unenthusiastic about being displayed, Sofia gradually becomes addicted to the admiration she receives. She narcissistically poses in front of a mirror, dressing and trying on her latest gift from Rubião. Indeed, the only time she steps outside herself—her compassion for Rubião's insanity—is also a mere extension of her own egoism because she believes herself to be the cause of his emotional state (299). Machado uses Sofia's and Palha's social climbing to illustrate their moral character, as reflected in their ability to cut off social ties no longer consistent with Palha's new social identity. This is apparent when Major Siqueira, testing Palha's and Sofia's repudiation of old friends, questions Palha about Sofia's birthday, an event to which Siqueira had always been invited. When the major does not receive an answer, he is fully aware that this snub is a direct result of Palha's and Sofia's new external identity resulting from their social ambition (271–72).

Rubiao's tragedy lies in his complete unawareness of the transformation he has undergone in his relationship with the external world (Haberly 1983, 84). His mental instability is clearly present in his moral characterization. The narrator analyzes his ambivalence over whether to stay in small-town Barbacena, where he has lived an insignificant and obscure existence, or go to live the brilliant life in fast-paced Rio de Janeiro (Nunes 1983, 127). Ironically, Rubião is unaware that his egoistic choice of leading a glamorous life at the Court in Rio de Janeiro will eventually bring him full circle to Barbacena and reduce him to even greater insignificance and obscurity than he had originally known. His initial goal is motivated by the egoistic promptings of his external self. But in Rio de Janeiro, he is a small fish in a large sea of political and financial sharks and upwardly mobile sophisticates for whom he is no match. This lack of awareness is what makes Rubião a pawn manipulated by Palha and others, and exploited by the ironical narrator, who suggests that Rubiao's story proves the survival-of-the-fittest framework of Quincas Borba's theory of Humanitism.

Far from leading readers to support this theory, Machado de Assis, through his ironic narrator, prompts them to arrive at the opposite conclusion: a social order dominated by materialist rationalism and its handmaiden, the external self, is inherently vicious and totally lacking in compassion and morality (Haberly 1983, 84). The narrator's irony leads them to conclude that such behavior is neither justifiable nor acceptable (Haberly 1983, 84). The insanity of Quincas Borba's philosophy is revealed in his conversation with Rubião: its irrational message becomes immediately apparent when Quincas Borba explains that the death of his grandmother, run down by a carriage, was neither accidental nor lamentable. The owner of the carriage was hungry; the coachman whipped his mules to get dinner for his master and fulfilled Humanitism. There was an obstacle that blocked this fulfillment: his grandmother. The obstacle had to be overcome and would have been the same had it been a cat or a mouse (112–13).

The only character in the novel to display any humanity is Quincas Borba the dog, whose internal self demonstrates unconditional love based on gentleness and sensitivity to the feelings of others, as well as a capacity for companionship, loyalty, and devotion. His simple, unsuspecting friendliness toward everyone holds no resentment, even toward those who rebuff him with kicks. At first, Rubião compares his own loyalty and friendliness for the philosopher Quincas Borba to that of Quincas Borba the dog. He also sees in the dog's loving and faithful glance the "soul" of the dead philosopher. At the novel's beginning, the narrator identifies Rubião's early traits with the dog's—and at the novel's end, both are merged into one. Even before his inheritance, however, signs of the egoistic desires of Rubião's external self are already visible among the more altruistic promptings of his internal self. Although battered about by a cruel society, Rubião is not so much the victim of the greed and egoism of others' external selves as he is of his own external self and internal moral weakness (Caldwell 1970, 132–33).

Esau and Jacob and *Ayres's Memorial* can be read as a single work linked by the character Counselor Ayres, who appears as the narrator and a character in both texts. The counselor is socially and financially secure, and almost immune to the dictates of the external self (Haberly 1983, 89). In *Esau and Jacob*, the struggle of the external self for upward mobility is portrayed in the careers of several minor characters. For example, Santos is an unscrupulous banker who amasses a financial fortune through his talent for making money by making others lose theirs. Baptista is obsessed with politics, and his ethical standards concerning political patronage appear somewhat questionable. Though Rubião's counterpart in becoming a millionaire, unlike Rubião, the friar Nóbrega is conscious of the transformation he has undergone in his relationship with the external world (Haberly 1983, 90). Unlike some of the characters in Machado's other novels, the characters in these two display temperaments that are more balanced. The dictates of ambition have not created the destructive choices between morality and success found in earlier novels. Interests of the external self, however, dominate the moral atmosphere of the social order through which they move (Haberly 1983, 90)—a world that, though not "conspicuously vicious," is empty and bankrupt, "frivolous, contemptuous of its heritage, and not averse to dishonesty" (Caldwell 1970, 168).

Although less offensive than the men, the women in this society are not without their faults. Despite her charm, Natividade is vain, selfish, snobbish, and unreasonable, though motherhood helps change some of this. Flora is an exception among the women, as her third suitor, the young bureaucrat-poet Gouvêa, is among the men. Genuine love is what distinguishes them. Innocent, modest, sweet, gentle, artistic, and poetically romantic, Flora seems to have but one flaw, her almost superhuman desire for perfection (Caldwell 1970, 169).

Financially and socially successful, as well as altruistic, all of the characters in *Ayres's Memorial* appear almost idyllic in their lack of concern for the pressures of the external self. There is Ayres, the cosmopolitan and humanistic diplomat, and his sister, the faithful widow Rita. Aguiar is a self-made banker, who is honest, kind, and concerned for everyone around him. His wife, Carmo, is not a socialite, as are so many of the female characters in Machado's other novels, but a homebody. A natural mother who has no children of her own, Carmo takes under her wing surrogate children like Fidélia and Tristão. Though a plantation mistress, Fidélia is nevertheless compassionate for the plight of her slaves. And though politically ambitious, Tristão is honest and ethical, not ruthless, as many of the political figures in Machado's novels are. All of the characters are transformed by one another's unselfish love (Caldwell 1970, 192).

In sum, Machado's gallery of characters is a composite of aberrations in a vicious and amoral world dominated by materialism, greed, and egoism, where more often than not the external self and the ambition for public success are at odds with the individual conscience, thus impeding or precluding a sense of balance and wholeness (Haberly 1983, 76). They are all victims of themselves and one another in an absurd existence where the cut of one's clothes, the size of one's bank account, and other such material considerations invariably supersede loving relationships (Nunes 1983, 140–41; Virgillo 1966, 778–86).

If Machado's characters perceive themselves as having free will in the pursuit of their goals, readers are aware of the tragic and erroneous choices these characters make in pursuing them. Instead of being helpless victims of circumstances beyond their control, Machado's characters fail to choose the one thing that might bring them wholeness—love—pursuing substitutes under the pressures of public success and the dictates of the external self (Nunes 1983, 140). Though Machado makes no direct statements or pronouncements, his ironical narration and allusions reflect a criticism of humanity, which he expresses through the recurring theme of humanity's inability to achieve wholeness. By holding up the mirror of his fictions, Machado hoped to make his readers see themselves and to point the way to a cure, however elusive (Haberly 1983, 140; Nunes 1983, 141).

SIX

THE HIDDEN RACIAL TEXT: RACIAL IDENTITY AND THE WRITINGS OF MACHADO DE ASSIS

A Black Song Without Color: Irony, Parody, and the Grotesque

Another important indication of Machado's fascination with subject-object duality and ambiguity is his dexterity in handling parody, irony, and the grotesque. These literary devices rely on the basic duality between life external to human consciousness and life as humans think it is or should be—or as they would like it to be (Brayner 1979, 101–3; Davis 1993, 21–22, 68–71; 90–97, 102, 158, 301; Gysin 1975, 27–32; Hodgson 1976, 7–9; McElroy 1989, ix–x, 1–29).

One of Machado's memorable examples of parody is in *Brás Cubas* when the narrator imagines himself on a horse from the medieval ballads, a device so overused by the Romantics that the Realist-Naturalists immortalized it in their novels. The fragmented and diffuse (or "spatialized") *Brás Cubas* narrative (Spencer 1971, 155–59), with its postmortem point of view, is a parody of autobiographical writings that usually start at the beginning, are related in chronological order, and written by a living author. Machado's use of the technique of appropriating a literary device but using it with an antithetical purpose is an indication of his erudition and understanding of opposing literary styles and genres (Cruz Júnior 2002, 180–82; Nunes 1983, 120, 143; Teixeira 1987, 77–88).

The grotesque juxtaposes or fuses contrasting, paradoxical, and incompatible elements. It brings us into the border region between fantasy and reality, beauty and ugliness, the tragic and the comic, the human and the nonhuman or superhuman, the living and the dead, the demonic and the ludicrous. Whether it is a character, an object, or a situation, the grotesque never belongs exclusively to one of these border regions, but always to two or more of them. The effect is a blend of anxiety and superiority, repulsion and fascination, disgust and pity, horror and amusement (Cassuto 1997, xii–xix; Cruz Júnior 2002, 180–82; Danow 1995, 5–31, 33–64; Gysin 1975, 27–32; Harpham 1982, 3–22; Hodgson 1976, 7–9; McElroy 1989, ix–x, 1–29).

The grotesque figure is a dehumanized human being or a humanized nonhuman. For humans, the grotesqueness may be due to physical deformity, as in the case of the once beautiful but later pockmarked, Marcela, or the beautiful but crippled Eugênia, both in *Brás Cubas*. Or it may be due to mental deformity, such as incoherent, compulsive, obsessive, or manic behavior in the cases of Rubião, Quincas Borba the philosopher, and the tragicomic Félix in *Resurrection* and the pathetic and comical Estêvão in *The Hand and the Glove*. The grotesque can also be achieved when humans take on the traits of animals, plants, landforms, or machines or when nonhuman figures assume human characteristics, as in the case of Quincas Borba the dog. And, finally, it can be achieved when the world of the living takes on qualities of death and the supernatural, as with Brás Cubas's postmortem narrative.

A grotesque situation is a state of affairs in which the incongruity of various elements evokes a concrete image of an estranged world through the contrast between expectation and fulfillment, the disturbance of space-time perception, or the relationship between cause and effect, which leaves readers acutely disoriented (Cruz Júnior 2002, 180–82; Danow 1995, 5–31, 33–64; Harpham 1982, 3–22; Hodgson 1976, 7; McElroy 1989, ix–x, 1–29). Frequently, this can be attributed to the manipulation and ultimate exposure of the devices that have been deployed to trap readers. The goal is to emphasize the artificial or subjective and therefore "Romantic" nature of the literary construct and, in so doing, to undermine the pretense of the Realist-Naturalist novel as being an objective description and sociopsychological analysis.

One example of Machado's use of a grotesque situation comes with Bento's ironic assurance in *Dom Casmurro* of a shared viewpoint that is deliberately undermined. This makes readers not only accomplices to the irony in the novel but also victims of it. In this as in other Machado novels, the narrator advises us to read attentively and sometimes goes out of his way to assist. A close reading of *Dom Casmurro* ultimately exposes Bento's conscious and unconscious devices to trap the reader into believing in Escobar's and Capitu's adultery. To achieve this effect, Machado concentrates on the verbal medium itself and the manner in which readers perceive it (Hodgson 1976, 7). He prepares readers for a familiar literary experience but then, by means of a radical, if subtly maneuvered shift, presents them with a situation in which they cannot resort to conventional literary responses. All of this makes the grotesque a subversive literary strategy, no matter how conservative Machado may appear otherwise (Gledson 1984, 5–6; 1987, 21).

The ironic gap between Machado and his characters is an aspect of his use of the grotesque. His characters are all victims of one another in an absurd existence characterized by irony and ambiguity, in which love is a rare occurrence. Egoism, as we have already noted, is the norm and the ultimate cause of all the psychological dis-ease within his novels. Material considerations invariably supersede love relationships. Machado's characters all experience a split between themselves and the outside world, between their conscious desires and deeper motivations and the choices they make between them. This can be seen in the narrative process itself, with its divided narrators: the defunct narrator Brás versus the living character, the spiritually dead Dom Casmurro versus the living Bento, Ayres the narrator versus Ayres the character, and Ayres the diarist who cannot love versus Ayres the character who finally can (Nunes 1983, 142).

These narrator-characters share the stage with a cast of other individuals, including wives and mothers who use their husbands and children as a means of self-aggrandizement, unable to give of themselves to their supposed loved ones. There are mad psychiatrists and philosophers who, far from healing humanity, are incapable of solving their own problems, and lawyers and physicians who seldom, if ever, apply their training except to join the elite legislature or pay lip service to the latest dictates of intellectual materialism. Clergymen seem better versed in the art of carving chickens than of understanding the intricacies of the human soul. Their military counterparts include scores of high-ranking officers whose primary claim to fame is their star-studded uniforms and whose whole existence hinges upon delivering speeches at banquets (Virgillo 1972, 70–80).

Richard Jackson, Antonio Boyd, Stanley Cyrus, and Martha Cobb argue that a narrative tone in fiction that deploys irony, parody, and the grotesque as literary devices draws on black and mulatto authors' shared confrontation with racist pressure and Eurocentric standards. These standards reward whiteness and restrict, if not negate, blackness in literature, as well as in society at large (Jackson 1979, 4–14; Boyd 1992, 36; Cyrus 1982, 29, 30, 31; Cobb 1974, 7–10). One unalterable fact in the lives of black and mulatto writers is their "consanguineal affiliation" as an oppressed group (Boyd 1975, 30). They can hardly project their art without showing some of the scars of racism (Jackson 1979, 4–14; Perkins 1970, 95). Whether they do so explicitly or not, the authors' psychology will in some way be governed by this phenomenon (Boyd 1975, 30). David Haberly suggests that Machado "continued to see himself, at some basic level of his existence, as a captive aboard the slave ship of the national past and of his own ancestors ... despite all his social and literary successes, despite his apotheosis as first president of the Brazilian Academy of Letters" (Haberly 1983, 98).

Generally, Machado's response to racist pressure and Eurocentric standards is not explicitly racial, as it is for Luís Gama and Lima Barreto, although his use of parody, irony, and the grotesque, like theirs, is often satirical. Yet Machado's techniques are more restrained, playful, and lighthearted, never quite descending to the level of bitter ridicule and mockery to be found in Lima Barreto's writings (Hutcheon 1985, 33; Marins 2004, 13–45). Instead, according to James Scott, they reflect the subtle yet powerful language of resistance that Machado deploys under the nose of—and often unrecognizable to—the oppressor (Scott 1990, 14–15, 27, 190–91). It is an indication of Machado's genius that he could write novels that appear so acceptable to the expectations of his literary public and yet are so subversive of those expectations. Indeed, as John Gledson explains:

> Machado presents his readers ... with the choice between two books, the one immensely readable, interesting, amusing; the other much more unsettling, giving uncomfortable insights into Brazilian upper-class society and its dependency on slavery, ... its repressiveness and callousness. With immense tact and daring, with a mixture of aggression and politeness which is the hallmark of his style, Machado kept his readers and was, in his own lifetime, a writer of considerable prestige. The only price he had to pay (and no doubt he was content to do so) was that part of his message went unperceived until long after his death. (Gledson 1987, 21)

Machado's writings reflect the paradoxical vantage point of an esteemed individual of African descent whose rise to social and literary prominence called into question the entire notion of dominant and subordinate by subverting the line between black and white (Reis 1992, 52–54). Roberto Reis and Octavio Ianni concur with Jackson, Boyd, and Cobb and suggest that Machado's use of irony, parody, and the grotesque serves as a vehicle for the expression of his humor. In a similar vein, Heloísa Gomes writes: "Ironic discourse has been the preferred option of authors like Machado de Assis, Herman Melville, and Mark Twain in the treatment of slavery and interracial relations. Instigating the intelligence and sensibility of their contemporaries with the exhibition of the grotesque masks of slavery—as Machado did in 'Father Against Mother' ...—they elaborated a social criticism that was aimed acutely at their time, but that transcended it" (Gomes 1994, 197–98).

To this, Murray Davis and Nicki Lisa Cole would add that humor is an articulation of the failure of institutions and individuals in society to live up to expectations and thus exposes the failures of the real world by comparing it to an ideal world (Davis 1993, 4–16, 21–33, 65, 93–94, 102, 158; Cole 2006, 23–24). Psychologically, humor allowed Machado to maintain a distance between himself and the traumas of living in a racist society. Sociologically, it allowed him to invert and disrupt structures—to subvert normative expectations of the racial order through a carnivalesque leveling of the social hierarchy (Miller 1988, 15; Gutwirth 1993, 50–51, 74–77, 100–115; Reis 1992, 53, 58).[1] The lords and ladies of high bourgeois society who populate his novels (whom we can assume to be overwhelmingly white, given the social stratification and racial demographics of the time) become instruments of their own undoing (Danow 1995, 5–31, 33–64; Ianni 1988, 94–95; Reis 1987, 71–97; 53, 58).

Machado provided his characters with all the social and economic freedom and privileges necessary to make a subtle and ironic yet poignant statement. As Luís Gama observed, slavery and racism oppressed and stripped African Brazilians of their humanity to the point of denying them even the freedom to be unhappy whenever and wherever they pleased (Gama in Sayers 1958, 392). The European Brazilian elite (and, by extension, late nineteenth-century Westerners) lived in a world dominated by materialist rationalism, egoism, and greed. Yet, according to Sayers, despite their free will and privileges or, rather, because they abused them, they, too, were stripped of their humanity and set adrift in a spiritual vacuum, where they were cheated out of the very happiness they so fervently sought (Sayers 1958, 392; 1993, 7; Nunes 1983, 140). Machado argued that humanity would never achieve a sense of wholeness within its own metaphorically mulatto nature as long as society judged individuals more by the dictates of public success and the external self than by their character.

The Black Racial Imagination: Literature, Identity Politics, and Black Liberation

Machado's oblique criticism of Brazil's racial and class hierarchy through irony, parody, and the grotesque generally escapes many Afrocentric literary critics—particularly radical Afrocentrists—who fail to see its relevance to black liberation.

Typically, these critics look for characters, settings, themes, and linguistic signs or a subaltern tone that mark a literary work as being "obviously" engaged in the struggle for black liberation or expressing Negritude or an Afrocentric aesthetic (Jackson 1979, 6; Leitch 1992, 86–87). Underpinned by an Afrocentric consciousness and championed by intellectuals of African descent who affirm a black identity, rearticulate the collective experience of blacks, and attach positive meaning and value to the concept of blackness, Negritude seeks to rehabilitate Africa and all individuals of African descent from Eurocentric ideology, which views blacks as inherently inferior to whites and which served, in part, to justify Western colonialism and imperialism (Bernd 1987, 14–44; Caute 1970, 17–28; Condé 1998, 1–7; Dathorne 1974, 307–338; Kennedy 1975, xix–xxix; Kesteloot 1965, 148–74).[2]

Negritude, the Cult of the Primitive, and "Hypocritical" Hybridity

Octavio Ianni considers Machado to be a seminal voice of Negritude in Brazilian literature (Ianni 1988, 92, 94, 95; Ianni in Fantini 2011, 152–53; Bernd 1987, 20, 69–71). Yet, given that traditional critics have viewed Machado's writings as lacking any affinity with either Negritude or Afrocentrism, it is worth digressing a bit to trace the origins of these movements in order to elucidate his relationship with them. As an interrogation of Eurocentric discourse among black intellectuals in the post–World War I era, the Negritude movement proper reflected a larger international trend. Many thinkers across the globe viewed the carnage of World War I as a failure of Western civilization itself (see, for example, Oswald Spengler's *Der Untergang des Abendlandes* [*Decline of the West*; 1922]). Or, as sociologist Pitirim Sorokin put it, the materialist rationalism, science, and technology of the "sensate" sociocultural mode, which gives preeminence to intellect and reason, were turning humanity not only away from the "ideational" sociocultural mode, which envisions the structure of the universe as profoundly divine, but also away from life itself (Sorokin 1957, 226–30, 272–83). Moreover, Sigmund Freud announced that bourgeois Christian morality, European civilization, and Western civilization generally were founded on the repression of instinct, which was the primary cause for the high incidence of mental dis-ease (Brookshaw 1986, 85–88; Franco 1970, 117–47).

These ideas led to an about-face on the part of many early twentieth-century Western thinkers in an era in which Europe had lost faith in its post-Enlightenment cultural claims. These thinkers sought to recapture all that had been marginalized in the ascent of intellect and reason that accompanied Europe's rise to global dominion (Philippou 2005, 248). A new "cult of the primitive" that culminated in the

1930s and 1940s in Europe, Africa, and the Americas questioned "white" Christian morality, which represented white as good and black as evil. Seeking to break away from the classical canons of Western art, avant-garde artists embraced the primitive; stylized forms of African sculpture, in particular, influenced the Cubist movement. African American musical forms such as blues and jazz became increasingly popular in Europe.

This "Black Modernism," combined with the influence of Sigmund Freud, Carl Gustav Jung, and the existentialist philosophers, symbolized liberation from the shackles of reason and intellect. Yet it was not the validation of blacks per se but the allure of the "black" forces of the subconscious that captured the interest of these early twentieth-century Western thinkers, who, in effect, "positively" rearticulated the stereotype wherein blacks were seen as a physical embodiment of humanity's forbidden and subconscious desires (Brookshaw 1986, 85–88; Franco 1970, 117–47). These ideas stimulated a fascination with African and African American life among white intellectuals in the United States, who used blackness as a tool in rebelling against the artificial restraint of Puritan morality. African American artists and thinkers in the 1920s and 1930s in the Harlem Renaissance were themselves influenced by the cult of the primitive.

More broadly, this primitivist cult meant that all peoples from developing nations would have their cultures re-valued and their cultural roots rehabilitated by their national elites as part of a new Romanticism and nationalism (Needell 1999, 8–10). This included the cult of "indigenism," which underpinned culturally nationalistic movements in Latin America of that time, and which was based on Native American culture in Mexico and the Andean countries and on black culture in other parts of Latin America and the Caribbean. Though these trends originated in Europe and were sanctioned by the prevailing cultural fashion there, avant-garde movements in the Americas had unique local origins and traits. As Ernest Gellner has pointed out, in highly charged and contested contexts, racial and cultural forces can serve as the basis for the self-transformation of an "inferior culture" into a "superior culture" (Gellner 1983, 168). And so it was that such forces, unleashed in the early 1900s, prepared the way for bringing the subdominant "native" element, which had until then been deemed "inferior," into the political and artistic mainstream in the 1920s and 1930s (Davis 1999, 56–60).

Under the impact of these trends, the Europhile culture prized by the Brazilian elite soon faded. This resulted in an inversion of the previous hierarchical relationship between the official, "high" Eurocentric culture of the nation and the "shameful" and "low" vernacular African Brazilian culture, which surrounded the elite and in which, to some extent, they participated. What emerged was a vibrant new vernacular Brazilian culture, often associated with Bahian migrants to Rio de Janeiro, who interacted with the port influences and wider audiences of the capital, a culture whose influence would be magnified by the cultural centrality of the capital—a national culture symbolized by the music and dance called the "samba," whose appeal transcended its African origins and regional specificity (Needell 1987b; 1999, 8–10; Philippou 2005, 253).

Brazil's vernacular culture, as part of the process of capitalist expansion in the late nineteenth and the early twentieth centuries, was part of the Atlantic world in which cross-cultural influence was rich and constant. It partook of a port culture in which, for example, Cuban music, Europeanized in France as the habanera, could find its way to Rio and influence the dance and music there in the *maxixe*, an immediate antecedent of the samba. Sometimes referred to as the "Brazilian tango," the maxixe appears to have originated in Rio de Janeiro around 1868, about the same time the tango was developing in Argentina.[3] Like the tango, the maxixe journeyed to Europe and the United States in the early part of the twentieth century (Needell 1987b; 1999, 8–10; Seigel 2009, 66–94; Wisnik 2008, 21–38).

The Brazilian modernist cult of "indigenism," much like the Negritude movement, rejected Western intellectualism and called for a return to a natural, atavistic world that repressive European culture had forced into the subconscious. Like its counterparts in other Western countries, the European Brazilian intelligentsia extolled Native Americans as symbols of a zest for life and artistic freedom and as contributors, both culturally and racially, to the formation of a Brazilian national identity. These intellectuals also praised African Brazilians' cultural contributions—but, in contrast, were notably silent about their racial ones (Brookshaw 1986, 85–88).

Yet with the important exception of musicians, modernist intellectuals rarely elaborated on African Brazilian concepts. Rather than actually engaging in a critical dialogue with the vernacular culture, they indiscriminately embraced that culture beneath the racial comportment line (Borges 1995, 72). Notwithstanding the greater prominence of African Brazilians in the modernist currents of the Northeast, mulattoes rather than blacks were generally viewed as playing a role in Brazil's racial blending by ultimately being bleached of their racial (though not their cultural) blackness. At its best, the modernist vision sought the full integration of all the various cultural elements of the country in the formation of a Brazilian national identity (Brookshaw 1986, 85–88, 99, 106–8; Davis 1999, 56–60; Franco 1970, 117–47; Philippou 2005, 247–49).

These social forces would become explicitly articulated in Brazil's racial democracy ideology, which emerged in the 1930s during the regime (1930–45) of Getúlio Vargas (died 1954) and defined Brazilian racial discourse for most of the twentieth century. Pervasive miscegenation, fluidity in racial markers, and the absence of legal barriers to racial equality led to the notion that class and culture, rather than race, determined one's status in the social hierarchy. Yet the whitening ideal bequeathed to Vargas by his nineteenth-century predecessors presented him with a serious dilemma. Explicit support of racial hierarchy and whitening contradicted Vargas's populist, developmentalist, and nationalist agenda. The resolution of this contradiction necessitated a new, inclusive, and uniquely "Brazilian" narrative of national identity that would legitimate Brazil as an emerging nation-state and its ambition to become a world power (Taylor 1978, 34).

Always the strategist, Vargas fully embraced and institutionalized racial democracy as the official national ideology and understood that his country's greatest liability—the "black peril"—could also become its greatest asset. This led to a reevaluation of African Brazilian cultural expression, which could now serve to advance his larger agenda for national integration under the rubric of brasilidade. Samba, candomblé, capoeira (which had been transformed into a stylized martial art dance form), and other forms of African Brazilian culture once viewed as "primitive" and "inferior" could now be considered emblematic of Brazil's racial democracy in action. Vargas's stance dovetailed with Gilberto Freyre's reinterpretation of Brazilian national identity as *lusotropicalismo* (Portuguese tropicality), which extolled Brazil as the outpost that reflected par excellence Portugal's unique history of creating racially and culturally blended egalitarian societies in the tropics. Through his writings, Freyre rearticulated Brazilian understandings of both "nation" and "race" by framing Brazil as an open and fluid racial and cultural order that was a synthesis of its three parent racial and cultural components. In addition, he recognized and legitimated the permanence and depth of the African Brazilian and Native American contributions to Brazilian national culture and society and celebrated the racial and cultural blending that many earlier authorities had considered abhorrent (Alberto 2011, 112–116; Burke and Pallares-Burke 2008, 59–62; Daniel 2006, 68–70; Philippou 2005, 253–54).

Consequently, Vargas made the racial democracy ideology a cornerstone of administrative policy for preserving African Brazilian cultural expression, while at the same time supporting whitening through miscegenation (Davis 1999, 83–177, 188). Brazil's racial democracy ideology was officially articulated as hybrid, integrationist, and egalitarian (fig. 1, dynamic a). Yet it bolstered rather than deconstructed hierarchy and thus supported racial and cultural blending as a means of perpetuating assimilationist (or inegalitarian integrationist) goals (fig. 1, dynamic b) and of deflecting attention away from pervasive patterns of exclusion and isolation (inegalitarian pluralism; fig. 1, dynamic f; Daniel 2005, 264; 2006, 38–39).

Afrocentrism, Strategic Essentialism, and Strategic Antiessentialism

Those who assert that Machado is a perfect case study of these problematic outcomes of Brazil's racial democracy and whitening ideologies fail to appreciate his affinity with an Afrocentric perspective, and thus the literature of Negritude broadly defined. Jerome Schiele believes that they do so in part because Afrocentrism has been used to convey different things, some of which obscure its deeper significance (Schiele 1991, 27). The most common perception of Afrocentrism is that it seeks to expose individuals, chiefly through the educational system, to the struggles, accomplishments, and contributions of individuals of African descent in the manner of egalitarian pluralism (fig. 1, dynamic c). Afrocentrism as a fully articulated system of thought emerged in the 1960s in the works of Senegalese thinker Cheikh Anta Diop (1923–86) and African American thinkers Maulana Karenga (1941–) and Molefi Asante (1942–) in particular. It was viewed as a response to social forces that conspired to ignore, if not erase, individuals of African descent from history and to deny them racial equality in the all areas of society. In response to these forces, Afrocentrism places African-descent individuals at the center of their analyses. Another prevailing view is that Afrocentrism is a new form of Black Nationalism and identity politics that exposes white racism, challenging the pervasive exclusion of inegalitarian pluralism (or apartheid) but also contesting the token inclusion of inegalitarian (or assimilationist) integration (hooks 1995, 23–31; Lowy 1998, 594–600; Marable 1995, 121–122; Nantambu 1998, 574; Schiele 1991, 27).

That said, following in the footsteps of apartheid (fig. 1, dynamic e), extreme or radical Afrocentrism replaces white superiority (or inegalitarian pluralism) with a new hierarchy premised on black superiority (fig. 1, dynamic f). Radical Afrocentrists often criticize the essentialist premises that underpinned scientific racism and sustained white supremacy while reinscribing essentialist notions of black identity (Asante 1980, 105–8; 1992, 17–22; Collins 1993, 52–55; hooks 1995, 23–31; Marable 1995, 121–22; Rattansi 1994, 57). They thus impose what Victor Anderson calls a myopic "ontological blackness" (Anderson 1995, 11), which rearticulates the notion of "purity" that underpinned the scientific racism associated with the Eurocentric paradigm (Keita 1994, 146–166).

To understand the relevance of Afrocentrism to Machado de Assis, it would be useful to discuss its relationship to Eurocentrism. Having emerged during the Renaissance in the fifteenth century, Eurocentrism developed during the Scientific Revolution and matured during the Enlightenment and the Industrial Revolution in the late eighteenth century; it has been a dominant mode of consciousness in Western civilization ever since. It views Europe as a self-contained entity and as the transcendental nexus of all particular histories—and European civilization as the consummate one by virtue of its unprecedented accomplishments in materialist rationalism, science, and technology and the extremes to which it progressed into "modernity" (Slater 1994, 88–90). The epistemological underpinnings of the Eurocentric paradigm and, ultimately, the entire modern worldview are rooted in what Sorokin called the "sensate" sociocultural mode, which gives preeminence to the intellect, reason, and the external self over other types of mentation, experience, and cultural expression.

This paradigm holds the scientific method to be the only valid approach to knowledge, an approach informed by the paradigm's empirical, rational perspective on nature: the external world has a logical order, which is the interplay of calculable forces, discernible rules, and measurable bodies. The paradigm thus views the universe as a mechanical system composed of elementary material building blocks, a system in which mechanical laws govern the movement of the planets, the changes on earth, and the structure of the smallest insects. Once grasped, these laws can be manipulated for human gain. It considers society to be a struggle for survival and subject to unlimited material progress, which can be achieved through economic growth and technological development (Lowy 1998, 594–600; Mazama 1998, 4; Sorokin 1957, 228–31, 275–83).

Europeans' accomplishments in the realms of science and technology enabled them to explore remote areas of the globe and to exploit the resources, including the human resources, they found there. European colonization of these areas, although complicated, fraught with conflicting aims and motives, and not without its European dissenters, turned fledgling European nation-states into commanding imperial powers that could dominate non-Europeans. The ruling classes of Western Europe, in their progressive evolution toward "enlightenment," tended to see the process of conquest and colonization as a contest between "civilization" and "barbarism."

The Eurocentric consciousness and its outgrowths, white racism and white supremacy, have had devastating consequences for the non-Western "Other," especially for individuals of African descent. This has been evident throughout the history of the Americas, where Eurocentrism served to justify African enslavement and to dichotomize whiteness and blackness into hierarchical categories of experience. However, these dichotomized categories have had the unintended consequence of legitimating and forging group identity among the "Other" (Daniel 2006, 171; Jones 1994, 201–21; Lemert 1996, 52). Originally a tool of oppression, it has thus become an important element of what Gayatri Chakravorty Spivak calls "strategic essentialism," and critical to the continuing struggle against racial inequality (Spivak in Landry and MacClean 1996, 7, 54–71, 159, 204, 295; Jones 1994, 201–10).

Strategic essentialism refers to a strategy that nationalities, racial, ethnic, or "minority" groups can use to present themselves to achieve certain goals. Significant differences may exist between members of these groups. Yet it can be advantageous for them to project their group identity in a reductionist manner that focuses on one axis of experience and identity and, ultimately, oppression (Landry and Maclean 1996, 7, 54–71, 159, 204, 295).[4] This has been most obvious in Brazil throughout the post-Abolition era in attempts to implement cultural (or discursive) initiatives aimed at mobilizing blacks (pretos) and mulattoes (pardos) under an identity as African Brazilians (negros). This was evident in the formation of the Frente Negra Brasileira (FNB; Brazilian Black Front) in the 1930s and the Teatro Experimental do Negro (TEN; Black Experimental Theater) in the 1940s. These strategies generally viewed group pluralism as a temporary tactic to mobilize against social inequities—and ultimately to fulfill the racial democracy ideology by integrating blacks and mulattoes into the social order as equals—rather than maintaining African Brazilians as a distinct group (Alberto 2011, 4–5, 10, 20–21; Butler 1998, 57–58, 88–112; Davis 1999, 182; Taylor 1978, 28–39, 57).

Nevertheless, Brazil's reputation as a racial democracy was tarnished by the findings of social scientists in the 1950s and 1960s, whose research indicated that the more phenotypically African individuals were, the lower they were in the social hierarchy in terms of education, occupation, and income—even in the absence of legal barriers to equality and the presence of fluid racial markers. During two decades of military rule (1964–85), however, the state prohibited Brazilian scholars from discussing racial inequality, claiming that no such problem existed.

With the gradual return of civilian rule in the 1970s and 1980s, the debate on racial inequality was reopened. The founding of the Movimento Negro Unificado (MNU; United Black Movement) in 1978 set the stage for a revitalized black movement. Activists argued that racial inequality, apart from class and culture, was a main factor in social stratification. They were supported by a new generation of social scientists (mostly white) whose findings supported their claims that the divide between the privileged few and the less privileged masses coincided with the racial divide between brancos and negros primarily and between pardos and pretos only secondarily (see, for example, Silva 1978 and Hasenbalg 1979, 1985). Analyses since the 1980s supported these findings (Daniel 2006, 188–93).

Activists began seeking to forge a politicized identity reminiscent and indeed derivative of the U.S. one-drop rule to sensitize individuals to the notion of African ancestry. They deployed a discourse that replaced the color terms "preto" and "pardo" with the racial term "negro" (African Brazilian) and more recently "afro-descendente" (African-descended). As before, group pluralism sought to integrate blacks and mulattoes into the social order as equals, but now it was considered a strategy for dismantling (rather than fulfilling) the racial democracy ideology and for recognizing a distinct African Brazilian racial and cultural group. Its objective was to draw clear racial boundaries, and more specifically, expand those of blackness and contract those of whiteness. By the 1990s, the debate crystallized around changing procedures for collecting and reporting official data on race in the decennial census—to tabulate pretos and pardos together, rather than as separate groups. By 2000, the debate included ways to implement affirmative action (Daniel 2006, 241–58, 285–92).

During the 1980s and 1990s and the first decade of the twenty-first century, critics such as Gilberto Freyre, Peter Fry, Yvonne Maggie, Ali Kamel, and António Risério began challenging the black movement's racial project (Fry 2000, 83–118; Nobles 2000, 116). They argued that imposing racial categories premised on ancestry is fraught with irreconcilable contradictions when applied to Brazil, where African ancestry and African phenotypical traits are widespread throughout the population, including large numbers of self-identified and socially designated whites (Daniel 2006, 292–93; Fry 2000, 83–118; Fry and Maggie 2007, 277–81; Kamel 2006, 17–41, 49–57; Risério 2007, 19, 24, 55, 67). French thinkers Pierre Bourdieu and Loïc Wacquant voiced similar criticism. To transform racial categories and strategies specific to a given context (e.g., the U.S. one-drop rule) into supposedly "natural, universal, and true" ones and impose these on all people in all situations amounted, in their opinion, to "cultural imperialism" and "symbolic violence" (Bourdieu and Wacquant 1999, 47–48).

The first organized resistance to this racial project emerged in 2001 with the formation of the multiracial movement (Movimento Pardo-Mestiço), which was established in Manaus, in the state of Amazonas. That this resistance first took place in Amazonas is not surprising given the region's high concentration of multiracial individuals with strong ties to Native American ancestry. According to movement president Jerson César Leão Alves, the goal is to support and rearticulate the historical process of racial and cultural blending (mestiçagem) that has characterized the Brazilian people and to affirm the right of individuals and the nation by extension to identify as "multiracial" (mestiço). Although Alves and other movement activists have stressed the importance of addressing black inequality and respecting a black identity, they argue that this should not be at the expense of individuals who identify as multiracial, nor should it be used to justify disregarding their grievances in the pursuit of equality.[5]

By 2007, the movement focused its efforts on gaining official recognition of a Day of Multiraciality (Dia do Mestiço) to celebrate this racial blending, recognition it secured at the municipal and state levels in several locales. The Dia do Mestiço occurs on June 27, three days after the Day of the Caboclo (Dia do Caboclo), the caboclos (individuals of Native American and European descent) being the first multiracial individuals to emerge in the colonial era. Its date refers to the twenty-seven multiracial representatives elected during the First Conference for the Promotion of Racial Equality, held in Manaus, Amazonas, from April 7 to 9, 2005. Its month refers to the month in which a multiracial woman was registered as the only multiracial representative at the First National Conference for the Promotion of Racial Equality, held in Brasilia, from June 30 to July 2, 2005. The multiracial movement has campaigned to get the Brazilian Institute of Geography and Statistics (IBGE) to replace the color term "pardo" with the racial designator "mestiço" in the collection of official data during the decennial census. The spirit of the campaign was captured in the slogan "Coloque de volta MESTIÇO no censo do IBGE" (Bring back MULTIRACIAL to the census of the IBGE).[6] The slogan alludes to the fact that, although the 1890 census used the term "mestiço," subsequent censuses replaced it with "pardo," reflecting a return to previous terminology (Nobles 2000, 89; Piza and Rosemberg 1999, 37–52).

On the other hand, activists and their supporters in the black movement believe that a multiracial identity is inimical to the goal of forging African Brazilians into a cohesive political force. Moreover, they argue that national racial and cultural identities in Brazil have been "hypocritically" shaped by multiracial ideologies that served to erase racial distinctions in the manner of what Eduardo Bonilla-Silva refers to as "color-blind racism" (Bonilla-Silva 2006, 25). This cornerstone of racial democracy ideology, supported by the state, deliberately masked persisting racial inequities, deflected public attention away from them, and undermined policies aimed at eradicating them (Daniel 2002, 170, 177; 2006, 257). Indeed, the black movement has voiced and displayed its sometimes aggressive antagonism toward the expression of multiraciality in the form of what multiracial activists refer to as "multiracialphobia" (*mestiçofobia*) or "antimultiracial racism" (*racismo antimestiço*).[7] This has involved denying, dismissing, and disrespecting multiraciality both through microaggressions, in the sphere of interpersonal relations, and through macroaggressions, where institutions structure the behavior of actors in the political and cultural economy (Johnston and Nadal 2010, 123–44).

Moreover, multiracial activists contend that this antagonism is now legitimated and abetted by the state. They believe that this is apparent in the Estatuto da Igualdade Racial (Statute of Racial Equality), submitted to the legislature in June 2000 and approved by the Senate in 2005. This legislation combines black and multiracial individuals into a single statistical category (*negros* or *afro-brasileiros*) so that patterns of discrimination and establishing racial quotas for achieving equity, particularly in the form of affirmative initiatives, might be tracked more aggressively. After considerable political wrangling, delay, and compromise, a revised bill (without mandatory racial quotas) was approved by the Chamber of Deputies in September 2009.[8] Yet the public debate over the efficacy of these racial equality policies continues apace, with some multiracial activists and their supporters contending that these policies will merely heighten group consciousness while having little, if any, impact on reducing racial inequality.

There can be no denying that the one-drop rule was implemented in the United States to deny equality to African Americans, but it also had the unintended consequence of forging group identity. This, in turn, enabled African Americans to organize and eventually culminated in the civil rights movement of the 1950s and 1960s, which dismantled Jim Crow segregation and achieved the passage of historic legislation that dissolved legal racial discrimination and inequality. Black movement activists argue that the absence of the negative factor of legal discrimination and the one-drop rule in Brazil has served to undermine African Brazilian unity in the struggle against racism. Imposing binary thinking grounded in ancestral definitions of identity is fraught with irreconcilable contradictions in Brazil. African ancestry (not to mention African phenotypical traits) is widespread throughout the population, to include large numbers of self-identified and socially designated whites, who may or may not be welcomed as "assumed blacks" (*negros assumidos*; Daniel 2006, 293). Indeed, the broader changes in racial identity sought by the black movement have not had a significant impact on the Brazilian masses. While the proportion of brancos in the total population decreased from 54 percent in 2000 to 48 percent in the 2010 census, the proportion of pardos increased from 40 percent to 43 percent. The small increase in the proportion of pretos over that same decade, from 6.2 percent to 7.6 percent, does not indicate a significant change in normative Brazilian racial identification (Barnes 2011). The 2010 census figures clearly establish that Brazil has an African Brazilian (or nonwhite) majority, though whites still make up almost half of the population, and that the overwhelming majority of African Brazilians are pardos.

The black movement's proposed formulation of a more inclusive blackness, whether in terms of statistics, public policy, or vernacular parlance, focuses primarily on eradicating a multiracial identification or absorbing it into a singular egalitarian African Brazilian identity. Consequently, it overlooks—or rejects outright—the possibility of a multiracial identity that is formulated on egalitarian premises (Conceição 2004; Fry 2000, 83–118; Fry and Maggie 2007, 277–81; Kamel 2006, 17–41, 49–57; Lemert 1996, 52; Vianna 2004). Yet, when based on egalitarian premises (e.g., "critical multiraciality") rather than the hypocritical and inegalitarian ethos that has historically characterized Brazilian racial and cultural blending, multiraciality has the potential to serve as an "intellectual weapon" and "theoretical wedge" (Zack 1994, 99) in the pursuit of "color-blind antiracism." Such a formulation posits a genuine racial democracy, where racial distinctions would play no significant, or at least a considerably less significant, role in determining an individual's social location in terms of wealth, power, privilege, and prestige.

Yet, when taken to radical Afrocentric extremes, the thinking espoused by the black movement and other Black Nationalist ideologies not only runs counter to this perspective on multiraciality; it also lends support to the oppressive dichotomization of whiteness and blackness inherent in Eurocentrism. Although related to Black Nationalist thought, Afrocentrism is more appropriately described as a paradigm predicated on traditional African philosophical assumptions, which is evident in its more moderate variants (Asante 1980, 105–8; 1992, 17–22; Daniel 1992, 133; hooks 1995, 23–31; Leitch 1992, 87–8; Marable 1995, 117–24; Rattansi 1994, 57; West 1993, 1–30). Moderate Afrocentrism opens up a long-overdue conversation about humanity's shared genetic, ancestral, and cultural heritage, which has been ignored, obscured, and denied by several hundred years of Eurocentric thought. Indeed, given that humans first evolved in eastern Africa millennia ago, everyone shares in this universal heritage. This also means that everyone in the Americas, not just descendants of the West African Diaspora, is in some sense an African-descent American.

Between 90,000 and 180,000 years ago, humans from an earlier African diaspora spread throughout Africa, Asia, Europe, and the Pacific; perhaps as early as 30,000 years ago but at least as recently as 15,000 years ago, they migrated to the

Americas. As they adapted to various environments, they evolved into geographical populations displaying differences in various bodily features. Some of the externally visible features—skin color, hair, and facial morphology—are commonly referred to as "racial traits." Yet these apparent physical differences reflect only 0.1 percent of humans' genetic inheritance, not the 99.9 percent that we all share.

Moreover, the boundaries delineating populations have always been eroded by contact—whether through migration, trade, or war. Indeed, racial blending has existed from time immemorial. And even though we recognize certain physical traits as marking off different populations, in fact, a "multiracial" lineage is the norm rather than the exception, regardless of one's racial identity. If you trace back twenty generations, each individual has more than a million ancestors (CBS 2007; Olson 2002, 32–48; 2006). If you trace back still further, the number of any one individual's ancestors—and of their possible "racial" combinations—is staggering.

Moderate Afrocentrism assumes that all elements of the universe have a metaphysical base, are created from a similar universal substance, and are functionally interconnected. It makes no absolute demarcation between the metaphysical (ideational and subjective) and the physical (sensate and objective) domains, and it extends this rejection of delineated boundaries to morality, temporality, and the meaning of reality. It places the same value on knowledge gained through intuition and feelings that it does on knowledge gained through the senses and the intellect. Finally, moderate Afrocentrism fosters a human-centered orientation that prizes interpersonal connections above material objects (Asante 1987, 3–18; Harris 1998, 15–26; Kershaw 1998, 27–44; Myers 1998, 1–14; Schiele 1991, 27).

In sum, moderate Afrocentrism rejects the dichotomization and hierarchical valuation of differences typified by Eurocentric and radical Afrocentric thinking, both of which divide people into mutually exclusive and unequal categories of value, privilege, and experience. It emphasizes instead contexts, relationships, and wholes. In what amounts to a fundamental epistemological shift, it seeks to move civilization away from the dominant either/or paradigm that originated in modernity (Asante 1987, 3–18; Hochschild 1995, 137–38; Myers 1988, 1–28; Schiele 1998, 73–88). Moderate Afrocentrism also questions notions of authentic and essentialist identity and thus also the mutually exclusive and essentialist construction of identities in modern Western consciousness. Rather, it provides the basis for what George Lipsitz defines as "strategic antiessentialism," which brings forward collective subjectivities in a complex manner that addresses more than one axis of experience, identity, and, ultimately, oppression, as well as the interlocking experiences of race, gender/sexuality, class, and so on and their accompanying identities

(Lipsitz 2003, 32–35). Moderate Afrocentrism seeks to incorporate concepts of "partly" or "both/neither" (Asante 1992, 5, 26, 28, 39; Daniel 2002, 180, 189; hooks 1995, 23–31; Rattansi 1994, 30; Rosenau 1992, 5–7; Seidman 1994, 8–9; Teitelbaum 1990, 24–42).

From a moderate Afrocentric perspective, it is critical to acknowledge not only that Machado was African Brazilian but also that he was a clearly multiracial individual of African and European descent in a racial order that prized whiteness and stigmatized blackness. This is crucial to understanding someone like Machado, who sought to transcend his blackness in response to Brazil's racial constraints.[9] These constraints were integral to the formation not only of Machado's racial identity but also of his literary sensibility, which is compatible with a moderate Afrocentric perspective.

Machado's criticism of modernity is, by extension, an interrogation of the Eurocentric dichotomization of the subjective (internal) and objective (external) aspects of human identity into mutually exclusive and antagonistic categories of experience. Although it is unclear whether Machado's framing of the internal identity (individual morality and conscience) includes a spiritual or metaphysical self in the ideational sense discussed both by Sorokin and in Afrocentric discourse, what is clear is that he expresses the need for reciprocity between the internal (ideational) and external (sensate) aspects of human identity (Hochschild 1995, 137–38). Machado's masterfully oblique critique of Brazil's racial and class hierarchy is thus an exquisite "black song without color" (Jackson 1976, 91) in the African Brazilian struggle for liberation.

SEVEN

TOWARD LITERARY INDEPENDENCE: NATIONAL IDENTITY AND THE WRITINGS OF MACHADO DE ASSIS

Race, Romanticism, and Anticolonialism: The Search for National Identity

Although Machado was critical of obsessive materialist rationalism and the attendant pathologies of modernity, he did not blame material "progress" in and of itself for Brazil's loss of spiritual direction and self-identity. Rather, he urged Brazilians to redeem their native genius without jettisoning their material accomplishments. At one and the same time, he criticized the excessive subjectivism of the Romantic idealists, the bourgeois materialism of the positivists, and the ponderous objectivism of the Realist-Naturalists, who had replaced blind allegiance to entrenched old tenets with slavish adherence to ephemeral new half-truths (*Oc*, 3:787; Almino 2005, 141; Caldwell 1970, 89–90, 113, 117; Fischer 1994, 191–214; Miskolci 2006, 352–77; Needell 1983, 94–96; Virgillo 1972, 73, 78).

Machado was outspoken in his opposition to literary figures who had fallen prey to the schism between old and new when defining Brazilian national cultural identity (*Oc*, 3:787; Virgillo 1972, 73, 78). During this era of rampant nationalism across the globe, the measure of a country's development and modernity was defined by the extent to which it had developed a unique national culture—which the Brazilian intelligentsia interpreted specifically to mean a literature and a literate public (Mazama 1998, 6, 8). Benedict Anderson argues that the development of "print capitalism," mass communication, and the press had a significant impact on nationhood, giving readers a feeling of belonging to an "imagined community" in a specific time and society, where they could observe characters playing their roles in a linear manner (Anderson 2006, 39, 6). Editorials aroused the same thoughts at the same time among members of a national culture based on a common language (Anderson 2006, 37–46). National sentiment—the feeling of a national community or nationhood—is a critical element in nation making. Indeed, in the words of Ernest Gellner, "nationalism is not the awakening of a nation to self-consciousness"; rather, "it invents nations where they do not exist" (Gellner 1964, 168).

Brasilidade and the "National Instinct"

As Brazil's most prominent nineteenth- and early twentieth-century writer, Machado, could not help but be preoccupied with the question of national identity (Baptista 1991, 43–63, 99–114; Cândido 1969, 2:115–16; Schwarz 1987, 29–48; 1992, xv, 100–106). Yet, during his lifetime, Machado's status as a representative Brazilian author was disputed by some of his contemporaries, and some even regarded him as a traitor to the national literary cause (Machado 1953, 95). According to Silvio Romero, writers' styles should conform to their temperament, providing a direct and immutable correspondence and imperceptible line between environmental, physical, and cultural traits as well as historical circumstances (Romero 1897, 12, 57, 61). Though Machado was a mulatto, Romero insisted that his pessimism, skepticism, and irony were incompatible with an authentic Brazilian and mestiço soul and that his novels were insipid, artificial attempts to imitate the humor of the eighteenth-century English novel (Romero in Kristal and Passos 2006, 21–22; Romero 1897, 66–67, 111, 122, 153, 161–67, 184, 255–56, 266–67, 285–86). Moreover, Machado's protagonists were not authentic expressions of the national character, nor did his novels convey a sense of his Brazilian surroundings (Romero 1897, 130, 307–8, 122). In sum, Romero argued that, by his indifference to Brazilian reality and his mindless imitation of foreign models, Machado delayed rather than advanced the development of an authentically Brazilian literature (Romero 1897, 79 80, 121–23; Douglass 1998, 1036–55; Kristal and Passos 2006, 21–22; Maciel 2007, 19–20).[1]

Efraín Kristal and José Passos assert that Romero's general criteria with respect to literature and national identity and his specific evaluation of Machado had a significant impact on the history of Brazilian literary criticism generally and

Machadian criticism in particular (Kristal and Passos 2006, 21–22). Thus José Veríssimo (1857–1916), while acknowledging Machado's genius, like Romero, faulted his writings for not being sufficiently nationalist. Later, Veríssimo would reconsider and write that Machado conveyed, albeit implicitly, a profound and perceptive understanding of the Brazilian soul and Brazilian society with an aptitude for synthesis that placed his works among the great universal masterpieces (Veríssimo 1894, 198; 1916/1963, 304, 310, 314; 1977, 105–6; Schwarz 2006, 820n5).

Writers Mario de Andrade (1893–1945), José Lins do Rego (1901–57), Aurélio Buarque de Holanda Ferreira (1910–89), and Cassiano Ricardo (1895–1974) and anthropologist Gilberto Freyre were all influenced by Romero's criteria in their appraisal of Machado (Kristal and Passos 2006, 21–22). Andrade expressed his admiration for Machado's literary genius and virtuosity but did not consider him a representative Brazilian author, and he observed that it was impossible to feel any affection for an author who held such a heartless view of humanity (Andrade 1974, 89, 90, 94, 101, 103, 105). Lins do Rego, acknowledging that no one was better able to convey the mysterious and dark recesses of the human psyche, sharply criticized Machado's contempt for humanity, his lack of compassion for human suffering, and his unwillingness to suggest any answers to society's most pressing concerns (Rego 1946, 45, 92, 97, 100). In much the same vein, Buarque de Holanda remarked that Machado "was lacking . . . a sentiment . . . of love for the land, the local setting, and his people" (Holanda 1939, 55); Ricardo called him a "great Brazilian writer with an anti-Brazilian spirit" (*Marcha para Oeste*, Ricardo 1959, 2:274–75). Freyre went even further, finding Machado to be an elitist and pretentious mulatto who denied not only his racial and class background but also everything specifically Brazilian, including the national landscape. Freyre summed up the deep Brazilian ambivalence toward Machado when he insisted that Alencar was the true father of Brazilian letters, notwithstanding Machado's unparalleled mastery of European literary forms (Freyre 1962, 115–16, 117, 118, 119). Indeed, as Kristal and Passos point out, many Brazilian writers have felt encumbered by Machado's legacy and have attempted to draw from his literary aesthetics, while at the same time writing novels that explicitly speak to social concerns relevant to Brazil (Kristal and Passos 2006, 21–22).

If some critics and writers dismissed Machado as unrepresentative of Brazil, others viewed him as "a puzzle with a Brazilian solution" (Kristal and Passos 2006, 22). Lúcia Miguel Pereira, in *Machado de Assis* (1936), noting that Machado was a self-taught, epileptic, near-sighted, and stuttering mulatto, argued that his protagonists serve as psychological projections that document, albeit indirectly, his struggles with his racial and socioeconomic background and his ambition for upward social mobility (Pereira 1936, 73, 164, 177). Any analysis of Machado's fiction, she argued further, must take into consideration this biographical information and the ways in which Machado triumphed over racial and socioeconomic inequalities (Pereira 1936, 13, 69, 73).

Pereira disagreed with Romero's conclusion that Machado was not a representative Brazilian author because he failed to convey a sense of brasilidade in his writings (Pereira 1936, 332). Instead, she considered Machado "the first great Brazilian author.... His writings are universal in thought, Brazilian in sensibility.... In truth, Machado de Assis was not simply a Brazilian author, but also a *carioca*, who was not merely national but also regional.... Not the type of regionalism that was preoccupied with local color, but rather,... a regionalism of sensibility" (Pereira 1936, 331, 332, 335).

Despite what some critics considered Pereira's overly interpretive psychobiographical analysis, other literary scholars shared her approach. Prominent among these were Augusto Meyer, José Barreto Filho, and Afrânio Coutinho. In his collection of essays *Machado de Assis* (1935), Meyer deconstructed the traditional image of a Machado as serene, skeptical, attentive, friendly, and prone to moderation. Drawing from Fyodor Dostoyevsky's *Notes from Underground* (1864), he unmasked what he considered to be the "real"—and more disturbing—Machado, an underground or subterranean (*subterrâneo*) man, a demonic and tragic misanthrope, whom Meyer found clearly reflected in his writings (Meyer 1935, 16, 13–20).

In *Introdução a Machado de Assis* (*Introduction to Machado de Assis*; 1947), Barreto Filho was one of the first to examine existential questions in Machado's work, particularly his focus on the tragic sense of life and the presence of evil in humanity. According to Barreto, Machado harbored a deep aversion toward the passage of time and its relationship to life and death and employed irony, humor, and pessimism as rhetorical tools to deal with this (Barreto Filho 1947, 17, 130–38). Barreto attributes his aversion to an internal demon that originated in Machado's own psychological suffering and that made itself felt throughout his writings, beginning with *Posthumous Memoirs of Brás Cubas* (Barreto Filho 1947, 112, 10, 29, 32, 136–37, 153).

Coutinho made similar arguments in *A filosofia de Machado de Assis* (*The Philosophy of Machado de Assis*; 1959) by examining the philosophical influences on Machado's temperament and literary production. Coutinho cited Blaise Pascal, Michel de Montaigne, and Arthur Schopenhauer as the main influences that informed Machado's pessimistic and skeptical conception of the world and humanity. Machado's contempt for humanity and indifference to human suffering in turn shaped his view on life and gave rise to his focus on humanity's capacity for evil (Coutinho 1959, 24–26, 43–44). Among the major biographical factors influencing Machado's worldview, Coutinho examined his physical frailty, the inner conflict resulting from his humble socioeconomic background and multiraciality, and his ambition for upward social mobility (Coutinho 1959, 34, 37), finding these contributed in large part to the dramatic transformation Machado underwent with the writing of *The Posthumous Memoirs of Brás Cubas*, published in serialized form in 1880. From that moment on, Machado's philosophical pessimism, disenchantment with humanity, lack of illusions, and newfound consciousness of human misery become more sharply defined (Coutinho 1959, 24). His epilepsy in particular may have been a key factor shaping the world represented in his works, which reflect the loss of illusions, hopes, and joy, a growing awareness of the presence of evil in life, and his contempt toward the society Machado considered the source of his psychological torment (Coutinho 1959, 55–56).

Lúcia Miguel Pereira's 1936 study paved the way for others that accepted her specific portrayal of Machado as a representative Brazilian author. Thus Astrojildo Pereira, in his essay "Machado de Assis: Novelist of the Second Reign" (1939), states: "It has been repeated many times—and with good reason—that Machado de Assis is the most universal of our writers; I should point out that what is missing in this statement is that he is also the most national, the most Brazilian of all. I would also add . . . that one quality comes from the other: . . . he is much more national than universal and much more universal than national. Other writers have more local setting; none has conveyed a more profound understanding of the Brazilian people" (Pereira 1944, 15).

Antônio Cândido draws from the work of Silvio Romero, Lúcia Miguel Pereira, Astrojildo Pereira, and José Barreto Filho to formulate his own insightful analysis of Machado in his landmark book *Formação da literatura brasileira* (*Formation of Brazilian Literature*; 1969; Kristal and Passos 2006, 23). Cândido argues that the Brazilian nation, having originated as a colony, sought to establish an autonomous cultural identity distinct from that of its colonial past, especially after political independence in 1822. Indeed, the struggle for cultural independence gained momentum between 1750 and 1880 with the growth of local themes that gradually shifted away from mere duplication of European forms. Cândido considers Machado the culmination of a lengthy process of literary emancipation from external models (Cândido 1969, 2:115, 214, 369). Along these same lines, Roberto Reis highlights Alencar's attempts to compose a vast mural of Brazil, writing urban, Indianist, rural, and historical novels that sketched a portrait of the nation. These efforts paralleled the political task of nation making undertaken with

Independence in 1822 and completed during the Second Reign (1840–89). Writers such as Alencar sought to give their works a specifically Brazilian character. Such a project perfectly matched the Romantic attachment to local color and nationalism and the idealization normative in literature of the time (Reis 1992, 47).

Although Machado recommended that writers welcome foreign literary influences (Caldwell 1972, 89–90; Douglass 1998, 1052),[2] he vigorously attacked the lingering colonial dependency of the Brazilian intelligentsia on European culture despite Brazil having gained political independence from Portugal in 1822.[3] This cultural dependency had led to a servile imitation of European models, which Machado referred to in an 1868 letter as a "plague that came from abroad and imposed itself upon Brazil's still unformed literary spirit, which as yet had no real consciousness of itself." Machado believed that "only a shadow of a literature had evolved, one without sustenance or ideals, false, and frivolous, consisting of poor imitations and bad copies." And he expressed despair at his own seeming impotence "to stem the invading tide" (*Brás Cubas, A semana, Correspondencia*, Assis 1968, 7:181–82; 1937, 31:89–90; Caldwell 1972, 89).

Machado sought to counter what he considered the mindless and indiscriminate copying of European fashion, literary and otherwise. He recommended borrowing from the finest, most enduring, and universal exemplars of European literature yet transforming these into something uniquely Brazilian (Bellei 1992, 45–46; Cândido 1968, 28–31; 1995, 129–35; Needell 1983, 94–96; Santiago 2001, 60–63, 151–52; Schwarz 1987 29–48; Schwarz 1992, xv, 100–106). The national culture was to be constructively engaged in the universal flow of human history, which had merely taken on the guise of a Western European synthesis (Arnason 1990, 210–13; Douglass 1998, 1048; Fischer 1994, 191–214; Friedman 1960, 520–21; Memmi 1967, 90–141; Passos 1997, 218; Pieterse 1994, 144; Rocha 2006, xxii–xxiv, xxx).

Published in celebration of the fiftieth anniversary of Brazil's political independence, Machado's essay "Notícia da atual literatura brasileira: Instinto de nacionalidade" (Notice on the Present State of Brazilian Letters: An Instinctive Sense of Nationality; 1873) was at once a masterful articulation of the importance of cultural independence and a thoughtful analysis of the advantages and disadvantages of developing local themes. Unlike political independence, Machado told his readers, literary independence "will not be achieved in a single day, but gradually, so that it will be more lasting; it will not be the work of one or two generations; many generations will labor until it has been completely accomplished" (*Oc*, 3:801). In an earlier essay, Machado observed that "it is much easier to transform a nation than it is to transform a literature. Indeed, the latter will not be achieved in one fell swoop, as was the case with the Grito de Ipiranga, but rather, only through long-term and consistent effort" (*Critica*, Oc, 3:787).[4]

Although an advocate for creating a uniquely Brazilian literary aesthetic, Machado constantly engaged with European models (Maciel 2007, 19). Indeed, José Merquior emphasizes that it was with Machado that Brazilian literature entered into a significant dialogue with the critical voices of Western literature (Merquior 1977, 154). Machado felt that Brazilian writers should draw both from their own cultural heritage and from foreign literary influences as they set about building a distinctly national literature—that all that was national should be in constant dialogue with all that was foreign.[5]

Homi Bhabha maintains that the "locality" of national culture is neither unified nor unitary in relation to itself, nor should it be viewed as simply as "Other" in relation to what is external (Bhabha 1990, 4). The boundary between internal and external necessarily involves a process of hybridity. National consciousness essentially takes place within liminal (or transnational) spaces (Whalen 2004, 1) "through which the meanings of cultural and political authority are negotiated" (Bhabha 1990, 4; 1995, 207).

Roberto Schwarz, in *Misplaced Ideas: Essays on Brazilian Culture* (1992), considers Machado's writings a reflection of these dynamics and their attendant complexities and tensions. Nationalist sentiment in Brazil, that is, the sense of separateness from Portugal and the Portuguese, had been growing since at least the middle of the seventeenth century (Haring 1968, 3). Yet, prior to the nineteenth century, the ruling class's imitation of Europe did not constitute a problem; indeed, its close association with the culture of Portugal and Western Europe and its social distance from the masses were the principal means by which it legitimated its dominance. All that would change with political independence, when tension between the local and the foreign escalated into a full-blown battle for supremacy (Schwarz 1992, 12–13).

At the same time, Brazil's adoption of European liberalism, which was evident in its judicial system and the Constitution of 1824, in a society so completely dependent on slavery, resulted in discontinuities that persistently exposed the nation's social inequalities (Schwarz 1977, 12; 1992, 19–24). The Constitution granted citizenship to all Brazilian-born individuals, including free African Brazilians and libertos—whose legal and constitutional status was still distinct from that of free individuals—but, by definition, excluding free Africans. Yet the document remained silent on slavery and contained no guarantees for slaveholders beyond universal protections of the civil liberties and property rights of all citizens (Garner 2007, 1, 4; Marquese 2006, 122–23). For much of the nineteenth century, liberalism remained a "misplaced idea." It could not be fully achieved because it diverged considerably from the many remaining social and economic features inherited from the colonial period (Schwarz 1992, 19–24).

According to Schwarz, Machado's writings portray brasilidade precisely in mirroring this situation and that one of the aesthetic expressions of this phenomenon is Machado's humor and ironic detachment, so prominent in his later works (Schwarz 1990, 168–72, 41, 40). On the other hand, this seeming anomaly was one of the reasons why some considered Machado the least authentically Brazilian writer (Schwarcz and Botelho 2008, 148–49). Instead of following models of the French novel, as was customary at the time, Machado looked to eighteenth-century British fiction as one of his main sources of inspiration, particularly Laurence Sterne's *Tristram Shandy*. This helped him devise the ideal vantage point to scrutinize late nineteenth-century Brazil in all its absurdity and illogicality (Reis 1992, 53–54; Rouanet 2005, 81–83). Yet, above all, Machado followed his own muse with narrative innovations, particularly his volubility, in exposing the hypocrisies, contradictions, and dysfunctionality of nineteenth-century Brazil, particularly the Second Empire. Indeed, Machado inverted and subverted numerous contemporary narrative and intellectual conventions in order to reveal the pernicious ends they served. These techniques and their masterful deployment have earned the praise of critics such as Cândido, Schwarz, John Gledson, and Sidney Chalhoub.

Yet some critics, such as Abel Baptista, author of *Em nome do apelo do nome* (*On Behalf of the Appeal of the Name*; 1991), take issue with them, faulting their sociohistorical framing of Machado's writings.[6] Cândido and others like him, Baptista argues, have fallen prey to intentionalism: they have sought to find the "true Machado" in the text (Baptista 1994, 150, 155; 2003b, 117–131), claiming that his writings and innovative narrative techniques represent a direct, immediate, and specific correspondence with nineteenth-century social reality and underscoring Machado's profound engagement in the nationalist project.

For his part, however, Baptista believes that this limited framing diminishes Machado's originality and greatness—that one can read Machado without reference to national or social contexts. He contends that Machado's unique narrative form reflects not the contradictions and dysfunctions of the social order but, rather, Machado's need to establish his own originality in relation to his literary predecessors. Essentially, Baptista maintains that Machado's literary trajectory was based on fashioning a national literature that took not Brazilian reality but broader literary imperatives into consideration (Baptista 2003b, 33–42; 98–99,

108–11; Caminhos Cruzados 2008; Leão 2008; Teixeira 2008; Olamblogue 2008). In a similar vein, Jeana Dennis states that, just as Machado's novels transcend time, they also transcend place and culture. Indeed, if one were to remove the geographical descriptions of Rio de Janeiro from his novels, the stories could occur in any location (Dennis 1990, 76).

Despite their validity, these arguments tend to fall into the binary and hierarchical thinking that Machado so opposed. On the one hand, Machado's narrative innovations, particularly his narrative volubility, may indeed reflect his objective of exposing the contradictions of nineteenth-century Brazil during the Second Empire and early Republic. Moreover, Machado expressed his deep engagement in the nationalist project by inverting and subverting various contemporary narrative and intellectual conventions in order to reveal the detrimental goals they sought to fulfill. On the other hand, Machado's unique narrative form may also reflect his need to establish his own originality. Thus it is more accurate to say that Machado's literary trajectory was based on fashioning a national literature that took into account *both* Brazilian reality *and* more universal literary concerns.

In any case, if earlier criticism characterized Machado as indifferent to Brazilian reality, this indifference, according to Baptista, referred not to Brazilian reality in its totality but as it was imposed by the national project derived from the Romantic imperative (Baptista 2003b, 31–33). Indeed, Machado was critical of writers of the Romantic tradition who merely sprinkled their writings with the names of local flora and fauna as "proof" of their authentic brasilidade.[7] From his perspective, the "majestic scenes of American nature certainly offered great possibility for the poet and the novelist" (*Crítica, Oc*, 3:802–3). Yet Machado gave eloquent voice to the perennial dilemma of the artist—how to develop nativistic and national themes while remaining universal in appeal—in "Notice on the Present State of Brazilian Letters: An Instinctive Sense of Nationality" (1873):

> I must add that on this point there is at times expounded an opinion, which I consider erroneous, that the national psyche can only be recognized in those works that deal in local color and themes, a doctrine that, to be exact, would limit the basic foundation of our literature.... National poets are not thus so because they have used in their verse a multitude of names referring to national birds and flowers; this indeed is the basis for a national lexicon, and nothing more.... True, there is no doubt that a literature, especially a newly developing one, should principally nourish itself upon subjects provided by its native region; but an absolute dependence on this doctrine would lead only to impoverishment. What must be expected of a writer,

above all else, is a certain intimate feeling, if you will, for the essence of a particular nation and its people at a particular moment, even if that subject matter is distanced in space or time. (*Crítica, Oc*, 3:803–7)

Machado called on writers to forge from Brazil's national essence a literature that would be at once universal and yet quintessentially Brazilian. He sought to achieve this by going beyond what he called laborious external descriptions of Brazilian flora, fauna, and racial types, or the excessive use of idiomatic language so typical of anticolonial nationalist writings seeking to affirm authentic brasilidade. Machado searched deep beneath the Brazilian epidermis, beyond the particularities of Brazilian language, culture, and physiognomy, to capture what he called the collective national "instinct" or soul. He then sought to link this Brazilian soul with an oversoul shared by all humanity. "Machado's imaginings of human motivation," Dain Borges tells us, "have revealed a Machado whose insights can speak to people and situations beyond Brazil" (Borges 2007, 246), to which Daniel Piza would add that Machado's writings demonstrate a "richness and relevance . . . to our own contemporary circumstances" (Piza 2005b, 282).

Furthermore, although the predominant setting of Machado's novels is Rio de Janeiro and, by extension, the greater nation of Brazil during the Second Empire and the early Republic, he presents this setting not as a panoramic catalogue of place-names and external descriptions (Cony 2008, 43–44) but, rather, as kaleidoscopic glimpses organically integrated into the narrative through the lives, experiences, and reactions of the characters (Fischer 1994, 191–214; Kristal and Passos 2006, 17–20). By setting his works in Rio de Janeiro, Machado places them at the epicenter of Brazil's transformation from a rural to an urban economy based on monetary and commercial relations. But, as Astrojildo Pereira has made clear, Machado's "carioca regionalism" is not limited to Rio de Janeiro. As the capital and thus point of convergence, Rio is a summation, an index of the entire nation (Pereira 1944, 15; Sevcenko 1983, 27–28). That said, writing in *Revista do Brasil* in 1940, Roger Bastide was of one of the first to argue that Machado was deeply engaged with the Brazilian landscape as meaningful subject matter expressed in literary form: "I regard Machado de Assis as one of the greatest Brazilian landscape artists, one of those who imbued the art of landscaping in literature with an impulse similar to that which was accomplished in a parallel fashion in painting, and that I shall describe, if you will allow me to use Mallarmé's expression, as a presence, but an almost hallucinatory presence of an absence . . . the landscape appears to be absent . . . yet it is actually a palpitating presence" (Bastide 1940, 1).

The map and mores of Rio de Janeiro and Brazil become the basis upon which Machado constructs a psychological universe that nevertheless remains outside space and time. Carlos Cony and other critics point out that Machado evokes the atmosphere of Tijuca, the gardens of Andraí, the opulent mansions of Botafogo and Laranjeiras, and the throngs of residents of Catete, Flamengo, and Gloria. He captures the hustle and bustle of the Centro (downtown area), its narrow and straight streets, which are inundated with carriages and pedestrians—particularly Rua do Ouvidor (Listener or Gossip Street)—the nerve center of the city, from which rumors, good and bad, disseminate, and for which reputations large and small were created and made to crumble (Cony 2008, 43–44).[8] Machado also chronicles the Paraguayan War, Abolition, the demise of the monarchy and the establishment of the Republic, as well as the social behavior of the times. In composite, these particulars render a Rio de Janeiro and Brazil that are both historical and temporal—but also universal (Fischer 1994, 191–214; Hansen 1997, 249; Lowe 1982, 87, 89; Pereira 1944, 15; Val 1977, 19–25).

Romantic Indianism

Machado's quest to universalize the particular and particularize the universal explains the lack of nationalist consciousness so apparent in the writings of his literary contemporaries and successors (Baptista 1991, 45–63, 99–111; Caldwell 1972, 89; Cândido 1995, 129–30, 135; Facioli 2002, 165; Pereira 1957, 14, 17; Santiago 2001, 151–52; Schwarz 1990, 9–13; 1992, xv, 101–3). This lack is perhaps most evident in his criticism of the Romantic idealization of Brazil as a paradise of Native Americans against a backdrop of tropical birds and palm trees (*Oc*, 3, 802–3). But Machado's criticism was intended neither to disparage Native Americans nor to belittle the Native American contribution to Brazilian culture or the legitimacy of Native Americans as a source of inspiration for the literary imagination but, rather, to convey his frustration with the Indianist movement. And though, at first glance, Machado's language might seem dismissive, his primary target was the Indianist "craze" that had swept Brazil as part of the search for a national symbol.

To understand Machado's position on this topic, it would be useful to briefly consider the Indianist movement, as well as stereotypes in abolitionist literature and Naturalism. Indianism became such a fad among the elite that many, including the emperor himself, fashioned Native American names for themselves (Haberly 1983, 10–17; Schwarcz 1998/2004, 117).[9] Cities were given indigenous names and efforts made to teach Native American languages and history in the schools. Aspirants to high society even sought to prove they were of noble Native American lineage. Tupí, the most widely spoken Native American language, was seriously proposed by some to replace Portuguese as Brazil's official language. This shift in opinion translated into the glorification of the Native American when the literary Indianist movement burst onto the scene in the writings of Domingos José Gonçalves de Magalhães (1811–62), Antonio Gonçalves Dias (1823–64), and José de Alencar (1829–77; Brookshaw 1988, 41–43; Driver 1942, 41–44; Haberly 1983, 10–17; Paulk 2005, 61–77; Philippou 2005, 247; Schwarcz 1998/2004, 96–117; Sommer 1991, 138–71).

Native Americans as a cultural symbol of Brazilian national identity emerged in response to mounting pressure to develop a sense of shared identity that would unify the former provinces into a nation-state. The primary promoter of this development was the Indianist literary movement, which drew from the idealization of Native Americans first asserted with Brazil's discovery. Moreover, the Jesuits had always attributed human dignity to Native Americans, Portuguese kings had customarily conferred nobility on certain chiefs who, in the sixteenth and seventeenth centuries, helped the Portuguese conquer, define, and defend the country's national boundaries, and Native American slavery had been definitively abolished by the middle of the eighteenth century. Brazil's Native Americans were now deemed noble savages, "personifying the pure virtue of the natural man" (Haberly 1983, 10–17), inherently good but desperately in need of being civilized. Indianist sentiment was further nurtured by the heated moral debate in the 1850s over the nature of Brazil's indigenous population. On one side were those who asserted that Native Americans were barbaric and should be forcibly civilized through subjugation and slavery and, on the other, those who advocated freedom for what they considered the original and rightful owners of Brazil (Hemming 1987, 466–81).

Brazil's elite traditionally turned to Europe as a source for ideas and inspiration, and the Indianist movement was no exception; the Native American appealed to the fashionable Western European Romanticism (Haberly 1983, 17). In keeping with the Romantic ethos, the Brazilian elite emphasized the extravagant virtue and talents of the Native Americans and their image as a noble people who lived in harmony with their natural surroundings and who embodied Brazilians' dreams of greater freedom (Brookshaw 1988, 33–34; Haberly 1983, 15–16; Reis 1992, 48). Yet there was more to the glorification of Native Americans than that.

Brazilian intellectuals turned to the past, just as emerging nineteenth-century Western European nation-states turned to medieval times, to find an appropriate symbol for their national future. The Portuguese colonizers were unacceptable:

they had been expelled from Brazil and represented colonial Brazil (Driver 1942, 41–44). Precolonial Native Americans, on the other hand, were regarded as heroic victims of colonial oppression, whose rebellion and resistance to slavery served as an ideal symbol of Brazil's own independence (Driver 1942, 72–73; Haberly 1983, 15–16; Hemming 1987, 468; Reis 1992, 48). Indianism drew heavily from Western European Romanticism. Yet the movement also differed from it by celebrating Brazil's "primitive" tropical environment, which European Romantics had characterized as a liability rather than an asset. Thus Indianism provided Brazilians with a means of asserting pride in their uniqueness.

Furthermore, the romanticization of Brazil's indigenous population—and indigenous ancestry—was made possible by the fact that the Native American threat to Brazilian territorial expansion had been sufficiently neutralized by disease and the ravages of colonization (Brookshaw 1988, 1–11; 1989, 33–34; Haberly 1983, 10–14; Hemming 1987, 466–81). Indeed, at the time of Portuguese colonization in the early sixteenth century, there were an estimated 2.5 million Native Americans in what would become Brazil (Hemming 1978/2004, 510; 1987, 5). By 1819, however, the indigenous population had fallen to 800,000—less than a third of what it had been in 1500—and Native Americans were being forced to retreat deeper into the nation's interior (Marcílio 1984, 41, 45). Consequently, they were seen as "curiosities." In light of this, Machado's comment that the indigenous contribution to Brazilian culture was minimal, at least as compared to that of African Brazilians, is not so far off the mark.

This brings us to a final reason for choosing the Native American as the national symbol. The "otherworldly" Native American espoused by the Indianist movement not only eclipsed the pressing social reality of Native Americans, but also caused Brazilians to turn a blind eye to another disturbing reality—the Africans and their descendants—thereby diverting attention from the issue of slavery (Paulk 2005, 61–77; Reis 1992, 50–52; Sommer 1991, 138–71). This effort to downplay the role of African Brazilians could be carried out with simple propaganda and the manipulation of racial statistics. However, nothing could be done about the overwhelming societal makeup of black and multiracial individuals. Since the early colonial era, there had been widespread miscegenation and the majority of Brazilians were, to varying degrees, of multiracial ancestry (including African antecedents), which the elite sought to ignore, if not deny. Consequently, multiraciality was also largely rejected as a choice for a national symbol partly because of contemporary beliefs that multiracial individuals were even more "inferior" than their parent racial groups. Thus the logical solution to this dilemma, as the Brazilian Historical and

Geographical Institute suggested to Pedro II, was to embrace Brazil's decimated Native Americans. This scheme also had the advantage of making it possible for the Brazilian elite to claim implicitly that racial and cultural blending had mostly involved the honorable Native Americans. It was thus an indirect sanctioning of multiraciality, as long as it involved Brazil's indigenous population, and made it possible to de-emphasize any connection with Africans.[10]

Romantic Abolitionism: Racial Whiteness and the Black Peril

If the Native American was the symbol of national identity and indigenous ancestry a source of pride, Africans were a troubling presence and African ancestry a source of shame, exacerbated by the presence of millions of slaves. African Brazilian slaves could hardly qualify as noble, and seeking to ennoble them would have meant granting them the freedom they lacked. Moreover, the existence of African and Portuguese centers of cultural reference, in which the demographic significance was heavily tilted in favor of a black majority, also meant that African culture had helped shape not only the evolving contours of African Brazilian culture but also the European core culture (Daniel 2006, 36). That said, David Brookshaw and David Haberly point out that the most conspicuous feature in the formation of Brazilian literature before 1850 is the almost complete absence of African Brazilian characters (Brookshaw 1986, 21; Haberly 1972, 31, 32). To the extent that African Brazilians were present in Indianist literature, they stood in contrast to Native Americans. Representing the reality of the colonized race, toiling as slave labor on the colonizer's plantation and by nature humble, resigned, and obedient, African Brazilians were no match—in terms of literary attraction—for the mythical Native Americans, by nature courageous and fiercely proud of their independence (Brookshaw 1986, 22).

The literary invisibility of African Brazilians was significantly diminished after 1850, thanks in large part to the emergence of abolitionist literature, though black and mulatto characters were still rare. Two powerful forces defined the basic character of literary abolitionism. First, it was influenced by the nation's literary tradition, the character of previous antislavery arguments, and, most important, the racial prejudices that were normative among white Brazilians. Second, it was influenced by the need to reach an overwhelmingly hostile or apathetic audience and take advantage of their new concerns about the slaves (Brookshaw 1986, 25; Haberly 1972, 32–33).

An examination of abolitionist literature reveals that it employed highly effective racial stereotypes that were both antislavery and antislave at the same time (Haberly 1972, 30; Bailey 1961, 24; Paulk 2005, 61–77; Sommer 1991, 138–55). Reflecting the racial attitudes of white authors as well as those of their readers, this literature helped smooth the way for abolition, but because slavery had a powerful and vocal constituency among the elite, it did not develop until after the middle of the nineteenth century (Haberly 1972, 30–31; Brookshaw 1986, 22). Although abolitionist literature was virtually without precedent in the nation's literary tradition and influenced by Victor Hugo and other foreign writers associated with Social Romanticism, the timing of the abolitionist transformation in Brazilian society strongly suggests that whites did not really see the African Brazilian masses that surrounded them until the end of the slave trade. That event not only endangered the continued existence of slavery but also greatly increased the value of individual slaves, now more expensive and difficult to replace. This, in turn, required slave owners to provide improved treatment of their human chattel (Brookshaw 1986, 21–23; Haberly 1972, 33).

According to Haberly, a key characteristic of abolitionist literature was the confusion of the institution of slavery and the individual slave (Haberly 1972, 33). Slavery, abolitionists asserted, was evil; but "evil," from the self-interested perspective of antislavery propaganda before 1850 simply meant harmful to white Brazilians. Although antislavery writers after 1850 could not entirely avoid the influence of long-standing humanitarian stereotypes in foreign literature, such as the "Pitiful Slave," the "Noble Slave," and the "Faithful Slave," these imported figures do not appear to have altered Brazilian racial attitudes or the racial bias of the nation's abolitionist movement.

White Brazilians, after 1850, were especially preoccupied with female slaves: there were relatively few women in the slave quarters, and their low fertility was a major obstacle to the continuation of slavery. The Pitiful Slave, typically a woman, achieved literary currency in Brazil, but only when the character was closely linked to specific concerns of the nation's overwhelmingly white elite. Whereas abolitionists interpreted her usual fate—suicide after immense suffering—as a great moral tragedy, the pro-slavery contingent must have been appalled by the "immoral" waste of good breeding stock (Brookshaw 1986, 24–25; Haberly 1972, 33–34).

The best-known example that combines aspects of the Pitiful, Noble, and to some extent the Faithful Slave stereotypes was Isaura, the heroine of Bernardo Guimarães's novel *A escrava Isaura* (*The Slave Isaura*; 1875). Not unlike her counterparts in U.S. abolitionist literature, Isaura is phenotypically European. This portrait of the noble near-white mulatto heroine as a sympathetic, faithful, helpless victim illustrated the gross injustice dealt her at the hands of the white master. It also revealed how the institution of slavery gave license to the sexual abuse of women, destroyed the family (by making rape and adultery profitable and by severing the natural bond between parent and child), and otherwise mocked the highest values the dominant culture claimed to cherish.

At the same time, this literary device also sustained certain sexist stereotypes. It pricked the conscience of white audiences in terms of slavery's injustices by bringing into sharp focus the fantasy (or nightmare) of white bondage. At the same time, it provided them with safe emotional and physical distance from the actual conditions of the enslaved black masses. This stereotype appealed to racist sentiments that reified the association of whiteness with freedom and blackness with slavery (Bailey 1961, 75–76; Branche 2006, 160–61; Brookshaw 1986, 24–25; Haberly 1972, 33–34; Reis 1992, 50–51). The existence of the stereotype of the Noble, Faithful, or Pitiful Slave did not call into question the institution of slavery itself. Much of this stereotypical literature was written in response to Harriet Beecher Stowe's *Uncle Tom's Cabin* (1852), translated into Portuguese and published twice during the 1850s—no doubt because it was a foreign bestseller, rather than because it dealt with slavery (Bailey 1961, 64; Brookshaw 1986, 24; Haberly 1972, 34).

Despite the popularity of the Pitiful, Noble, or Faithful Slave, the most prominent abolitionist works were generally concerned with two characters commonly encountered in the few scattered references to African Brazilians in literature before 1850—the "Immoral Slave" and the "Violent Slave." Both of these stereotypes had some basis in the reality of Brazilian slavery. The scarcity of African women and the plantation social order were conducive to immoral behavior, and there were numerous reports of fugitive or rebellious slaves (Brookshaw 1986, 24; Haberly 1972, 34). The high proportion of immoral and violent African Brazilian characters in Brazilian literature, both before and after 1850, nonetheless serves to illustrate the emotions and attitudes of white authors and their audiences. Abolitionists found the Violent Slave and the Immoral Slave useful because, after 1850, simple mathematics made slave owners sensitive about their female slaves—almost all Immoral Slaves were women—and about the danger, to their lives and their labor resources, of slave rebels and fugitives. Indeed, few immoral male slaves appear, either before or after 1850, largely because writers found it so difficult to define immorality for African Brazilian males (Brookshaw 1986, 27–28; Haberly 1972, 35–36).

Above all, the stereotypes of the Violent Slave and the Immoral Slave were effective because they tapped into the racial bias of the audience that abolitionism sought to reach with its own prejudices. Both images had long been used to justify slavery but now were turned against the institution. The most popular African Brazilian character in literature prior to 1850 was the Immoral Slave who joyfully conferred her bounteous favors (particularly those of a sexual nature) on the master, the overseer, and any other white male who happened along. The image of the perpetually willing female—implying both the greater desirability and superior sexual ability of white males—became both a national fantasy and a justification for a system that encouraged this type of miscegenation (Haberly 1972, 34–35). Moreover, the treatment of many female characters suggests that some abolitionists were working toward defining immorality as a matter of availability rather than character. Simply because they were present to tempt white males, black and mulatto women became dangerous creatures, unleashing violence and lust they could not control. Although this concept of latent immorality somewhat lessened white guilt, it also served to increase white fear. Even the most well-mannered black or mulatto woman was a ticking time bomb (Brookshaw 1986, 27–28; Haberly 1972, 35–36).

The other major stereotype of abolitionist literature in Brazil, the Violent Slave (Haberly 1983, 35–36), was not merely an expression of white disquiet. It also served to justify rigid social controls that sought to prevent or contain slave discontent. When abolitionist literature developed the image of violent slaves, it immediately became a powerful weapon. The actions of violent male slaves were frequently offered as a response to the mistreatment of female slaves. This was part of the campaign to convince slave owners that abolition was the only way to neutralize the threat posed by their cruel and dangerous chattel. Haberly states, however, that this stereotype brought Brazilian abolitionism into direct conflict with the European literary models that had influenced its vocabulary and style. The "Noble Black," in foreign literature, was frequently a typical Romantic hero—the solitary rebel who fought for freedom and avenged evil. For white Brazilians after 1850, who were increasingly mistrustful of the adult males in the slave quarters, this imported stereotype was not heroic, but frightening. In addition, when images from abroad were in conflict with that of the Violent Slave, humanitarianism was invariably sacrificed in the process (Haberly 1972, 37–38).

All of these antislave appeals were synthesized in Joaquim Manuel de Macedo's collection of short stories *As vítimas-algozes* (*The Victim Executioners*; 1869), which conjured up a laboratory of racial horrors. Simeão, the spoiled crioulo male house slave, massacres the master's family. Pai-Raiol, the *feiticeiro* (witch doctor), poisons the livestock, sets the cane on fire, and convinces Esméria the cook to seduce the slave master and poison his wife and her children.[11] Lucinda, the lascivious *mucama* (domestic), teaches her innocent young charge appalling perversions and assists her own lover in seducing the girl. These nightmarish accounts conveyed not only an explicit warning to whites about the evils of slavery but also an implied warning about the social catastrophe that lay ahead if new forms of social control were not implemented in slavery's aftermath. In sum, the message of abolitionist literature in Brazil is that the presence of blacks and mulattoes had disastrous consequences on the moral fiber of the social order because of the damages inflicted on them by slavery. Slavery should not only be abolished but African Brazilians also should be expunged from the social order as a remedy for their negative impact, both real and imagined, on whites (Bailey 1961, 48; Brookshaw 1986, 28–30; França 2007; Haberly 1972, 39; Sayers 1958, 331–40).

Race, Naturalism, and National Identity: "Order and Progress"[12]

By the time slavery was abolished in 1888, the literary stereotypes of African Brazilians that originated in abolitionist literature were firmly established. None stemmed from a reformed vision of blacks and mulattoes; rather, all were the product of the resentment of slave interests reeling from antislavery economics. As chattel, African Brazilians were regarded as subhuman. Their increased presence in late nineteenth-century literature, specifically Naturalist literature, which was buttressed by theories of scientific racism, helped confirm their subhumanity. The quantitative increase in the African Brazilian presence was not matched by a concomitant increase in quality.

Naturalism defined literature as a branch of science and the novel as a kind of microscope slide upon which the author placed certain organisms—some healthy, most diseased—and then observed and described their interaction with an objectivity devoid of moral judgments. The natural forces of heredity and environment determined the actions of animalistic characters in pursuit of the basic goals of survival, sex, and wealth. Human beings were animals trapped by deterministic environmental or hereditary influences that propelled them toward violence and immorality with the consequent dissolution of individual responsibility (Bosi 1970, 213; Coutinho 1969, 3:1–16, 63–67; Haberly 1972, 39–40).

Racial Whiteness and the Black Plague

The impact of Naturalism on Brazilian literature, as far as the novel is concerned, dates from 1881, the year Aluísio Azevedo published *The Mulatto*, which claimed to be an attack on slavery and the petty bigotry of provincial society. Set in Maranhão prior to Abolition, the story involves a tragic love, at least on the surface. Recently returned from Europe to collect his inheritance and seek information about his mysterious past, the protagonist Raimundo appears to be the perfect aristocrat—white, blue-eyed, highly educated, and exceptionally noble. Raimundo awakens the repressed passions of his sexually unfulfilled white cousin, Ana Rosa, and they embark on an affair. But when Raimundo finds out he is a mulatto and that his mother, the slave mistress of a wealthy Portuguese immigrant, was tortured and driven insane by her master's wife, he feels unworthy of Ana Rosa. Driven by her lust, however, she seduces him. Ana Rosa immediately discloses her pregnancy to her family, and demands marriage to Raimundo. An assortment of villains conspire to kill Raimundo; Ana Rosa is forced to marry a white man, a Portuguese clerk she despises.

The Mulatto was a resounding success, largely because of the frank description of Rosa's affair with Raimundo. It was in the abolitionist tradition and owes much to Romanticism in its portrayals of Raimundo (unaware of his mysterious, servile origins) and Ana Rosa. But the awakening of her lust and the ensuing love affair with Raimundo are interpreted through the lens of Naturalism. The tragic outcome of their relationship stems from the disastrous effect of mulatto passion upon weak feminine sensitivity. That said, many critics have been puzzled by the brief and idyllic epilogue. Five years after Raimundo's murder, Ana Rosa seems fulfilled as the wife of the clerk she once loathed. In terms of abolitionist and Naturalist stereotypes, however, this scene is completely logical. Any African Brazilian, regardless of status, education, character, or pigmentation, is inescapably a catalyst for immorality and violence. Raimundo's mother brought about immorality, cruelty, and her own insanity; Raimundo's uncontrollable effect on Ana Rosa aroused her libido and caused his death. A major lesson of *The Mulatto* for readers was that the tranquility of the social order could best be achieved maintained in the absence of African Brazilians (Haberly 1972, 42).

The ultimate African Brazilian immorality, in terms of the social values of the time, was encapsulated in Adolfo Caminha's *Bom-crioulo* (*The Good Black*; 1895), the first Brazilian novel to use a black as the main character. Caminha presents two diametrically opposed worlds: a phantom slaver, adrift on the most perverted currents of Brazil's past, and the city of Rio de Janeiro. The story is built around the same-sex love between Amaro, an escaped black slave turned seaman, and Aleixo, a white naval cadet and cabin boy. Amaro is an extremely strong yet gentle seaman, whose homosexuality Caminha attributes to his degenerate heredity and to the perversions and immorality of slave life he experienced as a young child. At sea, African Brazilians and whites are thrown together in the isolated confines of the ship's steamy hull, where Amaro, the Bom-Crioulo, comes to desire and possess the delicate, blond, blue-eyed, and pretty Aleixo. Once they return to land, in the "normal" world of the city, Amaro is unable to maintain his hold over Aleixo, and he loses him to the voluptuous and passionate Carolina, a middle-aged Portuguese prostitute. Yet immorality leads, as always, to violence, and Amaro, enraged by jealousy, murders the only person he has ever loved (Foster 1991, 9–22; 1994, 1–33; Haberly 1972, 43; Howes 2001, 41–62).

Finally, we have perhaps the strongest expression of antiblack sentiments in Brazilian literature (Bailey 1961, 103) and the most blatantly pornographic novel of Brazilian Naturalism, Júlio Ribeiro's *Carne* (*Flesh*; 1888). The sexual impulses of Lenita, the white heroine, are aroused by witnessing the promiscuous behavior of slaves on her father's estate in the utterly immoral environment of the coffee plantations of São Paulo's interior. Lenita's sudden awareness of the bronze statue of a naked gladiator, which symbolizes black sexuality, drives her into an affair with her cousin Barbosa and brings about a raving and self-destructive nymphomania, not unlike that of a lustful black female field slave.

Traditional critics, such as Sílvio Romero and José Veríssimo in the nineteenth century and Lúcia Miguel Pereira, Nelson Werneck Sodré, and Flora Süssekind in the twentieth, have considered the aforementioned novels simply as representing Naturalism's "mechanistic" view of existence and its preference for the unseemly, lowly, and revolting aspects of life.[13] Eva Bueno, however, provides a compelling reading of these texts that differs from what she calls the conventional and "unproblematic" interpretation (Bueno 1995, xi). After the fall of the Empire and with the rise of the Republic, the political moment necessitated an idea of Brazil that could be encapsulated under the positivistic slogan "Order and Progress." During this transition period, the uneven but successful integration of Comtean positivism in Rio de Janeiro and the provincial capitals sparked intellectual debates among various groups at different levels of society. The critical discourse of these new intellectuals demonstrates how the integration of various positivist philosophies ran parallel to the adoption of Naturalist aesthetics in Brazilian literature during the 1870s (Bueno 1995, 371–73, 391; Foster 1991, 9–22; Lins 1967, 37–46, 243–314; Skidmore 1974, 9–14).

Unlike positivism, however, Naturalism lacked political sponsorship. Its most widely recognized practitioners were from the provinces and incapable of expressing the "national spirit" of the bourgeoisie of the Court in Rio de Janeiro that so exemplified the progressive views of positivism. Bueno believes that this "ex-centricity" (or provinciality) of Brazilian Naturalism differed significantly from the utopian and essentially urban construct of positivism. It reflected the resistance of intellectuals from the periphery who saw a need to reconstitute the identities in danger of being expunged from the nation's history by the urban elite. The Naturalists were the first writers to view the totality of Brazilian society from the perspective of the periphery. They exposed a social order rife with contradictions and tensions caused by the sudden visibility of characters that previously enjoyed no aesthetic currency in Brazilian literature: blacks, mulattoes, masculinized women, feminized men, and homosexuals (Bueno 1995, 35, 37, 363–64; Foster 1991, 9–22).

Bueno argues that critics and historians have undervalued the Naturalist novel within Brazilian literature. Her explanation for this is that Brazilian Naturalism was forged in an embattled political climate, characterized by widespread disputes and divisions: the young members of the military against older officials and the monarchy; intellectuals from different regions of the country against the monarchy as well as one another; the civilian intellectuals against the military, which threatened their intellectual authority (Skidmore 1974, 9–14). Bueno views the disputes among and within these groups as "a site for irresolution, confusion, questioning, and demystifying" (Bueno 1995, 26) that articulate distinct forms of the national idea as well as struggles for dominance over who could best imagine this idea.

According to Bueno, each novel of the Naturalist pantheon provides a different lens through which to view the tensions and ruptures implicit in the ideological project of how Brazilian identity was formed after the fall of the Empire. Yet these novels display a common opposition to the *idea* of a nation that threatened to neutralize regional as well as gender, sexual, racial, and class differences through the projection of the unitary and centralized white, male, heterosexual, and bourgeois subject associated with the Republican regime. They sought to accomplish this, in part, by appropriating the very alignments of gender, race, and class they opposed (Bueno 1995, ix–iv, xxii; Foster 1991, 9–22).

Racial Whiteness and Black Extermination[14]

Notwithstanding Buenos's argument, Brookshaw, Haberly, and Borges point out that Naturalism was the literary counterpart of political Republicanism as well as of Darwinism in natural science. In fact, Herbert Spencer applied Darwin's theories of natural selection in plants and animals to human beings in order to biologically interpret the divisions of society as the basis for his Social Darwinism, according to which the strong would survive, whereas the weak would be eliminated, for the good of society as a whole. Social Darwinism drawn on racial lines was promptly exploited by Anglo–North Americans to explain the inherent inferiority of African Americans (Borges 1995, 60–61; Brookshaw 1986, 38–39; Haberly 1972, 40–41).

Ideological racism in Brazil could not be indulged with the same confidence as in the United States. Racial divisions had never been so formal, miscegenation was pervasive, and a substantial community of free coloreds had also developed during slavery. Nevertheless, the ideas of Spencer and the Social Darwinists found a ready audience in Brazil because they helped salve the white Brazilian conscience. On the one hand, abolition was necessary for the economic and social progress of the nation because it would sever the landowners' dependence on the labor of the inferior African Brazilians. On the other hand, this racial group could not be allowed to present a threat after Abolition because of its inherent inferiority. Exceptional mulattoes might be equal and even superior to individual whites, but Brazil would remain a nation dominated by whites (Brookshaw 1986, 38; Haberly 1972, 30–46; Skidmore 1974, 48–69; Torres 1969, 87–89).

These dynamics help explain why Realism, which was a significant movement in Europe, largely failed in Brazil, whereas Naturalism, which was its extreme and relatively minor offshoot, flourished. This break in the normal transatlantic flow of literary influences is understandable if one realizes that Naturalism in Brazil was in large part a prolongation and revitalization of the abolitionist literature of the previous Romantic generation. It did not, however, necessarily provide a more enlightened view of African Brazilians. Abolitionist literature is generally classified as part of Brazilian Romanticism, specifically Social Romanticism, which was beginning to wane by 1880. Haberly contends that a key reason for the decline of Brazilian Romanticism was the increasingly overt conflict between European Romanticism and the ideology of Brazilian abolitionism. The internal tension between foreign stereotypes and African Brazilian characters in Brazilian antislavery literature was paralleled by a more telling one, between Romantic individualism and the slaveholding mentality. The Romantic cult of the individual, who was capable of some control over his or her actions and responsible for them, placed a heavy burden of personal guilt upon the shoulders of the audience abolitionists were seeking to convert (Haberly 1972, 30–46).

As Haberly explains, Brazilian abolitionism was remarkably shortsighted. It concentrated upon its objective and almost entirely ignored the consequences of success. It preached the dangers of close contact between master and slave, yet was either unwilling or unable—even when abolition became inevitable—to come to grips with the future of the Brazilian social order once the violent and immoral creatures it had taught its readers to fear were finally unleashed. The results of the rising tide of manumission made it clear, however, that the traditional system of social controls had broken down. Large numbers of former slaves were inevitably drawn to the coastal cities, where a majority of Brazilian readers resided (Haberly 1972, 40–41).

Giorgio Marotti maintains that these critical problems for traditional abolitionism were largely resolved in Naturalism, which thrived on the abolitionists' racial prejudices. Naturalism's determinism legitimized new, less formal social controls that sought to separate African Brazilians and whites in urbanized areas. Writers like Aluísio de Azevedo, Adolfo Caminha, and Júlio Ribeiro, who as self-proclaimed abolitionists held these prejudices, could still openly oppose slavery and rejoice in its abolition (Marotti 1982, 66, 116–21). Naturalist novels, Haberly notes, clearly conveyed that the presence of African Brazilians was unhealthy because they had no control over their animal instincts. Since they had no morality, they could have disastrous consequences on the lives of those who did have, namely, whites. Thus these novels constituted a continuation of the ideas expounded in abolitionist literature. Naturalism abolished white guilt because all the crimes of the slave system were simply the result of uncontrollable natural forces. On the other hand, it also advised those safely outside that environment and free of those genes to avoid possible contagion through contact with those permanently damaged by environment and genealogy (Branche 2006, 160–61; Haberly 1972, 40–41; Marotti 1982, 116–21).

Naturalism's concern with clinical descriptions of the interaction of different social strata determined by natural forces seemed admirably suited to the needs of Brazilian writers and the elites preoccupied with ideas about racial heredity and the impact of the environment on human behavior. Naturalism's focus on poverty and squalor meant that full rein could be given to clinical study of African Brazilians, in which their bestiality could be illustrated. Moreover, the Naturalist novel lent itself to the treatment of African Brazilian immorality and violence by seeking out controversial and forbidden themes, particularly those of a sexual nature, and treating them with a frankness that often bordered on the pornographic. Finally, Naturalism's fully developed theory of human animalism gave rise to the animalization of African Brazilians (Haberly 1972, 40).

At the time, whites were particularly concerned about mulattoes, a group with some chance of upward social mobility. In Naturalist theory, mulattoes were considered dangerous and depraved because they received the weak and evil genes of both masters and slaves. Indeed, on the eve of Abolition, the mulattoes posed a greater numerical threat to the racial identity of the elite than did black slaves. Haberly points out that it is not surprising that Naturalism should have been so influential in Brazil's literary development by virtue of this concern. This was not only apparent in the descriptions but also the consideration of hitherto forbidden topics such as incest, homosexuality, sexual contact between the African Brazilian and the white woman, and uncontrollable black sensuality in general. The segregation, even the destruction, of African Brazilians literally and literarily could be considered a legitimate measure of white self-defense (Haberly 1972, 41).

Race, Postcolonialism, and the National Aesthetic: Critical Hybridity

Machado voiced no opinion on Realist-Naturalism's scientific racism and theories of mongrelization and hybrid degeneracy. His writings, however, seem to indicate a tacit disagreement with these notions (Daniel 1981, 5–7; Gledson 2002, 17). Of course, a multiracial background would not preclude an individual from agreeing with them. For example, Raimundo Nina Rodrigues (1862–1906), a prominent mulatto (albeit near-white) professor in Bahia's prestigious school of medicine, brought into being the most influential doctrinaire Brazilian racist thought of the era, linking behavior directly with biology. That said, Rodrigues countered theories of hybrid degeneracy with the ideology of whitening through miscegenation. He no doubt was as certain of the mulattoes'—and thus his own—superiority in proportion to their geno-phenotypical approximation to Europeans, as he was of the Africans' and Native Americans' inferiority (Blake 2011, 50–51, 59–66; Borges 1993, 240–42; Rodrigues 1894/1938, 161, 169, 215–17; Salvatore 1996, 204–7; Schwarcz 1999, 258–62; Skidmore 1974, 57–60).

From Canudos to Canaan

Machado's silence on such racist pronouncements is even more striking when we consider two late nineteenth- and early twentieth-century novels that confronted head-on questions of race and multiraciality as these related to whitening through miscegenation and the formation of Brazilian national identity—*Os sertões* (*The Backlands*; 1902) by Euclides da Cunha (1866–1909) and *Canãa* (*Canaan*; 1901) by José Pereira da Graça Aranha (1868–1931). *The Backlands* examines the fin de siècle war fought in the interior of Bahia between the military forces of the newly formed Republic and a messianic movement under the charismatic leadership of Antônio Vicente Mendes Maciel (1839–97). From the 1870s onward, the itinerant evangelist, mystic, and self-proclaimed prophet wandered through the backlands and lesser-inhabited areas of Brazil, bringing a message of consolation, hope, liberation, and a better life to the impoverished peasants as well as slaves of Bahia's interior and other provinces of the Northeast. Marciel soon became known as "Antônio Conselheiro" (Antônio the Counselor) among his growing band of followers.[15] In 1893, they settled on an abandoned farm in the northeastern interior of Bahia, called "Canudos." Over the years, landless farmers, former and fugitive slaves, Native Americans, and poor whites from across Bahia flocked to Conselheiro's increasingly prominent and largely self-sufficient community, seeking to live in Christian communion and simplicity (Graden 2006, 218; Madden 1993, 6–7).

The settlement grew rapidly, attracting poor and wealthy alike, although most settlers were peasants. Within a few years, they numbered between 18,000 and 25,000, making Canudos the second-largest urban center in Bahia after Salvador (Graden 2006, 216–23; Madden 1993, 7; Moniz 1987, 71). Landowners condemned it as a dangerous magnet for migrants and a drain on the supply of workers available to labor on estates. The Catholic Church condemned Conselheiro, whose growing appeal threatened its political power, as a religious fanatic and an impostor priest. Republicans claimed that Conselheiro supported the monarchy's return to power (Graden 2006, 216–23; Madden 1991, 60, 67–68). For the powerful and overwhelmingly white Brazilian elite, the struggle against Canudos was also a struggle to secure Brazil's future as modern nation-state under the positivist exigencies of "order and progress"—to protect it from being overrun by a barbaric and overwhelmingly nonwhite underclass (Blake 2011, 66–76; Graden 2006, 216–23).

These myriad concerns have led writers to arrive at wide-ranging conclusions about the conflict at Canudos and the circumstances surrounding it. Some considered it a political rebellion, others a civil war, and still others a struggle over racial questions (Madden 1993, 5). But whether Conselheiro's community represented a messianic or social movement or something else altogether, in late 1896, the Republic declared war on it, having branded its leader and his followers "monarchist rebels" conspiring against the new Republican regime (Madden 1993, 5). And when, after four military campaigns, the Republican army finally occupied Canudos in September 1897, it leveled the settlement and massacred most of its inhabitants (Blake 2011, 66–76; Borges 2006, 30; Graden 2006, 216–23; Levine 1992, 65, 102; Skidmore 1974, 104–9).

Costa Lima takes da Cunha to task for portraying Conselheiro and his disciples as regressive products of miscegenation in *The Backlands* (Lima 1988, 152–86). Yet da Cunha actually vacillates between the contemporary denigration of the mestiço and miscegenation and his admiration for the mestiço peasantry's hardiness, which he considered the bedrock of Brazil (Borges 2006, 30; Santos 2002, 75–77). Indeed, there is an unresolved tension in da Cunha's portrayal of the mestiço "monarchists." On the one hand, he describes Canudos's multiracial inhabitants as heroically defending their "primitivism" against the Republic and its representatives, who behave barbarically in first abandoning these inhabitants of the interior to poverty and ignorance and then responding with disproportionate violence to their religious movement. On the other hand, he frames the influences of race and environment in northeastern Brazil in deterministic terms: the *sertanejos* (inhabitants of the interior) are simply the unstable products of their primitive physical environment and their multiracial background. The few times that da Cunha steps outside his deterministic framework, he finds redeeming qualities in the multiracial individual of European and Native America descent—but none in the mulatto, toward whom his attitude is overwhelmingly negative (Blake 2011, 66–76; Borges 2006, 30, 34–36; Graden 2006, 220–23; Santos 2002, 75–77; Skidmore 1974, 104–9).

Along with da Cunha's *The Backlands*, one of the most widely read and discussed books in Brazil in the early part of the twentieth century was Graça Aranha's *Canaan*. Published in the same year as *The Backlands*, *Canaan* was more a novel of ideas than of actions but provided an equally striking dramatization of Brazilians' conflicting perspectives on miscegenation and multiraciality (Eakins 1980, 3–15; Santos 2002, 61–82). Its story is set in Espírito Santo, the central southern state where Aranha had spent several months as a local judge. Two German immigrants discuss their reactions to their new land and to the drama of a poor unmarried pregnant girl, Maria Perutz, born in Brazil to German settlers in an enclave settlement but not considered altogether "Brazilian" by the novel's characters. When Maria goes through childbirth unattended, the baby dies, and she is accused of murder. Although the theme of an aggrieved maiden may have made the book appealing for some readers, its real appeal lay in Graça Aranha's treatment of a burning issue of the time, whether Brazil's lush tropical land could become a center of civilization through the fusion of European immigrants and Brazilian mestiços (Eakins 1980, 3–15; Kathöfer 2008, 1–14; Santos 2002, 61–82; Skidmore 1974, 110–13).

Graça Aranha addressed this issue not with subtle devices but directly in dialogue between his immigrant protagonists. The optimist Milkau argues that Brazil would be redeemed and elevated by the merging of Europeans and multiracial Brazilians. His statement "Races are civilized through fusion" (Aranha 1901/1959, 42) affirms the "whitening through miscegenation" ideal, which was the Brazilian compromise with scientific racism (Skidmore 1974, 110–13; Eakins 1980, 3–15; Santos 2002, 61–82). For his part, the pessimist Lentz believes that the blend of two radically divergent racial groups would only result in an inferior race of unstable and conflicted mulattoes, due in large part to the African Brazilians' "bestiality and innate servility," and that progress could only come through the "replacement of a hybrid race, such as mulattoes, by Europeans" (Aranha 1901/1959, 43).

The author's sympathies lay with Milkau. Nonetheless, *Canaan*'s dialogue publicized the pseudoscientific theory of mulatto degeneracy, with all its grim implications for Brazil's population. Lentz was a portrait of the arrogant German who believed that the developing regions of the world could prosper only under a regime of strict European control. The Brazilians who read this book must have followed the debate between the two immigrants with considerable uneasiness. Nevertheless, Graça Aranha's treatment coincided with the beliefs of the most distinguished contemporary intellectuals, nearly all of whom praised *Canaan* both as a literary work and as a thoughtful portrayal of an important social problem. Far from contesting Lentz's racist views, prominent reviewers praised Graça Aranha's "honest" portrayal, ignoring the fact that his analysis was actually equivocal.

The success of *Canaan* thus provides insight into the racial attitudes of the Brazilian elite. Graça Aranha's presentation of the whitening ideology, on the one hand, and the determinist theory that relegated Brazil to permanent racial inferiority, on the other, reflected the parallel strands of racial thinking among the elite, who found it easiest to visualize the native-born Brazilian, especially the mestiço, in the terms of literary Romanticism, as an uncertain individual, lost in the vastness of an overwhelming nature. The equivocal nature of Graça Aranha's portrait was thus an accurate indicator of the equivocal feelings of many who were contemplating Brazil's future (Skidmore 1974, 110–13).

Whatever their positions on Brazil's basic dilemma, neither da Cunha nor Graça Aranha found any substance in late nineteenth- and early twentieth-century Neo-Romantic nationalism—*ufanismo*—which extolled Brazil as a multiracial paradise teeming with spectacular waterfalls and sumptuous landscapes (McCann 2003, 96–97; Skidmore 1974, 100–101).[16] This ethos seemed hopelessly naive in the face of harsh reality: the uncultivated land and the illiterate, diseased, superstitious, forgotten mestiços of the interior. Both authors struggled with racist theory. Da Cunha accepted the Native American as a cultural asset but thought the African a liability. Aranha seemed to favor the moderate views of Milkau but included a doctrinaire racist spokesperson in his dialogue in the figure of Lentz. The success of both *The Backlands* and *Canaan* was an indication of Brazilian preoccupations with whether the nation could survive in the face of both settlement by unassimilated superior immigrants and dehumanizing treatment of native-born Brazilians in the interior (Blake 2011, 66–76; Skidmore 1974, 100–101).

Machado's likely disagreement with the tenets of scientific racism and theories of mongrelization and hybrid degeneracy did not prevent him from supporting da Cunha's admission to the Brazilian Academy of Letters in 1903. Nor had Graça Aranha's not having published any books prevent Machado, along with Joaquim Nabuco and Lúcio Mendonça, from inviting him to be one of the forty founding members of the academy. The honor was most likely bestowed on Aranha by virtue of his close friendship with Machado and other Brazilian literati; Machado's vote in favor of da Cunha's admission to the academy was doubtless recognition of the literary merit of *The Backlands* (Gledson 2002, 31n9; Gibson 2006).

Machado did not explicitly concede—as did some late nineteenth- and early twentieth-century Neo-Romantics and early twentieth-century premodernists and Modernists—that the black, mulatto, caboclo or mameluco, and culture of Brazil's interior were representative of the national psyche (*Oc*, 3:804).[17] But he acknowledged that the culture of the interior best preserved national customs (*Oc*, 3:804). And he suggested that Brazil's future lay in the hands not of the predominantly white aristocracy or bourgeoisie but, rather, of the predominantly African Brazilian "proletarian intelligentsia" (*Oc*, 3:964).

Neocolonial and Postcolonial

The absence of explicit expressions of brasilidade tempts critics to characterize Machado's writings as "neocolonial," representing a prolongation of colonialism through other means (Shohat and Stam 1994, 1–54; Tiffin 1990, vii–xvi; Toro 1997, 36–37). Yet to determine whether such a characterization is valid requires a more nuanced analysis of the concepts of neocolonial and postcolonial and how these relate to colonialism.

Colonialism was the process by which European nation-states reached global economic, military, political, and cultural domination over "Others" through conquest, direct control and settlement of their lands, and distant control of their resources (Shohat and Stam 1994, 1–54; Tiffin 1990, vii–xvi). Patrick Williams and Laura Chrisman point out that the dismantling of Western European colonial empires through anticolonial struggles, which began in the late eighteenth and early nineteenth centuries, provided an opportunity for newly independent countries such as Brazil to cast off the shackles of Western colonial domination and exploitation and develop genuine postcolonial societies (Williams and Chrisman 1994, 1–19).

Yet Ella Shohat and Robert Stam contend that since the "post" in "postcolonial" suggests a stage "after" the demise of colonialism, it is imbued with a spatial and temporal, as well as a conceptual, ambiguity. "Postcolonial" is typically associated with developing or Third World countries that gained independence after World War II (Shohat and Stam 1994, 39). Yet it can include processes of liberation originating in all societies affected by colonialism, including areas in North and South America that gained political independence during the late eighteenth and early nineteenth centuries, although, in collapsing diverse chronologies, the term runs the risk of becoming meaningless.

Moreover, by implying that colonialism has ended, the term "postcolonial" fails to reflect the realities of post-independence power relations. Indeed, soon after former colonies gained their independence, it became apparent that the West had relinquished colonial domination and exploitation only to replace these with their neocolonial equivalents as its primary means of control (Shohat and Stam 1994, 1–54; Omi and Winant 1994, 66–69, 84, 115, 148). Shohat and Stam argue that the West maintained its influence in the post-independence era through a complex interweaving of economic, political, military, ideological, and cultural dynamics and power relations—and through selective inclusion and incorporation of opposition as well as interventionist politics (Shohat and Stam 1994, 1–54).

Notwithstanding these ambiguities and contradictions, the term "postcolonial" does indeed apply to Machado's quest for Brazil's cultural and literary independence. On the one hand, Machado challenged the widely held notion that Western European civilization was the "unquestioned and dominant center of the world" (Slater 1994, 88). Yet, on the other, he was also critical of anticolonial nationalism, which in seeking to dismantle the political domination of the colonial powers, spawned a superficial cultural essentialism and fundamentalism. In keeping with Bhabha's conceptualization of postcolonial thought, Machado searched for a radical nationalism that would generate a hybrid or intermediate space, one that would "contest the terms and territories of both" colonialism and anticolonial nationalism (Bhabha 1994, 28, 207–8).

As Joshua Lund and Robert Stam point out, however, Latin American critics have not been particularly receptive to Bhabha's work due in part to his perceived postcolonial appropriation of hybridity (Lund 2006, 47–48). Although Bhabha has been repeatedly "credited" with the concept of hybridity, in fact, this concept and its companions, "mestizaje," "syncretism," and "creolization," were a normative part of Latin American cultural analyses long before hybridity became fashionable in postcolonial studies (Lund 2006, 47–48; Stam 2000, 83, 91; Moehn 2008, 166). Indeed, largely under the rubric of "Modernism," these themes of hybridity were invoked by various cultural and intellectual programs in Latin America during the late nineteenth and the early twentieth centuries (Shohat and Stam 1994, 38–44).

That said, Latin American and postcolonial critics have actively incorporated hybridity both as part of their argument for the active participation in the flow of Western history and as a critique of the Eurocentric discourse that has dominated the West since the colonial era. Robert Young states that the celebration of hybridity counters the colonialist obsession with racial "purity" and hostility toward miscegenation encapsulated in pejorative terms such as "mongrelization" (Young 1995, 5). Renato Rosaldo, like many other critics, defines hybridity "as the ongoing condition of all human cultures, which contain no zones of purity because they undergo continuous processes of transculturation (mutual borrowing and lending between cultures)" (Rosaldo 1995: xi).

Yet hybridity is not inherently transcultural or transracial and therefore also not egalitarian (fig. 1, dynamic a). It is simply integrationist and premised on the deconstruction of dichotomous notions of purity. Shohat and Stam point out that this deconstruction should not obscure the potentially problematic agency of hybridity, which frequently ignores questions of hegemony (Shohat and Stam 1994, 38–44). This creates the illusion of equality and risks downplaying neocolonialism (inegalitarian integration; fig. 1, dynamic b), which effectively maintains forms of exploitation and control that reproduce hierarchies, racial and otherwise, in a new guise. Moreover, hegemonic structures and power relations deflect attention away from continuing patterns of exclusion and isolation (inegalitarian pluralism; fig. 1, dynamic f; Hardt and Negri 2000, 124–32, 143–46; Shohat and Stam 1994, 38–44).

Indeed, Joshua Lund and Rafael Pérez Torres point out that one cannot ignore the historical role of theories and practices of ethnocide, genocide, and rape in the emergence of hybridity's commitment to production and reproduction (Lund 2006, 51; Torres 2006, xii, 7). Moreover, national racial and cultural identities in Brazil and other parts of Latin America have been officially articulated as hybrid, egalitarian, and integrationist (fig. 1, dynamic a). Yet because these official identities have been premised on "hypocritical" rather than "critical" hybridity (Daniel 2005, 264; Lund 2006, 55) or "critical mestizaje" (Sandoval 2000, 72), they have tended to maintain, rather than critique, hierarchy. Hybridity euphemizes whitening and Europeanization through racial and cultural blending, which have perpetuated assimilationist or inegalitarian integrationist ideologies (fig. 1, dynamic b). Latin American nationalist theories and narratives of hybridity have frequently ended up being mere imitations (and poor ones at that) of the colonialist discourses they have supposedly contested.

Silviano Santiago believes that, to avoid these contradictions, Machado's national literary project involved elucidating a "duplicate with a difference" from European discourse: Brazilian writers were to rewrite European themes and reconfigure European forms yet at the same time avoid a neocoloniality that reduced intellectual and cultural production of the periphery to a second-order copy. Rather, Machado affirmed the value of the text of the colonized culture within what Santiago refers to as the "space-in-between" (*o entre-lugar*; Santiago 1978, 28). In Machado's schema, the notions of "original" and "copy" are deconstructed and the symbolic relationship between the center and periphery, colonizer and colonized is altered (Rocha 2005, xxiii, xxxi). They interact in a more intricate manner than the traditional binary and hierarchical opposition of these phenomena allows (Bhabha 1995, 206–12; Paolini 1999, 49–62; Shohat and Stam 1994, 38–44; Tiffin 1990, vii–xvi; Toro 1997, 36). Latin American cultural production is no longer deemed the "blind alley of dependency and incapable of articulating any originality" (Gazzola and Miranda 2000, 3). Furthermore, Santiago contends, this narration on the periphery retroactively has an impact on the text of the metropolis (or center), thus creating the possibility for a creative evaluation of the universality of the texts of the dominant culture (Santiago 1978, 3). Pedro Meira Monteiro argues that Antônio Cândido, Alfredo Bosi, and Roberto Schwarz have each sought to provide insight into cultural production, particularly literature, forged in a peripheral experience, specifically Brazilian. Typically, this culture develops in the shadow of models disseminated from the Northern Hemisphere, especially Europe, sometimes in consonance and sometimes in conflict with the ideals of these models. More broadly, Monteiro argues that the valorization of cultural production in the peripheral or liminal space is an essential part of a broader discussion applicable to all of Latin America (Monteiro 2008, 7).

Intellectuals and artists of Brazil's Modernist movement of the 1920s and 1930s were motivated by similar concerns in formulating the contours of a national culture. Frederick Moehn indicates that they were ambivalent both about imitating the models of "civilized" culture emanating from Europe and about incorporating elements of Native American and African Brazilian cultures, given the disparaging contemporary notions about the "barbarism" of these cultures (Moehn 2008, 171). Modernists sought to resolve this dilemma by exploiting what Roberto DaMatta refers to as the "virtue" of the middle and the "institutionalization of the intermediary" as the characteristic component of Brazilian social life (DaMatta 1990, 16–17; DaMatta in Moehn 2008, 171).

Originating in Modernist writer Oswald de Andrade's essay "Manifesto antropófago" (Cannibalist Manifesto; 1928), the concept of "cultural cannibalism" was another articulation of hybridity that emerged during this period. It was inspired by anthropological tales from the early colonial era about the imputed cannibalism of Native Americans, specifically the Tupinambá (also referred to as "Tupí"), who populated the forests of the State of Rio de Janeiro and who supposedly cannibalized their enemies in order to absorb the latter's strengths. Much like Machado, Andrade called for consuming only select elements of the West's cultural models and advanced technologies in the creation of an innovative, blended national culture that would be in dialogue with and suitable for exportation to the West (Andrade 1928; Moehn 2008, 172; Philippou 2005, 249–50).

None of Machado's works better captures aspects of cultural cannibalism than his short story "Um homem célebre" (A Famous Man), first published in the *Gazeta de Notícias* (*News Gazette*) in 1888 and later republished in Machado's *Various Stories* (1896). "A Famous Man" is set in Rio de Janeiro in 1875; its protagonist Pestana composes polkas, which bring him considerable fame and fortune. Yet Pestana despises his compositions because his true aspiration is to compose classical works along the lines of great Western European masters. Whenever Pestana tries to compose classical pieces, however, he realizes that every composition is a copy of something already authored by someone else. His memory has simply repeated the composition even though he was convinced that he was its originator. The cruel irony of fate dooms poor Pestana to composing polkas, which meet the limited expectations of popular taste. The debilitating effect of doing so leads to a fever and Pestana's demise in 1885.

At an existential or psychological level, "A Famous Man" examines the torment originating in the conflict between individual aspirations and the constraints that frustrate or prevent their fulfillment. At a sociological level, the story presents the dilemma artists must confront between capitulating to capitalist imperatives that force them to pander to fleeting popular tastes for the sake of financial survival rather than create something original and of lasting significance. Yet, José Wisnik argues, Pestana's conflict has a more racially marked subtext. Wisnik considers "A Famous Man"—published a few weeks after the Lei Áurea abolishing slavery in

1888—to be an oblique commentary on the slow and piecemeal process of abolition, as well as on some of the parallel sociocultural and artistic changes not included in the official history of the period (Wisnik 2008, 22–39). To illustrate his point, Wisnik examines the discussion between Pestana and his editor surrounding the best title for his first polka, composed in 1871. When Pestana selects the romantic and poetic title "Pingos de sol" (Sun Drops), his editor recommends instead "Candongas não fazem festa" (Candongas Don't Celebrate) or "A Lei de 28 de Setembro" (The September 28 Law), either of which, the editor insists, would be more popular (Wisnik 2008, 22–39, 58).

Wisnik also contends that Pestana's dilemma reflects the tension between the Europhile culture of the elite and the popular culture of the masses. Originally a Czech peasant dance, the polka was first introduced into the ballrooms of Prague in 1835. Although it became a European salon dance, Wisnik points out that it was a true prototype of a musical form for the masses. According to Idelber Avelar, the polka was introduced in Brazil in 1845 at the São Pedro Theater in Rio de Janeiro, just after the fifteen-year-long interruption of opera performances in the city between 1830 and 1845, when the waltz dominated elite dancing in Brazil. A great wave of polka dancing followed, and in 1846 a Polka Society was formed. Soon the dance replaced the waltz in the preferences of Rio's imperial elite (Avelar 2005, 163–67).

Yet, as African Brazilians began dancing and playing the polka, over time, the dance was transformed by African syncopation, polyrhythm, and total body articulations. Through a process of hybridization, the polka became a precursor of the largely African Brazilian–inflected dance form the maxixe, which derived its name from a cheap vegetable of African origin. Avelar maintains that, unlike the polka, the maxixe was not a ballroom but a street dance, directly and openly evoking the presence and performance of the African Brazilian body (Avelar 2005, 164). Influenced by various other African-derived or -influenced dance rhythms such as the tango, lundu, and habanera, the maxixe is considered one of the dances that contributed to the samba (Wisnik 2008, 22–39).

According to Wisnik, the term "maxixe" appeared as the title of a dance in 1897, although the dance itself may have emerged as early as the 1870s or 1880s (Wisnik 2008, 22–39). Nevertheless, Wisnik believes that the term "polka" was used to encompass not only the polka proper but also what he refers to as "polcas maxixadas" (maxixe-fied polkas; Wisnik 2008, 59), which were on their way to becoming the maxixe in the 1870s, when Machado had Pestana composing. Indeed, the titles of Pestana's compositions (e.g., "Candongas não fazem festa," "Não bula comigo, nhonhô") are clear referents to the African Brazilian vernacular. Avelar indicates that "nhonhô" is the name slaves called their masters, and the verb "bulir" (to play or tease) alludes to the constant sexual advances suffered by female slaves (Avelar 2005, 163–67). "Candonga," possibly of Angolan origin, was said to be the place where slaves sought refuge, typically to rest or recover from injuries they sustained on plantations. It was also the name of an African percussion instrument (Wisnik 2008, 59). Whatever the term's origin, Wisnik maintains that Candonga is an allusion to the post–September 28, 1871, bohemian world, which was far removed from the refined poetic sentiments of Pestana (Wisnik 2008, 22–39). Yet only if readers are familiar with the historical context and the lexicon used in those titles would they be aware of these allusions (Avelar 2005, 163–67).[18]

The significance of these cryptic referents becomes all the more meaningful when we consider that Brazil's elite considered the maxixe licentious, lascivious, and indecent. Indeed, Avelar adds that given the dance's implicit indication of African Brazilians "being active subjects of their own performances," it no doubt aroused considerable anxiety among the elite (Avelar 2005, 164). It should come as no surprise that even the name "maxixe" was taboo throughout the late 1870s and 1880s. The ban on the term led the foremost late nineteenth-century Brazilian pianist, Ernesto Nazareth, to devise a sanitized name, "tango brasileiro" (Brazilian tango), for his compositions that were in fact maxixes (Avelar 2005, 164; Wisnik 2008, 36–37). Initially diffused in the subaltern and bohemian environment of downtown Rio de Janeiro, the maxixe, like the samba, suffered, according to Wisnik, "a process of repression in the stylized and domestic spheres of whites" (Wisnik 2008, 23). Wisnik believes that Machado, well aware of the taboo and elite sensitivities surrounding it, was careful to avoid using the term "maxixe" in the short story (Wisnik 2008, 22–39).

That said, the ban on the maxixe was lifted when the dance was incorporated into the theatrical reviews (*teatro de revistas*) as a spectacle for white audiences (Avelar 2005, 163–67). During the 1920s, it took over the ballrooms of Rio de Janeiro. Micol Seigel points out, however, that the dance had to go through a process of refinement (or "whitening"): its "scandalous, improper choreography" and "lascivious, voluptuous, and undulating hip movements" had to be "tamed" before elite social clubs in Brazil would dance it (Seigel 2009, 73). Eventually, the maxixe traveled to Europe and North America as part of the transnational fascination with Afro-diasporic culture, where the cult of the primitive employed blackness as a tool in rebelling against the artificial restraints of Western morality (Seigel 2009, 67–94).

Wisnik considers "A Famous Man" a high point in the framing of a long-standing dilemma for those seeking to achieve an innovative synthesis of European and Brazilian cultural expression that could be both engaged with and exported to the West. The names of Pestana's compositions allude to the most important development of Brazilian popular music between the 1870s and the 1890s, namely, the process by which the polka was transformed by its encounter with African Brazilian forms. These eventually gave birth to the first distinctively Brazilian urban dance genre, the maxixe. Wisnik argues that Pestana was celebrated for composing a musical form that embodied this synthesis while remaining completely oblivious to this fact. The new hybrid art form that was evolving within the "space-in-between" was merely a torment that interposed itself between Pestana and the classic forms of Europe that he held in such high esteem (Wisnik 2008, 22–39).

Also relevant to analyses of Machado de Assis is Néstor García Canclini's theory of hybridity (1989), which largely echoes Santiago's "space in-between." Because, however, García Canclini fails to explicitly interrogate the potentially problematic agency of hybridity, some critics have concluded that he overlooks the unequal power relations and the ensuing exploitation that the implied conviviality of hybridity can easily obscure (Lund 2006, 32). Although García Canclini does contest the foundational status of European production and Eurocentrism's rigid binarism, he considers binarism and hybridity to be functions of each other, rather than completely antithetical, and views hybridity as a means of deconstructing binarism from within its own terms by destabilizing the categorical basis of the binary (Lund 2006, 33).

While acknowledging that hybridity shares in "mestizaje" and "syncretism," that all such terms can "designate the processes of hybridization" (Garcia Canclini in Lund 2006, 29), García Canclini has sought to distinguish his thinking on hybridity from that on racial and religious blending traditionally understood as "mestizaje" and "syncretism," respectively. He believes that the concept of hybridity encompasses not only racial blending but also the productions of traditional and modern technologies, social processes, and forms of thought (García Canclini 1989, 14–15; Lund 2006, 29). Toward this end, García Canclini calls for decoupling "traditional" and "modern" and other related binaries (urban and rural, elite and popular, and so on). Hybridity not only mediates but also fractures and reframes those binaries (Lund 2006, 29).

Similarly, for Machado, the concern was how to examine and draw social meaning from the juxtaposition of the traditional and modern, rather than simply from the existence of the traditional within the modern (Lund 2006, 31). Machado revealed the interdependence of these phenomena that emerges out of "a history in which modernization rarely operated through the substitution of the traditional" (García Canclini 1989, 72). He sought to render these partially integrated realities by means of what García Canclini refers to as "multitemporal heterogeneity" (García Canclini 1989, 72)—hybrid temporal frameworks that coexist within the same "national-cultural worlds" (Lund 2006, 31). These dynamics required Machado to move beyond Western conceptions of unity, purity, and hierarchy in order to forge a postcolonial national aesthetic that embraced contradictions, multiplicity, and ambiguity (Kraniauskas 2004, 740–58; Mignolo 2004, 276; Polar 2004a, 760–62; 2004b, 116–17; Santiago 1978, 13; Sarto 2004, 153–81; Toro 1997, 36–37; Wolff 1987, 44–45).

As part of the general assault on Eurocentrism, the postcolonial discourse on hybridity emphasizes an egalitarian integrationist perspective that challenges not only notions of cultural purity but also those of racial purity and hierarchy. It both critiques racial hierarchy and interrogates the idea that race is an objective reality absolutely fixed in biological data. Nonetheless, "deconstructive" postcolonial thinkers believe that all categories and identities—racial and otherwise—are largely sociocultural constructs that have no basis is "reality." In extreme cases, they recommend that the concept of race be cast into the dustbin of history. All uphold the belief that race should not determine an individual's social position in terms of wealth, power, privilege, and prestige, and most exponents seek to "transcend race" altogether in pursuit of universal humanism (Daniel 2002, 175–79). Yet this pursuit brings with it the real danger of shunting aside the need to address the social pathologies of white privilege and power (Frank and McPhail 2005, 573).

Indeed, some postcolonial thinkers challenge the notion that race is something we can or should somehow or transcend. These "constructive" postcolonial thinkers view racial formation as fundamental to structuring the social world, despite the contradictions inherent in the concept of race and the illusory and arbitrary nature of biophysical racial groupings and boundaries. They hold that there is a reality to the idea of race, if not race itself. From their perspective, the racialization process divides human bodies into presumed exclusive units and imposes upon them attributes and features that conform to ideological and social values. Racial categories in turn signify and symbolize social conflicts and interests and represent principles by which society allocates rewards and status.

These constructive thinkers acknowledge that the selection of particular human features for purposes of racial signification has changed over time and is always a sociohistorical process (Daniel 2002, 175–79). They consider race to be not only an element of social structure but also a dimension of human cultural representation and signification, a major mode of social differentiation grounded in our historical consciousness and in the structure of society's political, economic, religious, recreational, and other institutions. Constructivists argue that our goals should be to transcend essentialized notions of racial boundaries and categories and to deal more forthrightly with racial inequality. These postcolonial thinkers thus posit "racial transcendence" by acknowledging a more inclusive identity based on a multiplicity of ancestral backgrounds (Daniel 2002, 175–79).

Luís Gama and Lima Barreto have much in common with constructivist postcolonial thinking. They would argue that any notion of "transcending race"—even if it were possible or desirable—would dangerously deny continuing racial inequalities and indeed would be unthinkable until the struggle to achieve equality of racial difference was accomplished. Openly critical of the Brazilian ruling elite's obsession with whiteness and its discrimination against the African Brazilian masses, these authors also pointed out that centuries of miscegenation had imbued Brazilian racial categories and identities with an inescapable ambiguity. They therefore sought to operationalize the concept of hybridity by positing a "racial transcendence" that both acknowledged a more inclusive identity based on Brazil's multiplicity of ancestral and cultural backgrounds and called into question the whole notion of racial privilege (Daniel 2002, 175–79).

Machado's perspective is more akin to deconstructive postcolonial thinking, which seeks to "transcend race" in pursuit of universal humanism. Machado sought to operationalize the concept of hybridity by interrogating hierarchical, as well as essentialist and reductionist notions of categories of difference (and thus implicitly the concept of race and racial categories), thus pointing out the ambiguous, contradictory, and multiplicity of identities that exist within each individual. He went beyond the specificity of racial (and cultural) blending that has been a central tenet in the formation of Latin American national identities and ubiquitous in Latin American culture and thought (Torres 2006, xi). Rather than focusing on epidermal phenomena or parochial concerns, as did some of his contemporaries and those who followed him, in the search for a "mestizo" consciousness (Anzaldúa 1987, 77; Ramirez 1983, 6), Machado mirrored this consciousness by giving artistic expression to hybridity in a manner that encompassed broader contradictions and questions of multiplicity and ambiguity. He became Brazil's and Latin America's most deft and agile practitioner in this undertaking.

EIGHT

THE TRANSFORMATIVE VISION: SEEING WITH THE THIRD EYE

Betwixt and Between: Literature, Liminality, and Borderland Aesthetics

Traditional critics have divided Machado's novels into two distinct periods: a Romantic phase (1872–78) and Realist phase (1881–1908). Machado's earlier novels, *Resurrection, The Hand and the Glove, Helena,* and *Iaiá Garcia,* have been classified as "Romantic," and his later ones, *The Posthumous Memoirs of Brás Cubas, Quincas Borba, Dom Casmurro, Esau and Jacob,* and *Ayres's Memorial,* as "Realist." One of the most insightful studies to track the evolution of Machado's novels and short stories along these lines is Dieter Woll's *Machado de Assis: Die Entwicklung seines erzählerischen Werkes* (*Machado de Assis: The Development of His Narrative Works;* 1972). According to Woll, Machado's earlier prose fiction is characterized by linear narration and conventional romance but avoids falling into the melodramatic excesses of his contemporaries (Woll 1972, 42–53; Moser 1973, 267–69). Beginning, however, with *The Posthumous Memoirs of Brás Cubas,* published first in serialized form in *Revista Brasileira* in 1880 and in book form in 1881, Machado turns to the innovative structure of the psychological novel, which employs digressive and unreliable narration. Moreover, his ironic humor, which coexisted with an underlying optimism about human nature in the first phase, abruptly shifts to bitter sarcasm, absolute pessimism, and disillusionment in the second phase (Moser 1973, 267–69; Woll 1972).

These changes are generally attributed to the crisis in Machado's physical health—severe indigestion, insomnia, and frequent epileptic seizures—that occurred in December 1878. To these physiological stresses, Daniel Piza adds sociopolitical ones relating to the crisis of the Empire, particularly the abolitionist campaign and the emergence of Republican ideology (Piza 2005a, 193–216). Machado was forced to leave Rio de Janeiro to recuperate for three months at a health spa in Nova Friburgo in the mountains near the capital. His vision was in such poor condition that he was unable to read or write for six months, and his wife, Carolina, had both to read to him and to take dictation on numerous occasions. His three-month convalescence was a significant interruption for a writer who, between 1855 and the end of 1878, had to his credit 569 publications, including novels, short stories, plays, poems, criticism, and chronicles. Away from Rio de Janeiro and his work, Machado had time to meditate and process the lessons of 1878 (MacNicoll 1982, 36–37; Machado 1953, 116–17). Returning to Rio in 1879, with much improved health and an aesthetic epiphany, Machado began to compose *Brás Cubas* (some half dozen chapters of which he dictated to Carolina), which was to be a radical departure from his previous work (Caldwell 1970, 31; Kinnear 1976, 64; Pérez 1962, 83–84; Woll 1972, 113–14).

Woll argues that Machado's illness merely hastened the transformation of his worldview and aesthetics, which was already well under way. External developments coupled with an extended process of reflection, which included his negative reaction to the prosaic Naturalist aesthetics of the novels of Portuguese writer Eça de Queiroz (1845–1900), would have led to Machado's transformation quite apart from any epiphany originating in his illness (Moser 1973, 267–69; Woll 1972, 113–14).

Other critics have abandoned the two-phase division in favor of a more unified approach. They argue that there is a linear development in sophistication in Machado's earlier novels, which he refines further in his later novels. Indeed, Woll himself considers *Helena* and *Iaiá Garcia* as harbingers of Machado's shift from more one-dimensional characters to decidedly multidimensional and individualized ones that emerge in the second phase (Woll 1972, 77–80; Moser 1973, 267–69). Yet there is an undeniable difference between the later novels, which are quite innovative, and the earlier novels, which are considerably more in keeping with the literary canons of that time (Schwarz 2004, 15–34; 2006, 816–40). This difference reflects Machado's efforts to blend oppositional forms of consciousness embodied in nineteenth- and early twentieth-century aesthetic subjectivism and aesthetic objectivism. If anything, Machado's earlier novels have less in common with Romanticism and more with what has been called "Romantic Realism," just as his later novels display a greater affinity with was been termed "literary Impressionism" than with Realism-Naturalism (Castello 1969, 58; Fanger 1965, i–x, 3–27; Martins 1966, 83–88; Moisés 1959, 469–79).

Earl Fitz contends that Machado set out deliberately and systematically to transform the European novel (Fitz 2005, 43). In his earlier novels, Machado had already begun experimenting with the subjectivist aesthetics of Romanticism in a more realistic manner than his coevals and with the objectivist aesthetics of Realism in a more restrained fashion than anything that followed (Bagby Júnior 1993, 26–27). Although José de Alencar (particularly in *Lucíola, Diva*, and *Senhora*), and Manuel Antonio de Almeida (*Memoirs of a Police Sergeant*) took a somewhat similar approach in their works, most nineteenth-century Brazilian authors continued writing under the influence of Romanticism, whereas Machado sought to go beyond the stylistic limitations of the Romantic novel (MacNicoll 1982, 32).

Thus the direct, concise narrative of *Iaiá Garcia* is in striking contrast to the verbal, descriptive, emotional, and melodramatic excesses typical of the Romantics (Woll 1972, 42–53). Machado introduces five main characters, most of whom are required to conceal their thoughts and secrets from one another. This inaccessibility is a key element of Machado's technique of characterization in his later novels (MacNicoll 1982, 33). *Iaiá Garcia* also contains glimpses of the morbid irony that would become the hallmark of Machado's second phase, as when the aristocratic widow Valéria sends her only son off to the Paraguayan War rather than have him marry a young woman of lesser social standing. We also find hints of moral ambivalence that would become a staple of Machado's characterology in his later novels (MacNicoll 1982, 33).

Machado's detached treatment of Valéria's death in *Iaiá Garcia* was atypical of Romantic writers (MacNicoll 1982, 33). Furthermore, certain technical devices Machado honed during the 1870s, which would emerge in full force in 1880, are present in *Iaiá Garcia* (1878), albeit in a less developed form. For example, there are short inner monologues, the psychologically penetrating portrait of young Iaiá's sudden coming of age, and the dramatic depiction of dreams. That said, *Iaiá Garcia*'s chronological narration, omniscient narrator, and well-defined plot that leads to a logical, if not a happy ending, were compatible with the aesthetics of Romanticism, which continued to dominate the Brazilian literary scene in the 1870s (MacNicoll 1982, 33).[1]

It should also be pointed out, however, that philosophical materialism, rationalism, positivism, and the literature of Realism-Naturalism were becoming entrenched in Brazil's social, economic, and intellectual milieus while Machado was making the stylistic transformation that culminated in the complex, sophisticated, and innovative literary aesthetic of *Brás Cubas* (1881). The Realist-Naturalist works of both Émile Zola (in their original French) and José Maria Eça de Queiroz were becoming better known in Brazil (Loos 1955, 3–8). In fact, Eça's second major novel, *O primo Basílio* (*Cousin Basílio*; 1878), became a best seller in Brazil in large part because Eça, a passionate devotee of Zola, composed *Cousin Basílio* under the influence of French Naturalism, which was explicit, even clinical in its treatment of sexuality. Previously, the only novels available to Brazilians in Portuguese were late Romantic prose fiction, in which authors rarely even discussed the topic of sexuality; and even then, it was never broached directly. Eça was the first writer in the Portuguese language to break away from the moral restraints of Romanticism (MacNicoll 1982, 34).

The plot in *Cousin Basílio* is fairly straightforward. Luísa, a housewife trapped in a dull marriage with a mundane husband named Jorge, becomes intoxicated with romantic fantasies from reading romance novels and from idle conversations with her friend Leopoldina. In the midst of a suffocating summer when Jorge is away on business, Luísa's wealthy cousin and childhood friend Basílio, with whom she had previously exchanged romantic correspondence, unexpectedly visits her. Basílio has just returned from Paris, a place that further stimulates Luísa's romantic fantasies. Luísa eventually succumbs to Basílio's sexual advances. They rent a hideaway they name "O Paraíso" (The Paradise) and embark on an adulterous affair. The descriptions of the two together in their love nest, though tame by today's standards, were risqué and shocking to Brazilians in the 1870s. A prose fiction writer in the Portuguese language had never depicted adultery so explicitly (MacNicoll 1982, 34).

At this point, Eça introduces an unanticipated development: Luísa's jealous and vengeful domestic Juliana steals the letters Basílio wrote her during the affair and extorts money and other favors from Luísa. Eventually, Juliana stops doing her chores, which Luísa must now perform as if she were the domestic, and begins ordering her around as if Juliana were the mistress. Luísa approaches Basílio for financial assistance to help pay for Juliana's increasingly exorbitant demands and even proposes that they escape to Paris. Having lost interest in his relationship with Luísa, however, Basílio refuses; and, besides, he has no money. Just as Jorge is about to return, Basílio breaks off the love affair in a surprisingly uneventful manner by rushing off to Paris on business.

Given this seemingly hopeless situation, Luísa falls seriously ill, which causes Jorge concern, as does the odd role reversal between her and Juliana. Nevertheless,

Luísa has found a solution to her dilemma through the intervention of Sebastião, one of Jorge's friends, who, with the assistance of a law enforcement acquaintance, succeeds in retrieving Basílio's letters from Juliana by force. Shocked by the unexpected intervention, Juliana suffers a heart attack and dies. Luísa is ecstatic at this turn of events and quickly recovers from her illness. But her happiness is soon to be shattered. Answering a letter she had sent him in France, Basílio writes that he will send her enough money to silence Juliana. Jorge, however, intercepts and reads Basílio's letter. When he asks Luísa for an explanation, she falls seriously ill again, this time with a mysterious fever. Despite Jorge's forgiveness and valiant medical efforts to save her, Luísa eventually dies. Whereupon Jorge abandons his once-happy home and goes to live with Sebastião. Sometime later, Basílio returns to Lisbon and the now-shut house looking for Luísa. When informed that she has died, he turns pale, but responds with a mixture of cynicism and indifference.

Machado was appalled that such a tasteless and one-dimensional novel should garner so much public acclaim. Though he accepted Naturalist aesthetics within limits, he detested its excessive crudeness (Pujol 1934, 100). On April 16 and 30, 1878, writing under the pseudonym "Eleazar," Machado critiqued both the novel and the aesthetics of Realism-Naturalism in a two-part essay, published in O Cruzeiro (*Southern Cross*; Crítica, Oc, 3:903–13). He reproached Eça and the entire Realist-Naturalist movement for overemphasizing minute details with photographic exactitude. Indeed, by providing details ad nauseam, Eça had left little to the reader's imagination. Machado considered Eça's quasi-clinical descriptions to be excessive, tedious, and offensive. Eça had failed to explain why Luísa fell in love with her cousin Basílio, who in fact manipulated her like a lifeless object. Moreover, he had reduced the novel to simple physical attraction and pain and had disregarded any moral or psychological suffering. Luísa showed no sign of morality in her character and displayed no remorse when the affair ended (*Crítica, Oc,* 3:903–13; Faro 1977, 131–34; 162–75; Gledson 1997, xxi; MacNicoll 1982, 34–35; Nunes 1983, 13; Passos 2007, 90–99).

Machado also pointed out the imbalance in Eça's character development. For example, the servant, a secondary character, was the most complete figure in the novel; unlike Luísa's, her motivations were logical and in keeping with her psychological and social situation. With characteristically acerbic humor, Machado concluded that the only moral one could draw from *Cousin Basílio* was that the judicious choice of domestics was crucial to a discreet and successful love affair (*Crítica, Oc,* 3:907; Coleman 1980, 45–48; 124–32; Faro 1977, 131–34; 162–75; MacNicoll 1982, 35).[2]

Murray MacNicoll points out that, even on the eve of writing *Brás Cubas*, Machado remained implacably opposed to Realist-Naturalist aesthetics (MacNicoll 1982, 37). "This literary messianism," Machado inveighed, "has neither force of universality nor vitality; the only thing it contributes is decrepitude" (*Crítica, Oc*, 3:913). Although the deconstruction of Romanticism was a laudable goal, the Realist-Naturalists were simply exchanging one excess for another (Assis in MacNicoll 1982, 37): "This creates nothing new; it merely substitutes one agent of corruption for another" (*Crítica, Oc*, 3:912).

In late 1879, Machado published an even lengthier critique, "A nova geração" (The New Generation; *Crítica, Oc*, 3:809–34), which included an equally strong attack against Brazilian writers he felt had come under the pernicious spell of Realist-Naturalist aesthetics. Having emerged in the Northeast, specifically Recife, Realism-Naturalism had invaded Rio de Janeiro through literary critic and historian Sílvio Romero (1851–1914). The recommendations that Machado presented to Eça, Brazilian writers, and the Brazilian reading public were pivotal to his own aesthetic development and pointed toward a new path he would blaze in *Brás Cubas*, which became the antithesis of a Realist-Naturalist novel (MacNicoll 1982, 31–38). *Brás Cubas* would benefit not only from Machado's own creative insight and considerable technical skills but also from his encounter with the techniques and philosophies of eighteenth-century writers, especially Laurence Sterne.

Brás Cubas incorporates facets of Romanticism that Machado had absorbed during his formative years, along with a portion of carefully tempered Realism and a touch of morbid Naturalism (especially concerning death and physical decay; MacNicoll 1982, 31–38). Machado employs an innovative, "unreliable" first-person—rather than omniscient third-person—narrator. He characterizes through pointillist fragments, propelling the action with a spatialized narration built on psychological, rather than chronological, time. His focus is on the workings of the human consciousness, particularly the processes of perception. He intersperses mordant humor and irony to mitigate the seeming bleakness of the novel's underlying philosophy, which results from his relentless probing of human frailty. The result is a hybrid, highly individualistic novel alien to Brazilian literature, and even to European literature, of the time. Maria Wolff observes that Machado "is universally acknowledged as Brazil's major realist writer; nevertheless, the technical innovations that allow him to present his critical portrait of urban society also remove him from the mainstream of European Realism" (Wolff 1988, 274). Indeed, they antedate similar innovations of twentieth-century luminaries such as Proust, Kafka, Joyce, Mann, and others with whom Machado has a clear affinity (MacNicoll 1982, 31–38; Gledson 1997, xx; Levenson 1991, 57; Mortimer and Kolb 2002, 1–18; Schwarz 2004, 15–34; 2006, 816–40; Venâncio Filho 2000, 101–24).

In a sense, all five novels of Machado's second phase may be considered an assault on the then-dominant Realist-Naturalist paradigm (MacNicoll 1982, 31–38). Indeed, 1881 was not only the year Machado published *Brás Cubas* but also the year in which Aluísio Azevedo published *The Mulatto* (1881), which both critics and the public considered the first Brazilian Realist-Naturalist novel. It is interesting that Azevedo's novel does not appear in Machado's literary criticism, a lacuna all the more remarkable considering that Machado had been engaged in an open and at times acrimonious debate over the merits of the Realism-Naturalism. He had criticized not only Zola, the originator of the movement and his Portuguese disciple, Eça de Queiroz, but also other Brazilian authors who had fallen prey to their misguided aesthetics. Yet, given the polemic that crystallized around *The Mulatto*, its controversial subject matter, racial and otherwise, and Machado's own recommendations in such matters, it is not surprising that he would have passed over it in silence.

At the time of its publication, *The Mulatto* received far greater attention, and enjoyed far greater popularity, than *Brás Cubas*, both because of its scandalous subject matter (interracial marriage) and indictment of the Church and because it contained many elements of Romanticism (e.g., *costumismo* and melodramatic sentimentality)[3] that were a familiar part of the nineteenth-century Brazilian literary diet. Thus the Brazilian palate was better prepared for Azevedo's sentimental scandal than for Machado's literary innovation. *Brás Cubas*, with its veiled metaliterary probing of the human psyche, went largely unnoticed (Kinnear 1976, 55; Pereira 1957, 53–55; Sodré 1965, 174–80).

Machado's rejection of the representational framework of Realism-Naturalism and his probing investigation of the human psyche are important developments in the history of the Brazilian novel. Indeed, rather than having originated in a Eurocentric aesthetic as some have argued, they represented the first major attempt to wean cultivated Brazilian readers—and authors—away from both Western European Romanticism and Realism-Naturalism. Machado felt that each of these, as absolutes, was inappropriate to the formation of Brazilian literature and that they were equally detrimental to the terrain of art itself (Almino 2005, 141; Barreto Filho 1947, 78–79; Castello 1969, 33–36; Fitz 1989, 11–12; 2005, 50, 55; Hodgson 1976, 29; Kinnear 1976, 62; Nunes 1983, 13, 143; Santos 2005, 110).[4] "Let us look reality in the face," Machado wrote, but let us put Realism[-Naturalism] aside, so that we do not sacrifice aesthetic truths.... Realism ... totally negates the principles of art.... There is an untranscendable boundary between reality according to the canons of art, and reality according to nature.... If the mission of art were copying the facts, exactly the way they are in real life, then art would be useless; memory would be substituted for imagination.... If an exact copying of things were the ultimate goal of art, then indeed the best novel or play would be the shorthand reproduction from a court trial.... I do not, however, suggest that we cultivate a stuffy and decadent Romanticism either ... for, on the contrary, there is something of value in Realism that can be utilized to the advantage of our artistic and creative imagination. However, to free oneself from the excesses of one by falling into the excesses of the other is to transform nothing. (*Crítica, Oc,* 3:813, 912, 913)

Machado opposed the compulsive subservience of Brazilian authors to the authoritarian, heavy-handed, didactic, and humorless models of Realism-Naturalism as practiced by Zola and Eça, as well as the worn-out clichés of Romantic melodrama and *costumismo* imported from Europe. Machado's larger, metaphoric view of the mulatto experience was reflected in his exploration of liminality, ambiguity, and the dialectic between subject and object. Baptista argues that Machado's writings question the premises of mimesis, the possibility of representation, and even the existence of a meaningful objective reality. Baptista therefore believes that the term "Realist" is not an accurate description of Machado's aesthetics (Baptista 2003a, 396–400). On the other hand, John Gledson argues that, even though Machado's unreliable narrator, emphasis on memory, time, and ambiguity, discontinuous structure, and seemingly irrelevant narrative digressions have parallels in some twentieth-century anti-Realist fiction, they do not make Machado an anti-Realist (Gledson 1999, 12, 15). "Rather," Gledson explains, "they are part of Machado's continuous experiment to extend Realism's boundaries and capacities" (Gledson 1999, 15).

Machado's writings reflect an increasing sophistication in handling both the subjectivist aesthetics of Romanticism and the objectivist aesthetics of Realism-Naturalism. Although the novels Machado wrote before 1881 have more in common with Romantic Realism, unsatisfied with its limitations, he became more daring in his experiments with Romanticism and Realism in his later novels. Critics such as Afrânio Coutinho, Dirce Riedel, José Merquior, and Earl Fitz have suggested that Machado's later work has less of an affinity with unmitigated

Realism-Naturalism and more with the techniques of literary Impressionism. Indeed, Fitz believes that Machado provides "the 'missing link' between Flaubert and Proust . . . the writer whose best work presents us with the most profound and imaginative transition we have in the Western tradition from Realism to Modernism" (Fitz 2005, 44). Having shown striking similarities between Machado's later short stories, with their more concentrated, practically immobilized narration, and those of Anton Chekhov, whose writings are considered representative of Impressionist aesthetics, Woll concludes that Machado is actually more modern as a short story writer than as a novelist (Woll 1972, 149).

Romantic Realism and Impressionism: Bridging the Aesthetic Divide

Before examining specific aspects of Machado's novels that demonstrate his affinity with the techniques of Romantic Realism and Impressionism, it would useful to briefly analyze these currents within the context of nineteenth- and early twentieth-century aesthetics. Romantic Realist and Impressionist aesthetics were affected by the rise of subjectivism and Romanticism and by a belief in the inherent creative fertility and independence of the mind—"the Within" (Teilhard de Chardin 1955, 56)—that characterized the ideational culture of the first half of the nineteenth century. They were also influenced by objectivism and Realism-Naturalism—"the Without" (Teilhard de Chardin 1955, 56)—the truths and values of the reality external to consciousness, embodied at midcentury in sensate culture, which reached its apex in Naturalism in the latter half of the century. Impressionist aesthetics were affected by objectivism and Realism-Naturalism, which were followed by the neo-subjectivism of the late nineteenth and the early twentieth centuries (Wagar 1977, 53–62, 95–104, 135–43; Williams 1958, 30–48, 130–57). Influenced by an ideational cultural revival, the aesthetic embodiments of this new subjectivism, most notably the movements of Symbolism, Neo-Romanticism, and Expressionism, were even more daring than Romanticism in their exploration of "the Within," with its balletic flights and leaps of imagination beyond all matter, beyond even the speed of light (Barzun 1961, 96–114; Fleming 1974, 313–94; Hobsbawm 1962, 299–326; 1975, 307–36; Sorokin 1957, 103–283; Stromberg 1975, 197–245; Baumer 1977, 258–494; Fasel 1974; Mosse 1974, 1–10).

Caught in the midst of these endless changes, but sensitive to the "double aspect" of the universe—that, in the words of Pierre Teilhard de Chardin, "coextensive with the Without, there is a Within to things" (Teilhard de Chardin

1955, 56)—Romantic Realist and Impressionist prose fiction writers were embodiments of Pitirim Sorokin's "mixed (or blended) modalities" and sought to play both ends by embracing the middle. Romantic Realists adopted a hybrid literary style sometimes called "poetic" or "reluctant realism."[5] Continuing the Romantic Realist vision, but unsatisfied with its limitations, many authors in the late nineteenth century expressed their critique of unmitigated Realism-Naturalism through the hybrid techniques of Impressionism (Coelho 1974, 227; Fischer 1963, 71–75; Hauser 1951, 4:166–225; Heiney 1954, 243–75; Johnson 1973, 274; Kelley 1973, 252; Kronegger 1973, 32; Matz 2001, 1–45; Nagel 1980, 1–35).[6]

Heirs to the subjectivist and ideational aesthetics that reigned during the first half of the nineteenth century, Romantic Realists represent a blended sociocultural mode that sought to bring some balance into an altogether unbalanced world, as did the heirs to the objectivist and sensate aesthetics that became dominant beginning at midcentury, the Impressionists. Romantic Realists and Impressionists spurned the sensate mode's aesthetic objectivism and the ideational mode's aesthetic subjectivism as being only partial truths. Instead, they sought to combine both to achieve a more integrated whole. Sensitive to the "double aspect" of the universe during a period of transition, they stood out as bold representatives of a fleeting moment whose influence nevertheless remains to help us articulate our deepest notions about the inherent possibilities of human nature. However different they may appear to be in superficial aspects, these writers are for the most part what José Argüelles calls "transformative visionaries" (Argüelles 1975, 15).

Romantic Realism

Some novelists traditionally classified as "Romantics," such as Victor Hugo (1802–1885), had their realistic moments. Others traditionally classified as "Realist-Naturalists," such as Gustave Flaubert (1821–80) and Émile Zola (1840–1902), showed lingering traces of Romanticism, and even an affinity with Romantic Realists. Hugo, however, is a case in point where the balance is tipped more in the direction of Romantic than Realist; his works leave us with a stronger sense of the Within—the subjectivist aesthetics of Romanticism. On the other hand, Zola is unquestionably an apostle of the objectivist aesthetics of Naturalism. For his part, Flaubert was a "passionate Romantic" who ventured into Realism, becoming a "reformed idealist" and an advocate of the impersonal in art. His willed triumph over an inherent Romanticism in Madame Bovary and over the genteel Realism of William Thackeray (1811–63) in *L'éducation sentimentale* (*Sentimental Education*;

1869) represented the new aesthetics of Realism that drew upon the previous Romanticism only to challenge it (Fanger 1967, 242; Levine 1981, 137, 138, 140, 182). Thus the works of authors like Flaubert and Zola leave us with a stronger sense of the Without.

Romantics sought to maximize the Within in their novels at the expense of the Without, whereas Realist-Naturalists sought to maximize the Without in their novels at the expense of the Within. And Romantic Realists, at least in theory, sought to retain the relative importance of both while rejecting the absolute validity of either. As an amalgam of subjectivism and objectivism, they were "reluctant" Realist-Naturalists who brought elements of myth and imagination to their novels. They present us with what Charles Dickens called "the poetry of fact" or what Fyodor Dostoyevsky called "realism in a higher sense" (Dickens, Dostoyevsky in Fanger 1967, 65, 215), something that was less typical of the more prosaic and objectivist aesthetics of Realism-Naturalism (Auerbach 1953, 468–73; Becker 1980, 102–3; Bogart 1968, 269–70; Bosco 1959, 212–13; Brantlinger 1976, 18–25, 29–44; Carpeaux 1962, 4:1900, 1978, 1982, 1997, 1999–2007).[7]

NARRATIVE STRUCTURE AND POINT OF VIEW   Romantic Realists, above all else, sought to present sensory reality from a metaliterary perspective. Using the conversant and familiar style of the journalistic feuilleton to comment in a highly personal fashion on current goings-on, they sought to capture socioeconomic, political, intellectual, and cultural life in the nineteenth century—particularly the new urban setting—in its truth and familiarity as well as in its strangeness (Fanger 1967, 64; Hodgson 1976, 18, 29). This technique allowed them to achieve a multidimensional and complex narrative where the line between events taking place within and without the narration is blurred. It is for this reason that Romantic Realist novels are at once re-creations of specific times and places in history, and personal accounts that so often radiate a glow of subjective intensity absent from Realist-Naturalist novels (Fanger 1967, 40, 66).

Unlike the fact-bound Realist-Naturalists, Romantic Realists were interested in empirical details only as a means of achieving a higher dimension beyond spatiotemporal limitations. They imbued facts, characters, and events with a broader symbolic meaning and importance, revealing through the sensory world a "transcendent sphere of causes and effects" (Fanger 1967, 29). Romantic Realists found the magical empiricism of everyday reality to be constantly "outstripping the imagination of inventors," its boldness "rising to combinations so implausible or indecent as to be forbidden within the terrain of art unless the author trimmed them down"—or edited them out altogether (Fanger 1967, 13).

Readers are led not to view life from a consensual perspective, but rather to take part in the carnivalesque vision of a supersensory truth "as far above common sense as it is above common illusion" (Fanger 1967, 63). For Romantic Realists, everyday reality is a maze of subterranean marvels and full of unseen predators and dangers. It is a forest or jungle in its own right, whose inhabitants are linked by plot structures full of "strange coincidences," "plannings," "cross-purposes," and "wonderful chains of events" (Fanger 1967, 23, 25, 63). The comic and the tragic are constantly spilling over into each other, and the melodramatic is constantly verging on the trivial and the mundane (Fanger 1967, 115).

In their desire for subjective truths and values—that is, reality seen from within—Romantics typically used first-person narration, often in the form of diaries, letters, and the like; Realists, in their desire to faithfully report external reality and its facts, typically used third-person omniscient narration. Romantic Realists variously used both, most often combining first-person with third-person detached narration to produce double or suspended narration. Moreover, they used the conventions of drama to narrate as much as possible with no narrator present (showing) while at the same time exploiting the possibilities of narrative exposition and analysis (telling) through the "choral narrator" (Fanger 1967, 19, 34, 40, 42). Remaining outside the novel's events, the narrator—whether authorial or choral—was always guiding readers, manipulating the atmosphere, and periodically interpreting events, or conversing with and interrogating readers in the form of a depersonalized "I," whether in "exposition" or in "interstitial comment" (Fanger 1967, 66). Romantic Realist narrators were not only omniscient or semi-omniscient; they were also prescient. Such narrators allowed Romantic Realist authors both to present characters with maximum theatricality—that is, in dialogue independent of authorial comment—and to bring a correspondingly greater intensity and personality to their narrators when they did make their presence known.

SETTING AND CHARACTERIZATION   The Romantics sought to capture the poetry of nature or the exotic, preferring for their tableaux the countryside with its picturesque landscapes or the jungle with its lush vegetation. They considered the rationalized restraints, familiarity, and routine aspects of everyday reality generally unsuitable material for the arts. In contrast, Romantic Realists, like Realist-Naturalists, often found inspiration in everyday reality, particularly that of the city (Fanger 1967, 6, 21–22; Stowell 1980, 8–9). To capture contemporary life, they tended to include extensive external details about history and locale (Fanger 1967, 64; Hodgson 1976, 18, 29).

The nineteenth-century city was an important setting of Romantic Realist novels, although authors differed in terms of how they rendered the urban ambiance. Thus Charles Dickens and Honoré de Balzac personified or mythologized London or Paris with a panoramic catalogue of place-names, external descriptions, national history, and topography (Lowe 1982, 87, 89; Pereira 1959, 59–60), whereas Nikolai Gogol used the life of the city to create a new psychological universe that stood in "grotesque relation" to the real city (Fanger 1967, 120). Gogol portrayed a city of the mind, superimposing it on the map and mores of St. Petersburg. He presented the city less as an object seen through subjective eyes, or even as a personified object radiating a subjective glow, than as an elusive atmosphere (Lowe 1982, 87, 89; Pereira 1959, 59–60). And he integrated this atmosphere and the social behavior of the era into the narrative through the reactions of his characters, depicted in kaleidoscopic glimpses, which, in composite, brought to life a St. Petersburg that was both historical and temporal, but that remained outside time.

The psychological matrix of the characters in the fictional world of Romantic Realism is dominated by the principle of contrast and the tension created by the clash of opposites. Yet Romantic Realists shared the Realists' interest in examining ethical conflicts of characters in a given socioeconomic, political, intellectual, or cultural context. Their characters are free to choose from among alternatives presented to them. Romantic Realists rejected the Romantic dictum that characters could be divided into those who were morally good and those who were morally evil (Fanger 1967, 17–18). Their main characters are individuals of conflicting sentiments who present themselves in various shades of gray (Fanger 1967, 17–18). And though they have some qualities in common with the flat, two-dimensional characters associated with Romanticism—characters who in their purest form are archetypes, symbols, or caricatures constructed around a single idea expressed in a simple sentence—yet they also possess the qualities of the round, three-dimensional characters associated with Realism. They maintain a feeling of depth, of being fully developed personalities. They respond to their surroundings and change as they interact with them, thus appearing to be individuals drawn from real life, leading independent lives.

Impressionism

Some Realist-Naturalist novelists retained Romantic traits without becoming Romantic Realists. Likewise, some Symbolist, Neo-Romantic, or Expressionist novelists retained Realist-Naturalist traits or had "impressionistic moments."[8] What distinguishes literary Impressionists in the strictest sense from these authors is their seeking to retain the relative identity of both the Within and the Without while denying the absolute validity of either. Impressionists broke with the omniscient objectivity of Realism-Naturalism, on the one hand, and with the transcendent subjectivity of Neo-Romanticism, Symbolism, and Expressionism, on the other, to forge what Peter Stowell calls "subjective objectivism" (Stowell 1980, 4).

It is true that Symbolism and Impressionism affected each other in literature, painting, music, and the plastic arts. Thus the Symbolist novel was "impressionistic" in its optical, acoustic, and other sensory effects. The fact remains, however, that the Symbolist novel and, by extension, the Neo-Romantic and Expressionist novel were predominantly subjective, that is, transcendental, pararational, idealistic, or spiritual in approach, in sharp reaction against both Realism and Impressionism (Brumm 1958, 330–41; Freedman 1967, 135–43; Hauser 1951, 4:193–94; Matz 2001, 45–52; Moser 1952, 220, 276–77; Stephen 1972, 299–311; Uitti 1961, 37).

For its part, Impressionism viewed sense data as final and irreducible, regardless of how delicate its motifs may have been (Bradbury and McFarlane 1976, 192–205; Friedman 1976, 453–66; Scott 1976, 206–27; Stowell 1980, 9; Weisstein 1973, 15–28; Wellek 1982, 15–28). Whereas Symbolists and Neo-Romantics saw sensate reality as an elaborate, convoluted maze that was nonetheless often a sublimated world of the senses, Impressionists maintained a closer tie to the Realist-Naturalists' preoccupation with sensation than did their neo-subjectivist comrades (Ashton 1982, 519–27; Brody 1982, 483–92; Jullian 1982, 529–46; Moser 1952, 220, 276–77; Roditi 1982, 499–518; Schneider 1982, 471–81; Stephen 1972, 299–311; Vajda 1982, 29–41).

In the beginning, Impressionism, representing the apex and decline of the nineteenth-century Realist-Naturalist tradition, much as Romantic Realism represented the apex and decline of Romanticism, was hardly distinguishable within the total complex of Realism (consider the works of Edmund and Jules de Goncourt, for example). Yet, influenced by the new subjectivism, the Impressionists were more interested than their predecessors in the confluence of sensation with the secondary interpretation of feeling and intuition (Berg 1992, 29–60; Berrong 2006, 203–28; Bradbury and McFarlane 1976, 166, 174; Caramschi 1971, 287; Gibbs 1952, 180; Hauser 1951, 4:166; Leriche 2002, 192; Matz 2001, 11–15, 16, 45–52).[9]

Whereas the Realist-Naturalists presumed the existence of a harmonious relationship between external reality, sensory perception, and conceptualization,

Impressionists assumed that the relationship was more discordant, precipitated by factors that distorted sensory signals both within external reality (e.g., distance, fog, obscure sounds, light, darkness, obstructions, rain, smoke) and within the sensory mechanism or the perceiving interpretive intelligence (e.g., fears, dreams, fantasies, preoccupations; Berg 1992, 29–60; Berrong 2006, 203–28; Katz 2000, 13; Levenson 1991, 57; Matz 2001, 11–15, 16; Nagel 1980, 22; Peters 2001, 7–34). Nevertheless, they stopped short of accepting the subconscious, often mythical frameworks found in Symbolist, Neo-Romantic, and Expressionist novels. Instead, they relied on an explanation of reality grasped through sensory experience, interpreted by intellect, but more likely distorted by feelings, projections, or delusions. Realism depended on a one-to-one correlation between interpretation and perception. Impressionism suggested that this correspondence was always uncertain. This relates to the notion that any presentation of reality depends not only on how clearly it is perceived, but also on the fact that reality itself is ephemeral and constantly shifting—that it defies precise definition. In Impressionist fiction, characters are in a constant state of flux. They must continually interpret the objective world and distinguish the "real" from their own subjective views of it, yet they never fully comprehend their surroundings or themselves (Berg 1992, 29–60; Berrong 2006, 203–28; Katz 2000, 13; Levenson 1991, 57; Matz 2001, 11–15, 16; Moser 1952, 135; Nagel 1980, 22, 30; Peters 2001, 7–34).

Nonetheless, Impressionism in literature, unlike Impressionism in painting and music, broke away early on from the Realist tradition. Almost from its beginning, literary Impressionism was sympathetic to the reaction that would soon make itself felt in neo-subjectivist literary trends, but that would find expression in painting only after the dissolution of Impressionism in that art form (Daniel 1981, 9–10; Hauser 1951, 4:177; Matz 2001, 45–52). Impressionism in painting and music, while attempting to separate as much as possible the subjective workings of the conscious from the objective process of sensation, were essentially a continuation of photographic realism in painting and programmatic and descriptive realism in music: they sought a perpetuation of objectivist aims—optical realism in painting and acoustical realism in music (Berg 1992, 29–60; Frank 1952, 135–51; Jarocinski 1970, 90–107; Matz 2001, 45–52; Moser 1952, 220, 276–77; Palmer 1973, 19).

Yet the rise of Impressionism in the visual arts was also a reaction by painters to the newly established medium of photography, which produced lifelike still images. Initially photography's presence seemed to undermine the artist's ability to mirror objective reality. Photography inspired painters to pursue other means of artistic expression and, rather than compete with photography's ability to emulate reality, to focus on the one thing they could do better than photography, "by further developing into art form ... the very subjectivity that photography eliminated" (Levinson 1997, 47).

By contrast, literary Impressionism, through its partial alliance with neo-subjectivist trends, sought from the start to dissolve the distinction between subject and object—without, however, falling into the solipsism and intricate connotative language of Postimpressionism and without regressing to the denotative, sensory, or photographic reproduction of external reality. Instead, it focused on how the external reality beyond the eye, ear, or any other sense organ was influenced by the mind through which it was filtered. Objective reality was only relative, limited by the framework of our own subjective vantage points. Because literary Impressionism was descended from subjectivism, and thus closely related to Symbolism, Neo-Romanticism, and Expressionism, it and these movements helped dethrone the belief in an objective and external reality that existed apart from the perceiving subject. They shattered the objectivists' mirrorlike view of reality into myriad pieces, where each piece, while reflecting the objective whole, simultaneously had its own subjective and valid perspective.

Sharing a sensitivity to the Within, literary Impressionists, Symbolists, Neo-Romantics, and Expressionists all expressed a deep interest in the workings of the consciousness. Some authors were influenced by the psychological theories of the time (Freudian, Jungian, and Adlerian); others were opposed to them, while still others ignored them entirely. Many were interested in the unusual and demonstrated a certain flamboyance or ingenuity of language, a penchant for the fantastic, heroic, or superhuman in the human character. Some, especially the Symbolists, sought unabashedly to escape into a pararational world of dream; others, especially the Neo-Romantics, were attracted to geographical or historical escapism and exoticism. For the most extreme of them—the Expressionists—the dream atmosphere borders on the surreal, as if in a nightmare, though at least theoretically still set in the waking world. Everything is distorted, heightened, and the elements of conflict are presented in their bare essentials rather than encumbered with detail. Some Expressionists were strongly influenced by a religiosity and spiritualism that smacked of a desperate mysticism, whereas others clung to Catholicism. Still others, perceiving the fleeting validity of any religious or metaphysical absolutes, fell into a relativism bordering on the absurd, where the only truths and values were those of the individual and the only happiness that of the moment (Heiney 1954, 158–59).

Thus Impressionism, Symbolism, Neo-Romanticism, and Expressionism each in its own way attempted to maintain the validity of psychological reality in a fundamentally sensate-dominated world. As representatives in various degrees of a declining sensate cultural mode and a rising ideational one, and despite disagreement about many basic points, these movements were essentially unified in their purpose: to present human motivation more from the inside, from the point of view of the particular consciousness concerned, rather than from the perspective of an external observer. In its later forms of development, Impressionism was absorbed into the mainstream of the neo-subjectivist trends (e.g., Virginia Woolf, James Joyce; Coutinho 1976, 243; Scott 1976, 224), a process furthered by the fact that only the most radical Expressionists completely repudiated the sensate-rational world of the Realist-Naturalists.

What we find instead is a gradual shift of emphasis away from the predominantly sensate mode (the Without) and toward the ideational mode (the Within). Among the Impressionists, the Within and the Without combined in relatively equal proportions. First the Symbolists and Expressionists and later the Surrealists shifted their emphasis increasingly in favor of the Within, without, however, totally negating the sensate world, although their grasp on that world was indeed at times so tenuous as to appear almost nonexistent. Indeed, for all of their affinity with the Impressionists' dialectical vision, most of the neo-subjectivist trends, particularly Expressionism, took the novel into a radical and unprecedented interiorization that made Impressionism seem rather tame.

NARRATIVE STRUCTURE AND POINT OF VIEW   Impressionism, like Realism-Naturalism, required authors to disengage their consciousness from the text. Nearly all Impressionist narratives are presented from one or several points of view, one or several "restrictive central intelligences" (i.e., a parallax or prismatic narration). The points of view in Impressionist novels have less access to information derived from sources beyond empirical data than do the omniscient narrators in Realism-Naturalism (Nagel 1980, 24, 25, 27, 34). This consciousness serves as a channel through which the interpretation and, by extension, the turn of objective events are projected within the text (Nagel 1980, 25). Showing predominates, either indirectly through the continuous self-evocation of narrators (who are also characters in first-person narrations) or directly through the dramatically presented action, dialogue, interior monologue, dreams, daydreams, deliriums, or hallucinations of the characters.

Influenced by the experimental techniques of the new subjectivism of the late nineteenth and the early twentieth centuries, Impressionists abandoned the linear narrative that, for the most part, had been preserved by Romantic Realists and Realist-Naturalists. Impressionists replaced that structure with one more representative of the processes of consciousness itself. Structure became more important than effect; plot and action gave way to internal states, moods, and reactions of the characters (Heiney 1954, 243–44). Time became spatialized such that the normal causal relationship between beginning, middle, and end was altered through juxtaposition, fusion, reversal, or jumbling (Spencer 1971, 155–59). This brought to the narration a quality of being hauntingly stranded between beginning and ending, between being and becoming, without ever having been (Stowell 1980, 19, 20, 34–43). Naturalism and, to some extent, Realism, tended to build with sequential clarity and broader social significance (particularly Naturalism). Impressionism consisted of fragmentary episodic narrative units of discontinuous awareness that achieved unity through continuity of theme, scene, character, and association (Nagel 1980, 30, 35, 166).

SETTING AND CHARACTERIZATION   Due to its psychological focus, Impressionist fiction is neither dependent on nor restricted to an external spatiotemporal setting. Its emphasis is more on action within the boundless terrain of consciousness. Impressionists have little concern with details of external reality and setting, which they usually present in a fragmented, pointillist manner, with frequent use of synecdoche. Everything appears to be weightless, lacking in form, structure, or definition. Images of haze and rain, blurred outlines and half-dissolving shapes are transformed by atmosphere, moods, and memories. The consciousness that permeates the text at one and the same time plays over shapes and objects in the external environment, characters, dialogue, and gestures, such that they appear to be ingredients of the same atmosphere (Kronegger 1973, 47–48; Nagel 1980, 8, 10, 12, 29; Stowell 1980, 18, 20, 26, 39).

The traditional techniques of presenting characters as either solid figures or two-dimensional contours were for the most part preserved by Romantic Realists. With Impressionism, both the setting and characters are shattered into fragments. Characterization, like setting, is no longer achieved by means of reporting, but through rendering, that is, cumulatively by means of quick, significant pointillist fragments. Characters are evoked through dialogue and, in particular, interior monologue. These techniques bring readers into firsthand and immediate contact with characters' unvoiced thoughts and feelings, without the intervention of a narrator. Other devices of characterization include dreams, hallucinations, stream of consciousness, and altered states of consciousness (Nagel 1980, 12, 38, 53, 113, 116–24; Stowell 1980, 20, 23).

Impressionist fiction generally focuses on the truth-illusion theme, which depends on a character's ability to perceive, interpret, and communicate reality (Nagel 1980, 23; Kronegger 1973, 16). Reality itself constitutes a synthesis of pure sensation, filtered through consciousness and changed into impressions (Nagel 1980, 30; Kronegger 1973, 17). At worst, characters are full of uncertainty and delusions or experience a diminution in stature (Nagel 1980, 30). Throughout an entire novel, they may live in an illusionary world, unable to perceive reality accurately. They may receive restricted, distorted, disordered, or ambiguous information from the external world and constantly be limited to inconclusive judgments, or they may reason quite logically from unreliable and incomplete data and reach inaccurate conclusions (Nagel 1980, 23). This creates characters that are isolated psychologically from one another, who are uncertain of reality, and unable to communicate verbally what they experience within (Nagel 1980, 23; Stowell 1980, 28–29). Their awareness of the empirical limitations of their experiences often pushes them to the point of despair or crisis if they are forced to make ethical choices based on the data of their experience. At best, Impressionist characters may piece together fragments of information and experience that ultimately come together in a sudden moment of insight, or what Joyce called an "epiphany," which gives rise to some type of personal transformation or a new awareness (Nagel 1980, 23).

Although Impressionism shares with Realism-Naturalism an interest in sensate reality and a focus on the everyday, there are important differences within these shared traits. The basic premise of Realism is that external reality is known and quantifiable. Determining what is real is not as important as determining what to do about reality. Realism's primary emphasis is on ethical crises. Meanwhile, Impressionist themes and techniques are derived from the ambiguity of perceived reality and thus focus on attempting to define and understand it. Though ethical matters are not necessarily excluded from Impressionism, moral crises are not often used as a climax because protagonists do not yet understand reality enough to be able to decide which of a variety of choices they should make (Nagel 1980, 34). Realism, on the other hand, progresses from character definition to ethical conflict. Authors seek to capture a "photographic morality" in which the character's choice serves as the climax and denouement (Nagel 1980, 35, 167; Passos 2007, 87).

Although Realist characters have the free will to choose from among available choices, and thus assume full moral responsibility for their actions, Naturalism's deterministic framework precludes the possibility of moral choices (Nagel 1980, 31). The determinism may be biological, environmental, or both. When the deterministic force is biological, depraved, aberrant, and monomaniacal, characters are propelled by uncontrollable drives, which links their behavior to nonhuman nature as well as to humanity's hereditary past, where instinct dominates motives that are more volitional. When the deterministic force is environmental, most often social and economic, the emphasis is generally on the underclasses and their struggle to survive in a hostile society. Whether the deterministic force is biological or environmental, the plot usually winds down with linear and unwavering seriousness toward an inevitably tragic end (Hulet 1974, 2:2; Nagel 1980, 31, 165). Because Naturalist characters function primarily as representatives of social and economic groups, the ethical choices and individualization facilitated by Realist techniques are ruled out. Though Realist characters may also be representative of social aggregates, most are individuals confronting unique crises of intense moments abstracted from the universality of human experience.

The leveling effect of Naturalism, which focuses on the commonality of a character in relationship to individuals of the same group, both permits and calls for greater use of static characters who remain unchanged throughout an entire work (Nagel 1980, 32, 34, 118, 166). They are portrayed as being insignificant without being aware of that fact. They realize little beyond the abject misery inflicted on them without apparent meaning or justification. The stress is on their hopelessness and the futility of their reactions to unbearable circumstances (Nagel 1980, 102, 105). In Impressionist works, because perceptions vary from individual to individual, reality reveals only bits and pieces of its total complexity, making human knowledge inadequate to deal with world problems. The emphasis is not merely on individual insignificance, but also on how myriad tunnels of vision perpetuate a sense of isolation and alienation (Berg 1992, 29–60; Katz 2000, 13; Kronegger 1973, 46; Levenson 1991, 57; Nagel 1980, 102, 105).

Although Impressionist characters feel insignificant, they frequently achieve moments of deep and sensitive reflection and personal transformation that in and of themselves refute their lack of importance (Nagel 1980, 102). Whereas Naturalism would probably treat this feeling of insignificance tragically, Impressionism presents it ironically. Though compatible with Impressionism, where the emphasis is on the problematic relationship between truth and illusion, or Realism, where individual will plays a more important role than either chance or fate, the use of irony runs contrary to the logic of Naturalism, where the emphasis is on immutable biological or environmental forces(Nagel 1980, 165–69).

There is generally some disparity at the core of Realist and Impressionist fiction. In Realism, a character may make a fatally wrong choice in resolving an ethical conflict. In Impressionism, some perceptual distortion or misinterpretation generally provides the narrative with an ironic thrust beyond the mere structure of events. Frequently, the source of irony is self-inflation. Deflation forces characters to confront reality in Impressionism, or the consequences of their ethical choices in Realism, however uncomfortable, and may help them to better deal with the world. In Naturalism, biological or environmental forces are so overwhelming as to result in characters that are completely deflated and defenseless (Nagel 1980, 165–69).

Because the portrayal of biological or environmental forces beyond the control and comprehension of individuals cannot be rendered easily in terms of their consciousness, Realism-Naturalism tends to use an omniscient point of view, though Realism generally eschews the unlimited omniscience of Naturalism (Nagel 1980, 32, 166). Realist-Naturalist narrators provide voluminous expository data about characters and events—biography and background (names, dates, places), and objectively analyze the forces that propel characters toward their destinies (Nagel 1980, 166). Such information is most often provided directly, or a dramatic method is devised for its indirect revelation (Nagel 1980, 165–69). Telling (narrative description, analysis, exposition) tends to predominate over showing (dialogue, monologue, action), though Realism utilizes more showing than does Naturalism.

In sum, Impressionist and Romantic Realist authors in their different, but ultimately related, techniques sought to bridge aesthetic objectivism (the Without) and aesthetic subjectivism (the Within). Because they saw that a denial of aesthetic objectivism for aesthetic subjectivism, or vice versa, was a denial of the essential dual nature of humanity and of the universe itself, they viewed the two perspectives as being only partial visions of a greater integrated whole. As carriers of what Sorokin defines as "mixed" or hybrid styles, Impressionist and Romantic Realist authors espoused the "law of the included middle." They endeavored to bridge the various opposing nineteenth- and early twentieth-century embodiments of sensate culture's aesthetic subjectivism and ideational culture's aesthetic objectivism. Consequently, they shared in the metaphoric mulatto experience. Though Machado may not have directly been influenced by these authors, he was nevertheless among kindred souls.

MACHADO DE ASSIS: FROM ROMANTIC REALISM TO IMPRESSIONISM

The Poetry of Fact: Machado de Assis and Romantic Realism

Machado's fascination with subject-object duality, liminality, and ambiguity as they relate to human identity and experience in many ways reflected his own multiraciality. His synthesis of Romanticism and Realism-Naturalism likewise reflected his efforts to blend oppositional forms of consciousness embodied in nineteenth- and early twentieth-century aesthetic subjectivism and aesthetic objectivism. Thus his earlier novels have less in common with Romanticism and more with Romantic Realism (Castello 1969, 58; Fanger 1965, i–x, 3–27; Martins 1966, 83–88; Moisés 1959, 469–79).

The most prominent traits these novels share with Romantic Realism are their intrusive narrators and the conflicting and ambiguous inner nature of their characters. While remaining outside the action of his novels, Machado's narrators manipulate the atmosphere, interpret events, and guide, converse with, or interrogate readers in the form of a depersonalized "I," whether in "exposition" or in "interstitial comment" (Fanger 1965, 66). Moreover, they make it possible for Machado to constantly call attention to the act of writing within his novels, to challenge readers to question normative assumptions about literature, and to remind them that art is not a mirror of life, no matter how meticulously crafted the illusion (Nunes 1983, 15).

Narrative Structure

Machado's first four novels, *Resurrection*, *The Hand and the Glove*, *Helena*, and *Iaiá Garcia*, all begin in media res, following the Balzacian or Romantic Realist tradition. Each has a relatively well-defined beginning, middle, and end, with all the major narrative entanglements pertinent to the main plot resolved at the novel's conclusion. Though temporal references are chronological and objective, Machado extends the narration through psychological duration such that it reflects the most significantly experienced moments within the chronological sequence of narrative events (Nunes 1983, 24).

Resurrection (1872) is set in Rio de Janeiro during the Second Reign (1840–89), based on conjecture rather than specific narrative information. The events in the novel begin on New Year's Day and end on the same day one year later, with only vague temporal references such as "that evening," "a little while later," "the next day," "two weeks later," and "a few days later" to mark the passage of time (Nunes 1983, 23). Judging from narrator-author's statement "On that day—some ten years ago!" (63), the action unfolds in 1862–63. Although the bulk of the novel is told in the past tense and recounted ten years after the events, the last chapter, told in the present, is actually coeval with the events of the ten previous years, narrated in the earlier chapters. In a circular fashion, the novel closes as it opened. Félix begins a new year the way he ended the old, having gone through superficial changes, but essentially making no deep transformation, and thus falling short of a real rebirth or resurrection.

Machado's characters experience events psychologically and subjectively: whether they are calm or disturbed, we are made of aware of their states of mind in relation to sleep or the passage of night to day (Nunes 1983, 24). For example, when Félix ends his relationship with Lívia for the second time, he is so grief stricken that the day seems never to end, and the night seems even longer than the day. For the protagonists, as they wait to be married, the days seem endless, too, whereas for Menezes and Raquel, who are enamored with Lívia and Félix and unaware of their marriage plans, the days seem brief. We also see the psychological impact that seemingly neutral events have on characters, as when Lívia's son, Luís, asks Félix why he does not marry his mother, setting off a ripple of emotional shocks among Raquel, Lívia, Félix, and Meneses at Viana's birthday dinner

(Nunes 1983, 24). Though the narrative structure of *Resurrection* is not spatialized as it is in the later novels, where the recounting of the events is discontinuous, it reflects moments of greatest subjectivity within the objective sequence of the events narrated.

As in *Resurrection*, the events of *The Hand and the Glove* (1874) are related in relative linear order, though, once again, the narration takes place years after the actual events described, in this case, twenty years after. The action in *The Hand and the Glove* unfolds in 1853. Although, as before, the passage of time is marked by references such as the hour of day or night, "a little while later," "the next day," "one month later," "two weeks later" and "two years later" (Nunes 1983, 31), the novel's temporal framework is more complex in several respects. For one, it is also marked by significant events in the history of Rio de Janeiro, such as a cholera epidemic and a battle between fans of rival opera singers. For another, some episodes, particularly those relating to Guiomar's past, are narrated in flashback, and the narration refers to information given in previous chapters in order to clarify or link them with events in later chapters (Nunes 1983, 31).

As in *Resurrection*, the narrative in *The Hand and the Glove* is divided into chronological and psychological aspects. Thus, while Luís Alves tries to console Estêvão over his passion for Guiomar, the clock ticks on, oblivious to Estêvão's anguish (Nunes 1983, 32). Mrs. Oswald thinks of the heart in linear temporal terms (115), whereas the more enlightened narrator, in a metaliterary reference to his writing tasks, mockingly says: "But there, within that youthful and impatient heart, each minute seemed like, well, I shan't say a century—that would be to abuse my rights of style—but an hour, it certainly seemed like an hour to him" (71). In other words, though chronological time provides the framework of the characters' lives, and, by extension, the novel, it is psychological time—the intensity (or lack of intensity) of their subjective experience of external events—that determines the values and quality of those lives (Nunes 1983, 32).

The temporal framework of *Helena* (1876) is also chronological. The time sequences begin at eight o'clock on the night of April 25, 1859. The plot centers around the complications stemming from a testament left by the austere Councilor Valle, in which he recognizes his natural daughter Helena, a young lady of sixteen whose widowed mother, now deceased, had been his mistress. Helena subsequently comes to live with Valle's family, which consists of his son, Estácio, and his sister, Dona Ursula. At first, the Valle family feels a mixture of surprise and embarrassment at how Helena's existence and presence within the household might be viewed by society. Soon, however, they are won over by Helena's captivating presence. Estácio begins to fall in love with his half sister, though unaware of it, his passion being revealed to him by the family priest, Father Melchior. Helena is already aware of Estácio's attraction to her, as she also knows that in reality she is not the councilor's daughter, but only had been treated as such. With the discovery of Helena's real father this information is revealed, and Estácio, though by now engaged to Camargo's daughter, wants to marry Helena. His family and friends, concerned about the status quo, oppose this even though Helena is not his sister. Desperately struggling to repress her love for Estácio, while trying to conquer her feelings of remorse for having passed herself off as Valle's daughter, and tormented by her pride, which rebels against her having received an inheritance not rightfully hers, Helena dies of a broken heart.

In *Helena*, as in Machado's first two novels, the early segments are in part devoted to the depiction and introduction of the characters and their interaction, especially in moments of psychological crisis. The overall tone of the narration, however, is one of suspense and melodrama such that following the disclosure of the contents of Valle's will, the subsequent action centers around the question of Helena's identity, origins, and the enigma she presents. Thus *Helena* has elements of philosophical and psychological as well as chronological time (Nunes 1983, 36–37). Helena's eyes are the clock that measures a fateful hour, while the clock of affection and hope measures long hours. Helena tells Estácio that the most important thing is not to do a great deal in a short time, but to do a great deal that is gratifying and useful (88).

The plot of *Iaiá Garcia* (1878), the last of the earlier novels, centers on the lives and ambitions of three individuals—Iaiá Garcia, Estela Antunes, and Jorge Gomes. A love affair between Estela and Jorge, who is somewhat older, is quickly stymied both by Estela, whose pride will not allow her to endure their differences in social class, as well as by Valéria, Jorge's mother, for the same reasons. Valeria convinces Jorge to join the forces fighting in the Paraguayan War, hoping that he will forget his affair with Estela. After Jorge returns from war, he finds Estela married to Luís Garcia—a true marriage of convenience managed by Jorge's own mother—but he also finds that Luís Garcia's daughter, Iaiá, has become a beautiful young woman, now engaged to Procópio Dias (though we learn that Iaiá is secretly enamored with Jorge). The precocious Iaiá senses that her stepmother, Estela, now widowed because of Luís Garcia's death, could help her fulfill her love for Jorge but resolves nevertheless to do her duty. Iaiá sends her faithful black servant Raimundo to Procópio Dias with a letter accepting his marriage proposal. Raimundo decides, however, to turn back and tell Estela of Iaiá's true feelings. In a sublime gesture, Estela upstages even Iaiá's self-sacrifice by replacing Iaiá's letter with her own to be delivered to Jorge, stating that he is the god her stepdaughter worships and that she, Estela, favors their union. At this point, the novel shifts to São Paulo, where Estela has gone to reside and serve as head of a girl's school.

Iaiá Garcia continues the chronological narrations of the three earlier novels. The action begins on October 5, 1866, and ends in 1873, one year after Iaiá's father's death. As in *The Hand and the Glove*, there are several flashbacks, most of which are devoted to elaborating facts about the principal characters' lives (Nunes 1983, 40). Events of the story are dated with care; contemporary historical events such as the Paraguayan War are chronicled and woven into the novel's structure but serve only as a backdrop. The psychological and subjective aspects of time are again more important than the chronological. Because of Machado's greater dexterity in integrating the characters' emotional involvements into their behavior and the narration, the reader has a better sense of the subjective and psychological nature of time in their lives than in the earlier novels (Nunes 183, 41). As the narration draws out the suffering of separated or estranged lovers longing to be together again, minutes seem like hours and hours like days, while hurts of the past seem but a distant memory.

Narrative Point of View

The most obvious trait that Machado's earlier novels share with Romantic Realism is their use of a conversant and intrusive narrator. Romantics, particularly early Romantics, in their desire to convey subjective truths and values—reality seen from within—typically used first-person narration devoted to extensive introspective self-examination (often in the form of diaries, letters, and the like), whereas Realist-Naturalists, in their desire to faithfully report external reality and its facts, with maximum sensory verisimilitude and thus minimum emotional and imaginative content, typically used third-person omniscient narration. Machado combined first-person with detached third-person narration to produce double or suspended narration in the manner of Romantic Realism. This furthered his aim of achieving a multidimensional and complex narrative that blurred the line between subjectivity and objectivity, as well as between events taking place within and without the narration (Fanger 1965, 40, 66).

In addition, this narrative technique made it possible for Machado to present sensory reality from a metaliterary perspective in order to provide a glimpse of the socioeconomic, political, intellectual, and cultural transformation that was taking place in nineteenth-century Brazil, as the remnants of the traditional world continued to give way to the onslaught of modernity (Fanger 1965, viii, 64; Hodgson 1976, 18, 29). Although Machado's novels are re-creations of spatial domains at specific historical junctures, they are also personal and thus less typical of the more prosaic and objectivist aesthetics of Realism-Naturalism (Fanger 1965, 40, 66).

Machado sought to achieve a narrative that as nearly as possible implied no narrator (showing) while exploiting the possibilities of narrative exposition and analysis (telling; Fanger 1965, 19, 34, 40, 42). The most apparent examples of his use of this duality are the intrusive narrators of his earlier novels, who appear as quasi-subjective, referring to themselves as "I," but who are also not involved in the objective events narrated. Their subtle presence creates the illusion that past and present are occurring at the same time, much as a storyteller relating something that took place in the past does by being close to us in the present.

In the earlier novels, Machado's narrators, situated outside the events of the novel, are usually omniscient, having access to information both external and internal to the characters, often when the characters themselves do not. At other times, the narrators are only semi-omniscient and limited to partial or external information about the characters, having no inside view; readers are left to arrive at their own conclusions. The narrators at once present themselves as first-person subjects, coloring the mood of the narration, and as implied characters who "participate" in the narration without directly taking part in the events narrated. The narrators talk with and interrogate readers and intrude upon the narrative, revealing their plans and intentions and the techniques they use in writing (Castello 1969, 98). Because Machado expected his readers to be more than passively entertained by a straightforward story, he used his narrators to blur the line between author, narrator, reader, and character, between events within and without the novel. He brought readers into direct participation with characters, making both narrator and readers characters of a sort who, though not participating directly in the events narrated, were integral parts of the narrative process (Nunes 1983, 15, 19).

Machado's habit of giving readers access to privileged information is developed still more consciously in *The Hand and the Glove*, where readers gain insight into the characters even when the characters do not understand one another or themselves, and where Machado achieves both greater narrator-character-reader intimacy and a certain ironical effect (Nunes 1983, 22). As part of this greater intimacy, the narrator, addressing the readers directly, digresses to philosophize about love and life, or to express opinions about characters and events within the novel.

Sensing the readers' desire to get on with the story, as in *Resurrection*, the narrator in *The Hand and the Glove* scolds and teases them about this impatience while assuring them that all the gaps will be filled in at the proper time (100–101). Inherent in the narrator's confidential relationship with readers is an underlying assumption that readers are fully involved with the characters and that they are always one step ahead of the narrator, having already reached certain conclusions about the events (Nunes 1983, 30). In fact, however, Machado cleverly leads his readers to these conclusions through the narrative gaps and traps and sleight of hand of his cagey narrator.

Characterization

The technique of the intrusive narrator allowed Machado to bring greater presence and personality to the authorial narrative content without sacrificing the generic conventions of drama, which imply as nearly as possible no narrator at all. Through this subtle combination of showing and telling, Machado was able to present characters all at once or through a progressive analysis in which the narrator points out their motives and reactions. This device allowed Machado to reveal his characters both through their own thoughts, words, and actions and those of the other characters (Nunes 1983, 21, 25, 31). With the possible exception of *Helena* and *The Hand and the Glove*, Machado does so without including the extensive details of biography and attire so typical of Romantic Realists. Even there, however, his use of external data of this type is comparatively limited.

All four of Machado's earlier novels explore the complex and often contradictory aspects of the human psyche in a vicious and amoral world dominated by greed and egoism, where ambition for social success is at odds with individual morality. This focus, Machado's greater emphasis on character than on plot and action, and his use of the conversant narrator are the most obvious traits that align these earlier novels with Romantic Realism. Perhaps out of the need to adjust to squeamish Brazilian Victorianism, however, or to the prevailing demand for the inclusion of environmental influences on individual psychology, the second three, *The Hand and the Glove*, *Helena*, and *Iaiá Garcia* diverge somewhat from the more internal psychological thrust of *Resurrection*. The ethical conflicts and choices confronting the later protagonists, Guiomar, Helena, Estácio, Estela, and Iaiá, occur and gain significance within a socioeconomic context, whereas Félix's dilemma is primarily determined by factors internal to his character (Barreto Filho 1947, 112, 115; Nunes 1983, 28; Pereira 1959, 66–67).

Unlike most Romantic Realists, Machado does not include extensive external details about history and setting, even in these second three novels. In *The Hand and the Glove*, we are given details about the social and cultural life of the bourgeoisie during the Second Reign through descriptions of the estate on which Guiomar lives, groups of individuals gathered in the living rooms of great houses, and through historical street names. And in *Iaiá Garcia*, details of the Paraguayan War are carefully, if only schematically, chronicled (Nunes 1983, 31). But even here, most details elaborate the nuances of character psychology (Barreto Filho 1947, 19; Castello 1969, 98–99; Mota 1984, 330, 340).

As was frequently the case with Romantic Realism, Machado's primary means of characterization was through contrast and the creation of a psychological matrix dominated by the clash of opposites in a world of complex ethical choices. Thus, in *Resurrection*, Machado contrasts both the idealistic Lívia and the sincere, receptive, and loving Meneses, who is an echo of Lívia, with the realistic and cynical Félix (Nunes 1983, 26). In *The Hand and the Glove*, he contrasts the calculating and ambitious Guiomar with the sentimental romantic Estêvão, whose florid speech is riddled with bad metaphors, and with the affected and superficial dandy Jorge, and both Jorge and Estêvão, with Luís, who is the perfect match for Guiomar (Nunes 1983, 33). In *Helena*, Machado contrasts Estácio's unconscious incestuous desires for Helena with Camargo's explicitly incestuous desires for his daughter, Eugênia, whose frivolous nature he contrasts with Helena's reserved and sober temperament (Nunes 1983, 36). And finally, in *Iaiá Garcia*, he contrasts proud and self-confident Estela with her submissive father, Antunes, and the flighty adolescent Iaiá with the more subdued Estela (Nunes 1983, 43).

In keeping with Romantic Realism, Machado's characters are individuals of conflicting sentiments. Doubt is coupled with hope, pride, and egoism; greed and ambition are coupled with altruism, social responsibility, and self-sacrifice. Characters are free to choose from among the complex ethical alternatives presented to them in a society that judges individuals not by their character and moral integrity, but by the cut of their clothes, their family name, and their material wealth (Barreto Filho 1947, 138; Fanger 1965, 260). On the other hand, they are not helpless victims of biological or socioeconomic forces beyond their control, as would be the case with Naturalism. Rather, at various junctures in their lives, under the pressure for success, they have pursued substitutes for genuine love: they have victimized themselves. Yet this situation originates more in their own inner desires than in a natural design. Their destiny is determined more by the causes they set in motion than by the effects of a deterministic fate or the whims of chance.

In this sense, Machado's main characters, in keeping with Romantic Realism, are more three-dimensional even when they are caricatures. They not only respond to but change as they interact with their environment. They appear to be individuals drawn from real life, leading independent lives (Fanger 1965, 17). Though not as memorable as Balzac's or Dickens's, the main characters of Machado's earlier novels are closely identified with theme, which serves to characterize them (Nunes 1983, 20, 28, 35). Félix in *Resurrection* is identified with the theme of doubt; Guiomar in *The Hand and the Glove* and Helena in *Helena*, with the theme of upward social mobility; and Jorge and Valéria in *Iaiá Garcia*, with the marriage of convenience (Nunes 1983, 28, 35).

Life Behind the Veil: Machado de Assis and Impressionism

Machado continuously sought new ways of experimenting with the "transformative vision." Continuing in the Romantic Realist tradition but unsatisfied with its limitations, he became more daring in his experiments with Romanticism and Realism in his later novels (Brayner 1979, 72–73; Coutinho 1966, 30–31; Merquior 1977, 150–53, 166; Riedel 1959, 48, 59). As part of this process, he returned to the psychological line of development in *The Posthumous Memoirs of Brás Cubas* (1881) that he had begun in *Resurrection*, perhaps at least in part because, being better established as both an author and a salaried bureaucrat, he was less dependent on satisfying public taste for his financial security. In *Brás Cubas*, Machado continued to repudiate the denotative reproduction of external reality of Realism-Naturalism, on the one hand, while stopping well short of adopting the subconscious and often mythical framework and convoluted metaphorical solipsism and connotative language of Neo-Romanticism, Symbolism, and Expressionism, on the other.

Narrative Structure

The abandonment of straightforward, chronological for psychological, spatialized narration based on experiential time is what most obviously separates Machado's later novels from his earlier ones and what links them with Impressionism. This is quite evident in *Dom Casmurro* and even more so in *Brás Cubas*, with its unusual postmortem narration. Also, as with Impressionist novels, time itself is thematic in the later novels, representing the fleeting and inconsistent nature of existence. The focus is on time's cyclical repetition, tyranny over existence, intensity or lack of intensity in emotionally charged moments, and mutability through the free play of memory and psychological factors (Nagel 1980, 139; Venâncio Filho 2000, 101–24). Considering the temporal aspects of personal identity, Machado's narrations become symbolic attempts by characters such as Brás and Santiago to negate the leveling effects of time by seeking through their affective memory to recapture the past in an eternal present (the narration itself). Paradoxically, the narrations are also symbolic of the futility of their quest for time (Hansen 1997 248–60; Nagel 1980, 39, 103, 139; Venâncio Filho 2000, 1001–24).

As compared to *Dom Casmurro* and *Brás Cubas*, however, *Quincas Borba* and *Esau and Jacob* are more straightforward and linear in their narrations than most Impressionist novels. Moreover, unlike Machado's other later novels, which carefully chronicle temporal dates, *Quincas Borba* (1891) makes only indirect references to dates in its narrative sequences. Both *Quincas Borba* and *Esau and Jacob* begin in media res and are relatively straightforward chronological narrations of events, although there are several flashbacks as well as jumps over large spans of time in *Esau and Jacob*.

Whereas *Brás Cubas* and to some extent *Dom Casmurro* are spatialized narrations that encompass entire life spans, *Quincas Borba* encompasses only three years of Rubião's life, although these three years are emotionally intense and full of psychological duration (Nunes 1983, 97). The narrative focuses on Rubiao's psychological deterioration in chronological time as he slides into the atemporal world of insanity and delusion. As with *Brás Cubas*, *Quincas Borba* combines telling (narrative analysis, summary) with showing (scene, dialogue). The temporal rhythm is decelerated primarily through digressions and flashbacks and accelerated through jumps over spans of months. Simultaneous shifts in time and place help create a certain ironic effect because both the narrator and reader are allowed a multiple-angle view and understanding of events, whereas the characters' perceptions are veiled in ambiguity due to their egoistic perspectives and their consequent mutual misunderstanding of one another's motives (Hansen 1997, 250; Nunes 1983, 97).

Though *Dom Casmurro* (1899) has more of a plot than *Brás Cubas*, it is again nonlinear, discontinuous, and spatialized. Events are selected because of their personal value to the narrator Bento Santiago or because they help him build the case against his adulterous wife, Capitu, whom he blames for having transformed the outgoing and warm Bento Santiago into the withdrawn and morose Dom Casmurro. It is the contradiction between Bento Santiago of the past and Dom Casmurro of the present that serves as means of narrative development. Casmurro, though alive during the narration, is living a sort of spiritual death.

Like *Brás Cubas*, *Dom Casmurro* presents subjective, experiential, and psychological aspects of time alongside objective clock or calendar ones, which serve to frame them. And again as in *Brás Cubas*, the narrator begins his narration with explicatory chapters, one clarifying the title of the book and the other elaborating on his reasons for writing it.

As it does in *Brás Cubas* and *Dom Casmurro*, chronological time gives *Ayres's Memorial* (1908) its structure, but because the novel is written in diary form, the qualitative aspects of the quantitative units in the diary (days, weeks, hours) are more important than the dates themselves. And as with Impressionist novels written in diary or epistolary form, dates, sensory experiences, and other empirical phenomena serve as focal points for the evocation and rendering of emotional states that coincide with them (Kronegger 1973, 51, 53). In *Ayres's Memorial*, this includes digressions into philosophical discussions on social events, for example, Abolition, as well as discussions of art and the therapeutic effects of music (Nunes 1983, 59–60, 113).

Although plot is not as conspicuously absent in *Ayres's Memorial* as it is in *Dom Casmurro* or *Brás Cubas*, there is less emphasis on action. The tempo of the carefully dated narrative sequences is slow and weighed down with reflections, digressions, and regressions, though periodically accelerated through the alternation of summary, scene, and dialogue. The narrator's temporal frame of reference is close to that of the characters' because his diary entries are only a few days removed from when events occur. Ayres brings readers into the flow of events by sharing his reflections with them in such a way that, though it may seem that we are dealing with chronological time, we are actually dealing with psychological time (Nunes 1983, 59–60, 114). Indeed, more than anything else, *Ayres's Memorial* is an impressionistic investigation into the epistemology of perception, an autumnal sigh at the fleeting nature of life, the passing of time, and with it our hopes and dreams.[1]

Narrative Point of View

Whereas *Quincas Borba* and *Esau and Jacob* are essentially elaborations of the conversant narration Machado used in his earlier novels, *Brás Cubas*, *Dom Casmurro*, and *Ayres's Memorial* are extraordinarily intricate and daring probes into questions of narrator reliability and the interplay between author, narrator, and reader. In them, Machado's dramatized first-person narrators are not merely conversant but are also participants in the events narrated.

To overcome the sense of remoteness associated with time-removed first-person narration, and to capture the immediacy of experience so important to Impressionists, Machado most often fused the time of telling and action in a dramatic present time, creating the illusion that the events are being narrated by an individual who is experiencing, rather than writing, about them (Nagel 1980, 24–25). *Ayres's Memorial*, even with the slight time lag in Ayres's diary entries, is perhaps the most genuinely Impressionist of the later novels in that there is a comparatively greater immediacy of the narrator's rendering of experience.

Machado also made use of another Impressionist device in *Brás Cubas* and *Dom Casmurro*, uncertain and unreliable narration, where first-person narrators search for the truth and meaning of their experience and seek explanations and implications unrealized at the time of action (Nagel 1980, 24–40). The persistent self-conscious statements by the narrators Brás and Bento reflect the restrictions and questionable reliability of their commentary. As narrators, they are conscious of their perceptual limitations and the significance of their restricted vantage points and often find it necessary to rely on conjecture as to what "must," "might," or "appears" to have transpired (Nunes 1983, 40; Stowell 1980, 28). Reality becomes a function of the interpretive consciousness and subject to distortions of affective memory and other phenomena internal or external to the characters. Their impressions may or may not be rendered in detail; but, in either case, readers are forced to be skeptical of the reliability of narrator's assertions of judgment and fact (Kinnear 1976, 55–56; Nagel 1980, 21, 40; Venâncio Filho 2000, 101–24).

The omniscient narrators of *Esau and Jacob* and *Quincas Borba* have access to all information internal and external to characters, another technique potentially incompatible with Impressionist restrictions. In *Quincas Borba*, where the narrator is not also a character, as he is in the other later novels, Machado resolves this potential incompatibility by making him appear to identify with the protagonist, Rubião—tell the story from Rubião's perspective. The narrator's intrusions and evaluations either describe circumstances that cause Rubião to perceive his experiences in a particular manner or provide a superior perspective from which his distorted perceptions become ironic (Nunes 1983, 25).

That Ayres in *Esau and Jacob* (1904) is both omniscient narrator and character is not only implausible, but also antithetical to the Impressionist restriction on narrative intelligence. Machado distracts his readers from this basic implausibility and the narrator's necessarily restricted perspective as a character by having Ayres refer to himself in the third person, creating the illusion that *Esau and Jacob* is being related from the perspective of Ayres the character, just as *Quincas Borba* was related from the perspective of Rubião. Ayres the narrator maintains a respectful and polite distance regarding the characters, including himself. Indeed, he does not behave like an omniscient narrator at all, often admitting bewilderment and lack of penetration into the characters' deeper motivations (Caldwell 1972, 156); he deliberately leaves many gaps to be filled in, frequently warning readers to pay close attention and to reread (Wolff 1987, 46, 48).

In *Brás Cubas*, *Dom Casmurro*, and *Ayres's Memorial*, the dramatized first-person narrators, though conversant and intrusive as before, are participants in the events of the novel. We witness, in their guise as objective and reliable narrators, an ironic depiction of the subjective interference of their self-consciousness in the interpretation, and by extension, in the turn of objective events within the texts (Neto 1994, 12–17). Using this subjective viewpoint to project the interpretation of characters and events raises the question of perceptual relativity and unreliable commentary as it relates to the confluence of primary with secondary mentation—perception with conceptualization. Machado presents us with the narrative point of view from which such perception and conceptualization originate, the subjective first person (Neto 1994, 12–17).

Brás, Bento, and Ayres (in *Ayres's Memorial*) are all narrators who refer to themselves as "I" yet are also characters. The extent of their knowledge is determined by their relationship to the other characters and to events (Brayner 1979, 76–82; Hill 1976, 25–27; Nunes 1983, 64–64; Riedel 1959, 54–59). Brás Cubas furnishes us with complete details of his birth and what others said and did at that time. He also informs readers that because no one told him anything about his baptism, and because he was too young to remember, he is able to tell us little about this event. Brás is essentially a limited empiricist whose knowledge is determined by what he perceives and experiences.

Brás's assertion that the narrative process is unimportant when in fact it is alerts readers to his contradictory nature and suspect reliability. It puts us on guard for other statements, especially his assertion that, because he is dead, and therefore unaffected by the opinions of others, he can speak with complete candor about his mediocre and egoistic life (Nunes 1983, 67), even as he asks readers to judge for themselves what he says. We need only remember that how affected he was by the eulogies given at his funeral to confirm Brás's dishonesty in this matter (Nunes 1983, 68) and to see his dead man's candor for what it really is—his greatest form of deception.

Bento Santiago, the narrator of *Dom Casmurro*, is another limited empiricist. His knowledge is defined by the extreme subjectivity of his perceptions, experiences, and interpretations, which make the ambiguity of perception and conceptualization pivotal to interpreting the whole novel (Hansen 1997, 250; Nunes 1983, 66). In the introductory chapter "The Title," Bento tells us that "Dom Casmurro" refers to the nickname wrongly given him by an angry neighbor who thought Bento to be morose and withdrawn. The word "casmurro" also means "stubborn and wrong-headed" and is perhaps the important definition interpreting Bento's account of his life. As Helen Caldwell points out, we later find out that this name change from "Bento" (the Blessed) to "Casmurro," mirrors the narrator's transformation from the loving Bento to latter-day Iago, "the Christ-child that became the Prince of Evil" (Caldwell 1970, 146; Nunes 1983, 66).

In chapter 2, "The Book," Casmurro, alias Bento Santiago, states that his reason for writing is that he would like to restore the present in the past by piecing together the two ends of his life (Nunes 1983, 54). This period encompasses the story and deals with the details of Bento's supposed betrayal by his wife and his best friend, Escobar. Our suspicions of his unreliability are aroused by Bento's constant appeals to be alert, read carefully, and fill in narrative gaps—and exacerbated by his forgetfulness. Machado has carefully constructed Bento as both narrator and character to call our attention to the subjective nature of first-person narrations in which the narrator is also a major participant in the events narrated (Gledson 1984, 2; Nunes 1983, 56, 69, 76, 105).

At the conscious level, Bento gives us the objective case for his betrayal by Capitu and Escobar. Yet, as Marta de Senna argues, he is deft at crafting what she refers as the "strategy of deceit," which allows him "to build, on every other page, a kind of *trompe l'oeil* that conditions the reader's eyes to see what is not there, and not see what really is there to be seen" (Senna 2005, 407). With a criminal's urge to talk, as well as a lawyer's urge to at least to plead his case against Capitu, Bento discloses in carefully veiled metaphor that his jealousy may have originated in his own projected desires for Escobar, Sancha, or both, indications of which surface in 1871, shortly after Escobar proposes that the four of them take a trip to Europe. When Bento and Sancha shake hands, Bento tells the reader he felt a certain erotic impulse from her. And when Escobar, mentioning that he will swim the next day even though the sea is rougher than usual, asks Bento to feel his arms to show him how unafraid he is, Bento says Escobar's arms felt as if they were Sancha's.

Machado provides an almost Freudian rendering of these sentiments. The use of "as if" (*como se*) followed by "they were" (*fossem*)—the subjunctive—is the reason for this ambiguity in *Dom Casmurro* (230). The ambiguous language used to relate this vicarious adultery suggests Bento actually may have felt some type of same-sex attraction to Escobar. The fact that Bento is envious of both the thickness and strength of Escobar's arms when he feels them and of Escobar's ability to swim, something Bento could not do, plus his obvious self-doubts, lack of self-esteem, and personal inadequacy also seem to support this interpretation. We sense that one of Bento's underlying motives for writing his account, quite apart from presenting his case against Capitu, may actually have been his own unconscious sense of guilt about this attraction. The next day Escobar drowns; at his wake Bento, seeing how much Capitu is affected, becomes jealous (Linhares Filho 1978, 68–69; Novotny 1965, 44–45).

Convinced that Machado is testing readers to see whether and how much they will question Bento's "truth" about his wife's adultery, John Gledson imagines that they may be steered more by convention and emotion than by deduction in reaching their conclusions (Gledson 1999, 8). Indeed, Paul Dixon points out that, historically, Brazilian readers tended to side with Bento and to accept Capitu's adultery without question (Dixon 2009, 53). For her part, however, Caldwell was the first scholar to assert Capitu's innocence, arguing that, through the language of metaphor, the subjective mechanism of Bento's subconscious makes the "reality" he presents an illusion (Caldwell 1970, 143, 146; Nunes 1983, 56; Rimmon 1977, 12, 14, 16).

Roberto Schwarz, another of the earliest Brazilian scholars to assert Capitu's innocence, considers her a symbol of resistance to the holders of power in Brazil's patriarchal society, represented by her jealous husband. Schwarz attributes the unquestioning acceptance of Bento's accusation of his wife as a misreading of the novel, attributable to bias shaped by that same patriarchal society (Schwarz 1997, 24–25, 30, 33). Domício Proença Filho and Fábio Lucas, who agree with this assessment, argue that Capitu is the ultimate symbol of female resistance to Brazil's patriarchy, and she pays dearly for her agency, intellectual independence, and strength of character. Her behavior challenges the status quo at a time when women were expected to be seen but not heard (Proença Filho 2001, 90–91; Lucas 2009, 106–21). A modern feminist reading, Gledson notes, could not help but find that, by repeatedly invoking Capitu's "eyes like the tide" (*olhos de ressaca*), Bento was in fact demonizing her, whether consciously or unconsciously (Gledson 1999, 7).

Caldwell argues that, though Machado gives readers the freedom to decide on Capitu's guilt, he nevertheless wants readers to decide she is innocent and therefore intervenes in chapter 54 (Caldwell 1960, 150–60; Caldwell in Baptista 1994, 153). It is here that Bento tells of encountering a classmate from seminary who asked him if he remembered the "Panegyric of Saint Monica" he wrote. Bento responds: "Perfectly. . . . My dear classmate, I have never forgotten those days of the seminary, believe me" (145). Bento then confesses to readers that he remembered nothing of the panegyric, explaining, "It was a matter of courtesy, charity even, to recall some page or other" (145). In light of this confession, Caldwell believes that Machado is urging his readers to be suspicious of Bento's account of the events he claims support his case against Capitu.

For his part, Silviano Santiago argues that the only truth for which one should search is Bento's (Santiago 2000, 30), echoing Antônio Cândido, who writes, "But the fact is that, in Machado's universe, it does not matter much whether Bento's conviction is right or wrong, because the consequence is exactly the same in either case: whether it is imaginary or real, it destroys his household and his life" (Cândido 1970b, 256; see also 25–26). Gledson also believes Capitu's guilt or innocence is unimportant to Machado: it cannot be determined based on the text itself (Gledson 1984, 8; 1999, 9). Readers cannot know whether adultery actually occurred because all they know about it is confined to the extreme subjectivity of Bento's perceptions, experiences, and interpretations. This makes the ambiguity of perception and conceptualization pivotal to interpreting the whole novel, and is more important than whether Capitu is guilty or not. Furthermore, those who are drawn into questions of guilt or innocence are essentially conceding that the physical act of adultery is crucial, which Gledson argues is secondary to Machado (Gledson 1999, 9). If anything, this ambiguity of perception in *Dom Casmurro* affirms Machado's affinity with Impressionism and certainly stands in stark contrast to three prominent nineteenth-century Realist-Naturalist texts—Gustave Flaubert's *Madame Bovary*, José Maria Eça de Queiroz's *Cousin Basílio*, and Leo Tolstoy's *Anna Karenina*—that examine the question of adultery, and where the physical act of adultery is an undisputed fact. Yet Gledson believes Machado's creation of Bento is not an abandonment of Realism, but rather, a daring extension of it, in which Bento's manipulation of the plot and the narration and everything about him are a direct reflection on his character (Gledson 1999, 12, 14).

Nevertheless, the broader argument between Abel Baptista and those critics who have inherited Helen Caldwell's "legacy" is about intentionalism (Baptista 1994, 150, 155; Baptista in Gledson 1999, 2, 14). Baptista maintains that Caldwell and her successors erroneously seek to go behind Bento to find the "true Machado" in the text, when in fact the character Bento is the author in the sense that Machado has made him "write" *Dom Casmurro*. Indeed, Machado has Bento take full responsibility for everything in the book from the title to the last word. In addition, Gledson emphasizes that there is nothing in the book that can be isolated and taken as a direct statement by Machado. Yet he also acknowledges that it was of course Machado who decided on and wrote everything in *Dom Casmurro* and that the creative decision making in the novel must correspond to Machado's intentions (Gledson 1984, 156; Baptista 1994, 160; Baptista in Gledson 1999, 4–5, 12, 15).

What is at issue here is the ambiguous relationship between Machado and Bento—the implied (actual) author and the author-narrator. According to Baptista, one cannot exclude either Machado's or Bento's hand in crafting the novel in what he defines as a "double paradoxical injunction" (Baptista 1994, 146). Machado experiments with a narrative voice that, though it is not his own, could lead credulous readers to think that it is. Yet Gledson maintains that having Bento be author, narrator, and character at the same time is crucial to one of Machado's key ideas about fiction. Absent any direct, isolated authorial comment on the text, the readers' relationship with Bento is much more like a relationship with a real individual (Gledson 1999, 10, 11, 12–13).

Like the narrators in *Brás Cubas* and *Dom Casmurro*, the narrator of *Ayres's Memorial*, written in the form of a diary, speaks in the first person, though at times he also refers to himself in the third, as "old diplomat" or "my dear old Ayres." And though he sometimes addresses the paper of his diary: "Paper, dear foolscap, do not gather up everything this idle pen writes" (40), Ayres does not directly address the reader, as do Brás and Bento. On the other hand, like Brás's and Bento's, Ayres's knowledge of events and characters is limited to his subjective vantage point, but his perceptions (e.g., Tristão and Fidélia's love for each other and Dona Carmo's joyous excitement about their mutual affection) are often on target (Caldwell 1970, 184, 193).

As in the other two novels, all characters in *Ayres's Memorial* must eventually pass through the narrator's perceptions and conceptualizations. The only character who is revealed to us firsthand is Ayres himself, and even then, our image of him comes not from his self-analysis but through his observations and, above all, from his conjecture about and impressions of other characters, as does much of what we learn about the idyllic relationship between Carmo and Aguiar and the relationship between Tristão and Fidélia (17, 24, 135). Ayres tells us that Fidélia and Carmo are fond of each other and that his sister, Rita, feels they are worthy of this mutual regard. Though he doubts that Dona Carmo's motives are unselfish, he withholds absolute judgment until later (17). After the Aguiars' silver wedding anniversary, Ayres tells us how idyllic their marital harmony is, although he is careful to note the risk of making judgments about individuals at festive occasions (17). Ayres arrives at these and most of his conclusions about the other characters by a type of sophisticated inductive reasoning, where glances and gestures as well as spoken and, most of all, unspoken words reveal the deeper and "real" meaning and shed light on Ayres's own reliability or unreliability, as when his cynical doubt interferes in arriving at conclusions about a given character or situation (Caldwell 1970, 193).

The most common features shared by narrators Brás, Bento, and Ayres—aside from questions of their reliability (a feature they share with all of Machado's narrators)—are their conversational manner and their habit of digressing. As an integral part of Machado's metaliterary emphasis, these narrators, through their constant comparisons of the novel with other art forms such as theater and opera, their concerns about being published and read, and their philosophical meanderings draw our attention more to the narrator and the text than to the events being narrated. Moreover, all three narrators expect much more reader collaboration than was customary for novels of the time (Nunes 1983, 69, 72; Soares 1968, 68). Thus, in *Brás Cubas*, Brás makes this clear when he apologizes to impatient readers who are simply looking for a good story; he suggests that they skip passages like "the delirium." He points satirically to the two literary traditions that sought to give readers a straightforward story. Romanticism, he says, rode to death the high-spirited horse of the medieval ballads in its novels, whereas Realism-Naturalism, finding the poor horse lying dead and picked clean in the gutter, decided out of pity to immortalize it (127).

The narrator of *Quincas Borba* shares with the narrators of *Brás Cubas*, *Dom Casmurro*, and *Ayres's Memorial* the tendency to refer to himself as "I." Brás, Bento, and Ayres, however, are both narrator-subjects and character-objects at the same time, whereas the narrator in *Quincas Borba* is not actually a character, but an intrusive "I," like the narrators in Machado's earlier novels. Maria Nunes concludes that the dramatization implicit in having his narrators refer to themselves as "I" represents Machado's continued metaliterary emphasis and parody of the objectivist aesthetics of Realism-Naturalism (Nunes 1983, 65). This can be seen when the *Quincas Borba* narrator half-jokingly chastises himself about interrupting the flow of the narration in order to tease readers about rushing to judgment based on circumstantial evidence—evidence Rubião believes indicates an affair between Sofia and Carlos on the Rua de Harmonia (237). The narrator's expressed desire to follow the method of writers like Miguel de Cervantes, François Rabelais, Henry Fielding, and Tobias Smollett, who would frequently interrupt or suspend the narration in order justify their techniques, is additional evidence of Machado's metaliterary consciousness of art as art, as well as an attack on the mimetic techniques of Realism-Naturalism (245). Machado's strongest indictment of the materialist rationalist thinking behind Realism-Naturalism comes in Quincas Borba's Humanitism, an uncritical blend of the conclusions of Auguste Comte, Charles Darwin, and Thomas Malthus. Although the narration purports to prove the validity of Humanitism, the text in fact undermines it (Haberly 1983, 79; Nunes 1983, 50, 74; Vara 1976, 15–16).

Even though the foreword to *Esau and Jacob* tells us that Ayres's last two journals are narratives in which Ayres is also a character, as omniscient narrator, he can enter other characters' consciousness, and has unexplained access to facts about events that he did not witness (Nunes 1983, 65). Caldwell directs our attention to the fact that this dual role as narrator-subject and character-object enhances Ayres's literary power because all his behavior, thoughts, and dialogue as a character, together with all quotations from his diary, shed light on his mental processes as a narrator (Caldwell 1970, 155). Because, as the narrator in *Esau and Jacob*, he does not speak in the first person, readers more willingly suspend questions of Ayres's reliability: we forget that narrator and character—Ayres as subject and object—are one and the same (Caldwell 1970, 155).

In *Esau and Jacob*, the narrator discusses his intentions, intrudes upon the narration, addresses readers directly, and constantly calls attention to the fact that he is writing, as was the case with the narrators in previous novels. In addition, the narrator provides keys to deciphering the novel's allegorical component (Nunes 1983, 69). Saying that he speaks in images, the narrator drops numerous hints for breaking the novel's allegorical code, though his signals are somewhat cryptic and veiled in allusions to the other works of literature. As with Machado's other experimental techniques, interpreting the allegory requires the readers' collaboration and is based on the assumption that they have followed the narrator's instructions to read carefully (Nunes 1983, 58, 78).

Characterization

Aside from the spatialized narration, and questions of narrator reliability, the most obvious trait that Machado shares with other Impressionist writers is his interest in presenting characters from within. He seeks to explore the workings of their psyche, particularly with regard to the relationship between perceptions and conceptualizations of reality, and the consequences of the ethical choices the characters make based on the two. Thus his rendering of characters' subjective responses to objective reality is more complex compared to his earlier novels.

Machado's restriction on the narrative capacity to enter characters' minds omnisciently in *Dom Casmurro*, *Brás Cubas*, and *Ayres's Memorial* helps achieve this. What readers learn about characters emerges primarily from what characters perceive, do, and say, from what other characters perceive or say about them, and, in particular, from what is not said or perceived. Readers are compelled to participate in the characterization process as they sort through a fragmented and ambiguous reality. They must rely on composites built from quick, pointillist fragments, in contrast to the sharp delineation and extensive physical descriptions of characters in Realist-Naturalist novels.

In *Dom Casmurro*, it is primarily through Bento's perceptions that we see the characters, Capitu in particular, who at fourteen is described as tall with two braids, large dark eyes, a straight nose, a delicate mouth, and a rounded chin. Bento conveys her humble socioeconomic background by pointing out the poor manner in which she dresses, evident in her shoes, which are not only old, but which also have been mended by Capitu herself (84–85, Nunes 1983, 125). Bento's emphasis throughout the novel is on Capitu's moral development. She is womanly and reflects an inner spirituality. In particular, her mouth, arms, and eyes are described in synecdoche as a means of evoking her as a whole entity. José Dias describes Capitu's eyes as those of an "oblique and dissimulating gypsy" (113; Nunes 1983, 125). Capitu's "eyes like the tide" (114) with their treacherous magnetism, captivate and threaten Bento (Nunes 1983, 125). These and other fragments, such as Capitu's arms, dark luxurious hair, girlish reticence punctuated with sudden aggressiveness, sly wit, curiosity, and self-control in moments of crisis, coalesce into a portrait of her temperament over the course of the novel (Caldwell 1970, 144; Nunes 1983, 125). Escobar, like Capitu, is evoked through glimpses of his character in action at significant moments rather than through extensive physical description. Escobar's animated gestures, his curious and quickly wandering eyes, quick mind, mathematical genius, and disarming ways all contrast with Bento's features, as does Bento being the only son of a wealthy and aristocratic mother with Escobar being one of two children born to a poor mother (Caldwell 1960, 15).

As is typical of Impressionism, characters are revealed through one another's impressions. Capitu's eyes, her suspicious looks, and curiosity are impressions of José Dias; but Capitu also has her opinions about this meddlesome and fussy man. We also perceive Capitu through Escobar's eyes, whereas Escobar is perceived through the eyes of Cousin Justina, ever on the lookout for some small character fault not only in Escobar, but also in everyone else. Dona Gloria is perceived by the other characters to be a gracious landowning widow, who is deeply religious, severe, and ready to be old before her time. She is surrounded by relatives like Uncle Cosme, an obese lawyer who as a youth had been a political radical and womanizer, but who has lost interest in and energy for either, and by dependents like the pseudointellectual José Dias. Having much the same temperament as *Brás Cubas*'s Doctor Vilaça, José Dias is characterized as a charlatan and an opportunist, known for pompous phrases and generous use of hyperbole (Nunes 1983, 130–31). His remarks about the sense of duty that compelled him to remind Dona Gloria of her promise to enter Bento in a seminary actually reflect his gratuitous meddling in other people's affairs (Nunes 1983, 130–31).

Machado uses dreams and daydreams in *Dom Casmurro*, much as he did with the delirium in *Brás Cubas*, for indirect characterization and narrator self-evocation. A daydream reveals Bento's anxiety and preoccupation over entering the seminary: Emperor Dom Pedro II drives up in his coach to the front door of Bento's house, enters, and tells Dona Gloria to send him to medical school instead. A dream reveals Bento's jealousy, fears, and desires about Capitu: Bento sees Capitu talking with a suitor at a window. When he approaches, the suitor vanishes, and Bento finds Capitu's father Pádua standing next to her. The suitor had brought the list of lottery prizes, but Pádua's lottery ticket turned out to be a blank. Completely astounded, Pádua simply cannot believe he did not win the grand prize, considering the perfect symmetry of his ticket number: 4004. As Pádua speaks about the ticket, Capitu focuses her loving eyes on Bento. Pádua vanishes, along with his hopes for having the winning ticket. Bento quickly glances up and down the street but it is deserted. He clasps Capitu's hands, mumbles a few words, and wakes up alone in the dormitory (158–59).

If, with Nunes, we accept the Freudian importance of a woman's father in her choosing a husband, and Bento's equating of lottery prizes with happiness in married life—which he also did in the case of his parents—the lottery would appear to be a symbol of Bento's hope of winning the grand prize: happiness and fulfillment with Capitu. Pádua's failure to win the lottery may therefore be a prefiguration of Bento's failure in his relationship with Capitu (Nunes 1983, 132).

The characters in *Ayres's Memorial* reveal themselves slowly, and never completely. As in *Brás Cubas* and *Dom Casmurro*, they are evoked through the narrator's eyes, in this case Ayres's, and are filtered through his perceptions, whether in analysis and summary or in re-creations of actual conversations. Even these, however, are filtered through Ayres. Rita, Tristão, Fidélia, Aguiar, and Carmo are all evoked through biographical summary, Ayres's own physical descriptions, through their descriptions of one another, and through their interpretations of one another's actions and behavior. As is common in Impressionist novels, the illusive mood of the subjunctive prevails throughout the novel, such that things "seem to be" or "appear to be," although, in many instances, circumstances turn out to be just as Ayres had sensed they might be (e.g., Tristão and Fidélia's eventual marriage).

In each of his later novels, Machado's experimentation was primarily with the Impressionistic interplay between the implied or actual author (Machado), fictional narrator, the characters, and readers. In *Esau and Jacob*, though this interplay is present, the novel as a whole has more in common with Symbolism. It is true that most literature, even Realist-Naturalist literature, uses symbols of some sort as means of propelling the action (the essence of all art being some sort of metaphorical frame of reference). However, *Esau and Jacob*, much like other Symbolist novels, presents us with a deeper symbolic framework that tends toward the allegorical and archetypal, if not always mythical. Its characters and setting are more abstract ideas or concepts than simple poetic devices or organic metaphors.

Machado symbolically contrasts the twins in *Esau and Jacob* based on their divergent political opinions. And he symbolically contrasts Flora with the self-absorbed and egotistic characters surrounding her, though she, along with most of them, falls short of the ideal of wholeness she symbolizes. The novel closes with a reference to the proverbial flower ("Flora") that Ayres wears in his lapel, which symbolizes the ideal of balance, peace, and wholeness. This is in contradistinction to the twins, who symbolize the contradictory, though complementary, human impulses toward peace and justice, altruism and egoism, and who, like these impulses, remain at war with each other, as they were in their mother's womb. The conclusion suggests that, although humanity has the untapped, but usually distorted, potential to achieve wholeness, it will continue to live out its inherent contradictions, particularly in the political sphere, as long as it continues to pursue egotistic ideals (Nunes 1983, 107, 110).

In keeping with his expressed desire to give characters the autonomy to write their own story, Ayres has little use for the deterministic tell-all devices of the Realist-Naturalist novel. He shuns and ridicules long and baggy descriptions, especially those including physical details, and deliberately leaves many gaps to fill, frequently warning readers to pay close attention and to reread (Wolff 1987, 46, 48).

It is usually Ayres who evokes Flora, effecting her characterization through contrast, art metaphors, and an impressionistic outline of her physical appearance (Nunes 1983, 126). Ayres the narrator is conscious of his function of sketching as he suggests the lines of Flora's physical aspect. By nature, she is a sweet and thoughtful person. She has an aquiline nose, auburn hair, a slender face, and a half laughing mouth. Through Flora's speech, we sense that she is a spirit of conciliation and justice in defending both Pedro and Paulo. Her spirituality and philosophical connotations make her the most ethereal of the novel's characters, yet she shares with them an impressionistic characterization created through the sparse details of her physical description and enigmatic quality (Nunes 1983, 126).

Flora evokes both Pedro and Paulo through showing with her thoughts and imagination. She contemplates Paulo's adventurousness and radicalism, which will overturn the world in order to create another more perfect and just one. He is a perfectionist, and she imagines he would be a good husband. At the same time, she appreciates Pedro's love of peace, order, and harmony, which are equally desirable qualities in a prospective husband. His contentment with the world appeals to Flora's idea of eternal bliss. Flora's desire for both and her failure to make a choice between them before she dies symbolically configure humanity's (and specifically Brazil's) failure to achieve the two ideals at that moment in history (Nunes 1983, 128).

Indeed, Luiz Costa Lima considers Flora's inability to decide between her two suitors to be an accurate allegory of Brazil's political predicament in the late nineteenth century. The twins, who represent the Conservative and Liberal Parties, quarrel about everything and nothing because society requires them to exchange their greater similarity for a less significant difference that will clearly individuate them. In bickering and taking opposing positions, they convince themselves of their difference. Yet both Conservatives and Liberals were basically dominated by the interests of the landowners and were not essentially different. The interchangeability of the two parties is suggested, according to Costa Lima, by the fact that the twins switch parties after the Republic is installed, which also implies that the Republic was not that different from the Monarchy (Lima 1988, 192–98).

As a whole, the later novels, with their predominance of showing, absence of multiple-angle views of character, and lack of descriptive external details, are diametrically opposed to Realism-Naturalism, and further underscore Machado's affinity with Impressionism. This predominance of showing can be traced to their first-person narration, which permits the continuous dramatic self-evocations of the narrator-characters (Bento, Brás, and Ayres in *Ayres's Memorial*). These narrators, in turn, employ dramatic showing in evoking the other characters as well (Nunes 1983, 117, 126).

For the most part, the characters in *Quincas Borba* are evoked in schematic snapshots, and are revealed through fantasies, dreams, monologue, and synecdoche.

However, we do find a frequent use of showing through speech, gesture, facial expressions, and the accumulation of detail through a free indirect style, narrative summary, and multiple-angle views, including analysis and description. These are more conventional techniques associated with Realism-Naturalism than the dream and delirium sequences in *Dom Casmurro* and *Brás Cubas* (Nunes 1983, 138). Yet there is considerable impressionistic ambiguity concerning the inner meaning behind gestures, glances, and facial expressions; indeed, Rubião's dilemma stems from his misinterpretation in these areas (Nunes 1983, 52).

As a whole, *Quincas Borba* demonstrates that Machado was capable of handling Realist-Naturalist techniques, even when he chose to use them less extensively in his other later novels (Nunes 1983, 138). As Ivan Monteiro and Hairton Estrella have suggested, however, even in these cases, Machado's use of Realist-Naturalist techniques appears to have reflected more a parody of materialist-rationalist thinking than any real affinity for the techniques themselves (e.g., *Brás Cubas*; Monteiro and Estrella 1973, 39–47). Brás characterizes himself as one who loves parody, who is somewhat disdainful of the reader, and is satiric in his intentions (Nunes 1983, 67, 71). The recounting of his own death and funeral—a parody of the manner in which the traditional Romantic or Realist novel might be expected to begin—is one of the earliest indications of these satirical intentions (Nunes 1983, 119).

Throughout *Brás Cubas*, there are numerous examples of self-parody, as well as parody of Romanticism's excessive escapism and of overindulgence in the sordid and the profane by Realism-Naturalism and particularly by Naturalism (Nunes 1983, 120). Brás later parodies Romantic sentimentality when, in direct contrast to the suffering lovers in Romantic novels, who are unable to eat at the end of their love affairs, he gives a full account of the tasty lunch he had on the day that his affair with Virgília ended (257–58; Nunes 1983, 120). Brás continues to poke fun at Romantic idealization, and at the repugnant details of Naturalist characterization, when he asserts that he does not idealize Virgília's physical beauty because he is not writing a Romantic novel in which the author ignores "freckles and pimples," though he asserts that Virgília had none (152; Nunes 1983, 120).

Although Machado evokes Virgília through her heavy breathing, shining eyes, insatiable mouth, white bosom, and in particular, bare arms—synecdoche that he often uses to evoke female characters (Nunes 1983, 121)—these erotic details are discreetly toned down. They are mediated not by Romantic idealization but by art metaphors that describe Virgília in sculptural terms. Moreover, the lustful fantasy Brás has of Virgília undressing as he views her is a far cry from the explicit, almost pornographic Naturalist descriptions (Nunes 1983, 121). It seems reasonable to assume that, aside from evoking the predominantly physical attraction between Brás and Virgília, Machado's emphasis on physical detail may also be a means of parodying the Naturalist propensity for sensuous traits in characterization. In either case, it is an indictment of the overemphasis on the materialist component of reality. Brás and Virgília's affair itself seems to be a parody of both the idealized love of Romantic novels and the occasionally depraved love of Realist-Naturalist novels: their relationship is simply about the self-gratification of two egoists. Meanwhile, Eugênia, though also seen through Brás's eyes, is evoked neither in a sensuous manner nor through parody but through her moral character (Nunes 1983, 124).

As was common among Impressionist writers, Machado's preferred first to sketch his characters, then gradually unfold them through events, a process in which his original outline was to be at least partly filled in by the readers. His characters strive to stay afloat in the whirlpool of shifting consciousness, while responding to the changes in perceived events. Their success or failure is determined by their ability to overcome the possible division between the perception and conceptualization of their experiences, and they grow only in proportion to their ability to do so (Stowell 1980, 17, 21). Ultimately, Machado's characters, like those typical of literary Impressionism, are limited empiricists trapped by the reality of their senses, who must learn to sort out the "truths" scattered throughout their myriad perceptions (Stowell 1980, 22). They seek out reasons in order to plan their lives, only to have their view of a person or the world or their circumstances changed by some chance encounter, vague coincidence, or accidental occurrence.

Most of Machado's characters make errors in perception and interpretation, often tragic ones (e.g., Rubião and Bento). Isolated from others and locked into individual space-time vacuums of unfathomable mystery, these characters realize there is a vast hidden world within themselves that is inaccessible. With the exception of Ayres, who experiences a transformation by the end of his diary, most characters live in solitude. This is often indicated by the numerous ellipses that appear in the texts, or by the circular and enclosed nature of such narratives as *Dom Casmurro* and *Brás Cubas*. Characters struggle in isolation for accessibility, sometimes willfully, but always humanly, reaching out through generosity and kindness (Stowell 1980, 30).

As noted above, Machado's later novels demonstrate that he was primarily concerned with his characters' perceptions and conceptualizations of reality and the consequences of the choices they make based on these. Machado's characters face both the ethical crises typical of Realism and the cognitive and epistemological conflicts typical of Impressionism. Although this requires him to present more expository data on character, he does so briefly and in a truncated manner. Even when Machado diverges from his impressionistic paradigm for purposes of satire or parody, his background passages are minimal. He replaces the extensive expository descriptions so vital to the photographic and journalistic techniques of Realism-Naturalism with sparse external detail. Moreover, Machado relies on figurative devices such as synecdoche, where a recurring organic metaphor representing a fragment (e.g., "eyes like the tide") serves as a means of suggesting the whole (Capitu; Nagel 1980, 116, 117, 166, 167; Nunes 1983, 122, 125, 138).

Machado was more concerned with the dramatic revelation (showing) of his characters through action, dialogue, dream, daydream, fantasy, hallucination, and interior monologue than he was with any Realist-Naturalist photographic rendering of them. This is especially apparent in *Brás Cubas*, *Dom Casmurro*, and *Ayres's Memorial*. Except where characters are a narrative center, as Brás, Santiago, and Ayres are or the narrative center of intelligence relates the novel from the protagonist's or another character's perspective, revealing the mechanism of their consciousness, as it does in *Quincas Borba* and *Esau and Jacob*, Machado describes his characters briefly and often from the exterior. This restricts the depth of all but the major characters (Nagel 1980, 116).

Yet in first-person narrations like *Brás Cubas*, *Dom Casmurro*, and *Ayres's Memorial*, where readers are allowed access to the narrator-characters' unspoken thoughts and behavior in action and in dialogue, the restrictions and extreme subjectivity of their vantage points precludes their total development. Realist characters are highly individualized and fully developed. Machado's characters, more in keeping with Impressionism, are highly individualized, but only partially developed (Nagel 1980, 120). They appear as vague, enigmatic, elusive, and disembodied psyches and schematic anatomies that hover over the narration, giving us momentary glimpses of some significant psychological aspect. Combined with other such moments, they coalesce into a "kinetic portrait" (Nagel 1980, 116). In effect, these characters fragment the Realist-Naturalist concept of individuals, whose contours, motivations, and movements are clearly delineated. Instead, the outlines always leave something to the imagination. Machado thus makes more radical demands and requires significantly greater reader collaboration in the narration of his later than of his earlier novels. Readers are made into coauthors of a sort, who are placed in the position of having to participate in the creative process of bringing out the novel's meaning (Iser 1975, 29, 30, 40; Nunes 1983, 80, 118; Soares 1968, 68; Stowell 1980, 29).

In line with his interest in epistemological and ethical questions, Machado chose characters from the more privileged socioeconomic classes. Their social and financial security frees them from the basic imperatives for survival that confront the oppressed underclass characters that tend to populate Naturalist fiction. They are blinded by greed and egoism. Despite their free will, or rather due to an abuse of their free will, they are paradoxically oppressed, and are never inspired by their freedom to pursue genuine love, but rather bad copies and substitutes.

It is not surprising that, as do many Impressionist writers, Machado deals thematically with jealousy, best exemplified in *Dom Casmurro*, and to some extent in *Quincas Borba*. Perhaps more than any other single emotion associated with love, jealousy is nurtured by unseen or suspected relationships, by vague and hurried gestures, ambiguous and oblique glances, and barely audible whispers, which are nevertheless deeply felt (Stowell 1980, 46; Venâncio Filho 2000, 65–88). Machado's characters are not victims of uncontrollable biological urges, as would be the case with Naturalism. Rather, they are victims of perceptual ambiguity, hidden motives, and partial knowledge and they have the moral responsibility to choose from imperfectly understood alternatives. This focus on the phenomena of the psyche, which take place behind the veil of consciousness, allies Machado's later novels with literary Impressionism and places him in the vanguard of late nineteenth- and early twentieth-century Western literature (Almino 2005, 141–42; Fitz 1989, 3, 12, 16, 22; Nagel 1980, 113; Santiago 1978, 13; Wolff 1987, 44–45). Machado's novels do not display the tectonic complexity found in the writings of Marcel Proust, Henry James, Anton Chekhov, or Thomas Mann. Nonetheless, they share in the Impressionist aesthetic of these authors and are singular achievements that place Machado far ahead of his literary contemporaries in Brazil and Latin America (Armstrong 1999, 71, 75–76; Dennis 1990, 75–77; Gledson 1997, xx; Lisboa 1997, 172; Muricy 1988, 116, 118, 120; Nunes 1983, 140).

MACHADO DE ASSIS: AN ALTERNATIVE INTERPRETATION

G. Reginald Daniel with Gary L. Haddow

Modernity and Postmodernity: From "Either/Or" to "Both/Neither"

Machado's shared sensibility with Romantic Realist and Impressionist aesthetics reflects his broader experience of being *both* black and white, yet *neither*. By providing him with a sensitivity to the liminal space or "space-in-between" (*o entre-lugar*; Santiago 2000, 9), this experience enhanced Machado's ability to convey shades of meaning when discussing issues ranging from slavery to national literature, literary aesthetics, and modernity. Located in the late nineteenth and the early twentieth centuries, Machado's "both/neither" perspective, which views black and white as inherently relative and interlocking extremes on a continuum of grays, displays, according to novelist John Barth, a clear affinity with the postmodern sensibility (Barth in Fitz 1990, 15, 20–21).

To see how this is so, it is useful to trace the origins of postmodernism, whose symptomatic features first appeared in the works of Immanuel Kant (1724–1804) and Georg Hegel (1770–1831) during the early nineteenth century in German Romanticism and later in those of Friedrich Nietzsche (1844–1900) and Martin Heidegger (1889–1976; Rosenau 1992, 93). Foremost among those features are a recognition of and anxiety over the collapse of the faith and confidence in the capacities of intellect and reason (and its cultural embodiments in science and technology) and in the certitude of "progress" that had been hallmarks of the modern worldview (Harvey 1989, 27; Lowy 1998, 594–600; Rattansi 1994, 17). Postmodernism was a reaction against the sensate culture that had emerged out of the "Galilean-Cartesian-Baconian-Newtonian science" (Griffin 1993, viii), which spanned the Renaissance and became preeminent during the Enlightenment (Griffin 1993, vii; Hollinger 1994, 2–4, 13, 29; Rosenau 1992, 5–17), and which was bequeathed to the nineteenth and twentieth centuries, most notably through the various branches of philosophical positivism and scientific rationalism (Harvey 1989, 27).

Pitirim Sorokin captured this collapse of faith and confidence in his meticulous sociological analysis of Western history based on the regular cyclical waxing and waning of the sensate and the ideational paradigms, which influence trends in painting, sculpture, architecture, literature, economics, philosophy, science, and warfare. The ascendancy of the sensate paradigm that originated during the Renaissance was preceded by the ascendancy of its ideational counterpart during the rise of Christianity in the medieval era (Amin 1989, 71–76; Sorokin 1957, 268–75; Stromberg 1975, 4, 10, 14–16). Medieval Europeans saw themselves embedded in both physical (sensate) and spiritual (ideational) space. Their cosmology included a place not only for the body but also for the soul. Yet, with the advent of modern science in the sixteenth and seventeenth centuries, space came to be conceived in purely physical terms and the universe seen as a vast machine governed by mathematical laws. The extraordinary success of this scientific understanding had come at a price, however. By removing spiritual space from conceptions of reality, Modernists made any discussion of spiritual phenomena seem unreal, even illegitimate (Wertheim 1999, 17–43).

Moreover, the Modernist paradigm rested on a vision of the self or subject divorced from the empirical or sensory world of objects. The observer and mind were thought to be detached from the objective world of observed material phenomena. "The subjective and intersubjective domains were thus reduced to empirical studies ... and ... humans [themselves] became objects of information, never subjects of communication" (Wilber 1996, 270). The resulting "mirror of nature" worldview, often referred to as the "representation paradigm," was premised on the belief in one true, preordained empirical or objective reality, which was copied onto each individual's subjective consciousness. Knowledge (and thus truth) would be yielded solely by mirroring or reflecting—mapping— this one true world in the form of mimesis, objectively represented in scientific models (Rosenau 1992, 92–108; Wilber 1996, 59).

During the nineteenth and the early twentieth centuries, however, the limitations of the "mirror view of nature" became increasingly clear (Rosenau 1992, 92–96; Smith 1989, 9; Wilber 1996, 65–66); mapping the objective world left out the subjects who were making the maps in the first place and who brought something essential to the picture (Rosenau 1992, 46–49, 92–96; Smith 1989, 232–46; Wilber 1996, 57–86). Thus when the crisis of modernity came at last, it reflected one of the great transformations in human history. Indeed, the violent seismic shift during the nineteenth and twentieth centuries was comparable in magnitude to the profound shift from the ideational-dominated worldview of the medieval era to the sensate-dominated worldview of the Renaissance and Reformation that gave rise to modernity (Berman 1989, 72–78; Hoogvelt 1978, 25–26; Hollinger 1994, 25–26; Sorokin 1957, 622–23).

This "counter-Enlightenment," which became pronounced by the late nineteenth and the early twentieth centuries (Lyotard 1979, xxiii–xxv, 18–31), may be viewed as part of a broader transformation frequently referred to as "the postmodern turn" (Seidman 1994, 2). However, the term "postmodern" reflects a temporal ambiguity as well as an elusive, elastic, and equivocal sense of presence that defies any consensual definition (Slater 1994, 87). That said, postmodernism proper is generally said to have emerged in the early 1970s. It figures prominently in the works of twentieth-century Western European (particularly French) thinkers (Bertens 1993, 25–70; 1997, 103–20; Connor 1989, 27–64; Hollinger 1994, xii, 35, 47; Rosenau 1992, 12; Searle 1995, 28–48; Toro 1997, 29–33; Trey 1998, 31–68).[1]

Postmodern thinkers reject the Modernist notion that there is a linear connection between subjects and an objective world, whose reality is made transparent through the application of sensate culture's rationality and empiricism (Anderson 1995b, 4). Instead, they argue that humans construct reality, or rather realities, since their constructs are multiple or plural (Derrida 1979, 103). This argument has led postmodernists to dismiss the notion that the truth can be found in any impartial sense. Previously, arguments centered on which reality was "true." The postmodern position is that none is true in an absolute sense; all have some claims to validity (Rosenau 1992, 82–83; Smith 1989, 232–34; Toro 1997, 29–33).

A critical divide between the postmodern and modern worldviews is the proposition that all concepts and categories are largely sociocultural constructs, rather than unalterable essences (Hollinger 1994, 1–19; Natoli and Hutcheon 1993, ix–xiv; Rattansi 1994, 28; Rosenau 1992, 6–7, 67–82, 128–33; Seidman 1994, 1–21; Slater 1994, 87–90). If there is no singular reality but only multiple realities, each constructed and sponsored by its respective society and grounded in history, postmodernists argue that these multiple realities deserve equal respect in the manner of egalitarian pluralism (Rosenau 1992, 119, 128; Smith 1989, 232–34). That there are many centers and none of them holds delegitimizes any foundation upon which to secure a universal and objective reality. Instead, humans are "exposed to a babble of diverse and contradictory fragments" (Anderson 1995b, 4).

Deconstructive postmodernism, popularly considered most representative of postmodernism and perhaps its most vilified manifestation, maintains that there are no universal truths since all truth is relative (Natoli and Hutcheon 1993, ix; Rosenau 1992, 5–7, 14–17; Toro 1997, 29–33; Wilber 1996, 166, 187–92, 261–72).[2] Truth is culture bound and based on nothing much more than shifting tastes. Everything is "socially constructed"; different cultural worldviews are arbitrary, anchored in nothing but power or prejudice (Foucault 1980, 38–39; Rosenau 1992, 78). The only existing truth in the universe is the one some humans are able to force on others. Calling the very concept of universality into question, the deconstructive postmodern mind tends to be blurred and amorphous. It lacks an all-embracing outlook or metanarrative and actually doubts that it is any longer possible (or even desirable) to have one (Lyotard 1979, xxiii–xxv, 18–31; Smith 1989, 232–34).

In contrast to their deconstructive counterparts, constructive postmodernists have repudiated the scathing of grand narratives (Griffin 1993, 1–42; Rosenau 1992, 5–7, 14–17).[3] They argue that the deconstructive approach, when not counterbalanced by an integrative perspective, can lead to a debilitating relativism and ultimately to nihilism (Griffin 1993, 1–42; Rosenau 1992, 132) and that worldviews are not simply arbitrary but, rather, develop in history. In particular, Ken Wilber argues that these worldviews are constrained by currents in the objective environment that determine how much a culture can arbitrarily construct, which in turn prevents worldviews from being merely "collective hallucinations" (Wilber 1996, 61). The constructivist perspective investigates the actual history and unfolding of these worldviews as an evolutionary process governed in part by the currents of evolution itself. Most constructivists argue that each worldview gives way to its successor because certain inherent limitations in the previous worldview become apparent (Rosenau 1992, 105; Wilber 1996, 61–65).

Although accepting the notion that truth is constructed, not found, constructive postmodernists reject the idea that there is no objective world external to subjective consciousness. They argue that it is not necessary to deny the existence of the objective sensory world in order to acknowledge the creative influence of the subject, although both constructive and deconstructive postmodernists reject the notion of a substantial or unified and static self or ego (Anderson 1995b, 8). Human beliefs concerning the nature of reality are products of a creative interaction between the subjective consciousness and the external world. Moreover, ideas cannot be understood apart from the language that produced them (Anderson 1995b, 8; Baldwin 2008, 58–61; Smith 1989, 232–34; Wilber 1996, 61–5).

In sum, constructive postmodernism considers modern Western thought, including modern Western science and scholarship, as merely one way of thinking alongside others. It also abandons the quest for certainty and any solid foundation in an absolute sense on which to build constructive systems. Thus deconstructing much of the Western tradition is central to the project of constructive postmodernism (Baldwin 2008, 47–51; Rosenau 1992, 21). Yet constructive postmodernists argue that humanity will be even more severely limited if it seeks solely to deconstruct modernity—that the deconstruction of modernity should be accompanied by proposals for reconstruction (Rosenau 1992, 124).

Indeed, they believe humanity needs a new, more radically integrative or inclusive vision of reality (or metanarrative) than that originating in the modern worldview (Baldwin 2008, 47–51; Rosenau 1992, 124). By arguing that humans cannot respond to contemporary problems effectively with the modern way of thinking, however, constructive postmodernists are neither calling for a return to the traditional and premodern nor rejecting rational thought (Baldwin 2008, 47–51; Griffin 1993, 2, 11; Toro 1997, 29–33; Wilber 1996, 69–70). Rather, they are seeking to combine elements of the premodern and modern while at the same time transcending both the premodern world's supernaturalism and the modern world's anthropocentrism, individualism, materialist rationalism, and mechanism (Griffin 1989, 32–40). Their constructive stance is a response to the threats posed to humanity—and, indeed, to the entire planet Earth—by Modernism's sensate culture and materialist rationalist epistemology as well as by its negation of ideational culture, including its ecological impulses (Griffin 1993, ix–x). Their goal has been to avert the most insidious of all confrontations: humanity against humanity, life against itself (Rosenau 1992, 6–7).

Machado de Assis and the Postmodern Sensibility:
"The Centrality of the Middle"[4]

Despite their different trajectories, deconstructive and constructive postmodern sensibilities are both part of the critique of modernity and Western European society and culture as the normative standard against which all else is measured. Both reject modernity's dichotomous and hierarchical ranking of differences (inegalitarian pluralism) as well as its totalizing universalism, which resulted in the leveling of these differences (inegalitarian integration or assimilation; Baudrillard 1975, 88–89; Havel 1994; 1995, 232–38). Postmodernists have frequently sought to deconstruct this dichotomous hierarchy by highlighting "marginal," "hybrid" (or "mixed") phenomena that are "undecipherable with reference" to its framework (Rattansi 1994, 30; Sorokin 1957, 623–28, 699–704; Spieker 1995, 449–69). They do this to demonstrate the difficulties of defining one category of experience without including elements of another (Derrida 1978, 278–83; 1981, 42–43; Rosenau 1992, 5–7; Seidman 1994, 8–9; Söderlind 1994, 38–54). This strategy questions the hierarchical "grounds on which the dichotomy is erected" (Rattansi 1994, 30).

The deconstructive (both/and) and constructive (neither/nor) postmodern sensibilities are examples of Sorokin's "mixed mentalities" (Sorokin 1957, 49). The cyclical interplay between sensate and ideational modalities produces intermediate hybrid types or stages, which seek to express both modalities. One mixed mentality (which Sorokin refers to as "idealistic" or "integral") manifests itself most clearly in transition periods after ideational sociocultural dominance as a means of seeking to bring some reason into a world that appears to have taken leave of its senses. Another mixed mentality (which might be thought of as "neo-integral") tends to appear after periods of sensate sociocultural dominance. It is frequently accompanied by desperation and despair typically precipitated by a loss of faith in materialist rationalism, and its embodiments in science and technology, as the final arbiters of the truth. Ultimately, it reflects a spiritual crisis in which the goal is to offset the imbalance of a world that has gone to sensate extremes (Sorokin 1957, 49; 1964, 13–62).[5]

The periods of transition marked by these mixed mentalities not only serve as bridges between the ideational and sensate paradigms; they also bring forth individuals who seek to articulate the deepest notions of the inherent possibilities of human nature. Despite their temporal and stylistic differences, both integral and neo-integral mixed mentalities and their various historical articulations are premised on the belief that true reality has both sensate and ideational aspects (Sorokin 1957, 28–29). They interrogate the "either/or" perspective, with its "emphasis on the precision of interpretation and on the reduction of ambiguity" (Simone 1989, 141), complexity, and multiplicity, which constructs phenomena as different categories of experience that are viewed as mutually exclusive (or dichotomous), if not hierarchical, and that have an independent existence of their own. The resulting "monological" thinking (Wilber 1998, 141) that underpins the modern worldview considers singularity as the norm in terms of the construction of all categories of difference including race, gender, sexuality, and so on, as well as one's stance on critical social issues relating to morality and politics (Colker 1996, 1–10). The monological paradigm is part of what Pierre Bourdieu defines as the "doxa" (Bourdieu 1977, 159), that is to say, the sphere of sacred, sacrosanct, or unquestioned social concepts or dogmas that have acquired the status and effect of a force of nature. In contrast to this "either/or" perspective, these mixed mentalities reflect a composite both/neither perspective (Rattansi 1994, 30; Rosenau 1992, 5–7; Seidman 1994, 8–9; Wilber 1996, 69–70; 1997, 71–92; 2000, 167, 272, 278), which is premised on the "centrality of the middle" (Spieker 1995, 449).

Machado's consciousness was imbued with mixed mentality by virtue of his experience of being *both* black and white, yet *neither*, and the accompanying dualism he experienced between himself and the dominant European Brazilian culture. This gave rise to Machado's sensitivity to the borderland experience and to his more chromatic perspective on many contemporary topics. Correspondingly, Machado's insight into these concerns was informed not only by their immediate significance but also by their long-term and wide-ranging implications (Hansen 1997, 250–51; Nunes 1983, x).

For example, as someone who displayed this both/neither postmodern sensibility, Machado examined the larger existential questions of human bondage and its impact on *both* masters *and* slaves to arrive at his more nuanced indictment of slavery. That mainly white abolitionist authors argued along roughly similar lines to advance their cause might have made Machado's stance seem more acceptable to and indeed less subversive of contemporary literary social and literary norms. Yet such authors used their argument as a fear tactic to warn white readers of the potential social contagion of contact with individuals damaged by human bondage unless new forms of social control were implemented once slavery was abolished. Machado's argument was that slavery as form of racial oppression not only deprives subordinate groups of basic human amenities but also deprives dominant groups of their own humanity by preventing them from embracing the humanity of racialized "Others."

As part of this process, Machado juxtaposes the trials and tribulations of whites with those experienced by African Brazilians. Yet he does this without implying that the dehumanization experienced by masters was qualitatively or quantitatively equivalent to that of slaves. Machado's perspective should be understood neither as license to overlook the symbolic and social pathologies of white privilege and power nor as an appeal to those whose conception of racial equality reified the notion of white innocence and redemption (Frank and McPhail 2005, 573). Rather, Machado conceptualizes a space where racial groups may share common principles and the "transcendent value" of equity and justice (Shafer 2008). David Frank and Mark McPhail refer to this as the "rhetoric of consilience," which is an effective discursive strategy that emphasizes the essential nature of human equality and need for multiple agencies of responsibility and action (Frank and McPhail 2005, 573).

As a further reflection of the both/neither perspective, Machado's use of parody, irony, and the grotesque, though frequently satirical, is permeated with a lighthearted and restrained playfulness that combines dark comedy with light tragedy (Schwartz 2000, 38). Moreover, Machado's self-reflexive narrators address readers with "genial insolence, or with avuncular wisdom, or in the complicit tones of a confiding crony" (Schwartz 2000, 38). They openly display an interest in the processes of the narrative itself and the means by which it constructs both text and readers. Indeed, Machado requires readers to be active co-creators of meaning rather than passive consumers of the novel. Instead, he brings readers into direct participation with the characters, making both narrators and readers characters of a sort (Nicol 2009, 1–50).

That Machado deliberately undermines the narrators' ironic assurance to readers of a shared viewpoint makes readers not only accomplices to the irony in the novel but also in part at least victims of it (Hansen 1997, 246–48; Rosenau 1992, 25–41). Antonio Tosta refers to this narrative technique as being "entreabertura" (halfway open). The resulting sense of "in-betweenness" makes it possible for narrators to fully exercise their authorial power while at the same time giving readers creative license to fill in the gaps of the text, which helps bring the narration to life. Moreover, the narrators frequently lead readers to draw conclusions about the text, only to deconstruct them afterward (Tosta 2004, 37–55).

Machado concentrates on the verbal medium itself and the ways in which readers perceive it such that these perceptions and the language that produces them are intertwined. He prepares readers for a familiar literary experience but then, by means of a radical, if subtly maneuvered, shift, presents them with a situation in which they cannot resort to conventional literary responses. This technique, which relies on the contrast between expectation and fulfillment, the disturbance of space-time perception, and the relationship between cause and effect, leaves readers acutely disoriented. This is frequently attributable to Machado's manipulation and ultimate exposure of the devices he uses to trap readers (Cruz Júnior 2002,

180–82; Danow 1995, 5–31, 33–64; Hansen 1997, 246; Harpham 1982, 3–22; Hodgson 1976, 7; McElroy 1989, ix–x, 1–29; Reis 1992, 54–55; Rosenau 1992, 25–41).

Through these and other literary techniques, Machado seeks to interrogate, invert, subvert, and disrupt both the structures and the normative expectations of the social order. Indeed, as John Gledson has argued, Machado provides readers with two texts. One is transparent, interesting, and amusing. The other is less immediately apparent and provides unsettling insights into the repressiveness and callousness of the overwhelmingly white Brazilian elite (Gledson 1987, 21; Reis 1992, 53–54).

Likewise, Machado's writings are part of a larger oppositional framework that interrogates colonial discourse. Yet Machado sought to go beyond the limitations of anticolonial nationalist writings. In keeping with his both/neither framework, he recommended borrowing the finest and most enduring exemplars of European literature while at the same time transforming these into something at once uniquely Brazilian and yet universal in resonance and appeal (Baptista 1991, 43–63, 99–114; Cândido 1995, 129–30, 135; Douglass 1998, 1037; Facioli 2002, 165; Santiago 2001, 151–52; Schwarz 1990, 9–13; 1992, xv, 101–3).

Machado's search for a Brazilian national "instinct" or essence, though incompatible with deconstructive postmodernism, which views essentialism as one of modernity's greatest tyrannies, is altogether compatible with the constructive postmodern notion that there is an underlying "thematic Brazilian self" that provides a sense of connection, if not unity, to Brazil's developmental variations that have emerged through history. Machado's understanding of Brazil as a collective subjectivity or national essence is grounded in something akin to Pierre Bourdieu's "habitus." This is the cumulative, durable totality of cultural and personal life experiences that Brazilians carry with themselves—a collective subject or self that has its own characteristics, structures, development, and history. Although Brazil's national habitus is empirical, Machado would argue that it cannot be structured in the form of a substantial or unitary self (or ego), as was the case in the reductionist essentializing associated with modernity. Rather, this collective self is the strategic interplay of multiple inputs that postmodernists would argue is unique to Brazil, namely, the "national instinct," although it defies objectification and scientific generalization (Oc, 3:803–7; Bourdieu 1979/1984, 175; 1990, 52–53; Cândido 1995, 129–30, 135; Rosenau 1992, 57–61; Schwarz 1987, 29–48; 1990, 9–13; 1992, xv, 101–6).

Similarly, Machado's search for the universal, though incompatible with deconstructive postmodernism, would be compatible with constructive postmodernism.

Machado searched for commonality, a unifying thread that tied together the parts into a whole. The universal was reflected in the particular, and the particular was wedded to and grounded in the universal (Oc, 3:803–7; Cândido 1995, 129–30, 135; Schwarz 1987, 29–48; 1990, 9–13; 1992, xv, 101–6).

Also in keeping with this both/neither stance, Machado was essentially a radical skeptic (Gledson 1997, xviii; Muricy 1988, 17–19; Neto 1994, 8–10), who displayed what Jean-François Lyotard refers to as "an incredulity toward metanarratives" (Lyotard 1979, xxiv–xxv). He "maintained a position of unmitigated disbelief toward all philosophical systems and categorizations" (Rego 1997, xviii). According to Gledson, Machado believed that there is no "ultimate system of belief and everything can be relativized" (Gledson 1997, xix). He repudiated modernity's dominant sensate culture and materialist rationalist epistemology, as well as its patriarchal underpinnings, by virtue of the threat they pose to Brazil and, by extension, to humanity (Caldwell 1970, 89; Hansen 1997, 251; Miskolci 2006, 352–77; Needell 1983, 94–96).[6]

But despite being a radical skeptic, Machado did not completely dismiss spirituality as an aspect of ideational culture (although, based on the scanty information available, many critics have argued he was not only a philosophical skeptic but a religious one as well; Neto 1994, 7–11; Gledson 1997, xviii). In fact, Machado's stance on spirituality is not readily apparent, at least not in terms of the metaphysical connotation of the term. Some would suggest that Machado was an atheist, whereas others would argue he was an agnostic. That said, atheists typically express a disbelief in metaphysics, the existence of God or a "higher" power, and an afterlife, largely because of the lack of empirical evidence and rational explanations for the existence of these phenomena (Huxley 1992, 142–67; Mills 2006, 25–64). Although many self-identified atheists tend toward secular philosophies (e.g., humanism and naturalism), there is no single ideology or set of beliefs to which all atheists subscribe (Mills 2006, 25–64). On the other hand, agnosticism holds that the truth of theological claims regarding metaphysics, the existence of God, an afterlife, or even ultimate reality are unknown or, depending on the form of agnosticism, inherently unknowable due to the nature of subjective experience (Huxley 1992, 142–67; Mills 2006, 26). In both cases, agnosticism involves some form of skepticism. And, in Machado's case, the operative term is skepticism (Muricy 1988, 17–19; Neto 1994, 7–10).

Machado expressed what might appear to be a belief in metaphysical phenomena in a November 20, 1904, letter to Joaquim Nabuco, which conveyed a sense of his own imminent death: "Everything around me reminds me of my sweet and loving Carolina. Since I myself am on the edge of that eternal repose, I shall not be spending much time remembering her. I'll be going to see her, she'll be waiting for me ..." (*Oc*, 3:1071). Yet, shortly before his death, when asked whether he wanted a priest to perform last rites, Machado, who apparently remained lucid and coherent up until the last minute, refused this offer (*Oc*, 1:90; Caldwell 1970, 199). Indeed, he is reported to have said, "That would be hypocritical" (Assis in Fonseca 1968, 259; Magalhães Júnior 1981, 4:360; Viana Filho 1974, 287). Although, on the surface, Machado's refusal of last rites might seem to contradict his previous statement about Carolina, it was not necessarily a rejection of the sanctity of one's rite of passage into the afterlife. Rather, it had to do with what he clearly perceived as hypocritical—embracing Christian ritual in his final hours when he had rejected it most of his adult life (and reportedly had not attended church since his wedding).

Machado may have been "spiritual," but he was clearly not "religious" (Caldwell 1970, 10). He openly questioned religious politics as well as the institutionalization and ritualization of beliefs by the Church, which demanded fidelity to doctrine that in no small part encouraged religious hypocrisy and a conspicuous "calculating relativism, in which sins have values attached, and can be paid for 'quite literally' in currency of prayers, paternosters, and Ave Marias" (Gledson 1997, xx).[7] Machado was also disparaging of popular superstitions that more often than not spawned an uncritical acceptance of what he felt amounted to a questionable and vapid Spiritism (Douglass 1998, 1036–55; Machado 1983, 129–33, 183, 186).

"Spiritism" or "Spiritist Doctrine" was systematized by Hippolyte Léon Denizard Rivail (1804–69), better known by his pseudonym "Allan Kardec" (Moreira-Almeida and Neto 2005, 570). Kardec defined Spiritism as "a science that deals with the nature, origin and destiny of the spirits, as well as its manifestations with the corporeal world" (Kardec 1859/1995, 50). A synthesis of Protestantism, Catholicism, mysticism, and science (Hess 1991, 74), Spiritism differentiates itself from its Anglo-Saxon counterpart, Spiritualism, by its belief in reincarnation (Hess 1991, 16; Moreira-Almeida and Neto 2005, 571). Kardec considered Spiritism to be essentially a science (in its original sense) and a philosophy replete with moral concerns, rather than a religion. Spiritism implies a "reification" of the spiritual world in the sense that spirits are scientifically real. This reification in turn desacralizes the spirit or metaphysical world into an object of scientific analysis and presents an alternative interpretation of orthodox scientific thinking (although traditional scientists generally consider the Spiritist thesis as "pseudoscientific"; Hess 1991, 45–56; Moreira-Almeida and Neto 2005, 571).

The "Brazilianization" of Kardecism came about through the work of Adolfo Bezerra de Menezes Cavalcanti (1831–1900), particularly after the separation of Church and state that accompanied the founding of the Republic in 1889 left the Church institutionally weak (Moreira-Almeida and Neto 2005, 579–82). The Church's attempts to redress the situation through a program of "Romanization"—creating a large bureaucracy, importing foreign-born priests, and suppressing thaumaturgy (the working of wonders, miracles, and magic spells)—failed to diminish popular enthusiasm for the faith-healing and Spiritist practices of folk Catholicism. These were imbued with elements of indigenous religious expression throughout most rural areas where state influence was limited. Romanization had a similarly negligible impact on the appeal of African Brazilian religions among the masses in the urban areas (Hess 1991, 89–90). If anything, it served only to create a shortage of supply in the face of continued demand. Spiritists met this demand by replacing the Catholic folk healer's blessings and rituals of exorcisms with their magnetic and spiritual "passes" and "disobsession therapy" (Hess 1991, 89).

Spiritism provided an alternative to mainstream religion, whereas Kardecism attempted to fill a vacuum in the field of medical science. Bezerra de Menezes, who has been referred to as the "Brazilian Freud," persisted in promoting the Spiritist belief in reincarnation and formalizing the spiritual beliefs of the Brazilian masses despite being satirized by Machado and others. Machado on several occasions targeted Spiritists with his sardonic wit in his newspaper articles, astutely catching them at their most embarrassing moments (Hess 1991, 95–96).

In his short story "Uma visita de Alcibíades" (A Visit from Alcibíades), first published in *Journal das Famílias* (*Families' Journal*) and republished in revised form in his collection of short stories *Papéis avulsos* (*Oc*, 2:352–57), Machado unleashed a scathing attack against the Spiritist craze (Machado 1983, 129–31). Spiritist disciple Bezerra de Menezes considered belief in reincarnation to be part of "disobession therapy," which he believed could cure insanity. In the short story "A segunda vida" (The Second Life") and in *Quincas Borba*, Machado reversed the relationship, characterizing belief in reincarnation as a step on the road *to* insanity (Hess 1991, 95–96; Machado 1983, 129–33, 183, 186). Machado dismissed Bezerra de Menezes's attempt to bring scientific legitimacy to what he considered popular religion and superstition.

On September 28, 1886, one month after Bezerra de Menezes announced his conversion to Spiritism, Machado commented sarcastically that "one cannot serve two masters; either it be Baependi or Allan Kardec" (Assis 1956, 44). The Conde de Baependi (Brás Carneiro Nogueira da Costa e Gama) was the president of the Senate and a Conservative politician from Pernambuco, to whom Bezerra de Menezes was subservient. However, Bezerra de Menezes was from Ceará, not Pernambuco, and his subservience was a matter of party discipline, not regional origins (Hess 1991, 95–96). Yet, at the same time, Machado spoke out against the materialist positivists who, in perpetuating scientism and a scientific fundamentalism that considered the sensate mode as the absolute and only justifiable means of accessing the truth, displayed a new, almost religious devotion to mechanistic determinism and reductionism (Caldwell 1970, 89–91, 113, 124–25; Gledson 1997, xx; Hansen 1997, 251; Rocha 2006, xxxi; Virgillo 1972, 73).

That said, Machado clearly, though most often indirectly, expressed the need for a reciprocal relationship between the internal and external aspects of human identity. He argued that humans possess two souls, one on the inside (*alma interior*)—the subjective self—and one on the outside (*alma exterior*)—the objective self. These were roughly equivalent to the individual morality or conscience (the ideational or subjective aspect) and to the image reflected in the mirror through social interactions (the sensate or objective aspect) motivated by egoism and the dictates of public success (*Oc*, 2:345–52). Machado was highly critical of modernity's dominant either/or paradigm, which divided these two aspects of human identity into antagonistic categories of experience, thus impeding or precluding entirely a sense of mutuality between them (Boyd 1975, 45; Brookshaw 1986, 179; Daniel 1981, 11; Haberly 1983, 74–75; Hansen 1997, 250–51).

Most of Machado's main characters experience a crisis of identity as they confront their contradictory and ambiguous natures while navigating their kaleidoscopic selves. And all experience a split between themselves and the outside world, between conscious desires and deeper motivations and the choices they make among them. Because each character is caught between the objective reality of the senses and the subjective reality of the mind, material considerations often overpower the desire for loving relationships. Through their inability to achieve a balance between selfless love and self-love, most of the characters in Machado's novels become victims of themselves and of others (Daniel 1981, 12). Through them, and in keeping with the constructive postmodern sensibility, Machado thus expresses the need for a reciprocal relationship between the subjective and objective dimensions, or internal and external selves, however elusive such a relationship might be (Nunes 1983, 12, 82–84, 140, 142–43).

Machado's characters are confronted with the challenge of coming to terms with their multiple selves in lived experience by integrating their sensory awareness, perceptions, and relationship with the outside world. In this process, they are faced with having to accommodate ambiguity as they navigate through their diverse selves; their experiences cannot be structured or aggregated in the form of a unitary, stable, and transparent self or ego espoused by modernity. Rather, as subjects, Machado's characters are more in keeping with the postmodern understanding of the self that is the strategic interplay and balancing of multiple inputs, that is unique to each individual, and that can be neither objectified nor generalized (Powell 1997, 1481–1520; Rosenau 1992, 42–61). Indeed, João Hansen argues, they reflect Machado's critique of the empiricism and the "unity of the person" demanded by the "order and progress" of a positivist (and Modernist) society (Hansen 1999, 32).

Machado is highly adept at capturing the intricate and often contradictory identity and subjectivity that all human possess, or what Avery Gordon refers to as "complex personhood" (Gordon 1997, 4). All of us remember and have lapses in memory, are beleaguered by contradiction, and recognize and misrecognize ourselves and others. All of us suffer, whether selfishly or graciously, and are mired in the symptoms of our troubles, but all of us are also capable of transformation. Complex personhood means that the stories people tell about themselves, about their trials and tribulations, about their social worlds are "entangled and weave between what is immediately available" as a narrative and "what their imaginations are reaching toward" (Gordon 1997, 4). Gordon argues that complex personhood, at the very least, is about understanding that individuals are complex and often contradictory subjects who lead lives that are "simultaneously straightforward and full of enormously subtle meaning" (Gordon 1997, 5).

In contrast to the Modernist paradigm that posits the self or subject as separate from the sensory world of objects and materials, Machado supports a paradigm that deconstructs the dichotomization of subject and object. As someone of postmodern sensibility, Machado considers the assumption that humans actually perceive the objective world or reality to be naive. His characters' personal traits, structures, development, and history influence what they see in the objective world surrounding them. As subjects, they perceive the objective world quite differently at various times, based not so much on what is actually "out there" in some "pregiven" world as on what they bring to the picture (Hansen 1997, 248, 251; Rosenau 1992, 42–61).

Though not denying the existence of an objective sensory world external to the subjective consciousness, Machado dismisses the notion that the truth can be found in an impartial and fixed sense. Rather, through the characters in his novels, he conveys the belief that the external world cannot be understood apart from the language that produced it—that all human understanding of the nature of reality is the result of a creative interaction between the subjective consciousness and the external world (Moreci 2009; Rosenau 1992, 42–61).

To suggest the complexity and elusiveness of this creative interaction, Machado frequently resorts to descriptive haziness and vagueness. His novels are filled with crepuscular imagery and phrases of the type "not this, but not quite that," compounded by his generous use of the subjunctive, which with its "perhaps," "seems like," and "although" is the most ambiguous and elusive of all grammatical moods (Daniel 1981, 11). And Machado's frequent use of imperfect verb forms gives his novels the quality of being hauntingly stranded between beginning and ending, between being and becoming (Brayner 1979, 101–103; Daniel 1981, 11; Gysin 1975, 27–32; Hodgson 1976, 7–9).

Following this both/neither line of reasoning, Machado's goal was to disabuse cultivated Brazilian authors and readers alike of the folly of absolute reliance on either the objectivist aesthetics of Realism-Naturalism or the subjectivist aesthetics of Romanticism (Hansen 1997, 246). In order to capture reality without sacrificing aesthetic truths, Machado rejected such absolute reliance; he contended that becoming entangled in either extreme would be deleterious to the creative process. Speaking to one of those extremes, Hansen believes Machado's novels can be seen to interrogate a basic premise of Realist-Naturalist aesthetics—the validity of mimesis and the cultural assumptions sustaining it (Hansen 1999, 23–25, 31; Moreci 2009). In drawing from both Realism-Naturalism and Romanticism, the novels are informed by a transformative aesthetic, one Machado shares with other Romantic Realist and Impressionist prose fiction writers of his time (Hodgson 1976, 29; Nunes 1983, 13, 143; Schwarz 1977, 140–56). Just as Romantic Realists sought to extend Romanticism's boundaries and capacities, so Impressionists sought to extend those of Realism-Naturalism (*Oc*, 3:813, 913, 912; Barreto Filho 1947, 78–79; Castello 1969, 33–36; Fitz 1989, 11–12).

Indeed, from his first novel, *Resurrection*, to his last, *Ayres's Memorial*, Machado displays a kinship with Romantic Realist and Impressionist aesthetics. He sought to bridge sensate culture's aesthetic subjectivism and ideational culture's aesthetic objectivism while exploring the duality and ambiguity of the subjective and objective dimensions of human identity. Machado's integration of these aesthetic differences is based on critical hybridity. Borrowing from David Frank and Mark McPhail's "rhetoric of consilience" (Frank and McPhail 2005, 573), one could argue that Machado forged an "aesthetics of consilience." He sought to transform the dynamics of aesthetic division into an aesthetic reconciliation that emphasized the essential nature of aesthetic equality (Frank and McPhail 2005, 577–78). This approach still recognizes and indeed validates aesthetic difference but transforms the operations of negative difference into acts of positive coherence (McPhail 1996, 141–43). Machado endeavored to replace the either/or paradigm of modernity with a both/neither framework congruous with the postmodern sensibility. This ensures him a place in the vanguard of late nineteenth- and early twentieth-century Western thinking (Santiago 1978, 13; Wolff 1987, 44–45).

Though it may have been expedient at times for Machado to subdue one racial component to the other in his public life, what is often described as Machado's journey into whiteness was in fact his striving to achieve a meta-mulatto identity that reflected all colors—as does white—and absorbed them all—as does black—yet transcended racial specificity. In rejecting "the idea that descent is destiny," Machado presented a far-reaching challenge to identity politics (Hollinger 2008, 1034). Indeed, Machado's life and writings represent both a personal triumph over many of the social constraints imposed on individuals of African descent in nineteenth- and early twentieth-century Brazil and a significant contribution to the struggle for racial equality. Yet, in the mirror of his sorrows and triumphs as a mulatto reaching toward this goal, Machado saw a reflection of the struggles confronting all of humanity.

NOTES

Introduction

1. I use the words "mulatto" and "multiracial" interchangeably to refer to individuals of black and white backgrounds, although other backgrounds—particularly Native American—may be included in their lineage as well. I use "black" generally to refer to individuals who are considered completely or predominantly of African descent—but sometimes also as a synonym for "African Brazilian," "African American," "African-descent Brazilian," and "African-descent American," which encompass both "black" and "multiracial" individuals.

2. The multiracial movement in the United States, which emerged since the dismantling of Jim Crow segregation and the repeal of the last laws against racial intermarriage, has challenged the rule of hypodescent and moved the United States closer to the ternary racial order that has typified Brazil (Daniel 2006, 148–73).

3. See Caldwell 1970; Woll 1972; Riedel 1974; Sant'Anna 1975; Hill 1976; Linhares Filho 1978; Freitas 1981; Schüler 1978; Nunes 1983; Bagby Júnior 1993; Chagas 1994; Xavier 1994; Senna 1998, 2003; Sabino 1999; Décio 1999; Pereira 1999; Weschenfelder 2000; Madeira 2001; Moisés 2001; Niskier 2001; Bosi 1999, 2002, 2006; Facioli 2002; Venancio Filho 2000; Granja 2002; Freitas 2001; Cruz Júnior 2002; Baptista 2003a, 2003b; Silva 2002; Tufano 2003; Guimarães 2004; Nogueira 2004; Tosta 2004; Amaral 2005; Piza 2005a, 2005b; Gouvêa 2005; Lucas 2009. Translations from the Portuguese, whether of the titles to Machado's and other authors' works, of quotations from these works, or of various words and expressions, are my own unless otherwise noted.

4. See Haberly 1972, 1983; Param 1973; Boyd 1975, 1992; Nascimento 2002; Daniel 1981, 1995; Gledson 1984; Bernd 1987, 1988; Brookshaw 1986; Costa 1985; Foster 1987; Ianni 1988; Muricy 1988; Alvim 1989; Chalhoub 2001, 2003; Trípoli 2006; Duarte 2007a, 2007b; Bernardo, Michael, and Schäffauer 2010; Fantini 2011.

5. This paper did not become publicly available until 1995, when the conference proceedings were published in *Encruzilhadas: Symposium on Portuguese Traditions*, edited by Claude L. Hulet. My analysis draws from my master's thesis, "Luís Gama, José do Patrocínio, Machado de Assis, and Castro Alves: The Nineteenth-Century Brazilian Mulatto and the Author" (1973), my doctoral dissertation, "Machado de Assis and the Meta-Mulatto" (1987), and from my books, *More Than Black? Multiracial Identity and the New Racial Order* (2002) and *Race and Multiraciality in Brazil and the United States: Converging Paths?* (2006).

Chapter 1

This chapter title is borrowed from historian Carl Degler's pathbreaking *Neither Black nor White: Slavery and Race Relations in Brazil and the United States* (1971).

1. The Casa da Misericórdia (House of Charity) in Bahia, for example, sought to advance the state policies of marriages by providing dowries to offset this financial burden for some women

who might otherwise not have been able to marry or whose financial circumstances were so precarious that they might otherwise have been forced to become to prostitutes (Russell-Wood 1968, 176).

2. *Mameluco* is frequently used interchangeably with *caboclo*, which can, however, also refer to individuals of Portuguese, Native American, and African ancestry.

3. Pombal's reforms did not address slavery in the colonies, where it was a mainstay of the economy. He did abolish the African slave trade to Portugal in 1761, and in 1773, all slaves in Portugal were given their freedom. Yet slavery had been only one form of labor, and perhaps the least cost-effective one, used primarily to extend the work force. The absence of any real necessity for slavery, coupled with the relatively high price of slaves, made slave ownership more a luxury, a symbol of wealth and prestige, particularly associated with the Crown, nobility, and wealthy merchants (Saunders 1982, 2, 34, 85–86, 176–77).

4. The Afonsine, Manueline, and Filipine Ordinances were passed, respectively, during the reigns of Dom Afonso V (1432–81), Dom Manuel I (1469–1521), and Dom Filipe II (1578–1621).

5. Francis Dutra points out that this shift in attitudes and policies was particularly apparent in the Portuguese military orders (or religious-military orders), formed during the time of the reconquest of the Iberian Peninsula—the Crusade of the West—from the twelfth to the fifteenth centuries as part of the reclamation, protection, and defense of the territories conquered by the Muslims. Each of the three key orders—Christ, Santiago, and Avis—had very stringent requirements for admission (Dutra 2006, 113–15). The two chief requirements were "pureza de sangue" (purity of blood) and "qualidade" (quality). "Purity of blood" meant freedom from Muslim or New Christian ancestry or any other "infected race." However, there was no mention of African ancestry or color as an impediment to becoming a knight or commander in those orders. "Quality" meant nobility (noblemen, *fidalgos*, knights, and squires) and absence of any artisanal and manual labor on the part of the candidate and his antecedents into the grandparental generation. And even this defect could be countered by dispensation as a reward for services rendered to the Crown or in recognition of the necessary personal characteristics.

Between 1550 and 1609, it was even possible for pretos, that is, individuals deemed to be completely of African ancestry, to become knights in all three military orders. In other words, *sangue infecta* was never synonymous with "African ancestry" (Dutra 2006, 113–14). Between 1620 and 1720, however, the role played by African ancestry (increasingly associated with slavery and manual labor) became more complicated in terms of the military orders, particularly in Brazil, and increasingly emerged as a disqualifying factor. Associations between slavery, manual labor, and African ancestry were not necessarily made in cases where individuals were born elsewhere in the Portuguese Empire, including Portugal and even Africa, where slavery was not the mainstay of the economy, as it was in Brazil (Dutra 1999, 112–13; 2006, 139–40; 2011, 101).

6. The Paraguayan War, also known as the "War of the Triple Alliance," was fought between Paraguay and the allied countries of Argentina, Brazil, and Uruguay. The war has been attributed to various causes, including the aftereffects of colonialism in Latin America, the struggle for control over the strategic Río de la Plata region, Brazil's and Argentina's interference in the internal politics of Paraguay, Britain's economic interests in the region, and the expansionist ambitions of Paraguayan President Francisco Solano López. For many years, Paraguay had boundary disputes and tariff issues with Argentina and Brazil. After the Triple Alliance (Argentina, Brazil, and Uruguay) defeated Paraguay in conventional warfare, the conflict turned into a drawn-out guerrilla-style conflict that devastated the Paraguayan military and civilian population. The guerilla war lasted until Solano López was killed on March 1, 1870.

7. According to Zephyr Frank's perusal of 1,109 estate inventories in Rio de Janeiro, inheritance records indicate that 88 percent of wealth holders owned slaves (Frank 2004, 41).

8. Zephyr Frank bases the term "middling" on wealth holding rather than on social status. Indeed, the ranks of these middling wealth holders during the first half of the nineteenth century

included a wide range of individuals who typically would not be thought of as sharing the same, middle-class identity or status.

9. Charles Mills defines the racial contract as an ideological predisposition that informs both the beliefs whites have about themselves and racialized "Others" and the behaviors they have engaged in as a result of those beliefs. Unlike the social contract idealized in Western philosophy and politics, the racial contract reveals the inequitable ideological presuppositions, policies, and material conditions that have sustained the racial order (Mills 1997, 1–8).

10. The number of caboclos was miniscule in 1872, totaling 923, and was still quite small in 1890, totaling 17,445.

11. The numbers of caboclos (1,295,796) more than doubled since the 1872 census but still constituted a small proportion of the population (9.6 percent) in 1890.

12. Jeffrey Lesser points out that the largest numbers of European immigrants came from Italy, followed by those from Portugal and Spain, with those from Germany as a distant fourth. Immigrants from Syria, Lebanon, China, and Japan, being outside the historical black-white framework, had to carve out spaces that were largely unscripted. Some sought to achieve integration into the Brazilian racial order as close as possible to whiteness and its privileges. Others formed pluralistic enclaves that sought to maintain distinct societies, or they maintained identities as "hyphenated" Brazilians through various combinations of both of these trends (Lesser 1999, 1–12, 168–73).

13. Baron Georges-Eugène Haussmann (1809–91) transformed the old Paris of dense and irregular medieval alleyways into a rational city with long, wide, and straight boulevards lined with cafés, shops, and open spaces that extended outward far beyond the old city limits. These Haussmann renovations had a profound impact on the everyday lives of Parisians.

14. Thus, even though socioeconomic status appears to have been the key factor in residential patterns in the Bahian city of Salvador (Butler 1998, 134–40, 54) and statistics indicate no racially distinct enclaves, some racial clusters were discernible there.

15. Candomblé should be distinguished from Umbanda, which was a religion founded in the early twentieth century by combining African elements with Kardecism (see epilogue, "Machado de Assis and the Postmodern Sensibility: 'The Centrality of the Middle'"). Although candomblé and macumba are distinct religious expressions, candomblé is called "macumba" in some regions of Brazil, notably Rio de Janeiro and São Paulo (Butler 1998, 167, 187–88, 201–7).

16. Nevertheless, enforcing the proscriptions against African Brazilian religion required some legal maneuverings. The 1891 constitution declared freedom of religion and the separation of Church and state. The solution was to define African Brazilian religion as a civil threat to public health (Johnson 2001, 19; Blake 2011, 171–72).

17. That African Brazilian religious expression overwhelmed Catholicism was particularly true in Salvador, given the high concentration of African Brazilians and large number of terreiros there, although it was also true to a lesser extent in Rio de Janeiro, São Paulo, and other regions of Brazil (Graden 2006, 119, 130–31).

18. Capoeira is believed to have originated with slaves from Angola (Almeida 1986, 1–30; Butler 1998, 186–89).

Chapter 2

1. Vice President Nilo Peçanha assumed the presidency on June 15, 1909, upon the death of President Afonso Pena, and governed until November 15, 1910.

2. Derived from the official census, the statistics on illiteracy should be treated with caution. Historically, Brazil's official data have been notoriously unreliable and their collection plagued by methodological inconsistency.

3. The abbreviation *Oc*, used here and throughout main text and notes, refers to Machado's *Obra completa*, 3 vols. (Rio de Janeiro: Editora José Aguilar, 1962).

4. See also Ammermann 1987; DeVault 1990; Fiske 1989; Gottdiener 1985; Howard and Allen 1990; Iser 1974; Modleski 1982; Radway 1984; Rodgers 1991.

5. See also Bourdieu 1979/1984; DiMaggio 1987; Foucault 1977; Griswold 1983; Swidler 1986; Wuthnow 1987.

6. See also Gramsci 1971; Horkheimer and Adorno 1944; Bourdieu 1979/1984; Foucault 1977; Gitlin 1980; Hall 1984.

7. See also Becker 1982; Coser, Kadushin, and Powell 1982; Griswold 1983; Hirsch 1972; Long 1985; Peterson 1976; Powell 1985; Tuchman 1978; White and White 1965.

8. For a discussion of Negritude, see chapter 6, "The Black Racial Imagination: Literature, Identity Politics, and Black Liberation."

9. However conservative Silva Alvarenga may appear otherwise, he and other Arcadian poets—notably, Tomás António Gonzaga (1744–1810) and Cláudio Manuel da Costa (1729–89)—were involved in the ill-fated 1789 pro-independence movement referred to as the "Inconfidência Mineira" (Minas Gerais Conspiracy). Portuguese authorities arrested the main leaders and sentenced them to death. But the sentence was commuted to exile except in the case of physician Joaquim José da Silva Xavier (1748–92). Nicknamed "Tiradentes" (Tooth Puller) for his reputation for tooth extractions, Silva Xavier was hanged and quartered in public. Found dead in his cell, Cláudio da Costa was believed to have been murdered (Campos 2007, 195).

10. Contrary to popular belief, Caldas Barbosa did not secure the patronage of Portugal's premier, the Marquês de Pombal. That honor fell to Basílio da Gama, who was white, a point Caldas made clear in his autobiographical poem "A doença" (My Illness; Costigan 2007, 174).

11. The increasing resistance to the slave trade in Bahia is largely attributable to the Malês Revolt, the first slave uprising in Brazil in the 1830s and what some consider the largest slave rebellion in the Americas, undertaken by Muslim slaves in 1835 (Graden 2006, 22–33, 103–33).

12. Many libertos who migrated to the cities after the abolition of slavery joined or formed capoeira gangs—particularly in Rio de Janeiro. In fact, attorney and writer Lúcio de Mendonça (1854–1909) stated that Patrocínio himself had been trained in capoeira (on what it meant to be a "writer" in Brazil, see http://pt.wikipedia.org/wiki/Escritor; *Revista de Historia* 2008). In the transition to the Republic, these gangs, adept in both unarmed combat and the use of clubs and blade weapons, became associated with criminal or antigovernment activities and were enlisted by both monarchists and republicans to harass their opponents and disrupt their rallies. Capoeira was finally outlawed in 1892 (Almeida 1986, 1–30; Bueno 1996; Butler 1998, 186–89).

13. According to linguists, "Carioca" derives from the Tupí word "kara'i oca," roughly translated as "white house" or "house of whites," a term indigenous people used to refer to the houses built by the Portuguese. Eventually, the inhabitants of Rio de Janeiro took on the designation "Carioca" to refer to their city (St. Louis 2004, 12).

Chapter 3

This chapter title is borrowed from Thomas Skidmore's pioneering work *Black into White: Race and Nationality in Brazilian Thought* (1974).

1. The French novelist and author of *Madame Bovary* Gustave Flaubert (1821–80) was well known to have suffered from epilepsy throughout his life.

2. Masturbation was commonly thought to be the cause of epilepsy at that time. For his part, however, Queen Victoria's gynecologist-obstetrician and the originator of bromide therapy, Sir Charles Locock, felt it reduced libido and calmed sexual excitement. He considered encouraging

epilepsy patients to engage in it to be one of the reasons for his success in treating seizures (Pearce 2002, 412; Sun 2007, 108–9).

3. In 1836, there were only twenty schools in Rio, fourteen of them for the instruction of boys and six for girls, with 508 and 132 students in attendance, respectively. In addition, some instruction was provided by priests to the children of their parishioners (Massa 1969, 1:45).

4. Yv Scarlett Maciel argues that Machado actually translated *Oliver Twist* from a Dickens-authorized French translation by Alfred Gerardin rather than from the original English (Maciel 2007, 15–16).

5. There have been claims that Machado's stepmother, Maria Inês, asked Madame Gallot, who operated a bakery where he supposedly worked between the ages of seven and eleven, to provide him with daily informal instruction in French. Thus far, these claims have not been substantiated (Bagby Júnior 1975b, 227; Caldwell 1970, 24; Fonseca 1958, 81–86; Massa 1969, 1:77–79; Viana Filho 1974, 13).

6. According to some accounts, Machado received private, intensive instruction in Latin from Father Silveira Sarmento, again through the intervention of his stepmother, Maria Inês. However, these accounts remain uncorroborated (Bagby 1975, 228; Caldwell 1970, 24; Fonseca 1958, 86; Massa 1969, 1:77–79; Viana Filho 1974, 14).

7. "Black Legend" is a term coined by Spanish historian Julián Juderías in his book *La leyenda negra y la verdad histórica* (*The Black Legend and Historical Truth*; 1914) for what he considered to be the unfair depiction of Spain and Spaniards.

8. According to Leonardo Monteiro Monasterio, any free worker, including any ex-slave, could generally earn 200 milréis (200,000 réis) over the course of a year (Monasteiro 2009, 53). Earlier research by Mircea Buescu supports this conclusion (Buescu 1979, 83–85, 92). Moreover, Buescu's research on occupation and income from select parishes indicates that, for the years 1876–78, the average annual income for lawyers was 4,837 milréis (4.8 million réis), for physicians 4,379 milréis (4.4 million réis), for carpenters 715 milréis (715,000 réis), and for painters 945 milréis (945,000 réis). Indeed, based on 1872 census data, the average annual income for the majority of Brazilians was less than 750 milréis (750,000 réis; Buescu 1979, 94–95; Milanovic, Lindert, and Williamson 2007, 36–43).

9. Though Machado and Carolina had no children, they were devoted to their dog, Graziela, who died in 1891. Her grave in the garden of the Assis home on Rua Cosme Velho was surrounded by and covered with flowers (Caldwell 1970, 255n17; Machado 1953, 116; Pereira 1957, 173–74; Viana Filho, 144–45).

10. Given that Laura was still a minor at the time of Machado's death, her inheritance was under the guardianship of her father. The monies were released in 1909, when Laura married at age 15 and her husband, Second Lieutenant Estevão Leitão de Carvalho, requested an annulment of her status as a minor (Magalhães Júnior 1981, 4:378–79).

11. A few critics have asserted that photographers retouched images of Machado in order to lighten his complexion, a practice that was common at the time. Élcio Torres, who sketched Machado for *Raça Brazil* magazine, noted such retouching in photographs of Machado at the Brazilian Academy of Letters (Duarte 2007b, 135; Santos and Dias 2006).

12. This section heading is borrowed from Virginia Domínguez's *White by Definition: Social Classification in Creole Louisiana* (1986).

13. Brazilians today would most likely think of Machado in the same way that Brazilians of today would their two recent presidents, Fernando Henriques Cardoso and Luiz Inácio Lula da Silva, and millions of their other compatriots who have African ancestry but are neither identified nor designated as "mulato."

14. Linguistic evidence suggests that the Portuguese word "mulato" may actually be derived from "muwallad," the Arabic word for someone of blended African-Arab descent—a legacy of

the Moorish occupation of Iberia—and later evolved to refer to someone of blended African-European descent (Dozy 1869, 384; Forbes 1988, 131–50).

Chapter 4

"Unknown Machado" is borrowed from the translated title of Raimundo Magalhães Júnior's groundbreaking book *Machado de Assis desconhecido* (1955).

1. The Brazilian Theater Conservatory was an official agency of dramatic censorship in Rio de Janeiro charged with the task of perfecting Brazilian theater. Anything that was deemed offensive to Catholicism, the royal family, or Brazil's all-encompassing morality and public standards ("bons costumes") was subject to censorship, which ranged from excising vulgar expressions and risqué dialogue to significantly altering the plot (Faria 2008, 62; Jobim and Streeter 2004, 19–22).

2. These broader social reforms would not be implemented for another fifty years (Marotti 1982, 156).

3. See also Duarte 2007a, 47.

4. Machado was an active collaborator and a shareholder in the *Gazeta de Notícias*, one of Brazil's most widely circulated newspapers, which openly opposed slavery during the final years of the monarchy. He was also a chronicler in other periodicals where, writing under pseudonyms, he commented on slavery and other critical social issues. Machado's pseudonyms included "Lélio," in the newspaper section "Balas de Estalo" (The Sound of Bullets); "João das Regras" (John of the Rules) in *A + B*; "Malvólio," in the *Gazeta de Hollanda* (Holland Gazette); "Boas Noites" (Good Night), in the section "Bons Dias" (Good Morning); "Policarpo," in *Crônicas do Relojeiro* (The Watchmaker's Chronicles), and "Dr. Semana" (Dr. Week) in *Semana Ilustrada* (Illustrated Week; Duarte 2007b, 138).

5. Marotti points out that that the family name "Neves" (snow), "Cândido" (literally, "candid"; poetically, "snow-white") and "Clara" (light) variously reflect whiteness (Marotti 1982, 162–63).

6. Page numbers for Machado's nine novels (*Ayres's Memorial, Dom Casmurro, Esau and Jacob, The Hand and the Glove, Helena, Iaiá Garcia, The Posthumous Memoirs of Brás Cubas, Quincas Borba*, and *Resurrection*), cited parenthetically in the main text of chapters 4 and 5, refer to the critical editions listed in the references under their original Portuguese titles (Assis 1975b, 1977a, 1976, 1975a, 1977b, 1977c, 1977d, 1975c, 1975d, respectively).

7. The term "moleque" is usually translated as "youngster" or "kid" but actually has an implied racial connotation meaning "black kid" or "black youngster."

Chapter 5

1. *Memoirs of a Police Sergeant* was originally published in serialized form between June 1852 and July 1853 in the supplement "A Pacotilha" of the *Correio Mercantil*.

2. Although the term "malandro" can also be translated as "rogue" or "scoundrel," it is best translated as "trickster," a well-established trope in cultural and literary analyses. The trickster articulates a plot in which "individual desire and group authority cohabit within a network or web of relations; the dynamic is one of interaction rather than dominance and submission" (Ammons 1994, ix).

3. The Portuguese word "trapézio" in Faoro's title means both "trapezoid" and "trapeze" and, in this second sense, also refers to Brás Cubas's famous flying trapeze.

4. Arguments similar to those of Schwarz and Borges were made in the early 1960s by social scientists of the São Paulo School, which included Florestan Fernandes, Fernando Henriques

Cardoso, and Octavio Ianni. These scholars argued that capitalist development in Brazil had been distorted by ownership of slaves and slave labor (Borges 2007, 239; Schwarcz and Botelho 2008, 149). Moreover, they were among the first to challenge the racial democracy ideology and confirm the significance of race (or phenotype) apart from culture and class in social stratification (Daniel 2006, 180–89).

5. The Regency (1831–40) was rife with turmoil that threatened the social order and the integrity of the nation, which was politicized largely by partisan differences over the nature of the state. Fear of such turmoil among the ruling class was both considerable and most likely racialized, given Brazil's racial demographics, the memory of the 1799 slave uprising in Haiti, and the reality that people of color figured in most uprisings. Indeed, African Brazilian slaves did figure in very significant urban and also some rural uprisings. But the mass of Brazilians, who were people of color, did not appear to see their revolts as motivated by race so much as by politics, class, and nationalism. Race cannot therefore be separated out as the primary factor. Letter from Jeffrey Needell, September 15, 2011.

6. Ibid.

7. Irving Goffman, Daniel Renfrow, and Elaine Ginsberg point out that passing is a much broader phenomenon in which individuals seek to come to terms with social stigma that can involve other categories of difference (e.g., sex, gender, class; Goffman 1963, 48–51; Renfrow 2004, 486–88; Ginsberg 1996, 1–15). However, given the specificity of U.S. constructions of blackness in the annals of racial formation—the one-drop rule is unique to the United States and applied only to African-descent Americans—the topic of passing has attracted considerable attention from social scientists, historians, and fiction writers (Berzon 1978, 140–61; Spickard 1989, 333–35). Consequently, the experience of passing among African-descent Americans is in some ways a paradigmatic framework for discussion on this topic.

8. Continuous passing involves a complete and permanent break with the stigmatized community. Discontinuous passing involves more temporary forays across the social divide, whether sporadically or over a protracted period of time, in order to gain access to social opportunities (public facilities, employment, etc.) unavailable to individuals of the stigmatized group (Daniel 2002, 49–55; 2006, 116–22). Individuals essentially lead double lives, while necessarily taking care to keep each world separate to guard against the possibility of being exposed.

9. In Brazil, the more inclusive definition of whiteness, made possible by the mulatto escape hatch, complicates any discussion of this topic. An individual of African ancestry self-identified and socially accepted as white by Brazilian reckonings would not be thought of as passing (Daniel 1992, 92–94; 2002, 45–55).

10. See also Adler 1974, 23–40; Antonovsky 1956, 57–67; Gist 1967, 361–65; Goldberg 1941, 52–58; Green 1947, 167–71; Kerckhoff and McCormick 1955, 48–55; Miller 1992, 24–36; Poston 1990, 152–55; Wright and Wright 1972, 361–68.

Chapter 6

1. See also Price 2000, 190n3. In several chronicles, Machado was critical of the state's attempts to outlaw pre-Lenten carnival street celebrations called "entrudos," where participants threw mud, dirty water, flour balls, food, and strong-smelling liquids (often containing excrement and urine) at one another, which often led to riots (Pereira 1994, 149). For example, in a chronicle in *A semana* dated February 4, 1894, Machado commented that "the day the King of Carnival is banished from the world, the world will come to an end, because laughter is not only proper to humanity, it is a necessity. And there is only laughter and great laughter when it is public, universal,

inextinguishable, as was the case with Homer's gods, upon seeing the poor lame Vulcan" (*Crônica, A semana*, Oc, 3:558–59).

In another chronicle, dated February 16, 1896, Machado wrote typically ironic commentary on carnival's traditional image as a safety valve for releasing social tensions through its inversion of societal norms (Pereira 1994, 140–41). He argued that the pre-Lenten celebrations were only a temporary release that did not address the array of social tensions that accumulated over the course of the year. And, indeed, releasing tensions of such magnitude would require significantly more time than the brief interlude during carnival: "Frankly, . . . in a city the size of Rio de Janeiro, still not even sleeping, with its multitude of frights, sorrows, rages, and afflictions, which transpire the rest of the year, and not counting the tumultuous world of commerce, a week or even two weeks of laughter and merriment would not be too much. Generally speaking, the time is short, but the year is long" (*Crônica, A semana*, Assis 1957b, 28:110–11).

2. See also Mélone 1962, 99–132; Preto-Rodas 1970, 1–13; Sartre 1948/1963, 10, 12, 43–48.

3. Influenced by various other African-derived or -influenced dance forms such as the tango, lundu, and habanera and by those of European origin such as the polka, the maxixe was danced to rapid 2/4 time music.

4. It should be pointed out, however, that my use of the term "strategic essentialism" is not actually in keeping with Spivak's definition. She refers to strategic essentialism as a sort of temporary, rather than long-term, solidarity for the purpose of social action. Nevertheless, I think it is useful to apply her term here in order to understand the strategic importance of essentialist premises in mobilizing as well as in maintaining a sense of community among African Brazilians.

5. Personal e-mail communication with Jerson César Leão Alves, October 9, 2007.

6. See "Coloque de volta MESTIÇO no censo do IBGE," http://www.nacaomestica.org/.

7. See "Mestiçofobia É Racismo," http://www.nacaomestica.org/ and "Diga Não Ao Racismo Antimestiço," http://www.nacaomestica.org/.

8. See "Brasília–DF. Comissão Geral para debater o Estatuto da Igualdade Racial," http://www.nacaomestica.org/.

9. Jean-Paul Sartre praised Negritude and, by extension, Afrocentricity as strategic essentialism uniting individuals of African descent against Eurocentrism and white racism. He also envisioned them as emblematic of strategic antiessentialism. Blackness would be deployed as part of a larger project of abolishing all kinds of hierarchies, racial and otherwise. Ultimately, this would serve as a vehicle for the transcendence of blackness in a future global and universal humanism (Sartre 1948/1963, 57, 60–62).

Chapter 7

1. Notwithstanding Romero's critique of Machado on strictly aesthetic grounds, the harsh tone of his remarks appears to have been motivated in part by the stinging criticism Machado directed at him and the Realist-Naturalist movement at the beginning of Romero's career in an essay "A nova geração" (The New Generation; 1879; Jobim 2005, 574–75).

2. Though Brazilian Modernism began as an attempt by younger writers to introduce the latest European literary techniques, they eventually sought to capture new, more original Brazilian subject matter through those techniques. The Modernists of São Paulo not only introduced surrealism and other avant-garde techniques but also incorporated Native American and African Brazilian subject matter into the Brazilian arts. Their efforts culminated in the Week of Modern Art, a series of "festivals" of painting, sculpture, literature, and music held in the Municipal Theater of São Paulo in February 1922, which sought to assert Brazil's cultural independence during the centennial celebration of the nation's political independence from Portugal in 1822. The revolution

that was transforming artistic sensibilities in São Paulo extended to all the major states, although the Regionalist movement in the Northeast had strong local roots of its own (Brookshaw 1986, 99, 5–116; Skidmore 1974, 176–78).

3. Borrowing Linda Hutcheon's influential description of parody in the modern and postmodern periods, Ellen Douglass (1998, 1037) best captures and contrasts Machado's views on this matter of servile imitation in the phrase "repetition with critical difference" and in a combination of "respectful homage and ironically thumbed nose" (Douglass in Hutcheon 2000, 33). In other words, Machado's appropriation of and borrowing from European literature was "respectfully parodic," serving not only to reflect and propel the paradoxical processes of Brazilian literary culture in the late nineteenth century but also to critique the larger contemporary tendency of Brazilians to indiscriminately mimic European trends (Douglass 1998, 1037).

4. The "Grito de Ipiranga," literally, the "Ipiranga Shout," which is the defining moment of Brazil independence, stands out in sharp contrast to the violent national independence movements elsewhere in the Americas. On the banks of the Ipiranga River near the city of São Paulo, the regent Pedro (later Emperor Pedro I) issued his proclamation "Independência ou morte!" (Liberty or death!), declaring and essentially achieving Brazil's independence from Portugal on September 7, 1822.

5. A partial translation of Dickens's novel *Oliver Twist* (1838), Machado's *Oliveira Twist*, which appeared in serialized form in *O Jornal da Tarde* in 1870, is an excellent case study of his views on this cultural dialogue between Brazil and foreign lands. Machado began his translation in the early part of 1870 for the extra income he so much needed. Two months after he began publishing the first installments of *Oliveira Twist*, he was offered a position as officer for the secretary of state. Machado immediately notified the editors of *Jornal* of his decision to stop the translation and accepted the official position. Because he had a better command of French than English (indeed some scholars question whether Machado possessed any knowledge of English), Yv Scarlett Maciel, who conducted the first thorough examination of this work, argues that Machado based his translation on a Dickens-authorized French translation by Alfred Gerardin.

According to Maciel, Machado's close relationship with the original text of *Oliver Twist* provided him with an opportunity to give voice both to certain current cultural misconceptions regarding the value of all that is foreign and to contemporary tendencies that insisted on a certain type of Brazilianness through the misappropriation of Dickens's novel. Too often regarded as hackwork undertaken out of financial necessity, this translation demonstrates Machado's engagement with current themes and polemics. He imposes on Dickens's text modifications that, in the end, reveal more about the translator and his position in nineteenth-century Brazil than about the text itself. Prompted by the desire to turn the foreign into something less strange and to provide readers with the experience of recognizing their own culture in another, Machado transformed *Oliver Twist* into a text that exists between two worlds, that of the foreign and that of the national, London and Rio de Janeiro, a tale of two cites, so to speak (Maciel 2007, 11–20).

6. Baptista's *Em nome do apelo do nome*, first published in Lisbon, was edited and republished in Brazil as *A formação do nome* (*The Formation of the Name*; 2003).

7. José Jobim has pointed out that Machado did not maintain a consistent perspective on brasilidade over the course of his career, as indicated by the poems in his book *Americanas* (1875), which do indeed reflect local color and nativistic themes that were emblematic of brasilidade and the nationalist Romantic movement (Jobim 2005, 571–83). What Machado opposed was the single-minded focus on such color and themes to the exclusion of images that conveyed greater depth, profundity, and universality.

8. The word "Ouvidor" originally referred to an official position in the colonial/imperial bureaucracy, a sort of ombudsman or official auditor and magistrate. The "Ouvidor-geral" (General Ombudsman) was responsible for listening to the locals and, in theory, for taking their claims to

the central government. Therefore, the idea that the "Rua do Ouvidor" has to do with "gossip" is a stroke of irony.

9. Dom Pedro took as his Masonic alias "Guatimozim," the name of the last Aztec ruler of Mexico (Haberly 1983, 16).

10. Such sanctioning of interracial relations is exemplified in Indianist literature that centers on romantic interludes between Portuguese and Native American lovers. See particularly the poems of Antonio Gonçalves Dias, such as "Canto do Índio" and "Marabá," both from 1846, and the novels of José de Alencar, such as *O guaraní* (1857) and *Iracema* (1865). See also Brookshaw 1988, 1–11; Driver 1942, 51, 56; Haberly 1983, 10–14; Hemming 1987, 466–81; Paulk 2005, 61–77; Sommer 1991, 138–71.

11. The use of the term "feiticeiro" (witch doctor) is a disparaging reference to and trivialization of shamanism in African-derived religious expressions that would become part of the formation of African Brazilian candomblé in the personage of the male spiritual leader (*pai de santo*).

12. "Order and Progress" was a modification of the slogan of Auguste Comte, the founder of positivism, who proclaimed "L'amour pour principe et l'ordre pour base; le progrès pour but" (Love as a principle and order as the basis; progress as the goal). Brazilian disciples of Comte embraced the motto "Ordem e Progresso" (Order and Progress), which appears on the Brazilian flag, during Brazil's transition from a colonial monarchy to modern republic.

13. The pantheon of Naturalist novels also includes Aluísio Azevedo's *Casa de pensão* (*The Boarding House*; 1884) and *O cortiço* (*The Slum Tenement*; 1890) and Manuel de Oliveira Paiva's *Dona Guidinha do poço* (*Mrs. Guidinha of the Well*; 1897).

14. "Extermination" is defined as the act of killing with the intention of eradicating a demographic group within a population, although the term "genocide" is more often used when applied to humans. In Brazil, the goal was not the actual murder of African Brazilians but, rather, their eradication by means of what Haberly refers to as "laissez-faire genocide" (Haberly 1972, 46), whitening through miscegenation, along with social containment (or quarantine) through sharply lower levels of education, higher rates of poverty, malnutrition, disease, and infant mortality. The most widely used definition of "genocide" in international law is found in the 1948 United Nations Convention on the Prevention and Punishment of the Crime of Genocide. See http://www.hrweb.org/legal/genocide.html.

15. "Conselheiro" is how backlanders addressed a lay priest.

16. The term "ufanismo" is derived from Afonso Celso de Assis Figueiredo Júnior's short essay "Porque me ufano do meu país" (Why I Am Proud of My Country), one of the earliest efforts among late nineteenth- and early twentieth-century Brazilian intellectuals to turn racial and environmental determinism on its head. Ufanismo attached a positive valuation both to Brazil's miscegenated makeup and to its natural environment, described as a geographic paradise (Skidmore 1974, 99–102).

17. People of predominantly European and Native American ancestry live mostly in the North (caboclos), West (mamelucos), and the Sertão region of the Northeast (although the sertanejos as a rule have more African ancestry than the other two groups).

18. See also *Dicionário informal*, http://www.dicionarioinformal.com.br/buscar.php?palavra=candongas.

Chapter 8

This chapter title is borrowed from José Argüelles's insightful book The Transformative Vision: Reflections on the Nature and History of Human Expression (1975). The subtitle borrows conceptually from the term "third eye" in Eastern and esoteric thinking more generally. Also called the inner eye or mind's eye, this third (or "virtual") eye is said to be situated right between the two eyes, and expands up to the middle of the forehead. It is typically associated with the pineal gland, a small endocrine gland located near the center of the brain, between the two cerebral hemispheres, which synthesizes and secretes melatonin. According to spiritual traditions, when activated, the third eye imbues individuals with a higher (or expanded) awareness that transcends dichotomous and hierarchical thinking. The terms "third culture" or "third way" are similarly used to describe individuals who espouse a politics of the radical center that seeks conciliation between phenomena (e.g., subjectivism and objectivism, religion and science, socialism and capitalism, and various schools of thought on any particular issue), which are viewed as inherently antithetical, and often ranked hierarchically, in relationship to each other.

1. We also have it on Machado's authority based on a December 15, 1898, letter addressed to José Veríssimo that he clearly placed *Iaiá Garcia* (published in 1878, but dated 1877) in the first phase (*Epistolário, Oc*, 3:1044; Kinnear 1976, 54).

2. Although aware of the flaws Machado pointed out and quite pained by Machado's critique, Eça apparently took Machado's advice. His subsequent writings indicate a shift from his staunch adherence to pure or unmitigated representational Realism-Naturalism typified by *Cousin Basílio* to a variety of aesthetic approaches (MacNicoll 1982, 37; Santos 2005, 113).

3. *Costumismo* refers to the literary interpretation of local everyday life, mannerisms, and customs, especially of provincial, regional, and rural life in the nineteenth century. Related both to Realism-Naturalism and to Romanticism, costumismo shares Romanticism's interest in expression, as opposed to simple representation and to the Realist-Naturalist focus on precise representation of particular times and places.

4. See also Schwarz 1977, 140–56; 2004, 15–34; 2006, 816–40; Wolff 1987, 44–48.

5. Under the heading of Romantic Realism, Donald Fanger includes writings by Honoré de Balzac (1799–1850), Charles Dickens (1812–1870), Nikolai Gogol (1809–91), and Fyodor Dostoyevsky (1829–81). According to Robert Scholes and Robert Kellogg, Nathaniel Hawthorne (1804–64) and Herman Melville (1819–91) can also be included in this category (Scholes and Kellogg 1966, 89–91; Senna 1986, 12–15; Daniel 1981, 8–9).

6. See also Nettels 1977, 7, 21; Stauffer 1922, 14–29; Stowell 1980, 1–10; Watt 1979, 169–70. Peter Stowell, James Nagel, and other scholars have done extensive research on the history and techniques of Impressionism in literature. They have found some of the most representative examples of this literary aesthetic among the writings of Alphonse Daudet (1840–97), Marcel Proust (1871–1922), Joseph Conrad (1857–1924), Katherine Mansfield (1888–1923), Virginia Woolf (1882–1941), Dorothy Richardson (1873–1957), Henry James (1843–1916), Stephen Crane (1871–1900), Italo Svevo (1861–1928), Thomas Mann (1875–1955), and Anton Chekhov (1860–1904).

7. See also Carpeaux 1962, 5:2146–50; Carsaniga 1974, 235; Cizevskij 1971, 8; Current-García and Walton 1962, 14–26; Freeborn 1974, 87–88; Hauser 1951, 4:29–60, 106–160; Hemmings 1974, 36–67, 878; Levine 1981, 4–6, 9–15, 18–21; Lukács 1964, 66–78, 83–84; Norst 1966, 154–66; Ritchie 1974, 225–36; Scholes and Kellogg 1966, 89–91.

8. Symbolist, Neo-Romantic, or Expressionist writers with Realist-Naturalist or Impressionist tendencies include Joris-Karl Huysmans (1848–1907), Hermann Hesse (1877–1962), Oscar Wilde (1856–1900), D. H. Lawrence (1885–1930), Rudyard Kipling (1865–1936), André Gide (1864–1951), Franz Kafka (1883–1924), and James Joyce (1882–1941).

9. See also Merquior 1977, 150; Moser 1952, 135; Peters 2001, 7–34.

Chapter 9

1. Some critics have suggested that *Ayres's Memorial* is a veiled account of Machado's life with his wife, Carolina.

Epilogue

1. Notable French postmodernist thinkers include Jean-François Lyotard (1924–98), Michel Foucault (1926–84), Jean Baudrillard (1929–2007), Gilles Deleuze (1925–95), Félix Guattari (1930–92), and Jacques Derrida (1930–2004).

2. Judging from their writings, Lyotard, Foucault, Baudrillard, Deleuze, Guattari, and Derrida are all deconstructive postmodernists. Science (the grand tool of the modern mind and a curse to the postmodern mind) may very well be the undoing of postmodernism's radical pluralism, for twentieth-century science found the universe to be far more interconnected and integrated than postmodernist pluralism has supposed (Smith 1989, 241). Paradoxically, the stance that there are no universal truths itself claims to be universally true and is perhaps the most obvious contradiction in all deconstructive postmodern thought (Rosenau 1992, 90; Wilber 1996, 62–63).

3. These constructive postmodernists include Henri Bergson (1859–1941) and, in certain respects, Karl Marx (1818–83), Hegel, Nietzsche, and Heidegger, as well as North American thinkers such as Charles Peirce (1839–1914), William James (1842–1910), and Charles Hartshorne (1897–2000) and British thinker Alfred North Whitehead (1861–1947).

4. "The Centrality of the Middle" is the title of Sven Spieker's 1995 article in *SEER: Slavonic and East European Review*.

5. Sorokin considers medieval scholasticism an integral (or idealistic) mixed mentality that synthesized the ideational modality of Christian faith and the sensate modality of Aristotelian empiricism. It originated in the need to reconcile the realities of a burgeoning economic prosperity of the physical world of the Renaissance and Reformation with the metaphysical tradition of medieval consciousness, which displayed a preoccupation with "otherworldly" concerns and a notable indifference toward those of the secular world (Sorokin 1957, 26–40). Sorokin describes the other (neo-integral) mixed mentality as a tormented and unintegrated declining sensate sociocultural modality, mired in its own decadence. Arnold Hauser and Wylie Sypher sharply disagree, finding it to be a vibrant style in its own right, one that seeks (albeit sometimes desperately) to achieve a balance between the ideational and sensate modalities. They refer to this "postsensate" mixed mentality as "Mannerism," a term derived from the style that emerged in the transition from the sensate dominance of the high Renaissance to the ideational dominance of the Baroque (Hauser 1951, 2:97–106; Sypher 1978, 100–117).

6. Paul Dixon has argued for a provocative and radical reinterpretation of *Dom Casmurro* as a novel that not only interrogates patriarchy but also posits matriarchy as a balancing or equalizing force for society (Dixon 1989, 71–91). Some would argue, however, that matriarchy is not simply the antithesis of patriarchy but, rather, is premised on a partnership model, where, beginning with the most fundamental difference in the human species between male and female, diversity and difference are not ranked in a dichotomous hierarchy based on inferiority or superiority, dominator or dominated, and so on (Eisler 1988, xii–xxiii).

7. Machado makes these antireligious sentiments abundantly clear in his short story "Igreja do diabo" (The Devil's Church), collected in his *Histórias sem data* (*Oc*, 2:368–74).

REFERENCES

Adams, Julia. 2005. "The Rule of the Father: Patriarchy and Patrimonialism in Early Modern Europe." In *Max Weber's Economy and Society: A Critical Companion*, edited by Charles Camic, Philip S. Gorski, and David M. Trubek, 237–66. Stanford: Stanford University Press.
Adler, Peter S. 1974. "Beyond Cultural Identity: Reflections on Cultural and Multicultural Man." In *Topics in Cultural Learning*, edited by R. Brislin, 23–40. Honolulu: East-West Center.
Aiex, Anoar. 1990. *As idéias sócio-literárias de Lima Barreto*. São Paulo: Vertice.
Alberto, Paulina L. 2011. *Terms of Inclusion: Black Intellectuals in Twentieth-Century Brazil*. Chapel Hill: University of North Carolina Press.
Alden, Dauril. 1963. "The Population of Brazil in the Late Eighteenth Century: A Preliminary Study." *Hispanic American Historical Review* 43 (May): 173–205.
———. 1996. *The Making of an Enterprise: The Society of Jesus in Portugal, Its Empire, and Beyond, 1540–1750*. Stanford: Stanford University Press.
Algranti, Leila Mezan. 1988. *O feitor ausente: Estudo sobre a escravidão urbana no Rio de Janeiro*. Petrópolis: Vozes.
Almeida, Bira. 1986. *Capoeira, a Brazilian Art Form: History, Philosophy, and Practice*. 2nd ed. Berkeley: North Atlantic Books.
Almeida, Manuel Antônio de. 1854. *Memórias de um sargento de milícias* [*Memoirs of a Police Sergeant*]. Rio de Janeiro: Typographia Brasiliense de Maximiano Gomes Ribeiro.
Almino, João. 2005. "Machado de Assis: Contemporary Writer." *Portuguese Literary and Cultural Studies*, special issue, *The Author as Plagiarist: The Case of Machado de Assis*, nos. 13–14 (Fall–Spring): 141–42.
Alvim, Clara. 1989. *Os discursos sobre o negro no século XIX: Desvios da enunciacão machadiana*. Rio de Janeiro: CIEC.
Amaral, Andrey do. 2005. *O máximo e as máximas de Machado de Assis*. Rio de Janeiro: Quartet.
Amin, Samir. 1989. *Eurocentrism*. New York: Monthly Review Press.
Ammermann, Nancy T. 1987. *Meaning and Moral Order: Explorations of Cultural Analysis in the Modern World*. New Brunswick: Rutgers University Press.
Ammons, Elizabeth. 1994. "Introduction." In *Tricksterism in Turn-of-the-Century American Literature: A Multicultural Perspective*, edited by Elizabeth Ammons and Annette White-Parks, vii–xii. Hanover: University Press of New England.
Anderson, Benedict. 2006. *Imagined Communities: Reflections on the Origin and Spread of Nationalism*. London: Verso.
Anderson, Victor. 1995. *Beyond Ontological Blackness: An Essay on African American Religious Criticism*. New York: Continuum.
Anderson, Walter Truett. 1995. "Introduction." In *The Truth About the Truth: De-Confusing and Re-Constructing the Postmodern World*, edited by Walter Truett Anderson, 1–11. New York: Jeremy P. Tarcher/Putnam.

Andrade, Mario de. 1974. *Aspectos da literatura brasileira*. São Paulo: Martins.
Andrade, Oswald de. 1928. "Manifesto antropófago." *Revista de Antropofagia* 1, no. 1 (May): 3, 7.
Andrews, George Reid. 1991. *Blacks and White in São Paulo, Brazil, 1888–1988*. Madison: University of Wisconsin Press.
Antonovsky, Aaron. 1956. "Toward a Refinement of the 'Marginal Man' Concept." *Social Forces* 35 (October): 57–67.
Anzaldúa, Gloria. 1987. *Borderlands: La Frontera—The New Mestiza*. San Francisco: Spinsters/Aunt Lute.
Aranha, José Periera de Graça. 1901/1959. *Canaã [Canaan]*. Rio de Janeiro: F. Briguiet.
Araújo, Mozart de. 1963. *A modinha e o lundu no século XVIII*. São Paulo: Ricordi.
Argüelles, José A. 1975. *The Transformative Vision: Reflections on the Nature and History of Human Expression*. Berkeley: Shambhala.
Armstrong, Piers. 1999. *Third World Literary Fortunes: Brazilian Culture and Its International Reception*. Lewisburg: Bucknell University Press; London: Associated University Presses.
Arnason, Johann P. 1990. "Nationalism, Globalization, and Modernity." *Theory, Culture, and Society* 7, no. 2: 207–36.
Asante, Molefi. 1980. *Afrocentricity: The Theory of Social Change*. Buffalo: Amulefi.
———. 1987. *The Afrocentric Idea*. Philadelphia: Temple University Press.
———. 1992. *Kemet, Afrocentricity, and Knowledge*. Trenton: Africa World Press.
Ashton, Dore. 1982. "The Other Symbolist Inheritance in Painting." In *The Symbolist Movement in the Literature of European Languages*, edited by Anna Balakian, 519–27. Budapest: Akademiai Kiado.
Assis, Joaquim Maria Machado de. 1937. *Obra completa*. 31 vols. Rio de Janeiro: W. M. Jackson Editôres.
———. 1957a. *Obra completa*. 30 vols. Rio de Janeiro: W. M. Jackson Editôres.
———. 1957b. *Obra completa*. 31 vols. Rio de Janeiro: W. M. Jackson Editôres.
———. 1959. *Obra completa*. 3 vols. Rio de Janeiro: Editora José Aguilar.
———. 1962. *Obra completa [Oc]*. 3 vols. Rio de Janeiro: Editora José Aguilar.
———. 1968. *Obras illustradas*. 7 vols. São Paulo: Linografica Editora.
———. 1975a. *A mão e a luva [The Hand and the Glove]*. Rio de Janeiro: Civilização Brasileira; Brasília: INL.
———. 1975b. *Memorial de Aires [Ayres's Memorial]*. Rio de Janeiro: Civilização Brasileira; Brasília: INL.
———. 1975c. *Quincas Borba*. Rio de Janeiro: Civilização Brasileira; Brasília: INL.
———. 1975d. *Ressureição [Resurrection]*. Rio de Janeiro: Civilização Brasileira; Brasília: INL.
———. 1976. *Esaú e Jacó [Esau and Jacob]*. Rio de Janeiro: Civilização Brasileira; Brasília: INL.
———. 1977a. *Dom Casmurro*. Rio de Janeiro: Civilização Brasileira; Brasília: INL.
———. 1977b. *Helena*. Rio de Janeiro: Civilização Brasileira; Brasília: INL.
———. 1977c. *Iaiá Garcia*. Rio de Janeiro: Civilização Brasileira; Brasília: INL.
———. 1977d. *Memórias póstumas de Brás Cubas [The Posthumous Memoirs of Brás Cubas]*. Rio de Janeiro: Civilização Brasileira; Brasília: INL.
Auerbach, Erich. 1953. *Mimesis: The Representation of Reality in Western Literature*. Translated by Williard R. Trask. Princeton: Princeton University Press.
Avelar, Idelber. 2005. "Machado de Assis on Popular Music: A Case for Cultural Studies in Nineteenth-Century Latin America." *Portuguese Literary and Cultural Studies*, special issue, *The Author as Plagiarist: The Case of Machado de Assis*, nos. 13–14 (Fall–Spring): 161–76.
Azevedo, Aluísio. 1881/1971. *O mulato [The Mulatto]*. São Paulo: Martins Editora.
Azevedo, André Nunes de. 2003. "A reforma Pereira Passos: Uma tentativa de integração urbana." *Revista Rio de Janeiro*, no. 10 (May–August): 39–79.

Azevedo, Elciene. 1999. *Orfeu de Carapinha: A trajetóira de Luiz Gama na imperial cidade de São Paulo*. Campinas, São Paulo: Editora da UNICAMP, Centro de Pesquisa em História Social da Cultura.
Azevedo, Thales de. 1955. *As elites de côr*. São Paulo: Companhia do Brasil.
Bagby Júnior, Alberto I. 1975a. "Eighteen Years of Machado de Assis: A Critical Annotated Bibliography for 1956–1974." *Hispania* 58:648–83.
———. 1975b. "Machado de Assis and Foreign Languages." *Luso-Brazilian Review* 12, no. 2 (Winter): 225–33.
———. 1993. *Machado de Assis e seus primeiros romances*. Porto Alegre: EDIPUCRS.
Bailey, Dale S. 1961. "Slavery in the Novels of Brazil and the United States." Ph.D. diss., Indiana University.
Bailey, Stanley R. 2009. *Legacies of Race: Identities, Attitudes, and Politics in Brazil*. Stanford: Stanford University Press.
Bakhtin, M. M. 1981. *The Dialogic Imagination: Four Essays*. Edited by Michael Holquist. Translated by Caryl Emerson and Michael Holquist. Austin: University of Texas Press.
Baldwin, John D. 2008. *Ending the Science Wars*. Boulder: Paradigm.
Baptista, Abel Barros. 1991. *Em nome do apelo do nome*. Lisbon: Litoral Edições.
———. 1994. "O legado Caldwell, ou o paradigma do pé atrás." *Santa Barbara Portuguese Studies* 1:145–77.
———. 2003a. *Autobibliografias: Solicitação do livro na ficção de Machado de Assis*. Campinas: Universidade Estadual de Campinas.
———. 2003b. *A formação do nome: Duas interrogações sobre Machado de Assis*. Campinas: UNICAMP, Universidade Estadual de Campinas.
Barbosa, Domingos Caldas. 1944. *A viola de Lereno*. 2 vols. Edited by Francisco de Assis Barbosa. Rio de Janeiro: Imprensa Nacional, Ministério de Educação e Saúde.
———. 1958. *Poesia*. Edited by Luís da Câmara Cascudo. Rio de Janeiro: Livraria Agir Editora.
Barbosa, Francisco de Assis. 1959. *A vida de Lima Barreto*. Rio de Janeiro: Livraria José Olympio Editora.
Barnes, Taylor. 2011. "For the First Time, Blacks Outnumber Whites in Brazil," May 24, http://www.miamiherald.com/2011/05/23/v-fullstory/2231323/for-the-first-time-blacks-outnumber.html#ixzz1Vjw8qUwa.
Barreto, Afonso Henriques de Lima. 1956. *Diário íntimo*. Obra completa, vol. 14. São Paulo: Brasiliense.
Barreto Filho, José. 1947. *Introdução a Machado de Assis*. Rio de Janeiro: Agir.
Barvosa, Edwina. 2008. *Wealth of Selves: Multiple Identities, Mestiza Consciousness, and the Subject of Politics*. College Station: Texas A&M University Press.
Barzun, Jacques. 1961. *Classic, Romantic, and Modern*. Chicago: University of Chicago Press.
Bastide, Roger. 1940. "Machado de Assis: Paisagista." *Revista do Brasil* 3, no. 29 (November): 1–14.
———. 1943. *A poesia afro-brasileira*. São Paulo. Livraria Martins Editora.
———. 1961. "Dusky Venus, Black Apollo." *Race and Class* 3, no. 1: 10–8.
Baudrillard, Jean. 1975. *The Mirror of Production*. St. Louis: Telos Press.
Baumer, Franklin L. 1977. *Modern European Thought: Continuity and Change in Ideas, 1600–1950*. New York: Macmillan.
Beattie, Peter. 2001. *The Tribute of Blood: Army, Honor, Race, and Nation in Brazil*. Durham: Duke University Press.
Becker, George J. 1980. *Realism in Modern Literature*. New York: Frederick Ungar.
Becker, Howard. 1982. *Art Worlds*. Berkeley: University of California Press.
Béhague, Gerard. 1968. "Biblioteca da Ajuda (Lisbon) Mss 1595–1596: Two Eighteenth-Century Anonymous Collections of Modinhas." *Anuario* 4:44–81.

Bellei, Sergio. 1992. *Nacionalidade e literatura: Os caminhos da alteridade.* Florianópolis: Editora da UFSC.
Bello, José Maria. 1966. *A History of Modern Brazil, 1889–1964.* Translated by James L. Taylor. Stanford: Stanford University Press.
Benchimol, Jaime Larry. 1990. *Pereira Passos: Un Haussman tropical, revovação urbana da cidade do Rio de Janeiro no início do século XX.* Rio de Janeiro: Secretaria Municipal de cultura, Turismo e Esportes, Departamento Geral de Documentação e Informação Cultural, Divisão de Editorão.
Berg, William J. 1992. *The Visual Novel: Emile Zola and the Art of His Times.* University Park: Pennsylvania State University Press.
Berman, Morris. 1989. *Coming to Our Senses: Body and Spirit in the Hidden History of the West.* New York: Bantam Books.
Bernardo, Gustavo, Joachim Michael, and Markus Schäffauer, eds. 2010. *Machado de Assis e a escravidão.* São Paulo. Annablume Editora.
Bernd, Zilá. 1987. *Negritude e literatura na América latina.* Porto Alegre: Mercado Aberto.
———. 1988. *Introdução à literatura negra.* São Paulo: Editora Brasiliense.
Berrong, Richard M. 2006. "Modes of Literary Impressionism." *Gene: Forms of Discourse and Culture* 39, no. 2 (Summer): 203–28.
Bertens, Hans S. 1993. "The Postmodern *Weltanschauung* and Its Relation to Modernism: An Introductory Survey." In *A Postmodern Reader*, edited by Joseph P. Natoli and Linda Hutcheon, 25–71. Albany: State University of New York Press.
———. 1997. "The Sociology of Postmodernity." In *International Postmodernism: Theory and Literary Practice*, edited by Han S. Bertens and Douwe Fokkema, 103–20. Philadelphia: John Benjamins.
Berzon, Judith. 1978. *Neither White nor Black: The Mulatto Character in American Fiction.* New York: New York University Press.
Bhabha, Homi K. 1990. "Introduction." In *Nation and Narration*, edited by Homi K. Bhabha, 1–8. New York: Routledge.
———. 1994. *Location of Culture.* New York: Routledge.
———. 1995. "Cultural Diversity and Cultural Differences." In *The Post-Colonial Studies Reader*, edited by Bill Ashcroft, Gareth Griffiths, and Helen Tiffin, 206–12. New York: Routledge.
Bicudo, Virgínia Leone. 1947. "Estudo de atitudes raciais de pretos e mulatos em São Paulo." *Sociologia* 9, no. 3: 195–219.
Bim, Leda Marana. 2010. "Amor e morte: Uma comparação dos contos 'Pai contra Mãe' e 'Mariana.'" In *Machado de Assis e a escravidão/Machado de Assis und die Sklaverei*, Hamburg Conferences, edited by Gustavo Bernardo, Joachim Michel, and Markus Schäffauer, 115–24. São Paulo: Annablume.
Blake, Stanley E. 2011. *The Vigorous Core of Our Nationality: Race and Regional Identity in Northeastern Brazil.* Pittsburgh, Pa.: University of Pittsburgh Press.
Bogart, Doris Van de. 1968. *Introduction to the Humanities: Painting, Sculpture, Architecture, Music, and Literature.* New York: Harper and Row.
Bone, Robert. 1958. *The Negro Novel in America.* New Haven: Yale University Press.
Bonilla-Silva, Eduardo. 2006. *Racism Without Racists: Color-Blind Racism and the Persistence of Racial Inequality in America.* Lanham, Md.: Rowman and Littlefield.
Booth, Wayne C. 1961. *The Rhetoric of Fiction.* Chicago: University of Chicago Press.
Borges, Dain Edward. 1992. *The Family in Bahia, Brazil, 1870–1945.* Stanford: Stanford University Press.
———. 1993. "'Puffy, Ugly, Slothful and Inert': Degeneration in Brazilian Social Thought, 1880–1940." *Journal of Latin American Studies* 25, no. 2 (May): 235–56.

———. 1995. "The Recognition of Afro-Brazilian Symbols and Ideas, 1890–1940." *Luso-Brazilian Review, Culture and Ideology in the Americas: Essays in Honor of Richard M. Morse* 32, no. 2 (Winter): 59–78.
———. 2006. "Euclides da Cunha's View of Brazil's Fractured Identity." In *Brazil in the Making: Facets of National Identity*, edited by Carmen Nava and Ludwig Lauerhass Jr., 28–44. Lanham, Md.: Rowman and Littlefield.
———. 2007. "The Relevance of Machado de Assis." In *Imagining Brazil*, edited by Jessé Souza and Valter Sinder, 235–51. Lanham, Md.: Lexington Books.
Bosco, Umberto. 1959. *Realismo Romantico*. Rome: Salvatore Scisscia Editore, 1959.
Bosi, Alfredo. 1970. *História concisa da literatura brasileira*. São Paulo: Cultrix.
———. 1983. "A máscara e a fenda." In *Machado de Assis*, edited by Bosi et al., 437–57. São Paulo: Ática.
———. 1999. *Machado de Assis: O enigma do olhar*. São Paulo: Ática.
———. 2002. *Machado de Assis*. São Paulo: Publifolha.
———. 2004. "Raymundo Faoro: Leitor de Machado de Assis." *Estudos Avançados* 18, no. 51: 355–76.
———. 2006. *Brás Cubas em três versões: Estudos machadianos*. São Paulo: Companhia das Letras.
———. 2008. *Colony, Cult, and Culture* [*Dialética da colonização: Colônia, culto e cultura*]. Edited by Pedro Meira Monteiro. Translated by Robert P. Newcomb. Dartmouth: University of Massachusetts Dartmouth.
Bourdieu, Pierre. 1979/1984. *Distinction: A Social Critique of the Judgment of Taste*. Translated by Richard Nice. Cambridge, Mass.: Harvard University Press.
———. 1990. *The Logic of Practice*. Translated by Richard Nice. Cambridge: Polity Press.
———. 1996. *The Rules of Art*. Translated by Susan Emanuel. Cambridge: Polity Press.
Bourdieu, Pierre, and Loïc Wacquant. 1999. "On the Cunning of Imperialist Reason." *Theory, Culture, and Society* 16, no. 1: 47–48.
Boxer, Charles R. 1957. *A Great Luso-Brazilian Figure: Padre Antonio Vieira, S. J., 1608–1697*. London: Hispanic and Luso-Brazilian Councils.
———. 1963. *Race Relations in the Portuguese Colonial Empire, 1415–1825*. Oxford: Clarendon Press.
———. 1969. *The Portuguese Seaborne Empire, 1415–1825*. New York: Knopf.
Boyd, Antonio Olliz. 1975. "The Concept of Black Aesthetics as Seen in Selected Works of Three Latin American Writers: Machado de Assis, Nicolás Guillén, and Adalberto Ortiz." Ph.D. diss., Stanford University.
———. 1992. "The Social and Ethnic Context of Machado de Assis's 'Dom Casmurro.'" *Afro-Hispanic Review* 11, nos. 1–3: 34–41.
Bradbury, Malcolm, and James McFarlane. 1976. "Movements, Magazines, and Manifestos: The Succession from Naturalism." In *Modernism*, edited by Malcolm Bradbury and James McFarlane, 192–205. Harmondsworth, UK: Penguin Books.
Branche, Jerome C. 2006. *Colonialism and Race in Luso-Hispanic Literature*. Columbia: University of Missouri Press.
Brantlinger, Patrick. 1976. *The Practice of Psychoanalytic Criticism*. Detroit: Wayne State University.
Brayner, Sonia. 1979. *Laberinto do espaço romanesco: Tradição e renovação da literatura brasileira, 1880–1920*. Rio de Janeiro: Civilização Brasileira; Brasília: INL.
Broca, Britto. 1957. *Machado de Assis e a política e outros estudos*. Rio de Janeiro: Organização Simões, Editora.
Brody, Elaine. 1982. "Musical Settings of Symbolist Poems." In *The Symbolist Movement in the Literature of European Languages*, edited by Anna Balakian, 438–92. Budapest: Akademiai Kiado.
Brookshaw, David. 1986. *Race and Color in Brazilian Literature*. Metuchen, N.J: Scarecrow Press.

———. 1988. *Paradise Betrayed: Brazilian Literature of the Indian*. Amsterdam: Center for Latin American Research and Documentation.
Brumm, Ursula. 1958. "Symbolism and the Novel." *Partisan Review* 25 (Summer): 330–41.
Bruzzi, Nilo. 1959. *José do Patrocinio: Romancista*. Rio de Janeiro: Editora Aurora.
Budasz, Rogério. 2007. "Black Guitar Players and Early African-Iberian Music in Portugal and Brazil." *Early Music* 35, no. 1 (February): 2–21.
Bueno, Eva Paulina. 1995. *Resisting Boundaries: The Subject of Naturalism in Brazil*. New York: Garland.
Buescu, Mircea. 1979. *Brasil: Disparidades de renda no passado: Subsídios para o estudo dos problemas brasileiros*. Rio de Janeiro: APEC.
Burdick, John. 1992. "The Myth of Racial Democracy." *North American Congress on Latin America Report on the Americas* 25, no. 4 (February): 40–42.
Burke, Peter, and Maria Lúcia G. Pallares-Burke. 2008. *Gilberto Freyre: Social Theory in the Tropics*. Oxford: Peter Lang.
Burns, E. Bradford. 1970. *Latin America: A Concise Interpretive History*. Englewood Cliffs: Prentice-Hall.
———. 1993. *A History of Brazil*. 3rd ed. New York: Columbia University Press.
Butler, Kim. 1998. *Freedoms Given, Freedoms Won: Afro-Brazilians in Post-Abolition São Paulo and Salvador*. New Brunswick: Rutgers University Press.
Caldwell, Helen. 1960. *The Brazilian Othello of Machado de Assis*. Berkeley: University of California Press.
———. 1970. *Machado de Assis: The Brazilian Master and His Novels*. Berkeley: University of California Press.
———. 1972. "Machado de Assis, Independence, Liberty." In *UCLA Semana de Arte Moderna Symposium (1922–1972): Commemorating the 50th Anniversary of the Semana de Arte Moderna in São Paulo and the 150th Anniversary of Brazilian Independence, February 7–12, 1972*, edited by Claude L. Hulet, 89–99. Los Angeles: University of California, Los Angeles.
Câmara, Joaquim Mattoso. 1962. *Ensaios machadianos*. Rio de Janeiro: Livraria Academica.
Caminhos Cruzados. 2008. "Roberto Schwarz sobre o 'Sentimento Íntimo do País' em Machado de Assis. Intervenção de Roberto Schwarz no Simpósio 'Caminhos Cruzados: Machado de Assis pela Crítica Mundial,' dia 26 de agosto de 2008, Após Palestra de Abel Barros Baptista na Mesa-Redonda 'Machado de Assis: Nacional e Universal.'" http://www.youtube.com/watch?v=BGIR1mfvEYU.
Campos, Maria Consuelo Cunha. 2011. "Luiz Gama." In *Literatura e afrodescendência no Brasil: Antologia crítica*, vol. I: *Precursores*, edited by Eduardo de Assis Duarte, 127–42. Belo Horizonte: Editora UFMG.
Cândido, Antônio. 1968. "Literature and the Rise of Brazilian National Identity." *Luso-Brazilian Review* 5, no. 1 (June): 27–43.
———. 1969. *Formação da literatura brasileira*. 2 vols. São Paulo: Livraria Martins Editora.
———. 1970a. "Dialética da malandragem: Caracterização das *Memórias de um sargento de milícias*" [The Dialectic of Tricksterism: Characterization in *Memoirs of a Police Sergeant*]. *Revista do Instituto de Estudos Brasileiros* 8:67–89.
———. 1970b. "Esquema de Machado de Assis." In *Vários escritos*. São Paulo: Duas Cidades, 15–32.
———. 1995. *On Literature and Society*. Translated, edited, and introduced by Howard S. Becker. Princeton: Princeton University Press.
Caramschi, Enzo. 1971. *Réalisme et impressionisme dans l'oeuvre des Frères Goncourt*. Pisa: Libreria Soliardica.
Carlson, Marin A. 1993. *Theories of the Theatre: A Historical and Critical Survey from the Greeks to the Present*. Expanded ed. Ithaca: Cornell University Press.

Carneiro, Maria Luiza Tucci. 2005. *Preconceito racial em Portugal e Brasil colônia: Os cristãos-novos e o mito da pureza de sangue.* São Paulo: Editôra Perspectiva.
Carpeaux, Otto Maria. 1962. *História da literatura occidental.* 8 vols. Rio de Janeiro: Edições O Cruzeiro, 1962.
Carsaniga, S. M. 1974. "Realism in Italy." In *The Age Realism,* edited by F. W. J. Hemmings, 323–55. Harmondsworth, UK: Penguin Books.
Carvalho, José Murilo de. 1980. *A construção da ordem: A elite política imperial.* Rio de Janeiro: Editora Campus.
———. 1989. *Os bestializados: O Rio de Janeiro e a república que não foi.* São Paulo: Companhia das Letras.
———. 1996. *A campanha abolicionista: José do Patrocínio.* Rio de Janeiro: Fundação Biblioteca Nacional.
Cassuto, Leonardo. 1997. *The Inhuman Race: The Racial Grotesque in American Literature.* New York: Columbia University Press.
Castello, José Aderaldo. 1969. *Realidade e ilusão em Machado de Assis.* São Paulo: Companhia Editora Nacional.
Castro, Hebe Maria Mattos de. 1995. *Das cores do silêncio: Os significados da liberdade no sudoeste escravista Brasil, século XIX.* Rio de Janeiro: Arquivo Nacional.
Caute, David. 1970. *Frantz Fanon.* New York: Viking Press.
CBS. 2007. "Roots." *60 Minutes,* October 7.
Chagas, Wilson. 1994. *A fortuna crítica de Machado de Assis.* Porto Alegre: Movimento.
Chalhoub, Sidney. 1990. *Visões da liberdade: Uma história das últimas décadas da escravidão na corte.* São Paulo: Companhia das Letras.
———. 2001. "What Are Noses For? Paternalism, Social Darwinism, and Race Science in Machado de Assis." *Journal of Latin American Cultural Studies* 10, no. 2 (August): 171–91.
———. 2003. *Machado de Assis: Historiador* [*Machado de Assis: Historian*]. São Paulo: Companhia das Letras.
Chapman, A. H., and Miriam Chapman-Santana. 2000. "Machado de Assis's Own Writings About His Epilepsy: A Brief Clinical Note. *Arquivos de Neuro-Psiquiatria* 58, no 4: (December): 1153–54.
Chaves, Flávio Loureiro. 1974. *O mundo social do "Quincas Borba."* Porto Alegre: Movimentos; Brasília: INL.
Cizevskij, Dmitrij. 1971. *Comparative History of Slavic Literatures.* Translated by Richard Noel Porter and Martin P. Rice. Vanderbilt University Press.
Cobb, Martha. 1974. "The Black Experience in the Poetry of Nicolás Guillén, Jacques Roumain, and Langston Hughes." Ph.D. diss., Catholic University of America.
Coelho, Haydée Ribeiro. 2011. "Lima Barreto." In *Literatura e afrodescendência no Brasil: Antologia crítica,* vol. I: *Precursores,* edited by Eduardo de Assis Duarte, 291–310. Belo Horizonte: Editora UFMG.
Coelho, Nelly Novais. 1974. *Literatura e linguagem: A obra literária e a expressão lingüística.* Rio de Janeiro: Livraria José Olympio Editora.
Cohen, David W., and Jack P. Greene. 1972. "Introduction." In *Neither Slave nor Free: The Freemen of African Descent in the Slave Societies of the New World,* edited by David W. Cohen and Jack P. Greene, 1–23. Baltimore: Johns Hopkins University Press.
Cole, Nicki Lisa. 2006. "Not 'Just' Satire: Decoding the Racial Narratives of Saturday Night Live." Master's thesis, University of California, Santa Barbara.
Coleman, Alexander. 1980. *Eça de Queirós and European Realism.* New York: New York University Press.
Colker, Ruth. 1996. *Hybrid: Bisexuals, Multiracials, and Other Misfits Under American Law.* New York: New York University Press.

Collins, Patricia Hill 1993. *The Black Scholar* 23, nos. 3–4 (Fall): 52–55.
Conceição, Fernando. 2004. "As cotas contra o apocalipse." *Folha de São Paulo Caderno Mais*, June 27.
Condé, Maryse. 1998. "O Brave New World." *Research in African Literatures* 29, no. 3: 1–7.
Connor, Steven. 1989. *Postmodern Culture: An Introduction to Theories of the Contemporary.* Oxford: Blackwell.
Conrad, Robert. 1972. *The Destruction of Brazilian Slavery, 1850–1888.* Berkeley: University of California Press.
Conselho Nacional de Estatística (CNE). 1961. *Contribuições para o estudo da demografia no Brasil.* Rio de Janeiro.
Cony, Carlos Heitor. 2008. "Confluências." In *Cadernos de literatura brasileira: Machado de Assis*, 41–45. Rio de Janeiro: Instituto Moreira Salles.
Coon, Carlton S. 1965. *The Living Races of Man.* New York: Knopf.
Corção, Gustavo. 1965. *O desconcerto do mundo.* Rio de Janeiro: Livraria Agir Editora.
Cordeiro, Francisca de Basto. 1961. *O Machado de Assis que eu vi.* Rio de Janeiro: Livraria São José.
Coser, Lewis, Charles Kadushin, and Walter Powell. 1982. *Books: The Culture and Commerce of Publishing.* New York: Basic Books.
Costa, Christine. 2005. Machado de Assis: The Apprentice Journalist." *Portuguese Literary and Cultural Studies*, special issue, *The Author as Plagiarist: The Case of Machado de Assis*, nos. 13–14 (Fall–Spring): 561–69.
Costa, Emilia Viotti da. 1985. *The Brazilian Empire: Myths and Histories.* Chicago: University of Chicago Press.
Costigan, Lúcia Helena. 2007. "Domingos Caldas Barbosa (1740–1800): A Precursor of Afro-Brazilian Literature." *Research in African Literatures* 38, no. 1 (Spring): 172–80.
Costigan, Lúcia Helena, and Russell G. Hamilton. 2007. "Introduction." *Research in African Literatures* 38, no. 1 (Spring): 5–8.
Coutinho, Afrânio. 1940. "Machado de Assis e o problema do mestiço." *Revista do Livro*, 3rd ser., vol. 3, no. 20 (February): 22–29.
———. 1959. *A filosophia de Machado de Assis e Outros Ensaios.* Rio de Janeiro: Livraria São José.
———. 1966. *Machado de Assis na literatura brasileira.* Rio de Janeiro: Livraria São José.
———. 1969. *A literatura no Brasil.* Direção de Afrânio Coutinho. 2nd ed. 5 vols. Rio de Janeiro: Editorial Sul Americana.
———. 1976. *Introdução à literatura brasileira.* Rio de Janeiro: Civilização Brasileira.
———. 1989. "El fenómeno de Machado de Assis." *Brasil Kultura* 14, no. 63: 8–12.
Coutinho, Carlos Nelson. 1974. "O significado de Lima Barreto na literatura brasileira." In *Realismo and anti-realismo na literatura brasileira*, edited by Carlos Nelson Coutinho, Gilvan Ribeiro, José Paulo Neto, Leandro Konder, and Luiz Sergio N. Henriques, 1–56. Rio de Janeiro: Paz e Terra.
Coutinho, Eduardo de Faria. 2010. "A desconstrução de estereótipos na obra de Machado de Assis: A questão da escravidão." In *Machado de Assis e a Escravidão/Macchado de Assis und die Sklaverei*, Hamburg Conferences, edited by Gustavo Bernardo, Joachim Michel, and Markus Schäffauer, 93–100. São Paulo: Annablume.
Cox, Oliver 1970. *Caste, Class, and Race: A Study in Social Dynamics.* New York: Monthly Review Press.
Cruz, Jon. 1999. *Culture on the Margins: The Black Spiritual and the Rise of American Cultural Interpretation.* Princeton: Princeton University Press.
Cruz Júnior, Dilson Ferreira da. 2002. *Estratégias e máscaras de um fingidor: A crônica de Machado de Assis.* São Paulo: Nankin Editorial: Humanitas: FAPESP.
Cunha, Euclides da. 1902. *Os sertões.* Rio de Janeiro: Laemmert.

Current-García, Eugene, and Patrick R. Walton. 1962. *Realism and Romanticism in Fiction*. Chicago: Scott, Foresman.
Cyrus, Stanley A. 1982. "Ethnic Ambivalence and Afro-Hispanic Novelists." *Afro-Hispanic Review* 1, no. 1 (January): 29–32.
DaMatta, Roberto. 1990. "For an Anthropology of the Brazilian Tradition or A Virtude Está no Meio." Working Paper no. 182, Latin American Program, Wilson Center. Washington, D.C.
Daniel, G. Reginald. 1973. "Luís Gama, José do Patrocínio, Machado de Assis, and Castro Alves: The Nineteenth-Century Brazilian Mulatto and the Author." Master's thesis, Indiana University.
———. 1981. "Machado de Assis: Racial Identity and the Brazilian Novelist." Paper presented at the Symposium on Portuguese Traditions, University of California, Los Angeles.
———. 1988. "Machado de Assis and the Meta-Mulatto." Ph.D. diss., University of California, Los Angeles.
———. 1992. "Passers and Pluralists: Subverting the Racial Divide." In *Racially Mixed People in America*, edited by Maria P. P. Root, 91–108. Newberry Park, Calif: Sage.
———. 1995. "Machado de Assis and the Meta-Mulatto." In *Encruzilhadas: Symposium on Portuguese Traditions*, edited by Claude L. Hulet, 4:64–67. Los Angeles: University of California, Los Angeles, Department of Spanish and Portuguese.
———. 2002. *More Than Black? Multiracial Identity and the New Racial Order*. Philadelphia: Temple University Press.
———. 2005. "Beyond Eurocentrism and Afrocentrism: Globalization, Critical Hybridity, and Postcolonial Blackness." In *Critical Globalization Studies*, edited by Richard P. Appelbaum and William I. Robinson, 259–68. New York: Routledge.
———. 2006. *Race and Multiraciality in Brazil and the United States: Converging Paths?* University Park: Pennsylvania State University Press.
Daniel, Mary L. 1996. "Ethnic Love/Hate in the 'Inéditos' of Lima Barreto." *Hispania* 79, no. 3 (September): 389–99.
Danow, David K. 1995. *The Spirit of Carnival: Magical Realism and the Grotesque*. Lexington: University of Kentucky Press.
Dathorne, Oscar Ronald. 1974. *The Black Mind: A History of African Literature*. Minneapolis: University of Minnesota Press.
Dávila, Jerry. 2003. *Diploma of Whiteness: Race and Social Policy in Brazil, 1917–1945*. Durham: Duke University Press.
Davis, Darien. 1999. *Avoiding the Dark: Race and the Forging of National Culture in Modern Brazil*. Aldershot, UK: Ashgate.
Davis, Murray. 1993. *What's So Funny? The Comic Conception of Culture and Society*. Chicago: University of Chicago Press.
Day, Caroline Bond. 1932. *A Study of Some Negro-White Families in the United States*. Cambridge, Mass.: Harvard University Press.
Décio, João. 1999. *Retorno ao romance eterno: "Dom Casmurro" de Machado de Assis e outros ensaios*. Blumenau: Editora da FURB.
Degler, Carl N. 1971. *Neither Black nor White: Slavery and Race Relations in Brazil and the United States*. New York: Macmillan.
Dennis, Jeana E. Paul. 1990. "Aspects of Plot Structure, Narration, Theme, and Characterization in Major Novels of Machado de Assis." Master's thesis, Texas Tech University.
Derrida, Jacques. 1979. *Spurs: Nietzsche's Styles*. Translated by Barbara Harlow. Chicago: University of Chicago Press.
———. 1978. *Writing and Difference*. Translated by Alan Bass. Chicago: University of Chicago Press.

Desan, Philippe, Priscilla Parkhurst Ferguson, and Wendy Griswold. 1989. "Editors' Introduction." In *Literature and Social Practice*, edited by Philippe Dessan, Priscilla Parkhurst Ferguson, and Wendy Griswold, 1–10. Chicago: University of Chicago Press.
DeVault, Marjorie L. 1990. "Novel Readings: The Social Organization of Interpretation." *American Journal of Sociology* 95, no. 4: 887–921.
DiMaggio, Paul. 1987. "Classification in Art." *American Sociological Review* 52, no. 4 (August): 440–55.
Directoria Geral de Estatística. 1872. *Recensamento da população do Imperio do Brasil a que se procedeu no dia 1º de agosto de 1872*. Rio de Janeiro.
———. 1898. *Sexo, raça e estado civil, nacionalidade, filiação, culto e analphabetismo da população recenseada em 31 de dezembro de 1890*. Rio de Janeiro: Officina de Estatística.
———. 1986. *Resumo histórico dos inquéritos censitários realizados no Brasil: Recenseamento do Brasil*. Originally published in *Recenseamento do Brasil*, vol. 1, Introdução, 1920. São Paulo: IPE-USP, edição facsimilada, 169–251.
Dixon, Paul. 1989. *Retired Dreams: "Dom Casmurro": Myth and Modernity*. West Lafayette, Ind.: Purdue Research Foundation.
———. 2009. "Machado de Assis, the 'Defunto Autor' and the Death of the Author." *Luso-Brazilian Review* 46, no. 1: 45–56.
Domingues, Petrônio. 2004. *Uma história não contada: Negro, racismo, e branqueamento em São Paulo no pós-abolição*. São Paulo: Editora Senac.
Domínguez, Virginia. 1986. *White by Definition: Social Classification in Creole Louisiana*. New Brunswick: Rutgers University Press.
Douglass, Ellen H. 1998. "Machado de Assis's 'A Cartomante': Modern Parody and the Making of a 'Brazilian' Text." *Modern Language Notes* 113, no. 5 (December): 1036–55.
Dozy, Reinhart Pieter Anne. 1869. *Glossaire des mots espagnols et portugais derivés de l'arabe*. Leiden: E. J. Brill.
Driver, David Miller. 1942. *The Indian in Brazilian Literature*. New York: Hispanic Institute in the United States.
Duarte, Eduardo de Assis. 2007a. *Machado de Assis afro-descendente: Escritos de caramujo (antologia)*. Rio de Janeiro/Belo Horizonte: Pallas/Crisálidas.
———. 2007b. "Machado de Assis's African Descent." *Research in African Literatures* 38, no. 1 (Spring): 134–51.
Duggan, Paul Vincent. 1976. "Social Themes and Political Satire in the Short Stories of Lima Barreto." Ph.D. diss., City University of New York.
Dutra, Francis A. 1999. "A Hard-Fought Struggle for Recognition: Manuel Gonçalves Doria, First Afro-Brazilian to Become a Knight of Santiago." *Americas* 56, no. 1 (July): 91–113.
———. 2003. "The Vieira Family and the Order of Christ." *Luso-Brazilian Review* 40, no. 1 (Summer): 17–31.
———. 2006. "African Heritage and the Portuguese Military Orders in Seventeenth- and Early Eighteenth-Century Brazil: The Case of Mestre de Campo Domingos Rodrigues Carneiro." *Colonial Latin American Historical Review* 15, no. 2 (Spring): 113–41.
———. 2011. "Ser mulato em Portugal nos primórdios de época moderna." *Tempo* 16, no. 30: 101–14.
Eakins, Marshall C. 1980. "Race and Ideology in Graça Aranha's *Canaã*." *Ideologies and Literature* 3, no. 14 (September–November): 3–15.
Egejuru, Phanuel Akubueze 1978. *Black Writers, White Audience: A Critical Approach to African Literature*. Hicksville: Exposition Press.
Eisler, Riane. 1988. *The Chalice and the Blade: Our History, Our Future*. San Francisco: HarperCollins.
Epilepsia. 2003. "The History and Stigma of Epilepsy." *Epilepsia* 44, no. S6 (September 1): 12–14.

Epp, Michael H. 2003. "Raising Minstrelsy: Humour, Satire, and the Stereotype in *The Birth of a Nation* and *Bamboozled*." *Canadian Review of American Studies* 33, no. 1: 17–35.
Expilly, Charles [Jean-Charles Marie]. 1935. *Mulheres e costumes do Brasil*. São Paulo: Companhia Editôra Nacional.
Facioli, Valentim. 2002. *Um defunto estrambótico: Análise e interpretação das "Memórias póstumas de Brás Cubas."* São Paulo: Nankin Editorial.
Fanger, Donald. 1965. *Dostoevsky and Romantic Realism: A Study of Dostoevsky in Relation to Balzac, Dickens, and Gogol*. Chicago: University of Chicago Press.
Fanon, Frantz. 1952/1967. *Black Skin, White Masks*. Translated by Charles Lam Markmann. New York: Grove Press.
———. 1963/1968. *The Wretched of the Earth*. Translated by Constance Farrington. New York: Grove Press.
Fantinati, Carlos Erivany. 1978. *O profeta e o escrivão: Estudo de Lima Barreto*. HUCITEC: São Paulo.
Fantini, Marli. 2011. "Machado de Assis." In *Literatura e afrodescendência no Brasil: Antologia crítica*, vol. I: *Precursores*, edited by Eduardo de Assis Duarte, 143–72. Belo Horizonte: Editora UFMG.
Faoro, Raymundo. 1958/1975. *Os donos do poder: Formação do patronato político brasileiro* [*The Owners of Power: Formation of Brazilian Political Patronage*]. 2 vols. Porto Alegre: Editora Globo.
———. 1974. *Machado de Assis: A pirâmide e o trapézio* [*Machado de Assis: The Pyramid and the Trapezoid*]. São Paulo: Companhia Editora Nacional.
———. 1976. *Machado de Assis: A pirâmide e o trapézio* [*Machado de Assis: The Pyramid and the Trapezoid*]. 2nd ed. São Paulo: Companhia Editora Nacional.
Faria, João Roberto. 2008. *Machado de Assis: Do teatro. Textos críticos e escritos diversos*. Compiled, edited, and with an introduction and notes by João Roberto Faria. São Paulo: Perspectiva.
Faro, Arnaldo. 1977. *Eça e o Brasil*. São Paulo: Companhia Editora Nacional, Editora da Universidade de São Paulo.
Fasel, George. 1974. *Modern Europe in the Making: From the French Revolution to the Common Market*. New York: Dodd, Mead, and Company.
Fernandes, Florestan. 1969. *The Negro in Brazilian Society*. Translated by Jacqueline D. Skiles, A. Brunel, and Arthur Rothwell. Edited by Phyllis B. Eveleth. New York: Columbia University Press.
Fernandes, Paula T., Priscila C. B. Salgado, Ana Lúcia A. Noronha, Fernanda D. Barbosa, Elisabete A. P. Souza, and Li M. Li. 2004. "Stigma Scale of Epilepsy: Conceptual Issues." *Journal of Epilepsy and Clinical Neurophysiology* 10, no. 4: 213–18.
Figueiredo, Maria do Carmo Lanna. 1995. *O romance de Lima Barreto e sua recepção*. Belo Horizonte, Minas Gerais: Editora Lê.
Fischer, Ernst. 1963. *The Necessity of Art: A Marxist Approach*. Translated by Anna Bostock. Middlesex, England: Penguin Books.
Fischer, Sibylle Maria. 1994. "Geography and Representation in Machado de Assis." *Modern Language Quarterly* 55, no. 2 (June): 191–214.
Fiske, John. 1989. *Understanding Popular Cultural*. New York: Routledge.
Fitz, Earl. 1989. *Machado de Assis*. Boston: G. K. Hall.
———. 1990. "*Memorias Póstumas de Brás Cubas* as (Proto) Type of the Modernist Novel: A Problem in Literary History and Interpretation." *Latin American Literary Review* 18, no. 36 (July–December): 7–25.
———. 2005. "Machado de Assis' Reception and the Transition of the Modern European Novel."

Portuguese Literary and Cultural Studies, special issue, *The Author as Plagiarist: The Case of Machado de Assis*, nos. 13–14 (Fall–Spring): 43–57.
Fleming, William. 1974. *Arts and Ideas*. New York: Holt, Rinehart, and Winston.
Flory, Thomas. 1977. "Race and Social Control in Independent Brazil." *Latin American Studies* 9, no. 2 (November): 199–224.
Fonseca, Godín da. 1968. *Machado de Assis e o hipopótamo: Uma biografia honesta e definitiva; A última palavra sôbre Machado de Assis*. Rio de Janeiro: Edição de Ouro.
Forbes, Jack D. 1988. *Black Africans and Native Americans: Color, Race, and Caste in the Evolution of Red-Black Peoples*. London: Blackwell.
Foster, David. 1987. *Handbook of Latin American Literature*. New York: Garland.
———. 1991. *Gay and Lesbian Themes in Latin American Writing*. Austin: University of Texas Press.
———. 1994. "Adolfo Caminha's *Bom-Crioulo*: A Founding Text of Brazilian Gay Literature." In *Latin American Writers on Gay and Lesbian Themes: A Bio-Critical Sourcebook*, edited by David William Foster, 1–33. Westport, Conn.: Greenwood Press.
Foucault, Michel. 1977. *Discipline and Punish*. New York: Vintage.
———. 1980. *Power/Knowledge: Selected Interviews and Other Writings, 1972–1977*, edited by Colin Gardner. New York: Pantheon Books.
França, Jean Marcel Carvalho. 2007. "Questão negra: O medo da senzala." *Trópico*. http://p.php.uol.com.br/tropico/html/textos/1419,1.shl.
Franco, Jean. 1970. *The Modern Culture of Latin America: Society and the Artist*. Rev. ed. Middlesex, UK: Pelican Books.
Frank, David A., and Mark Lawrence McPhail. 2005. "Barack Obama's Address to the 2004 Democratic National Convention: Trauma, Compromise, Consilience, and the (Im)Possibility of Racial Reconciliation." *Rhetoric and Public Affairs* 85, no. 4: 571–94.
Frank, Paul L. 1952. "Realism and Naturalism in Music." *Journal of Aesthetics and Art Criticism* 10, no. 2 (December): 135–51.
Frank, Zephyr L. 2004. *Dutra's World: Wealth and Family in Nineteenth-Century Rio de Janeiro*. Albuquerque: University of New Mexico Press.
———. 2005. "Wealth Holding in Southeastern Brazil, 1815–1860." *Hispanic American Historical Review* 85, no. 2: 223–57.
Freeborn, R. H. 1974. "Realism in Russia to the Death of Dostoyevsky." In *The Age of Realism*, edited by F. W. J. Hemmings, 69–141. Harmondsworth, UK: Penguin Books.
Freedman, Ralph. 1967. "Symbol as Terminus: Some Notes on Symbolist Narrative." *Comparative Literature Studies* 4, nos. 1–2: 135–43.
Freitas, Luiz Alberto Pinheiro de. 2001. *Freud e Machado de Assis: Uma interseção entre psicanálise e literatura*. Rio de Janeiro: Mauad.
Freitas, Maria Eurides Pitombeira de. 1981. *O grotesco na criação de Machado de Assis, Gregório de Matos*. Rio de Janeiro: Presença.
Freyre, Gilberto. 1962. "Reinterpretando José de Alencar." In *Vida, forma, e cor*, 115–33. Rio de Janeiro: José Olympio.
———. 1963a. *The Mansions and the Shanties*. Translated by Harriet de Onís. New York: Knopf.
———. 1963b. *The Masters and the Slaves*. Translated by Harriet de Onís. New York: Knopf.
———. 1970. *Order and Progress*. Translated and edited by Rod W. Horton. New York: Knopf.
Friedlander, Walter J. 2001. *The History of Modern Epilepsy: The Beginning, 1865–1914*. Westport, Conn.: Greenwood Press.
Friedman, John. 1960. "Intellectuals in Developing Societies." *Kyklos* 13, no. 4: 513–44.
Friedman, Melvin. 1976. "The Symbolist Novel: Huysmans to Malraux." In *Modernism*, edited by Malcolm Bradbury and James McFarlane, 453–465. Penguin Books.
Fry, Peter. 2000. "Politics, Nationality, and the Meaning of Race." *Daedalus* 129, no. 2: 83–118.

Fry, Peter, and Yvonne Maggie. 2007. "Política social de alto risco." In *Divisões perogosas: Políticas raciais no Brasil contemporâneo*, edited by Peter Fry, Yvonne Maggie, et al., 277–81. Rio de Janeiro: Civilização Brasileira.

Furtado, Júnia Ferreira. 2008. *Chica da Silva: A Brazilian Slave of the Eighteenth Century*. New Approaches to the Americas. New York: Cambridge University Press.

Gama, Luís Gonzaga Pinto da. 1904. *Primeiras trovas burlescas*. 3rd ed. Edited by Antônio dos Santos Oliveira and João da Rosa e Cruz. São Paulo: Bently Júnior.

García Canclini, Néstor. 1989. *Culturas híbridas*. Mexico City: Grijalbo.

———. 2003. "Cultural Studies and Revolving Doors." In *Contemporary Latin American Cultural Studies*, edited by Stephen Hart and Richard Young, 12–23. London: Arnold; New York: Oxford University Press.

Garner, Lydia M. 2007. "State and Race in the Brazilian Empire." *Forum on Public Policy: A Journal of the Oxford Round Table*, March 22, 1–21.

Gates, Henry Louis, Jr. 1986. "Editor's Introduction: Writing Race and the Difference It Makes." In *Race, Writing, and Difference*, edited by Henry Louis Gates, 1–20. Chicago: University of Chicago Press.

Gayle, Addison, Jr. 1976. *The Way of the New World: The Black Novel in America*. New York: Doubleday.

Gazzola, Ana Lúcia, and Wander Melo Miranda. 2000. "Introduction." In Silviano Santiago, *Uma literatura nos trópicos: Ensaios sobre depedência cultural*, 1–8. Rio de Janeiro: Rocco.

Gellner, Ernest. 1964. *Thought and Change*. London: Weidenfeld and Nicolson.

———. 1983. *Nations and Nationalism*. Oxford: Blackwell.

Gellner, Ernest, and Anthony D. Smith. 1996. "The Nation: Real or Imagined? The Warwick Debates on Nationalism." *Nations and Nationalism* 2, no. 3: 357–70.

Gibbs, Beverly Jean. 1952. "Impressionism as a Literary Movement." *Modern Language Journal* 36: 175–82.

Gibson, Lydialyle. 2006. "Race in Brazil." *University of Chicago Magazine* 98, no. 55. http://magazine.uchicago.edu/0606/investigations/race.shtml.

Ginsberg, Elaine K. 1996. "Introduction: The Politics of Passing." In *Passing and the Fictions of Identity*, edited by Elaine K. Ginsberg, 1–18. Durham: Duke University Press.

Gist, Noel P. 1967. "Cultural Versus Social Marginality: The Anglo-Indian Case." *Phylon*, 28 (Winter): 361–65.

Gitlin, Todd. 1980. *The Whole World Is Watching*. Berkeley: University of California Press.

Gledson, John. 1984. *The Deceptive Realism of Machado de Assis*. Liverpool Monographs in Hispanic Studies. Liverpool: Francis Cairns.

———. 1986. *Machado de Assis: Ficção e história*. Translated by Sonia Coutinho. Rio de Janeiro: Paz e Terra.

———. 1987. "Brazilian Fiction: Machado de Assis to the Present." In *Modern Latin American Fiction: A Survey*, 18–40, edited by John King. London: Faber and Faber.

———. 1997. "*Dom Casmurro*: A Foreword." In *"Dom Casmurro": A Novel by Joaquim Maria Machado de Assis*, translated by John Gledson, xi–xxvii. New York: Oxford University Press.

———. 1999. "Realism and Intentionalism Revisited." In *Machado de Assis: Reflections on a Brazilian Writer*, edited by Richard Graham, 1–22. Austin: University of Texas Press.

———. 2002. "Machado de Assis and Graciliano Ramos: Speculations on Sex and Sexuality." In *Luso-Sex: Gender and Sexuality in the Portuguese-Speaking World*, edited by Susan Canty Quinlan and Fernando Arenas, 12–34. Minneapolis: University of Minnesota Press.

Godoi, Rodrigo Camagro de. 2009. "'Altamente literário' e o 'altamente moral': Machado de Assis e o conservatório dramático brasileiro (1859–1864). *Olho d'Água* (São José do Rio Preto) 1, no. 2: 109–24.

Goffman, Irving. 1963. *Stigma: Notes on the Management of Spoiled Identity*. Englewood Cliffs: Prentice-Hall.
Goldberg, Milton M. 1941. "A Qualification of the Marginal Man Theory." *American Sociological Review* 6, no. 1: 52–58.
Gomes, Eugênio. 1958. *Machado de Assis*. Rio de Janeiro: Livraria São José.
———. 1967. *O enigma de Capitu: Ensaio de interpretação*. Rio de Janeiro: Livraria José Olympio.
———. 1979. *Machado de Assis: Influências inglesas*. Rio de Janeiro: Pallas Editora e Distribuidora.
Gomes, Heloísa Toller. 1994. *As marcas da escravidão: O negro e o discurso oitocentista no Brasil e nos Estados Unidos*. Editora UFRJ: EDUERJ.
———. 2007. "Afro-Brazilian Literature: Spaces Conquered, Spaces In-between." *Research in African Literatures* 38, no. 1 (Spring): 152–228.
Gordon, Avery. 1997. *"Ghostly Matters": Haunting and the Sociological Imagination*. Minneapolis: University of Minnesota Press.
Gottdiener, Mark. 1985. "Hegemony and Mass Culture: A Semiotic Approach." *American Journal of Sociology* 90, no. 5 (March): 979–1001.
Gouvêa, Fernando da Cruz. 2005. *Visão política de Machado de Assis e outros ensaios*. Recife Companhia Editora de Pernambuco.
Graden, Dale Torston. 2006. *From Slavery to Freedom in Brazil: Bahia, 1835–1900*. Albuquerque: University of New Mexico Press.
Graham, Richard. 1972. *Britain and the Onset of Modernization in Brazil, 1950–1914*. London: Cambridge University Press.
Gramsci, Antonio. 1971. *Selections from the Prison Notebooks*, edited by Quentin Hoare and Geoffrey Nowell Smith. New York: International.
Granja, Lúcia. 2002. *Machado de Assis, escritor em formação: A roda dos jornais*. São Paulo: FAPESP Campinas: Mercado de Letras.
Green, Arnold W. 1947. "A Re-Examination of the Marginal Man Concept." *Social Forces* 26 (December): 167–71.
Green, James N. 1999. *Beyond Carnival: Male Homosexuality in Twentieth-Century Brazil*. Chicago: University of Chicago Press.
Grieco, Agrippino. 1960. *Machado de Assis*. 2nd ed. Rio de Janeiro: Conquista.
Griffin, David Ray. 1989. *Varieties of Postmodern Theology*. Albany: State University of New York Press.
———. 1993. "Introduction: Constructive Postmodern Philosophy." In *Founders of Constructive Postmodern Philosophy: Peirce, James, Bergson, Whitehead, and Hartshorne*, edited by David Ray Griffin, 1–42. Albany: State University of New York.
Griswold, Wendy. 1983. "The Devil's Technique: Cultural Legitimations and Social Change." *American Sociological Review* 48 (October): 668–80.
———. 1993. "Recent Moves in the Sociology of Literature." *Annual Review of Sociology* 19 (August): 455–67.
Grupo de Estudos da História do Brasil. 2006. "Machado de Assis." Historia do Brasil, November 18. http://br.groups.yahoo.com/group/HISTORIADOBRASIL/message/2201.
Guerreiro, Cendes F. 1992. "Machado de Assis's Epilepsy." *Arquivos de Neuro-psiquiatria* 50, no. 3 (September): 378–82.
Guimarães, Hélio de Seixas. 2004. *Os leitores de Machado de Assis: O romance machadiano e o público de literatura no século 19*. São Paulo: Editora da Universidade de São Paulo/Nankin.
Gutwirth, Marcel. 1993. *Laughing Matter*. Ithaca: Cornell University Press.
Gysin, Fritz. 1975. *The Grotesque in American Negro Fiction: Jean Toomer, Richard Wright, Ralph Ellison*. Bem: A. Franke A. G. Verlay.

Haberly, David T. 1972. "Abolitionism in Brazil: Anti-Slavery and Anti-Slave." *Luso-Brazilian Review* 9, no. 2 (Winter): 30–6.

———. 1983. *Three Sad Races: National Identity and National Consciousness in Brazilian Literature*. New York: Cambridge University Press.

———. 1985. "The Deceptive Realism of Machado de Assis by John Gledson." *Hispania* 68, no. 1 (March): 79–80.

Hall, Stuart. 1984. "Cultural Studies at the Center: Some Problematics and Problems." In *Culture, Media, Language*, edited by Stuart Hall, Dorothy Hobson, Andrew Lowe, and Paul Willis, 15–47. London: Hutchinson.

Hall, Stuart, and Bill Schwarz. 1998. "Breaking Bread with History: C. L. R. James and the Black Jacobins." *History Workshop Journal* 46:17–32.

Hansen, João Adolfo. 1997. "*Dom Casmurro*, the Fruit and the Rind: An Afterword." In *"Dom Casmurro": A Novel by Joaquim Maria Machado de Assis*, translated by John Gledson, 245–58. New York: Oxford University Press.

———. 1999. "*Dom Casmurro*: Simulacrum and Allegory." In *Machado de Assis: Reflections on a Brazilian Master Writer*, edited by Richard Graham, 23–50. Austin: University of Texas Press.

Hapke, Ingrid. 2010. "Tomando liberadades: O escravo 'fora do lugar.'" In *Machado de Assis e a escravidão/Machado de Assis und die Sklaverei*, Hamburg Conferences, edited by Gustavo Bernardo, Joachim Michel, and Markus Schäffauer, 101–14. São Paulo: Annablume.

Harding, Rachel Elizabeth. 2006. "É a Senzala: Slavery, Women, and Embodied Knowledge in Afro-Brazilian Candomblé." In *Women and Religion in the African Diaspora: Knowledge, Power, and Performance*, edited by R. Marie Griffith and Barbara Dianne Savage, 3–18. Baltimore: Johns Hopkins University Press.

Hardt, Michael, and Antonio Negri. 2000. *Empire*. Cambridge, Mass.: Harvard University Press.

Haring, Clarence. H. 1968. *Empire in Brazil: A New World Experiment with Monarchy*. New York: Norton.

Harpham, Geoffrey. 1982. *On the Grotesque: Strategies of Contradiction in Art and Literature*. Princeton: Princeton University Press.

Harris, Marvin. 1964. *Patterns of Race in the Americas*. New York: Norton.

Harris, Norman. 1998. "A Philosophical Basis for an Afrocentric Orientation." In *Afrocentric Visions: Studies in Culture and Communication*, edited by Janice D. Hamlet, 15–26. Thousand Oaks, Calif.: Sage.

Hart, Stephen, and Richard Young. 2003. "Introduction." In *Contemporary Latin American Cultural Studies*, edited by Stephen Hart and Richard Young, 1–11. London: Arnold; New York: Oxford University Press.

Harvey, David. 1989. *The Condition of Postmodernity: An Enquiry into the Origins of Cultural Change*. Cambridge: Basil Blackwell.

Hasenbalg, Carlos. 1979. *Discriminação e desigualdades raciais no Brasil*. Rio de Janeiro: Graal. Translation of "Race Relations in Post-Abolition Brazil: The Smooth Preservation of Racial Inequalities." Ph.D. diss., University of California, Berkeley, 1978.

———. 1985. "Race and Socioeconomic Inequalities in Brazil." In *Race, Class, and Power in Brazil*, edited by Pierre-Michel Fontaine, 25–41. Los Angeles: University of California, Los Angeles, Center for African American Studies.

Hauser, Arnold. 1951. *The Social History of Art*. 4 vols. Translated by Stanley Godman. New York: Random House.

Havel, Václav. 1994. "The Need for Transcendence in the Postmodern World." Speech made in Independence Hall, Philadelphia, July 4.

———. 1995. "The Search for Meaning in a Global Civilization." In *The Truth about the Truth: De-Confusing and Re-Constructing the Postmodern World*, edited by Walter Truett Anderson, 232–38. New York: Putnam.
Havighurst, Robert James, and João Moreira. 1965. *Society and Education in Brazil*. Pittsburgh: University of Pittsburg Press.
Heiney, Donald W. 1954. *Essentials of Contemporary Literature*. Great Neck, N.Y.: Barron's Educational Series.
Hemming, John. 1978/2004. *Red Gold: The Conquest of the Brazilian Indians*. London: Macmillan.
———. 1987. *Amazon Frontier: The Defeat of the Brazilian Indians*. London: Macmillan.
Hemmings, F. W. J. 1974. "Realism in the Age of Romanticism." In *The Age of Realism*, edited by F. W. J. Hemmings, 36–67. Harmondsworth, UK: Penguin Books.
Herron, Robert. 1968. "The Individual, Society, and Nature in the Novels of Lima Barreto." Ph.D. diss., University of Wisconsin.
Hess, David J. 1991. *Spirits and Scientists: Ideology, Spiritism, and Brazilian Culture*. University Park: Pennsylvania State University Press.
Hill, Amariles Guimarães. 1976. *A crise da diferença: Uma leitura das "Memórias póstumas de Brás Cubas."* Rio de Janeiro: Cátedra; Brasília: INL.
Hirsch, Paul M. 1972. "Processing, Fads, Fashions: An Organization-Set Analysis of Cultural Industry Systems." *American Sociological Review* 77, no. 4: 639–59.
Hobsbawm, E. J. 1962. *The Age of Revolution, 1789–1848*. New York: New American Library.
———. 1975. *The Age of Capital, 1848–1875*. New York: New American Library.
Hochschild, Jennifer L. 1995. *Facing Up to the American Dream: Race, Class, and the Soul of the Nation*. Princeton: Princeton University Press.
Hodgson, Peter. 1976. *From Gogol to Dostoevsky: Jakov Butkov, a Reluctant Naturalist in the 1840's*. Munich: Wilhelm Fink.
Hoetink, H[arramus]. 1973. *Slavery and Race Relations in the Americas: Comparative Notes on Their Nature and Nexus*. New York: Harper and Row.
Holanda, Aurélio Buarque de. 1939. "Linguagem e estilo de Machado de Assis Revista do Brasil," 3rd ser., vol. 2, no. 13 (July): 54–77.
Hollinger, David A. 2008. "Obama, the Instability of Color Lines, and the Promise of a Postethnic Future." *Callaloo* 31, no. 4 (Fall): 1033–37.
Hollinger, Robert. 1994. *Postmodernism and the Social Sciences: A Thematic Approach*. Thousand Oaks, Calif.: Sage.
Hoogvelt, Ankie M. M. 1978. *The Sociology of Developing Societies*. 2nd ed. London: Macmillan.
hooks, bell. 1995. *Yearning: Race, Gender, and Cultural Politics*. Boston: South End Press.
Horkheimer, Max, and Theodor Adorno. 1944. "The Culture Industry: Enlightenment of Mass Deception." In *Dialectic of Enlightenment*, edited by Max Horkheimer and Theodor Adorno, 534–52. New York: Seabury Press.
Howard, Judith A., and Carolyn Allen. 1990. "The Gendered Context of Reading." *Gender and Society* 4, no. 4: 534–52.
Howes, Robert. 2001. "Race and Transgressive Sexuality in Adolfo Caminha's 'Bom-Crioulo.'" *Luso-Brazilian Review* 38, no. 1 (Summer): 41–62.
Hulet, Claude L. 1974. *Brazilian Literature*. 3 vols. Washington, D.C.: Georgetown University Press.
Hutcheon, Linda. 1985. *A Theory of Parody*. New York: Metheun.
Huxley, Thomas Henry. 1992. *Agnosticism and Christianity and Other Essays*. Buffalo, N.Y.: Prometheus Books.
Ianni, Octávio. 1988. "Literatura e consciencia." *Revista do Instituto de Estudos Brasileiros: Edição comemorativa do centenário da abolição da escravidão*, no. 28: 91–99.

IBGE (Instituto Brasileiro de Geografia e Estatistica). 1870. "Mappa da população da Côrte e província do Rio de Janeiro em 1821." *Revista do Instituto Histórico e Geográfico Brasileiro* 33 (40): 135–42.
Innes, Catherine Lynette. 1978. "Through the Looking Glass: African and Irish Nationalist Writing." *African Literature Today* 9:10–24.
Iser, Wolfgang. 1974. *The Implied Reader*. Baltimore: Johns Hopkins University Press.
Isfahani-Hammond, Alexandra. 2008. *White Negritude: Race, Writing, and Brazilian Cultural Identity*. New York: Palgrave Macmillan.
Jackson, Richard L. 1976. *The Black Image in Latin American Literature*. Albuquerque, New Mexico: University of New Mexico Press.
———. 1979. *Black Writers in Latin America*. Albuquerque: University of New Mexico Press.
———. 1988. *Black Literature and Humanism in Latin America*. Athens: University of Georgia Press.
Jaguaribe, Beatriz. 2001. "Modernist Ruins: National Narratives and Architectural Forms." *Alternative Modernities*, edited by Dilip Parameshwar Gaonkar, 327–48. Durham: Duke University Press.
Jarocinski, Stefan. 1970. *Debussy, impressionnisme, et symbolisme*. Translated by Theresa Douchy. Paris: Éditions du Seul.
Jobim, José Luís. 2005. "Machado de Assis and Nationalism: The *Americanas* Case." *Portuguese Literary and Cultural Studies*, special issue, *The Author as Plagiarist: The Case of Machado de Assis*, nos. 13–14 (Fall–Spring): 571–83.
Jobim, José [Luís], and Mark Streeter. 2004. "Censorship and Morality: Machado de Assis, Émile Augier, and the National Theater Institute." *Luso-Brazilian Review* 41, no. 1 (2004): 19–36.
Jodorosky, Alexandro. 1971. *El Topo: A Book of the Film*. Edited by Ross Firestone. New York: Douglas/Links.
Johnson, J. Theodore, Jr. 1973. "Literary Impressionism in France: A Survey of Criticism." *L'Esprit Créateur* 13, no. 4 (Winter): 271–97.
Johnson, Paul Christopher. 2001. "Law, Religion, and 'Public Health' in the Republic of Brazil." *Law and Social Inquiry* 26, no. 1 (Winter): 9–33.
Johnston, Marc P., and Kevin L. Nadal. 2010. "Multiracial Microaggressions: Exposing Monoracism." In *Microaggressions and Marginality: Manifestation, Dynamics, and Impact*, edited by Derald Wing Sue, 123–44. Hoboken: Wiley.
Jones, Rhett S. 1994. "The End of Africanity? The Bi-Racial Assault on Blackness." *Western Journal of Black Studies*, 18, no. 4: 201–10.
Juederías, Julián. 1914. *Leyenda negra y la verdad histórica*. Madrid: Editora Nacional.
Jullian, Philippe. 1982. "The Esthetics of Symbolism in French and Belgian Art." Translated by Edouard Roditi. In *The Symbolist Movement the Literature of European Languages*, edited by Anna Balakian, 529–46. Budapest: Akademiai Kiado.
Kamel, Ali. 2006. *Não somos racistas: Uma reação aos que querem nos transformar numa nação bicolor*. Rio de Janeiro: Editora Nova Fronteira.
Karasch, Mary. 1975. "From Portage to Proprietorship: African Occupations in Rio de Janeiro, 1808–1850." In *Race and Slavery in the Western Hemisphere: Quantitative Studies*, edited by Stanley Engerman and Eugene Genovese, 366–94. Princeton: Princeton University Press.
———. 1987. *Slave Life in Rio de Janeiro, 1808–1850*. Princeton: Princeton University Press.
Kardec, Allan [Hippolyte Léon Denizard Rivail]. 1859/1995. *O que é o espiritismo?* Rio de Janeiro: FEB.
Kathöfer, Gabi. 2008. "The Phantasm of the German Migrant or the Invention of Brazil." *Flusser Studies* 7 (November): 1–14. http://www.flusserstudies.net/pag/07/kathofer-german-migrant.pdf.

Katz, Tamar. 2000. *Impressionist Subjects: Gender, Interiority, and Modernist Fiction in England.* Urbana: University of Illinois Press.

Keita, Maghan. 1994. "Deconstructing the Classical Age: Africa and the Unity of the Mediterranean World." *Journal of Negro History* 79, no. 2 (Spring): 146–66.

Kelley, Alice van Buren. 1973. *The Novels of Virginia Woolf: Fact and Vision.* Chicago: University of Chicago Press.

Kennedy, Ellen Conroy. 1975. *The Negritude Poets: An Anthology of Translations from the French,* edited by Ellen Conroy Kennedy. New York: Viking Press.

Kennedy, James. 1974. "Luís Gama: Pioneer of Abolition in Brazil." *Journal of Negro History* 59, no. 3 (July): 255–67.

Kerckhoff, Alan C., and Thomas C. McCormick. 1955. "Marginal Status and Marginal Personality." *Social Forces* 34, no. 1 (October): 48–55.

Kershaw, Terry. 1998. "Afrocentrism and the Afrocentric Method." In *Afrocentric Visions: Studies in Culture and Communication,* edited by Janice D. Hamlet, 27–44. Thousand Oaks, Calif.: Sage.

Kesteloot, Lilyan. 1965. *Les écrivains noirs de langue française: Naissance d'une littérature.* Brussels: Université de Bruxelles.

Kinnear, J. C. 1976. "Machado de Assis: To Believe or Not to Believe?" *Modern Language Review* 71, no. 1 (January): 54–65.

Klein, Herbert S. 1969. "The Colored Freedmen in Brazilian Slave Society." *Journal of Social History* 3, no. 1 (Autumn): 30–52.

———. 1971. "The Internal Slave Trade in Nineteenth-Century Brazil: A Study of Slave Importations into Rio de Janeiro in 1852." *Hispanic American Historical Review* 51, no. 4 (November): 567–85.

———. 1972. "Nineteenth-Century Brazil." In *Neither Slave Nor Free: The Freemen of African Descent in the Slave Societies of the New World,* edited by David Cohen and Jack P. Greene, 309–34. Baltimore: Johns Hopkins University Press.

———. 1986. *African Slavery in Latin America and the Caribbean.* New York: Oxford University Press.

———. 1995. "European and Asian Migration to Brazil." In *The Cambridge Survey of World Migration,* edited by Robin Cohen, 208–14. Cambridge: Cambridge University Press.

Klein, Herbert S., and Francisco Vidal Luna. 2000. "Free Colored in a Slave Society: São Paulo and Minas Gerais in the Early Nineteenth Century." *Hispanic American Historical Review* 80, no. 4 (November): 913–41.

Knight, Franklin W. 1974. *The African Dimension in Latin American Societies.* New York: Macmillan.

Kraniauskas, John. 2004. "Hybridity in a Transnational Frame: Latin Americanist and Postcolonial Perspectives on Cultural Studies." In *The Latin American Cultural Studies Reader,* edited by Ana del Sarto, Alicia Ríos, and Abril Trigo, 740–58. Durham: Duke University Press.

Kristal, Efraín, and José Luiz Passos. 2006. "Machado de Assis and the Question of Brazilian National Identity." In *Brazil in the Making: Facets of National Identity,* edited by Carmen Nava and Ludwig Lauerhass Jr., 17–28. Lanham, Md.: Rowman and Littlefield.

Kronegger, Maria Elizabeth. 1973. *Literary Impressionism.* New Haven: College and University Press Services.

Lajolo, Marisa, and Regina Zilberman. 2005. "Machado and the Cost of Reading." *Portuguese Literary and Cultural Studies,* special issue, *The Author as Plagiarist: The Case of Machado de Assis,* nos. 13–14 (Fall–Spring): 249–61.

Landry, Donna, and Gerald MacClean, eds. 1996. *The Spivak Reader: Selected Works of Gayatri Chakravorty Spivak.* New York: Routledge.

Lange, Brad. 2008. "Importing Freud and Lamarck to the Tropics: Arthur Ramos and the Transformation of Brazilian Racial Thought, 1926–1939." *Americas* 65, no. 1 (July) 9–34.

Leitch, Vincent B. 1992. *Cultural Criticism, Literary Theory, Poststructuralism*. New York: Columbia University Press.
Lemert, Charles. 1996. *Sociology After the Crisis*. Boulder: Westview Press.
Lemos, Celina Borges. 1995. "The Modernization of Brazilian Urban Space as a Political Symbol of the Republic." Translated by Elizabeth Jackson. *Journal of Decorative and Propaganda Arts* 21, Brazil theme issue: 218–37.
Leriche, Françoise. 2002. "Proust: An 'Art Noveau' Writer." In *Proust in Perspective: Visions and Revisionst*, translated by Jane Kuntz and edited by Armine Kotin Mortimer and Katerine Kolb, 189–212. Urbana: University of Illinois Press.
Lesser, Jeffrey H. 1991. "Are African-Americans African or American? Brazilian Immigration Policy in the 1920s." *Review of Latin American Studies* 4, no. 1: 115–37.
———. 1999. *Negotiating National Identity: Immigrants, Minorities, and the Struggle for Ethnicity in Brazil*. Durham: Duke University Press.
Lessing, Gotthold Ephraim. 1968. *Gesammelte Werke*. 2nd ed. 10 vols. Edited by Paul Rilla. Berlin: Aufbau.
Levenson, Michael. 1991. *Modernism and the Fate of the Individual: Character and Novelistic Form from Conrad to Wolf*. Cambridge: Cambridge University Press.
Levine, George. 1981. *The Realistic Imagination: English Fiction from Frankenstein to Lady Chatterley*. Chicago: University of Chicago Press.
Levine, Robert M. 1992. *Vale of Tears: Revisiting the Canudos Massacre in Northeastern Brazil, 1893–1897*. Berkeley: University of California Press.
Levinson, Paul. 1997. *The Soft Edge: A Natural History and Future of the Information Revolution*. London and New York: Routledge.
Lima, Luiz Costa. 1988. *Control of the Imaginary: Reason and Imagination in Modern Times*. Translated by Ronald W. Sousa. Minneapolis: University of Minnesota Press.
Linhares Filho, José. 1978. *A metáfora do mar no "Dom Casmurro."* Rio de Janeiro: Edições Tempo Brasileiro.
Lins, Ivan. 1967. *História do positivismo no Brasil*. 2nd ed. São Paulo: Companhia Editora Nacional.
Lins, Osman. 1976. *Lima Barreto e o espaço romanesco*. São Paulo: Editora Ática.
Lipsitz, George. 2003. "Noise in the Blood: Culture, Conflict, and Mixed Race Identities." In *Crossing Lines: Race and Mixed Race Across the Geohistorical Divide*, edited by Marc Coronado, Rudy P. Guevarra, Jeffrey Moniz, and Laura Furlan Szanto, 32–35. Santa Barbara: Multiethnic Student Outreach; Center for Chicano Studies, University of California, Santa Barbara.
Lisboa, Maria Manuel. 1996. *Machado de Assis and Feminism: Re-Reading the Heart of the Companion*. Lewiston, N.Y.: Edwin Mellen Press.
———. 1997. "Machado de Assis and the Beloved Reader: Squatters in the Text." In *Scarlett Letters: Fictions of Adultery from Antiquity to the 1990s*, 160–173, edited by Nicholas White and Naomi Segal. New York: St. Martins Press.
Lockhart, James, and Stuart B. Schwartz. 1987. *Early Latin America: A History of Colonial Spanish America and Brazil*. New York: Cambridge University Press.
Long, Elizabeth. 1985. *The American Dream and the Popular Novel*. London: Routledge and Kegan Paul.
Loos, Dorothy S. 1955. "The Influence of Émile Zola on the Five Major Naturalistic Novelists of Brazil." *Modern Language Journal* 39, no. 1 (January): 3–8.
Lopes, Elisângela Aparecida. 2007. "'Homem do seu tempo e do seu país'": Senhores, escravos, e libertos nos escritos de Machado de Assis." Ph.D. diss., Universidade Federal de Minas Gerais.
Lopes, José Leme. 1981. *A psiquiatria de Machado de Assis*. 2nd ed. Rio de Janeiro: Agir Editora.
Lowe, Elizabeth. 1982. *The City in Brazilian Literature*. East Brunswick, N.J.: Associated Press.

Lowy, Richard. 1998. "Development Theory, Globalism, and the New World Order: The Need for a Postmodern, Antiracist, and Multicultural Critique." *Journal of Black Studies* 28, no. 5 (May): 594–615.
Lucas, Fábio. 2009. *O núcleo e a periferia de Machado de Assis*. São Paulo: Amarilys.
Lukács, George. 1964. *Studies in European Realism*. New York: Grosset and Dunlop, 1964.
Luna, Francisco Vidal, and Herbert S. Klein. 2003. *Slavery and the Economy of São Paulo, 1750–1850*. Stanford: Stanford University Press.
Lund, Joshua. 2006. *The Impure Imagination: Toward a Critical Hybridity in Latin American Writing*. Minneapolis: University of Minnesota Press.
Lyotard, Jean-François. 1979. *The Postmodern Condition: A Report on Knowledge*. Translated by Geoff Bennington and Brian Massumi. Minneapolis: University of Minnesota Press.
Machado, José Bettencourt. 1953. *Machado of Brazil: The Life and Times of Machado de Assis*. New York: Bramerica.
Machado, Maria Cristina Texeira. 2002. *Lima Barreto: Um pensador social na Primeira República*. Goiânia: Editora da Universidade de São Paulo.
Machado, Ubiratan. 1983. *Os intelectuais e o espiritismo: De Castro Alves a Machado de Assis*. Rio de Janeiro: Edições Antares; Brasília: INL.
Maciel, Yv Scarlett. 2007. "Machado de Assis's *Oliveira Twist*: Translation and the Making of a Novelist." Master's thesis, University of North Carolina.
MacNicoll, Murray Graeme. 1982. "Machado de Assis in 1878." *Luso-Brazilian Review* 19, no. 1 (Summer): 31–38.
Madden, Lori. 1991. "Evolution in the Interpretations of the Canudos Movement: An Evaluation of the Social Sciences." *Luso-Brazilian Review* 28, no. 1 (Summer): 59–75.
———. 1993. "The Canudos War in History." *Luso-Brazilian Review* 30, no. 2, special issue, "The World Out of Which Canudos Came" (Winter): 5–22.
Madeira, Wagner Martins. 2001. *Machado de Assis: Homem lúdico: Uma leitura de "Esaú e Jacó."* São Paulo: Annablume, FAPESP.
Magalhães Júnior, Raimundo. 1955. *Machado de Assis desconhecido*. Rio de Janeiro: Civilização Brasileira.
———. 1956. "Prefácio." In *Diálogos e reflexões de um relojoeiro*, by Joaquim Maria Machado de Assis, 10–28. Rio de Janeiro: Civilização Brasileira.
———. 1958a. *Ao redor de Machado de Assis*. Rio de Janeiro: Civilização Brasileira.
———. 1958b. *Machado de Assis, funcionário público: No Império e na República*. Rio de Janeiro: Ministério de Viação e Obras Públicas, Serviço de Documentação.
———. 1969. *A vida turbulenta de José do Patrocínio*. Rio de Janeiro: Sabiá.
———. 1981. *Vida e obra de Machado de Assis*. 4 vols. Rio de Janeiro: Editora Civilização Brasileira.
Malinoff, Jane M. 1981. "Domingos Caldas Barbosa: Afro-Brazilian Poet at the Court of Dona Maria I." In *From Linguistics to Literature: Romance Studies Offered to Francis M. Rogers*, edited by Bernard H. Bichakajan, 195–240. Amsterdam: John Benjamins.
Mamigonian, Beatriz Gallotti. 2002. "To Be a Liberated African in Brazil: Labour and Citizenship in the Nineteenth Century." Ph.D. diss., University of Waterloo.
Mannheim, Karl. 1956. *Essays on the Sociology of Culture*. London: Routledge and Kegan Paul.
Marable, Manning. 1995. *Beyond Black and White: Transforming African American Politics*. New York: Verso.
Marcílio, Maria Luisa. 1984. "The Population of Colonial Brazil." In *The Cambridge History of Latin America*, vol. 2, *Colonial Latin America*, edited by Leslie Bethell, 37–63. New York: Cambridge University Press.
Marins, Álvaro. 2004. *Machado e Lima: Da ironia à sátira*. Série Ensaios Brasileiros, no. 1. Rio de Janeiro: Utópos.
Marotti, Giorgio. 1982. *Il negro nel romanzo brasiliano*. Rome: Bulzoni Editore.

Marques, Reinaldo Martiniano. 2011. "Domingos Caldas Barbosa." In *Literatura e afrodescendência no Brasil: Antologia crítica*, vol. I: *Precursores*, edited by Eduardo de Assis Duarte, 49–60. Belo Horizonte: Editora UFMG.

Marquese, Rafael de Bivar. 2006. "The Dynamics of Slavery in Brazil: Resistance, the Slave Trade, and Manumission in the Seventeenth to Nineteenth Centuries." *Novos Estudos, CEBRAP,* no. 2, 74, 107–23.

Martins, Heitor. 1983. "Um primitivo documento inédito da consciência negra em língua portuguesa." In *Do barroco a Guimarães Rosa*, 119–26. Belo Horizonte: Editora Itatiaia; Brasília: INL, Fundação Nacional Pró-Memória.

Martins, Hélcio. 1966. "Sobre o realismo de Machado de Assis." *Luso-Brazilian Review* 3, no. 2 (December): 83–88.

Martins, Luciana L., and Mauricio A. Abreu. 2001. "Paradoxes of Modernity: Imperial Rio de Janeiro, 1808–1821." *Geoforum* 32, no. 4: 533–50.

Massa, Jean-Michel. 1969. *La jeunesse de Machado de Assis (1839–1870): Essai de biographie intellectuelle*. 2 vols. Aix-en-Provence: Rennes.

———. 2001. "A biblioteca de Machado de Assis." In *A biblioteca de Machado de Assis*, edited by José Luís Jobim, 21–90. Rio de Janeiro: Academia Brasileira de Letras/Topbooks Editora.

Mathews, Thomas G. 1974. "The Question of Color in Puerto Rico." In *Slavery and Race Relations in Latin America*, edited by Robert Brent Toplin, 299–323. Westport, Conn.: Greenwood Press.

Mattos, Ilmar Rohlof de. 1987. *O tempo Saquarema: A formação do estado imperial*. São Paulo: Editora Hucitec.

Mattoso, Katia M. de. 1986. *To Be a Slave in Brazil, 1550–1888*. New Brunswick: Rutgers University Press.

Matz, Jesse. 2001. *Literary Impressionism and Modernist Aesthetics*. Cambridge: Cambridge University Press.

Mazama, Ama. 1998. "The Eurocentric Discourse on Writing: An Exercise in Self-Determination." *Journal of Black Studies* 29, no. 1 (September): 3–16.

McCann, Frank D. 2003. *Soldiers of the Patria: A History of the Brazilian Army, 1889–1937*. Stanford: Stanford University Press.

McElroy, Bernard. 1989. *Fiction of the Modern Grotesque*. Basingstoke, UK: Macmillan.

McPhail, Mark Lawrence. 1996. *Zen in the Art of Rhetoric: An Inquiry into Coherence*. Albany: State University of New York Press.

Meade, Teresa. 1986. "'Civilizing Rio de Janeiro': The Public Health Campaign and the Riot of 1904." *Journal of Social History* 20, no. 2 (Winter): 301–22.

———. 1996. *"Civilizing Rio": Reform and Resistance in a Brazilian City, 1889–1930*. University Park: Pennsylvania State University Press.

Meade, Teresa, and Gregory Alonso Pirio. 1988. "In Search of the Afro-American Eldorado: Attempts by North American Blacks to Enter Brazil in the 1920s." *Luso-Brazilian Review* 25, no. 1 (Summer): 85–100.

Mélone, Thomas. 1962. *De la négritude dans la littérature négro-africaine*. Paris: Présence Africaine.

Memmi, Albert. 1967. *The Colonizer and the Colonized*. Boston: Beacon Press.

Mendonça, Renato. 1973. *A influência africana no português do Brasil*. Rio de Janeiro: Civilização Brasileira.

Menezes, Lená Medeiros de. 2000. "Jovens portugueses: Histórias de trabalho, histórias de sucessos, histórias de fracassos." In *Histórias de imigrants e de imigração no Rio de Janeiro*, edited by Angela de Castro Gomes, 164–82. Rio de Janeiro: Viveiros de Castro Editora.

Merquior, José Guilherme. 1977. *De Anchieta a Euclides: Breve história da literatura brasileira*. Rio de Janeiro: Livraria José Olympio Editora.

———. 1998. "Machado em perspectiva." In *Machado de Assis: Uma revisão*, edited by Antonio Carlos Secchin et al., 33–45. Rio de Janeiro: In-Fólio.
Meyer, Augusto. 1935. *Machado de Assis*. Porto Alegre: Globo.
Mignolo, Walter. 2004. "The Movable Center: Geographical Discourses and Territoriality During the Expansion of the Spanish Empire." In *The Latin American Cultural Studies Reader*, edited by Ana del Sarto, Alicia Ríos, and Abril Trigo, 262–90. Durham: Duke University Press.
Milanovic, Branko, Peter H. Lindert, and Jeffrey G. Williamson. 2007. "Measuring Ancient Inequality." Policy Research Working Paper 4412. World Bank Development Research Group Poverty Team (November). http://www-wds.worldbank.org/external/default/WDSContentServer/WDSP/IB/2007/11/28/000158349_20071128113445/Rendered/PDF/wps4412.pdf.
Miller, Jonathan. 1988. "Jokes and Joking: A Serious Laughing Matter." In *Laughing Matters: A Serious Look at Humour*, edited by John Durant and Jonathan Miller, 5–16. New York: Longman Scientific and Technical.
Miller, Robin. 1992. "The Human Ecology of Multiracial Identity." In *Racially Mixed People in America*, edited by Maria P. P. Root, 24–36. Thousand Oaks, Calif.: Sage.
Mills, Charles W. 1997. *The Racial Contract*. Ithaca: Cornell University Press.
Mills, David. 2006. *Atheist Universe: The Thinking Person's Answer to Christian Fundamentalism*. Berkeley: Ulysses Press.
Miskolci, Richard. 2006. "Machado de Assis, O outsider estabelecido." *Sociologias* 8, no. 15 (January–June): 352–77.
Modleski, Tania. 1982. *Loving with a Vengeance: Mass Produced Fantasies for Women*. Hamden, Conn.: Archon Books.
Moehn, Frederick. 2008. "Music, Mixing, and Modernity in Rio de Janeiro." *Ethnomusicology Forum* 17, no. 2 (November): 165–202.
Moisés, Massaud. 1959. "Machado de Assis e o realismo." *Anhembi* 35, no. 105 (August): 469–79.
———. 2001. *Machado de Assis: Ficção e utopia*. São Paulo: Editora Cultrix.
Monasterio, Leonardo Monteiro. 2010. "Brazilian Spatial Dynamics in the Long Term (1872–2000): 'Path Dependency' or 'Reversal of Fortune'?" *Journal of Geographical Systems* 12, no. 1 (August): 51–67.
Moniz, Edmundo. 1984. *O espírito das épocas: Dialéctica da ficção*. 4th ed. Rio de Janeiro: Elo Editora e Distribuidora.
———. 1987. *Canudos: A guerra social*. 2nd ed. Rio de Janeiro: Elo Editora.
Monteiro, Ivan C., and Hairton M. Estrella. 1973. *Metalinguagem em "Quincas Borba" de Machado de Assis*. Rio de Janeiro: Livraria Acadêmica.
Monteiro, Pedro Meira. 2008. "Preface: The Dialectic of Resistance: Alfredo Bosi, Literary Critic." In *Colony, Cult, and Culture*, by Alfredo Bosi, edited by Pedro Meira Monteiro, and translated by Robert P. Newcomb, 7–17. Dartmouth: University of Massachusetts Dartmouth.
Moraes, Renata Figueiredo. 2009. "'Pai contra mãe': A permanência da escravidão nos contos de Machado de Assis." In *4º Encontro Escravidão e Liberdade no Brasil Meridional: de 13 a 15 de maio de 2009, Curitiba, Universidade Federal do Paraná: caderno de resumos*, edited by Carlos Alberto Medeiros Lima. http://www.labhstc.ufsc.br/ivencontro/pdfs/comunicacoes/RenataMoraes.pdf.
Moreci, Michael. 2009. "False Truths: How Fact Is Fiction in Machado de Assis." *Quarterly Conversation*, December 7, http://quarterlyconversation.com/false-truths-how-fact-is-fiction-in-machado-de-assis.
Moreira-Almeida, Alexander, and Francisco Lotufo Neto. 2005. "Spiritist Views of Mental Disorders in Brazil." *Transcultural Psychiatry* 42, no. 4 (December): 570–95.

Morse, Richard M. 1974. *From Community to Metropolis: A Biography of São Paulo, Brazil*. New York: Farrar, Straus, and Giroux.
Mortimer, Armine Kotin, and Katherine Kolb. 2002. "Introduction: Proust 2000—Sketches for a Profile." In *Proust in Perspective: Visions and Revisions*, edited by Armine Kotin Mortimer and Katerine Kolb, 1–18. Urbana: University of Illinois Press.
Moser, Gerald. 1973. "Machado de Assis: Die Entwicklung seines erzählerischen Werkes." *Luso-Brazilian Review* 10, no. 2 (Winter): 267–69.
Moser, Ruth. 1952. *L'impressionisme français*. Geneva: Librairie Droz.
Mosse, George I. 1974. *The Culture of Western Europe: The Nineteenth and Twentieth Centuries*. Chicago: Rand McNally College.
Mota, Artur. 1984. "Machado de Assis." *Revista da Academia Brasileira de Letras* 147 (March): 320–52.
Motta, Felipe Ronner Pinheiro Imalu. 2008. "Literatura, fatalidade, e história: O journalismo engajado de José do Patrocínio, 1877–1905." Ph.D. diss., Pontifícia Universidade Católica de São Paulo. http://www.sapientia.pucsp.br//tde_busca/arquivo.php?codArquivo=6308.
Moura, Clovis. 1983. *Brasil: As raízes do protesto negro*. São Paulo: Global Editora.
Murat, Luís. 1926. "Machado de Assis e Joaquim Nabuco." *Revista da Academia Brasileira de Letras* 21, no. 54 (June): 146–48.
Muricy, Katia. 1988. *A razão cética: Machado de Assis e as questões de seu tempo*. São Paulo: Companhia de Letras.
Myers, Linda James. 1988. *Understanding an Afrocentric World View: Introduction to an Optimal Psychology*. Dubuque: Kendall/Hunt.
———. 1998. "The Deep Structure of Culture: Relevance of Traditional African Culture in Contemporary Life." In *Afrocentric Visions: Studies in Culture and Communication*, edited by Janice D. Hamlet, 1–14. Thousand Oaks, Calif.: Sage.
Nabuco, Joaquim. 1938. *O abolicionismo*. Rio de Janeiro: Civilização Brasileira.
———. 1983. *Discursos parlamentares*. Brasília: Câmara dos Deputados.
Nagel, James. 1980. *Stephen Crane and Literary Impressionism*. University Park: Pennsylvania State University Press.
Nantambu, Kwame 1998. "Pan-Africanism versus Pan-African Nationalism: An Afrocentric Analysis." *Journal of Black Studies* 28, no. 5 (May): 561–74.
Naro, Nancy Priscilla Smith. 1996. "Fact, Fantasy, or Folklore? A Novel Case of Retribution in Nineteenth-Century Brazil." *Luso-Brazilian Review* 33, no. 1 (Summer): 59–80.
Nascimento, Abdias do. 1979. *Mixture or Massacre? Essays on the Genocide of a Black People*. Translated by Elisa Larkin Nascimento. Buffalo: Puerto Rican Studies and Research Center, State University of New York at Buffalo.
Nascimento, Gizêlda Melo do. 2002. "Machado: Três momentos negros." *Terra Roxa e Outras Terras: Revista de Estudos Literários* 2:53–62.
National Educational Television. 1965. "Brazil: The Vanishing Negro." History of the Negro People Series Studies. Released by Indiana University Audio-Visual Center.
Natoli, Joseph, and Linda Hutcheon. 1993. "Introduction." In *A Postmodern Reader*, edited by Joseph Natoli and Linda Hutcheon, ix–xiv. New York: State University of New York Press.
Nazzari, Muriel. 1996. "Concubinage in Colonial Brazil: The Inequalities of Race, Class, and Gender." *Journal of the Family* 21, no. 2 (April): 107–24.
Needell, Jeffrey D. 1983. "Rio de Janeiro at the Turn of the Century: Modernization and the Parisian Ideal." *Journal of Interamerican Studies and World Affairs* 25, no. 1 (February): 83–103.
———. 1987a. "The Revolta Contra Vacina of 1904: The Revolt Against 'Modernization' in Belle Époque Rio de Janeiro." *Hispanic American Historical Review* 67, no. 2 (May): 233–69.

———. 1987b. *A Tropical Belle Époque: Elite Culture and Society in Turn-of-the-Century Rio de Janeiro*. New York: Cambridge University Press.

———. 1999. "The Domestic Civilizing Mission: The Cultural Role of the State in Brazil, 1808–1930." *Luso-Brazilian Review* 36, no. 1: 1–18.

———. 2001. "Provincial Origins of the Brazilian State: Rio de Janeiro, the Monarchy, and National Political Organization, 1808–1853." *Latin American Research Review* 36, no. 3: 132–53.

———. 2006. *The Party of Order: The Conservatives, the State, and Slavery in the Brazilian Monarchy, 1831–1871*. Stanford: Stanford University Press.

Neto, Antônio Luís Machado. 1973. *Estrutura social da República das letras: Sociologia da vida intelectual brasileira, 1870–1930*. São Paulo: Editora da Universidade de São Paulo.

Neto, Couto de Magalhães de. 1976. "Machado de Assis e o negro." *Dom Casmurro* (Outras Mascaras) 15, no. 6 (40): 5.

Neto, José Raimundo Maia. 1994. *Machado de Assis, The Brazilian Pyrrhonian*. West Lafayette: Purdue University Press.

Nettels, Elsa. 1977. *James and Conrad*. Athens: University of Georgia Press.

Nicol, Bran. 2009. *The Cambridge Introduction to Postmodern Fiction*. Cambridge: Cambridge University Press.

Nishida, Meiko. 2003. *Slavery and Identity: Ethnicity, Gender, and Race in Salvador, Brazil, 1808–1888*. Bloomington: Indiana University Press.

Niskier, Arnaldo. 2001. *O olhar pedagógico em Machado de Assis*. Rio de Janeiro: Expressão e Cultura.

Nobles, Melissa. 2000. *Shades of Citizenship: Race and the Census in Modern Politics*. Stanford: Stanford University Press.

Nogueira, Nícea Helena de Almeida. 2004. *Lawrence Sterne e Machado de Assis: Tradição da sátira menipéia*. Rio de Janeiro: Editora Galo Branco.

Nogueira, Oracy. 1954/1985. "Preconceito racial de marca e preconceito racial de origem: Sugestão de um quadro de referência para a interpretação do material sobre relações raciais no Brasil." In *Tanto preto quanto branco: Estudo de relações raciais*, edited by Oracy Nogueira, 78–79. São Paulo: T. A. Queiroz.

Norst, M. J. 1966. "Biedermeier." In *Periods in German Literature*, edited by J. M. Ritche, 154–66. London: Oswald Wolff.

Novotny, Peter. 1965. "A Poetic Corroboration of Psychoanalysis." *American Image* 22, no. 1: 40–46.

Nunes, Maria Luisa. 1979. *Lima Barreto: Bibliography and Translations*. Boston: G. K. Hall.

———. 1983. *The Craft of an Absolute Winner: Characterization and Narratology in the Novels of Machado de Assis*. Westport, Conn.: Greenwood Press.

Nunes, Rosana Barbosa. 2000. "Portuguese Migration to Rio de Janeiro, 1822–1850." *Americas* 57, no. 1 (July): 37–61.

Oakley, Robert J. 1986. "The Deceptive Realism of Machado de Assis: A Dissenting Interpretation of 'Dom Casmurro.'" *Modern Language Review* 81, no. 4 (October): 1028–29.

O'Hare, Greg, and Michael Barke. 2002. "The Favelas of Rio de Janeiro: A Temporal and Spatial Analysis." *GeoJournal* 56, no. 3 (March): 225–40.

Olamblogue. 2008. "Abel Barros Baptista sobre Machado de Assis." Interview, November 18, 2008. http://olamtagv.wordpress.com/2008/11/18/abel-barros-baptista-sobre-machado-de-assis.

Oliveira, Emanuelle K. F. 2007. *Writing Identity: The Politics of Afro-Brazilian Literature*. West Lafayette, Ind.: Purdue University Press.

Oliveira, Franklin de. 1958. "O artista em sua narração: A fortuna crítica de Machado de Assis, 1912–1958." *Revista do Livro* 3, no. 11 (September): 61–9.

Oliveira, João Pacheco de. 2000. "Entering and Leaving the 'Melting Pot': A History of Brazilian Indians in the National Censuses." *Journal of Latin American Anthropology* 4, no. 2 (March): 190–211.

Oliveira, Ney dos Santos. 1996. "Favelas and Ghettos: Race and Class in Rio de Janeiro and New York City." *Latin American Perspectives* 23, no. 4 (Fall): 71–89.

Olson, Steve. 2002. *Mapping Human History: Discovering the Past Through Our Genes*. New York: Houghton Mifflin Company.

———. 2006. "We Are All Jesus' Children: Go Back a Few Millenniums, and We've All Got the Same Ancestors," *Slate*, March 15. http://www.slate.com/id/2138060.

Omi, Michael, and Howard Winant. 1994. *Racial Formation in the United States: From the 1960s to the 1990s*. New York: Routledge.

Orico, Osvaldo. 1953. *O tigre da abolição: José do Patrocínio*. Rio de Janeiro: Gráfica Olímpica Editora.

Ortiz, Fernando. 1947. *Cuban Counterpoint*. Translated by Harriet de Onís. New York: Knopf.

Palmer, Christopher. 1973. *Impressionism in Music*. London: Hutchinson University Library.

Paolini, Albert J. 1999. *Navigating Modernity: Postcolonialism, Identity, and International Relations*, edited by Anthony Elliot and Anthony Moran, 49–62. Boulder: Lynne Rienner.

Param, Charles. 1973. "The Negro and Slavery in the Novels of Machado de Assis." In *Proceedings: Pacific Northwest Conference on Foreign Languages, 24th Annual Meeting*, 24:240–46. May 4–5, 1973, Western Washington State College. Corvallis: Oregon State University.

Park, Robert. 1928. "Human Migration and the Marginal Man." *American Journal of Sociology* 33 (May): 881–93.

Passos, Gilberto Pinheiro. 1997. "Afterword: Cosmopolitan Strategies in the Posthumous Memoirs of Brás Cubas." In *Posthumous Memoirs of Brás Cubas: A Novel by Joaquim Maria Machado de Assis*, translated by Gregory Rabassa, 205–19. New York: Oxford University Press.

Passos, José Luiz. 2007. *Machado de Assis: O romance com pessoas*. São Paulo: EDUSP, Nankin Editora.

———. 2009. "O mal e a metamorfose em Machado de Assis." *Luso-Brazilian Review* 46, no. 1: 57–74.

Pastore, Ferruccio. 2001. "Nationality Law and International Migration: The Italian Case." In *Towards a European Nationality: Citizenship, Immigration, and Nationality Law in the EU*, edited by Randall Hansen and Patrick Weil, 95–117. Basingstoke, UK: Palgrave.

Patrocínio, José do. 1877/2003. *Motta Coqueiro ou pena de morte*. Virtual Books Online, Pará de Minas: M e M Editores.

Paulk, Julia C. 2005. "(Re)Writing Patriarchy and Motherhood in José de Alencar's Allegorical Antislavery Plays, O Demônio Familiar and Mãe." *Luso-Brazilian Review* 42, no. 1: 61–77.

Pearce, J. M. S. 2002. "Bromide, the First Effective Antiepileptic Agent." *Journal of Neurology, Neurosurgery, and Psychiatry* 72:412.

Peard, Julyan G. 2000. *Race, Place, and Medicine: The Idea of the Tropics in Nineteenth-Century Brazil*. Durham: Duke University Press.

Pereira, Astrojildo. 1944. *Interpretações*. Rio de Janeiro: Casa do Estudante do Brasil.

———. 1959. *Machado de Assis*. Rio de Janeiro: Livraria José Olympio Editora.

Pereira, Edimilson de Almeida. 1995. "Survey of African-Brazilian Literature." *Callaloo* 18, no. 4, *African Brazilian Literature: A Special Issue* (Autumn): 875–80.

Pereira, Leonardo Affonso de Miranda. 1994. *O carnaval das letras*. Rio de Janeiro: Secretaria Municipal de Cultura, Departamento Geral de Documentação e Informação Cultural, Divisão de Editoração.

Pereira, Lúcia Miguel. 1936. *Machado de Assis*. São Paulo: Companhia Editora Nacional.

———. 1957. *História da literatura brasileira: Prosa de ficção, 1870–1920*. 2nd ed. Rio de Janeiro: Livraria José Olympio Editora.

———. 1994. "Colcha de retalhos." In *Escritos da maturidade*, 15–22. Rio de Janeiro: Graphia.
Pereira, Ruben Alves. 1999. *Fraturas do texto: Machado e seus leitores*. Rio de Janeiro: Sette Letras.
Peres, Phyllis. 1998. "Domingos Caldas Barbosa e o conceito de 'crioulização do Caribe.'" *Revista Iberoamericana* 64, nos. 182–83: 209–18.
Pérez, Renard. 1962. "Esboço biográfico: Machado de Assis e a sua circunstância." In Joaquim Maria Machado de Assis, *Obra Completa*, 1:65–90. Rio de Janeiro: Editora José Aguilar.
Perkins, Eugene. 1970. "The Changing Status of Black Writers." *Black World*, June, 18–23, 95–98.
Peters, John G. 2001. *Conrad and Impressionism*. New York: Cambridge University Press.
Peterson, Richard A. 1976. *The Production of Culture*. Beverly Hills: Sage.
Philippou, Styliane. 2005. "Modernism and National Identity in Brazil, or How to Brew a Brazilian Stew." *National Identities* 7, no. 3 (September): 245–64.
Pierson, Donald. 1942/1967. *Negroes in Brazil: A Study of Race Contact at Bahia*. Carbondale: Southern Illinois University Press.
Pieterse, Jan Nederveen. 1994. "Unpacking the West: How European Is Europe?" In *Racism, Modernity, and Identity: On the Western Front*, edited by Ali Rattansi and Sallie Westwood, 130–46. Cambridge: Polity Press.
Pietrani, Anélia Montechiari. 2000. *O enigma mulher no universo masculino machadiano*. Niterói: Editora da Universidade Federal Fluminense.
Piza, Daniel. 2005a. *Machado de Assis: Um gênio brasileiro*. São Paulo: Imprensa Oficial São Paulo.
———. 2005b. "The Place of Machado de Assis in the Present." *Portuguese Literary and Cultural Studies*, special issue, *The Author as Plagiarist: The Case of Machado de Assis*, nos. 13–14 (Fall–Spring): 281–84.
Piza, Edith, and Fúlvia Rosemberg. 1999. "Color in the Brazilian Census." In *Race in Contemporary Brazil: From Indifference to Equality*, edited by Rebecca Reichmann, 37–52. University Park: Pennsylvania State University Press.
Polar, Antonio Cornejo. 2004a. "Mestizaje and Hybridity." In *The Latin American Cultural Studies Reader*, edited by Ana del Sarto, Alicia Ríos, and Abril Trigo, 760–64. Durham: Duke University Press.
———. 2004b. "Mestizaje, Transculturation, Heterogeneity." In *The Latin American Cultural Studies Reader*, edited by Ana del Sarto, Alicia Ríos, and Abril Trigo, 116–19. Durham: Duke University Press.
Pontes, Eloy. 1939. *A vida contradictoria de Machado de Assis*. Rio de Janeiro: Livraria José Olympio Editora.
Poppino, Rollie E. 1961. *Brazil: The Land and the People*. Oxford: Oxford University Press.
Porter, Dorothy B. 1951. "Padre Domingos Caldas Barbosa: Afro-Brazilian Poet." *Phylon* 12, no. 3: 264–71.
———. 1952. "The Negro in the Brazilian Abolition Movement." *Journal of Negro History* 3, no. 1 (January): 54–80.
Poston, W. S. Carlos. 1990. "The Biracial Identity Model: A Needed Addition." *Journal of Counseling and Development* 69 (November/December): 152–55.
Powell, John A. 1997. "The Multiple Self: Exploring Between and Beyond Modernity and Postmodernity." *Minnesota Law Review* 81 (June): 1481–1520.
Powell, Walter. 1985. *Getting into Print: The Decision-Making Process in Scholarly Publishing*. Chicago: University of Chicago Press.
Prado, Antonio Arnoni. 1976. *Lima Barreto: O crítico e a crise*. Rio de Janeiro: Editora Cátedra; Brasília: INL.
Prado Júnior, Caio. 1969. *The Colonial Background of Modern Brazil*. Translated by Suzette Macedo. Berkeley: University of California Press.
Preto-Rodas, Richard A. 1970. *Negritude as a Theme in the Poetry of the Portuguese-Speaking World*. Gainesville: University of Florida Press.

Price, Darby Li Po. 2000. "Mixed Laughter." In *We Are a People: Narrative and Multiplicity in Constructing Ethnic Identity*, edited by Paul Spickard and W. Jeffrey Burroughs, 179–91. Philadelphia: Temple University Press.

Proença Filho, Domício. 2001. "Capitu: A moça dos olhos de água." In *Personae: Grandes personagens da literatura brasileira*, edited by Lourenço Dantas and Benjamin Abdala Júnior, 69–99. São Paulo: Editora SENAC São Paulo.

———. 2004. "A trajectória do negro na literatura brasileira." *Estudos Avançados* 18 (50): 161–93.

Pujol, Alfredo. 1934. *Machado de Assis*. 2nd ed. Rio de Janeiro: Livraria José Olympio Editora.

Queirós [Queiroz], José Maria de Eça de. 1878. *O primo Basílio: Episódio doméstico*. Porto: Livraria Chardron.

Rabassa, Gregory. 1965. *O negro na ficção brasileira: Meio século de história literária*. Translated by Ana Maria Martins. Rio de Janeiro: Edições Tempo Brasileiro.

———. 1967. "Negro Themes and Characteristics in Brazilian Literature." *African Forum* 2 (Spring): 20–34.

Rachum, Ilan. 1977. "Feminism, Woman Suffrage, and National Politics in Brazil: 1922–1937." *Luso-Brazilian Review* 14, no. 1 (Summer): 118–34.

Radway, Janice. 1984. *Reading the Romance: Women, Patriarchy, and Popular Culture*. Chapel Hill: University of North Carolina Press.

Raimon, Eve Allegra. 2004. *The "Tragic Mulatta" Revisited: Race and Nationalism in Nineteenth-Century Antislavery Fiction*. New Brunswick: Rutgers University Press.

Ramirez, Manuel, III. 1983. *Psychology of the Americas: Mestizo Perpsectives on Personality and Mental Health*. New York: Pergamon Press.

Rattansi, Ali. 1994. "'Western' Racisms, Ethnicities, and Identities in a 'Postmodern' Frame." In *Racism, Modernity, and Identity: On the Western Front*, edited by Ali Rattansi and Sallie Westwood, 15–86. Cambridge: Polity Press.

Rego, Enylton de Sá. 1997. "Preface." In *Posthumous Memoirs of Brás Cubas: A Novel by Joaquim Maria Machado de Assis*, translated by John Gledson, xi–xix. New York: Oxford University Press.

Rego, José Lins do. 1946. *Conferências no prata: Tendências do romance brasileiro*. Rio de Janeiro: Casa do Estudante do Brasil.

Reis, Roberto. 1987. "Brazil." In *Handbook of Latin American Literature*, edited by David William Forster, 71–99. New York: Garland.

———. 1992. *The Pearl Necklace: Toward an Archaeology of Brazilian Transition Discourse*. Translated by Aparecida De Godoy Johnson. Gainesville: University Press of Florida.

Renfrow, Daniel G. 2004. "A Cartography of Passing in Everyday Life." *Symbolic Interaction* 27, no. 4 (Fall): 485–506.

Renn, Kristen. 2004. *Mixed Race Students in College*. Albany: State University of New York Press.

Rennó, Adriana Campos. 1999. *Violando as regras: Uma (re)leitura de Domingos Barbosa*. São Paulo: Arte e Ciência.

———. 2001. "Domingos Caldas Barbosa: Textos recolhidos." Ph.D. diss., vol. 2, "Assis," Universidade Estadual Paulista, São Paulo.

Revista de Historia. 2008. "É duro viver de letras: Contratos com editora e salários no serviço público mostram a evolução da renda do maior escritor brasileiro." February 9, 2008. *Revista de Historia.com.br*. http://www.revistadehistoria.com.br/secao/capa/e-duro-viver-de-letras.

Ricardo, Cassiano. 1959. *Marcha para oeste: A influência da "Bandeira" na formação social e política do Brasil*. 2 vols. Rio de Janeiro: Livraria José Olympio Editora.

Ricupero, Bernardo. 2004. *O romantismo e a idéia da nação no Brasil, 1830–1870*. São Paulo: Martins Fontes.

Riedel, Dirce Côrtes. 1959. *O tempo no romance machadiano*. Rio de Janeiro: Livraria São José.

———. 1974. *Metáfora: O espelho de Machado de Assis*. Rio de Janeiro: Livraria F. Alves Editora.

Rimmon, Shlomith. 1977. *The Concept of Ambiguity: The Example of James.* Chicago: University of Chicago Press.
Risério, António. 2007. *A utopia brasileira e os movimentos negros.* São Paulo: Editora 34 Ltda.
Ritche, James MacPherson. 1974. "Realism in Germany from the Death of Goethe." In *The Age of Realism*, edited by F. W. J. Hemmings, 218–64. Harmondsworth, UK: Penguin Books.
Rocha, João Cezar de Castro. 2006. "Introduction: The Location of the Author." *Portuguese Literary and Cultural Studies*, special issue, *The Author as Plagiarist: The Case of Machado de Assis*, nos. 13–14 (Fall–Spring): xix–xxxix.
Rockquemore, Kerry Ann, and David L. Brunsma. 2002. *Beyond Black: Biracial Identity in America.* Thousand Oaks, Calif.: Sage.
Rodgers, M. F. 1991. *Novels, Novelists, and Readers: Toward a Phenomenological Sociology of Literature.* Albany: State University of New York Press.
Roditi, Edouard. 1982. "The Spread and Evolution of Symbolist Ideals and Art." In *The Symbolist Movement in the Literature of European Languages*, edited by Anna Balakian, 499–518. Budapest: Akademiai Kiado.
Rodrigues, Raimundo Nina. 1894/1938. *As raças humanas e a responsabilidade penal no Brasil.* São Paulo. Companhia Editora Nacional.
Romero, Sílvio. 1897. *Machado de Assis: Estudo comparativo de literatura brasileira.* Rio de Janeiro: Laemmert.
Rosaldo, Renato. 1995. "Forward." In *Hybrid Cultures: Strategies for Entering and Leaving Modernity*, translated by Christopher L. Chiappari and Silvia L. López, xi–xvii. Minneapolis: University of Minnesota Press.
Rosenau, Pauline Marie. 1992. *Postmodernism and the Social Sciences: Insights, Inroads, and Intrusions.* Princeton: Princeton University Press.
Rouanet, Sergio Paulo. 2005. "The Shandean Form: Laurence Sterne and Machado de Assis." *Portuguese Literary and Cultural Studies*, special issue, *The Author as Plagiarist: The Case of Machado de Assis*, nos. 13–14 (Fall–Spring): 81–103.
Russell-Wood, Anthony John R. 1968. *Fidalgos and Philanthropists: The Santa Casa da Misericórdia of Bahia, 1550–1755.* Berkeley: University of California Press.
———. 1972. "Colonial Brazil." In *Neither Slave Nor Free: The Freemen of African Descent in the Slave Societies of the New World*, edited by David W. Cohen and Jack P. Greene, 84–133. Baltimore: Johns Hopkins University Press.
———. 1982. *The Black Man in Slavery and Freedom in Colonial Brazil.* Palgrave Macmillan.
Sabino, Fernando Tavares. 1999. *Amor de Capitu: O romance de Machado de Assis sem o narrador Dom Casmurro; Recriação literária.* São Paulo: Editora Ática.
Salgueiro, Maria Aparecida Ferreira de Andrade. 2005. "Machado de Assis: A Keen Look at Nineteenth-Century Brazilian Identity." *Portuguese Literary and Cultural Studies*, special issue, *The Author as Plagiarist: The Case of Machado de Assis*, nos. 13–14 (Fall–Spring): 281–91.
Salvatore, Ricardo D. 1996. "Penitentiaries, Visions of Class, and Export Economies: Brazil and Argentina Compared." In *The Birth of the Penitentiary in Latin America: Essays on Criminology, Prison Reform, and Social Control, 1830–1940*, edited by Ricardo D. Salvatore and Carlos Aguirre, 194–223. Austin: University of Texas Press.
Sandoval, Chela. 2000. *Methodology of the Oppressed.* Minneapolis: University of Minnesota Press.
Sant'anna, Affonso Romano de. 1975. *Análise estrutural de romances brasileiros.* 3rd ed. Petrópolis: Editora Vozes, Ltda.
Santiago, Silviano. 1978. "O entre-lugar no discurso latino-americano." In *Uma literatura nos trópicos: Ensaios sobre dependência cultural*, 9–26. São Paulo: Perspectiva.

———. 1982. *Vale quanto pesa: Ensaios sobre questões político-culturais*. Rio de Janeiro: Paz e Terra.
———. 2000. "Retórica da Verossimilhança." In *Uma literatura nos trópicos: Ensaios sobre depedência cultural*, 27–46. São Paulo: Perspectiva.
———. 2001. *The Space In-Between: Essays on Latin American Culture*. Edited by Ana Lúcia Gazzola. Durham: Duke University Press.
Santos, Hermetério dos. 1908. "Machado de Assis." *Gazeta de Notícias*, November 29.
Santos, João Camilo dos. 2005. "Machado de Assis, Critic of Eça de Queirós—A Symptomatic Misunderstanding." *Portuguese Literary and Cultural Studies*, special issue, *The Author as Plagiarist: The Case of Machado de Assis*, nos. 13–14 (Fall–Spring): 105–28.
Santos, Jussara. 2011. "José do Patrocínio." In *Literatura e afrodescendência no Brasil: Antologia crítica*, vol. I: *Precursores*, edited by Eduardo de Assis Duarte, 205–22. Belo Horizonte: Editora UFMG.
Santos, Lilliane, and Carlos Dias. 2006. "Carta da redação: História sem retoques." *Raça Brasil* 95 (February). http://racabrasil.uol.com.br/Edicoes/95/artigo14890-1.asp.
Santos, Sales Augusto dos. 2002. "Historical Roots of the 'Whitening' of Brazil." *Latin American Perspectives* 29, no. 1 (January): 61–82.
Sarto, Ana Del. 2004. "The 1980s: Foundations of Latin American Cultural Studies." In *The Latin American Cultural Studies Reader*, edited by Ana del Sarto, Alicia Ríos, and Abril Trigo, 153–81. Durham: Duke University Press.
Sartre, Jean-Paul. 1948/1963. *Black Orpheus*. Translated by S. W. Allen. Paris, Présence Africaine.
Saunders, A. C. de C. M. 1982. *A Social History of Black Slaves and Freedmen in Portugal, 1441–1555*. Cambridge: Cambridge University Press.
Sayers, Raymond S. 1958. *O negro na literatura brasileira*. Translated by Antônio Houaiss. Rio de Janeiro: O Cruzeiro.
———. 1993. *A sociedade brasileira na ficção de Machado de Assis: Papéis avulsos*. Translated by Oswaldino Marques. Brasília: Thesaurus/Presença.
Schiele, Jerome H. 1991. "Afrocentricity for All." *Black Issues in Higher Education*, September 26–27.
———. 1998. "Rethinking Organizations from an Afrocentric Viewpoint." In *Afrocentric Visions: Studies in Culture and Communication*, edited by Janice D. Hamlet, 73–88. Thousand Oaks, Calif.: Sage.
Schneider, Joseph W., and Peter Conrad. 1980. "In the Closet with Illness: Epilepsy, Stigma Potential, and Information Control." *Social Problems* 28, no. 1 (October): 32–44.
Schneider, Marcel. 1982. "Symbolist Music." In *The Symbolist Movement in the Literature of European Languages*, translated by Edouard Roditi and edited by Anna Balakian, 471–78. Budapest: Akademiai Kiado.
Scholes, Robert, and Robert Kellogg. 1966. *The Nature of Narrative*. London: Oxford University Press.
Schüler, Donaldo. 1978. *Plenitude perdida: Uma análise das seqüências narrativas no romance "Dom Casmurro" de Machado de Assis*. Porto Alegre: Editora Movimento.
Schultz, Kirsten. 2001. *Tropical Versailles: Empire, Monarchy, and the Portuguese Royal Court in Rio de Janeiro, 1808–1821*. New York: Routledge.
Schulz, John. 2008. *The Financial Crisis of Abolition*. New Haven: Yale University Press.
Schwarcz, Lília Moritz. 1998/2004. *The Emperor's Beard: Dom Pedro II and the Tropical Monarchy of Brazil*. Translated by John Gledson. New York: Hill and Wang.
———. 1999. *The Spectacle of the Races: Scientists, Institutions, and the Race Question in Brazil, 1870–1930*. Translated by Leland Guyer. New York: Hill and Wang.
Schwarcz, Lília Moritz, and André Botelho. 2008. "Ao vencedor as batatas 30 anos: Crítica da cultura e processo social." Interview with Roberto Schwarz. *Revista Brasileira de Ciências Sociais* 23, no. 67: 147–94.

Schwartz, Lynne Sharon. 2000. "Playing with Realism." *New Leader* 83, no. 5 (November): 38–40.
Schwartz, Stuart. 1987a. "Formation of Colonial Identity in Brazil." In *Colonial Identity in the Atlantic World, 1500–1800*, edited by Nicholas Canny and Anthony Pagden, 15–50. Princeton: Princeton University Press.
———. 1987b. "Plantations and Peripheries, c. 1580–c. 1750." In *Colonial Brazil*, edited by Leslie Bethell, 67–144. New York: Cambridge University Press.
Schwartzman, Simon. 2003. "Atualidade de Raymundo Faoro." *DADOS: Revista de Ciências Sociais* 46, no. 2: 207–13.
Schwarz, Roberto. 1977. *Ao vencedor as batatas: Forma literária e processo social nos inícios do romance brasileiro* [*To the Winner Go the Potatoes: Literary Form and Social Process in the Beginning of the Brazilian Novel*]. São Paulo: Duas Cidades.
———. 1987. *Que horas são?, Ensaios*. São Paulo: Schwarcz.
———. 1990. *Um mestre na periferia do capitalismo: Machado de Assis*. São Paulo: Duas Cidades.
———. 1992. *Misplaced Ideas: Essays on Brazilian Culture*. Translated by John Gledson. New York: Verso.
———. 1996. "The Historical Meaning of Cruelty in Machado de Assis." *Modern Language Quarterly* 57, no. 2 (June): 165–79.
———. 1997. *Duas meninas*. São Paulo: Companhia de Letras.
———. 1998. "A novidade das *Memórias póstumas de Brás Cubas*." In *Machado de Assis: Uma revisão*, edited by Antonio Carlos Secchin et al., 47–64. Rio de Janeiro: In-Fólio.
———. 1999. *Seqüências brasileiras*. São Paulo: Companhia das Letras.
———. 2004. "A viravolta machadiana." *Novos Estudos CEBRAP*, no. 69 (July): 15–34.
———. 2006. "*Posthumous Memoirs of Brás Cubas*." In *The Novel*, vol. 1: *History, Geography, and Culture*, edited by Franco Moretti, 816–40. Princeton: Princeton University Press.
Scott, Clive. 1976. "Symbolism, Decadence, and Impressionism." In *Modernism*, edited by Malcolm Bradbury and James McFarlane, 192–205. Penguin Books.
Scott, James. 1990. *Domination and the Arts of Resistance: Hidden Transcripts*. New Haven: Yale University Press.
Searle, John R. 1995. "Postmodernism and the Western Rationalist Tradition." In *Campus Wars: Multiculturalism and the Politics of Difference*, edited by John Arthur and Amy Shapiro, 28–48. Oxford: Westview Press.
Secchin, Antonio Carlos, José Maurício Gomes de Almeida, and Ronaldes de Melo e Souza. 1998. *Machado de Assis: Uma revisão*. Rio de Janeiro: In-Fólio.
Seidman, Steven. 1994. "Introduction." In *The Postmodern Turn: New Perspectives on Social Theory*, edited by Steven Seidman, 1–21. New York: Cambridge University Press.
Seigel, Micol. 2009. *Uneven Encounters: Making Race and Nation in Brazil and the United States*. Durham: Duke University Press.
Senna, Jorge de. 1986. "Machado de Assis and His Carioca Quartet." *Latin American Literary Review* 14, no. 27 (January–June): 9–18.
Senna, Marta de. 1998. *O olhar oblíquo do bruxo; Ensaios em torno de Machado de Assis*. Rio de Janeiro: Nova Fronteira.
———. 2003. *Alusão e zombaria: Considerações sobre citações e referências na ficção de Machado de Assis*. Rio de Janeiro: Fundação Casa de Rui Barbosa.
———. 2005. "Strategies of Deceit: *Dom Casmurro*." *Portuguese Literary and Cultural Studies*, special issue, *The Author as Plagiarist: The Case of Machado de Assis*, 13–14 (Fall–Spring): 407–18.
Sereno, Renzo. 1947. "Cryptomelanism: A Study of Color Relations and Personal Insecurity in Puerto Rico." *Psychiatry* 10, no. 3 (August): 261–69.
Sevcenko, Nicolau. 1983. *Literatura como missão: Tensões sociais e crição cultural na Primeira República*. São Paulo: Editora Brasiliense.

Shafer, Jack. 2008. "How Obama Does That Thing He Does: A Professor of Rhetoric Cracks the Candidate's Code." *Slate Magazine*, February 14. http://www.slate.com/id/2184480.
Shohat, Ella, and Robert Stam. 1994. *Unthinking Eurocentrism: Multiculturalism and the Media*. New York: Routledge.
Silva, Hélcio Pereira da. 1976. *Lima Barreto: Escritor maldito*. Rio de Janeiro: Civilização Brasileira.
Silva, Ivete Helou da. 2002. *Machado de Assis: O cronista míope*. Rio de Janeiro: Galo Branco.
Silva, Luiz. 1989. "Luiz Gama: Uma trajetória além do seu tempo." *Estudos Afro-Asiáticos* 16, no. 2: 59–69.
Silva, Nelson do Valle. 1978. "White-Nonwhite Income Differentials: Brazil." Ph.D. diss., University of Michigan.
Simone, Timothy Maliqalim. 1989. *Race in Postmodernn America*. New York: Autonomedia.
Skidmore, Thomas E. 1974. *Black into White: Race and Nationality in Brazilian Thought*. New York: Oxford University Press.
Slater, David. 1994. "Exploring Other Zones of the Postmodern: Problems of Ethnocentrism and Difference Across the North-South Divide." In *Racism, Modernity, and Identity: On the Western Front*, edited by Ali Rattansi and Sallie Westwood, 87–125. Cambridge: Polity Press.
Smedley, Audrey. 1993. *Race in North America: Origin and Evolution of a Worldview*. Boulder: Westview Press.
Smith, Huston. 1989. *Beyond the Post-Modern Mind*. 2nd rev. ed. Wheaton, Ill.: Theosophical Publishing House.
Soares, Maria Nazaré Lins. 1968. *Machado de Assis e a análise da expressão*. Rio de Janeiro: Instituto Nacional do Livro.
Söderlind, Syliva. 1994. "Margins and Metaphors: The Politics of Post-***." In *Liminal Postmodernisms: The Postmodern, the (Post-)Colonial, and the (Post-)Feminist*, edited by Theo D'haen and Hans Bertens, 35–54. Amsterdam: Rodopi.
Sodré, Nelson Werneck. 1965. *Naturalismo no Brasil*. Rio de Janeiro: Editora Civilização Brasileira.
Sommer, Doris. 1991. *Foundational Fictions: The National Romances of Latin America*. Berkeley: University of California Press.
Sorokin, Pitirim A. 1957. *Social and Cultural Dynamics: A Study of Change in Major Systems of Art, Truth, Ethics, Law, and Social Relationships*. Rev. and abr. ed. Boston: Porter Sargent.
———. 1964. *The Basic Trends of Our Time*. New Haven: College and University Press Services.
Sousa, J. Galante de Sousa. 1958. "Cronologia de Machado de Assis." *Revista do Livro* 3 (September): 141–81.
Souza, Grayce Mayre Bonfim. 2008. "Uma trajetória racista: O ideal e pureza de sangue na sociedade ibérica e na América portuguesa. *Politeia: História e Sociedade, Vitória da Conquista* 8, no. 1: 83–103.
Spencer, Sharon. 1971. *Space, Time, and Structure in the Modern Novel*. Chicago: Shallow Press.
Spengler, Oswald. 1922. *Der Untergang des Abendlandes* [*Decline of the West*]. Munich: C. H. Beck.
Spickard, Paul R. 1989. *Mixed Blood: Intermarriage and Ethnic Identity in Twentieth-Century America*. Madison: University of Wisconsin Press.
Spieker, Sven. 1995. "The Centrality of the Middle: On the Semantics of the Threshold in Gogol's Arabeski." *SEER: Slavonic and East European Review* 73, no. 3 (July): 449–69.
Spitzer, Leo. 1989. *Lives in Between: Assimilation and Marginality in Austria, Brazil, and West Africa, 1780–1945*. New York: Cambridge University Press.
Spix, Johann Baptist von, and Carl Friedrich Philipp von Martius. 1824. *Travels in Brazil, in the Years 1817–1820: Undertaken by Command of His Majesty the King of Bavaria*. Vol. 1. London: Longman, Hurst, Res, Orme, Brown, and Green.
Stam, Robert. 2000. "Tropical Detrius: *Terra em Transe*, Tropicália and the Aesthetics of Garbage." *Studies in Latin American Popular Culture* 19:83–92.

Stauffer, Ruth M. 1922. *Joseph Conrad: His Romantic-Realism*. Boston: Four Seas.
Stein, Ingrid. 1984. *Figuras femininas em Machado de Assis*. Rio de Janeiro: Paz e Terra.
Stepan, Nancy Leys. 1991. *The Hour of Eugenics: Race, Gender, and Nation in Latin America*. Ithaca: Cornell University Press.
Stephen, Philip. 1972. "Naturalist Influences on Symbolist Poetry, 1882–86." *French Review* 46, no. 2 (December): 299–311.
St. Louis, Regis. 2004. *Rio de Janeiro*. 4th ed. Oakland: Lonely Planet.
Stonequist, Everett W. 1937. *The Marginal Man*. New York: Russell and Russell.
Stowell, Peter H. 1980. *Literary Impressionism, James, and Chekhov*. Athens: University of Georgia Press.
Stromberg, Roland N. 1975. *An Intellectual History of Modern Europe*. 2nd ed. Englewood Cliffs: Prentice-Hall.
Sun, Haowei. 2007. "From Leeching to Anaphrodisiacs: Treatments of Epilepsy in the Nineteenth Century." *University of Toronto Medical Journal* 84, no. 2 (March): 107–10.
Süssekind, Flora. 1982. *O negro como arlequim: Teatro e discriminação*. Rio de Janeiro: Achiamé/Socii.
———. 1990. *O Brasil não é longe daqui: O narrador, a viagem*. São Paulo: Companhia das Letras.
Swidler, Ann. 1986. "Culture in Action: Symbols and Strategies." *American Sociological Review* 51, no. 2 (April): 273–86.
Sypher, Wylie. 1978. *Four Stages of Renaissance Style: Transformation in Art and Literature, 1400–1700*. Gloucester, Mass.: Peter Smith.
Tauscher, Dennis. 2010. "Escravidão e abolição em *Memorial de Aires* e 'O Caso da Vara.'" In *Machado de Assis e a escravidão/Machado de Assis und die Sklaverei*, Hamburg Conferences, edited by Gustavo Bernardo, Joachim Michel, and Markus Schäffauer, 135–146. São Paulo: Annablume.
Taylor, Quintard. 1978. "Frente Negra Brasileira: The Afro-Brazilian Civil Rights Movement, 1924–1937." *Umoja* 2, no. 1: 25–40.
Teilhard de Chardin, Pierre. 1955. *The Phenomenon of Man*. Translated by Bernard Wael. New York: Harper and Row.
Teitelbaum, Stanley. 1990. "Making Everything Perfectly Fuzzy." *Los Angeles Times Magazine*, April 1, 24–42.
Teixeira, Ivan. 1987. *Apresentação de Machado de Assis*. São Paulo: Livraria Martins Fontes Editora.
Teixeira, Jerônimo. 2008. "Machado, um verdadeiro imortal." *VEJA* Edição 2079, September 24. http://veja.abril.com.br/240908/p_160.shtml.
Temkin, Owsei. 1971. *The Falling Sickness: A History of Epilepsy from the Greeks to the Beginning of Modern Neurology*. 2nd rev. ed. Baltimore: Johns Hopkins Press.
Thompson, Era Bell. 1965. "Does Amalgamation Work in Brazil?" *Ebony*, August, 27–30, 32–34, 41.
Tiffin, Helen. 1990. "Introduction." In *Past the Last Post: Theorizing Post-Colonialism and Post-Modernism*, edited by Ian Adam and Helen Tiffin, vii–xvi. Calgary: University of Calgary Press.
Tinhorão, José Ramos. 2004. *Domingos Caldas Barbosa: O poeta da viola, do modinha, e do lundu, 1740–1800*. São Paulo: Editora 34.
Toplin, Robert Brent. 1981. "Reinterpreting Comparative Race Relations: The United States and Brazil." In *Freedom and Prejudice: The Legacy of Slavery in the United States and Brazil*, edited by Robert Brent Toplin, 9–103. Westport, Conn.: Greenwood Press.
Toro, Alfonso de. 1997. "The Epistemological Foundations of the Contemporary Condition: Latin America in Dialogue with Postmodernity and Postcoloniality." In *Latin American Postmodernisms*, edited by Richard A. Young, 29–51. Amsterdam: Rodopi.
Torres, João Camilo de Oliveira. 1969. *Interpretação da realidade brasileira*. Rio de Janeiro: Livraria José Olympio Editora.

Torres, Rafael Pérez. 2006. *Mestizaje: Critical Uses of Race in Chicano Culture*. Minneapolis: University of Minnesota Press.
Tosta, Antonio Luciano. 2004. "Machado de Assis: A obra entreaberta." *Luso-Brazilian Review* 41, no. 1: 37–55.
Trey, George. 1998. *Solidarity and Difference: The Politics of Enlightenment in the Aftermath of Modernity*. Albany: State University of New York Press.
Trigo, Abril. 2004. "General Introduction." In *The Latin American Cultural Studies Reader*, edited by Ana del Sarto, Alicia Ríos, and Abril Trigo, 1–14. Durham: Duke University Press.
Trípoli, Mailde Jerônimo. 2006. *Imagens, máscaras, e mitos: O negro na obra de Machado de Assis*. Campinas: Editora Unicamp.
Trochim, Michael R. 1988. "The Black Guard: Racial Conflict in Post-Abolition Brazil." *Americas* 44, no. 3 (January): 287–88.
Tuchman, G. 1978. *Edging Women Out: Victorian Novelists, Publishers, and Social Change*. New Haven: Yale University Press.
Tufano, Douglas. 2003. *Machado de Assis: Questões éticas em discussão*. São Paulo: Paulus.
Turner, Victor Witter. 1969. *The Ritual Process: Structure and Anti-Structure*. New York: Cornell University Press.
Uitti, Karl D. 1961. *The Concept of Self in the Symbolist Novel*. Hague: Mouton.
Uricoechea, Fernando. 1978. *O minotauro imperial. A burocratização do estado patrimonial brasileiro no século XIX*. Rio de Janeiro: Difusão Europeia do Livro.
Vajda, Gyorgy M. 1982. "The Structure of the Symbolist Movement." Translated by Eva Palmai. In *The Symbolist Movement in Literature of European Languages*, edited by Anna Balakian, 29–41. Budapest: Akadeimai Kiado.
Val, Waldir Ribeiro do. 1977. *Geografia de Machado de Assis*. Rio de Janeiro: Livraria São José.
Vara, Teresa Pires. 1976. *A mascarada sublime: Estudo de "Quincas Borba."* São Paulo: Duas Cidades, Secretaria da Cultura, Ciência, e Tecnologia.
Venâncio Filho, Paulo. 2000. *Primos entre si: Temas em Proust e Machado de Assis*. Rio de Janeiro: Nova Fronteira.
Veríssimo, José. 1894. *Estudos brasileiros: Segunda série, 1889–1893*. Rio de Janeiro: Laemmert.
———. 1916/1963. *História da literatura brasileira: De Bento Teixeira (1601) a Machado de Assis (1908)*. 4th ed. Brasília: Biblioteca Básica Brasileira.
———. 1977. *Estudos de literatura brasileira*. 6th ed. Belo Horizonte: Italiaia.
Viana Filho, Luiz. 1974. *A vida de Machado de Assis*. São Paulo: Livraria Martins Editora.
Vianna, Hermano. 2004. "Mestiçagem fora de lugar." *Folha de São Paulo Caderno Mais*, June 27.
Virgillo, Carmelo. 1966. "Love and the 'Causa Secreta' in the Tales of Machado de Assis." *Hispania* 49, no. 4 (December): 778–86.
———. 1972. "Machado de Assis and the Myth of Brazil." In *UCLA Semana de Arte Moderna Symposium (1922–1972): Commemorating the 50th Anniversary of the Semana de Arte Moderna in São Paulo and the 150th Anniversary of Brazilian Independence, February 7–12, 1972*, edited by Claude L. Hulet, 70–80. Los Angeles: University of California, Los Angeles.
Wagar, Warren W. 1977. *World Views: A Study in Comparative History*. Hinsdale, Ill.: Dryden Press.
Waizbort, Leopoldo. 2007. *A passagem do três ao um: Crítica literária, sociologia, filologia*. São Paulo: Cosac Naify.
Washington, Robert E. 2001. *The Ideologies of African American Literature: From the Harlem Renaissance to the Black Nationalist Revolt*. Lanham, Md.: Rowman and Littlefield.
Wasserman, Renata R. Mautner. 2008. "Race, Nation, Representation: Machado de Assis and Lima Barreto." *Luso-Brazilian Review* 45, no. 2: 84–106.
Watt, Jan. 1979. *Conrad in the Nineteenth Century*. Berkeley: University of California Press.

Waugh, Patricia. 1984. *Metafiction: The Theory and Practice of Self-Conscious Fiction*. London: Waugh Methuen.
Weber, Max. 1947. *The Theory of Social and Economic Organization*. Translated by A. M. Henderson and Talcott Parsons. New York: Free Press.
———. 1968. *Economy and Society*. 2 vols. Berkeley: University of California Press.
Weisstein, Ulrich. 1973. "Introduction." In *Expressionism as an International Literary Phenomenon*, edited by Ulrich Weisstein, 15–28. Paris: Gidier.
Wellek, René. 1982. "What Is Symbolism?" In *The Symbolist Movement in the Literature of European Languages*, edited by Anna Balakian, 15–28. Budapest: Akademiai Kiado.
Wertheim, Margaret. 1999. *The Pearly Gates of Cyberspace: A History of Space from Dante to the Internet*. New York: Norton.
Weschenfelder, Eládio Vilmar. 2000. *A paródia nos contos de Machado de Assis*. Passo Fundo: Universidade de Passo Fundo.
West, Cornell. 1993. *Beyond Eurocentrism and Multiculturalism*. Vol. 1. Monroe, Maine: Common Courage Press.
Whalen, Tracy. 2004. "Introduction: Rhetoric as Liminal Practice." RHETOR 1. http://uregina.ca/~rheaults/rhetor/2004/whalen.pdf.
White, Harrison C., and Carolyn A. White. 1965. *Canvases and Careers: Institutional Change in the French Painting World*. Chicago: University of Chicago Press.
Wilber, Ken. 1996. *A Brief History of Everything*. Boston: Shambhala.
———. 1997. "An Integral Theory of Consciousness." *Journal of Consciousness Studies* 4, no. 1 (February): 71–92.
———. 1998. *The Marriage of Sense and Soul: Integrating Science and Religion*. New York: Random House.
———. 2000. *Integral Psychology: Consciousness, Spirit, Psychology, Therapy*. Boston: Shambhala.
Wilcken, Patrick. 2005. "'A Colony of a Colony': The Portuguese Royal Court in Brazil." *Common Knowledge* 11, no. 2: 249–63.
Williams, Lorna T. 1987. "Recent Works on Afro-Hispanic Literature." *Latin American Research Review* 22, no. 2: 245–54.
Williams, Patrick, and Laura Chrisman. 1994. "Colonial Discourse and Post-Colonial Theory: An Introduction." In *Colonial Discourse and Post-Colonial Theory: A Reader*, edited by Patrick Williams and Laura Chrisman, 1–19. New York: Columbia University Press.
Williams, Raymond. 1958. *Culture and Society, 1780–1950*. New York: Harper and Row.
Wisnik, José Miguel. 2008. *Machado maxixe: O caso pestana*. São Paulo: Publifolha.
Wolff, Maria Tai. 1987. "Inexplicating the Nineteenth-Century Novel: *Esaú e Jacó*." In *Transformations of Literary Language in Latin American Literature: From Machado de Assis to the Vanguards*, edited by K. David Jackson, 45–52. Austin: University of Texas, Department of Spanish and Portuguese; Abaporu Press.
———. 1988. "Realism." In *Dictionary of Brazilian Literature*, edited by Irwin Stem, 272–74. Westport, Conn.: Greenwood Press.
Woll, Dieter. 1972. *Machado de Assis: Die Entwicklung seines erzählerischen Werkes* [*Machado de Assis: The Development of His Narrative Works*]. Braunschweig: G. Westermann.
Woodridge, Benjamin M., Jr. 1986. "The Deceptive Realism of Machado de Assis." *Hispanic Review* 54, no. 2 (Spring): 239–40.
Wright, Roy Dean, and Susan W. Wright. 1972. "A Plea for a Further Refinement of the Marginal Man Theory." *Phylon* 33 (Winter): 361–68.
Wuthnow, Robert. 1987. *Meaning and Moral Order: Explorations of Cultural Analysis*. Berkeley: University of California Press.

Xavier, Therezinha Mucci. 1986. *A personagem feminina no romance de Machado de Assis*. Rio de Janeiro: Presenca.
———. 1994. *Verso e reverso do favor no romance de Machado de Assis*. Viçosa: Universidade Federal de Viçosa, Imprensa Universitária.
Yacubian, Elza Márcia Targas. 2002. "A epilepsia retratada ao longo da história." *Com Ciência: Revista Electrôica de Journalismo Científico*, July 10. http://www.comciencia.br/reportagens/epilepsia/ep19.htm.
Yoshino, Kenji. 2006. *Covering: The Hidden Assault on Our Civil Rights*. New York: Random House.
Young, John K. 2006. *Black Writers, White Publishers: Marketplace Politics in Twentieth-Century African American Literature*. Jackson: University Press of Mississippi.
Young, Robert J. C. 1995. *Colonial Desire: Hybridity in Theory, Culture, and Race*. New York: Routledge.
Zack, Naomi. 1994. *Race and Mixed Race*. Philadelphia: Temple University Press.
Zackodnik, Teresa C. 2004. *The Mulatta and the Politics of Race*. Jackson: University Press of Mississippi.

INDEX

abolicionismo, O (Abolition) (Nabuco), 123
abolition of slavery
   in Brazil: Black Guard after, 53; free coloreds on, 18–19; Machado's writings on, 79–84, 97–100, 185, 244–45; mass manumissions before, 51, 82; for Native Americans, 164; Naturalism and, 174–76; parliamentary debates over, 80–81; passage of law enacting, 51, 53; political and economic reasons for, 19–20; social reforms needed with, 51, 79–82, 174–75, 260 n. 2; state's gradual approach to, 80; in ternary racial order, 18–21, 30–31; urban expansion after, 34
   in Portugal, 256 n. 3
   vs. true emancipation, 100
   in U.S., 79
Abolitionist Confederation (Confederação Abolicionista), 52
abolitionist literature
   characteristics of, 166–67
   emergence of, 166
   Naturalism as continuation of, 174–76
   stereotypes in, 55, 163, 166–70
abolitionist movement
   African Brazilian participation in, 36, 50–51
   free coloreds in, 18–19
   Gama (Luís) in, 50–51, 101
   journals supporting, 36
   Paraguayan War and, 18
   Patrocínio in, 52–56, 101
   rise of, 18–19
   in ternary racial order, 18–21
Abreu, Mauricio, 23, 24
absolutism, colonial, combined with industrial capitalism, 24
Academia Brasileira de Letras. *See* Brazilian Academy of Letters
activist organizations, African Brazilian, 146–47
Adler, Peter, 122
adultery, in *Dom Casmurro*, 224–26
affirmative action, 147, 149

Afonsine Ordinances, 16, 256 n. 4
Afonso V (king of Portugal), 256 n. 4
Afonso VI (king of Portugal), 17
Africa
   culture of, in Brazilian culture, 22, 166
   origins of humanity in, 150–51
African Americans
   as immigrants to Brazil, 28–30
   one-drop rule in definition of, 3
   one-drop rule in group identity of, 149
   passing as white, 120, 261 n. 7
   political mobilization of, 149
   skin color of, 1–2
   in Social Darwinism, 174
   synonyms for, 255 n. 1
African Brazilian(s) (mulattoes and blacks)
   in abolitionist movement, 36, 50–51
   in black movement, 146–50
   in colonial era, 11, 13
   divide between mulattoes and blacks, 35, 53
   goal of eradication of, 176, 264 n. 14
   Indianist movement and, 165–66
   in literature (*see* African Brazilian characters; African Brazilian writers)
   Machado accused of indifference to, 67–68, 71–72, 77
   Machado as, 4, 152
   mulattoes' views on blacks, 35
   Naturalist view of, 170–76
   in Old Republic, 34, 35
   polka transformed by, 185
   population of, 26–27, 150
   in purity of blood statutes, 16, 17
   in racial hierarchy, 35
   religions of, 33, 249
   as statistical category, 149
   synonyms for, 255 n. 1
   upward mobility of, 34, 35, 73
   with white status, 35
African Brazilian characters
   in abolitionist literature, 166–70

African Brazilian characters (*continued*)
  in cultivated tradition, 43
  female, 104, 167–70
  Machado's use of, 84–102; in novels, 84, 89–100, 101; in short stories, 84–89
  as main character, first novel with, 171–72
  vs. Native American characters, 166
  in Naturalism, 170–73
  rarity of: before 1850, 166, 168–69; in Machado's works, 84, 101–2
  sexuality of (*see* sexuality)
  stereotypes of (*see* stereotypes)
  in tradition of opposition, 54–56
African Brazilian organizations
  Black Guard's effect on attitudes toward, 53
  rise of modern activist, 146–47
  strategic essentialism in, 146
African Brazilian vernacular. *See* vernacular
African Brazilian writers
  African Brazilian vernacular used by, 41–42
  cultivated tradition of, 42–44
  European orientation of, 40–41
  as interpreters of black experience, 41
  racial consciousness in, 36–37, 40–42
  social status of, 39–40, 73
  tradition of opposition of, 42–43, 48–61
  vernacular tradition of, 42–43, 44–48
  white audience of, 37, 40
  "white" literature by, 42–43
African slaves. *See* slaves
African-descent individuals
  in Afrocentrism, 144
  all Americans as, 21, 27, 150
  black movement's use of term, 147
  Machado as, 4
  in purity of blood statutes, 15–17
Afrocentrism, 144–52
  black movement in Brazil and, 146–50
  essentialism in, 144, 151, 262 n. 9
  Eurocentrism's relationship to, 144–46, 150–51
  Machado's relationship to, 139–40, 144–45, 152
  moderate, 150–52
  origins of, 140, 144
  radical, 144, 150, 151
  views of, 144, 150–52
afro-descendente. *See* African-descent individuals
agnostic, Machado as, 247
agregados (free clients or dependents)
  and literary culture, 39
  Machado as, 70, 115
  in Machado's writings, 112–13, 115
  in patriarchal families, 39, 112–13, 115
agriculture
  free coloreds in, 14–15
  modernization of, 60
Agriculture, Commerce, and Public Works Ministry, Machado's career at, 68–69, 80–81
Alencar, José de
  Indianist literature of, 164, 264 n. 10
  Machado's reviews of plays by, 78
  nationalist literature of, 112, 155, 157–58
  and Romanticism, 192
Alencar, Mario de, 63
allegory, in *Esau and Jacob*, 229, 232, 233
Almeida, Manuel Antônio de, 106–7, 192, 260 n. 1
Alvarenga, Manuel Inácio da Silva, 43–44, 258 n. 9
Alves, Jerson César Leão, 148
Alvim, Cesário, 57
Amado, Jorge, 42
Amazonas, multiracial movement in, 147–48
ambiguity, 124–34
  in human experience, 7–8, 121, 124
  in Impressionist novels, 208, 224, 226
  in Machado's characters: agregado, 112, 113, 115; mulatto, 102, 105; narrative voice of, 83; postmodern sensibility in, 250–51
  in Machado's personal experience, 121–22, 124
ambition, conflict between individual morality and, 8, 124–34
American literature, Machado's study of, 64
American Verses (*Americanas*) (Machado), 79, 263 n. 7
ancestry, of Brazilian elite, 22, 23, 27
ancien régime, 23
Anderson, Benedict, 153–54
Anderson, Victor, 144
Andrade, Mario de, 56, 155
Andrade, Oswald de, 184
"Angel, An" ("Um anjo") (Machado), 71
Anglo–North America
  interracial marriage in, 12
  one-drop rule in, 3
  Social Darwinism in, 174
Anna Karenina (Tolstoy), 226
anticolonial nationalism, Machado's critique of, 181, 246
antiessentialism, strategic, 151–52, 262 n. 9
antimultiracial racism, 149
apartheid, 144. *See also* inegalitarian pluralism
Aranha, José Pereira da Graça, 176, 178–80

Araújo, Jovita Maria de, 69
Arcadian movement, 43, 258 n. 9
archetypes
    tragic mulatto, 103–4
    trickster, 107
architecture, 25
Argentina, in Paraguayan War, 256 n. 6
Argüelles, José, 199, 264
aristocracy, Brazilian. *See* elite
artisans
    free coloreds as, 15
    multiracial individuals as, 14
artists, social status of, 39
Asante, Molefi, 144
assimilation
    after abolition, 35
    in African Brazilian literature, 37
    in colonial Brazil, 13
    and masquerading as white, 119–20
    in racial democracy ideology, 30, 144
Assis, Francisco José de, 65, 66, 71, 73
Assis, Joaquim Maria Machado de. *See* Machado de Assis, Joaquim Maria
atheist, Machado as, 247
audience
    of Machado, 37–38; and book sales, 37–38; intellectual demands placed on, 38; narrators' shared viewpoint with, 114, 136–37; postmodern sensibility in approach to, 245–46; subversion of expectations of, 138–39; urban bourgeoisie as, 102
    white: of abolitionist literature, 166–68; of black literature, 37, 40
Augusta, Amália, 56
authors. *See* writers; *specific authors*
autobiographical writing
    Ayres's Memorial as, 265 n. 1
    Machado's lack of, 72, 124
    Machado's parody of, 135
avant-garde, 262 n. 2
Avelar, Idelber, 185–86
Ayres's Memorial (Machado)
    as autobiographical novel, 265 n. 1
    dual identities in, 133–34
    earnings from, 69
    as Impressionist novel: in characterization, 230, 231–32, 235, 236; in narrative point of view, 221–23, 227–28; in narrative structure, 221
    lack of interracial unions in, 103
    as Realist novel, 190
    slavery in, 97–100, 101

Azevedo, Aluísio
    O mulato, 102–3, 170–71, 196
    Naturalist novels of, 264 n. 13
    racial prejudices of, 175
    Realist-Naturalist writings of, 196
Azevedo, Maria de, 16

Baependi, Conde de (Brás Carneiro Nogueira da Costa e Gama), 249–50
Bagby Júnior, Alberto, 64
Bahia
    Canudos settlement in, 177–78
    marriage in, 255–56 n. 1
    slave rebellions in, 48, 258 n. 11
Balzac, Honoré de, 202, 265 n. 5
Bandeira, Manuel, 47
Baptista, Abel, 160, 161, 197, 226, 227
barbarism, 184
Barbosa, António de Caldas, 45
Barbosa, Domingos Caldas, 45–48, 258 n. 10
Barreto, Afonso Henriques de Lima, 56–61
    civil service career of, 57
    and constructive postcolonialism, 189
    death of, 57
    education of, 57
    exploration of human behavior by, 105
    family of, 56–57
    Machado's influence on, 59
    mockery in tone of, *vs.* Machado, 101, 138
    novels of, 59–61
    response to Eurocentric standards, 138
    in tradition of opposition, 56–61
Barreto Filho, José, 156, 157
Barroso, Maria José de Mendonça, 70
Barth, John, 238
Barvosa, Edwina, 123
Bastide, Roger, 44, 106, 162
batuque, 33
Baudrillard, Jean, 266 n. 1
Belle Époque (1880–1914), 26–33, 58
Bergson, Henri, 266 n. 3
Bernadelli, Rodolfo, 72
Bhabha, Homi, 159, 181–82
Bilac, Olavo, 52
binarism, in relation to hybridity, 187
binary racial order, in U.S.
    multiracial movement as challenge to, 255 n. 2
    one-drop rule in, 3
    origins of, 3–4
black, use of term, 255 n. 1. *See also* blackness
black Americans. *See* African Americans
black Brazilians. *See* African Brazilian(s); pretos

black experience
  African Brazilian vs. European Brazilian writers as interpreters of, 41–42
  Machado on risks of examining, 103
  in Machado's narrative voice, 137–38
Black Experimental Theater (Teatro Experimental do Negro), 146
Black Front, Brazilian (Frente Negra Brasileira), 146
Black Guard (Guarda Negra), 53
"Black Legend," 67, 259 n. 7
black liberation, Machado's relevance to, 139–40
Black Modernism, 141
black movement, in Brazil, 146–50
  vs. civil rights movement in U.S., 149
  critics of project of, 147–48
  on multiracial identity, 148–49, 150
  on racial hierarchy, 146–47, 150
Black Nationalism, 144, 150
black superiority, in Afrocentrism, 144
blackness
  Afrocentrist views of, 144, 150–52
  in Brazil: black movement on expansion of, 147, 150; continuum of, 4, 73; European Brazilian views of, 35; social advancement not associated with, 35; ternary racial order of (see ternary racial order)
  Eurocentric views of, 145–46
  in U.S.: binary racial order of, 3–4; informal definitions of, 3; legal definitions of, 3; in one-drop rule, 2–3
"Boas Noites" (pseudonym), 82, 260 n. 4
Bocage, Manuel Maria Barbosa du, 47
boçal (African-born) slaves, 22
"Bodarrada, A" (The Goat Herd) (Gama), 49
bodes (goats), 49
Bom-crioulo (The Good Black) (Caminha), 171–72
Bonilla-Silva, Eduardo, 148
Borges, Dain, 110–12, 162, 173
Bosi, Alfredo, 105, 106, 113, 125, 183
both/neither perspective
  characteristics of, 124
  of Machado, 9, 238, 244–47
  in moderate Afrocentrism, 152
  in postmodernism, 244
Bourdieu, Pierre, 147, 244, 246
bourgeoisie
  African Brazilian, 34
  as entrepreneurs, in social order, 111
  interracial marriage by, in colonial era, 13
  white Brazilian, 102
Boxer, Charles, 16, 17

Boyd, Antonio, 137, 138
brancos (whites). See also European Brazilian(s)
  Machado as, 4
  population of, 27, 149–50
  in ternary racial order, 4
Brás Cubas. See Posthumous Memoirs of Brás Cubas
brasilidade (Brazilianness). See also national identity
  Machado on other authors' use of, 161–62, 263 n. 7
  in Machado's writings, 8–9, 115, 156, 160, 180
  in racial democracy ideology, 143
Brazil
  colonial (see colonial Brazil)
  end of slavery in, 34, 51, 53, 79–80
  independence from Portugal (1822), 13, 157–59, 263 n. 4
  laws of (see legal system)
  literature of (see literary culture; specific genres and writers)
  official language of, 164
  in Paraguayan War, 256 n. 6
  as racial democracy (see racial democracy)
  racial order in (see ternary racial order)
  as state vs. kingdom under Portugal, 24
Brazil, Empire of (1822–89)
  abolitionist movement in, 50, 53
  Black Guard support for, 53
  imposition of national culture by, 25–26
  Machado as civil servant in, 68–69
  public education in, 38–39
  Regency governments in (1831–40), 25, 118, 261 n. 5
  Second Reign in (1840–89), 112, 158, 160, 161
  social uprisings in collapse of, 118, 261 n. 5
Brazil, Federative Republic of (1964–85), racial inequality in, 146
Brazil, Old Republic of (1889–1930)
  Black Guard in, 53
  economic shifts in, 34
  establishment of, 25, 34
  inegalitarian pluralism in, 31
  public education in, 39
  separation of church and state in, 249
  in war of Canudos, 177–78
Brazilian Academy of Letters (Academia Brasileira de Letras)
  Aranha as founding member of, 180
  and Barreto, 59, 60
  Cunha's admission to, 180
  Machado as president of, 63, 66

photos of Machado at, 259 n. 11
Brazilian Black Front (Frente Negra Brasileira), 146
Brazilian Historical and Geographical Institute, 25, 165–66
Brazilian Institute of Geography and Statistics (IBGE), 148
Brazilian Theater Conservatory, 78, 260 n. 1
Brazilianness. *See* brasilidade
British liberalism, 24
British literature. *See* English literature
Brito, Paul, 66
bromide, 75–76
Brookshaw, David, 42, 124, 166, 173
Bueno, Eva, 56, 172–73
Buescu, Mircea, 259 n. 8
Burdick, John, 15, 28
bureaucratic estate, 108–9
burial, of Machado, 67, 70

caboclos
  day celebrating, 148
  vs. mamelucos, 256 n. 2
  population of, 26, 257 nn. 10–11
cafusos, 14
Caldas, António Pereira de Souza, 45–46
Caldwell, Helen
  on *Dom Casmurro*, 224, 225, 226
  on *Esau and Jacob*, 229
  on Machado's English skills, 64
  on Machado's family, 71
Câmara, Maria Leopoldina Machado da, 65, 66, 70, 71, 73
Caminha, Adolfo, 171–72, 175
Canãa (Canaan) (Aranha), 176, 178–80
Cândido, Antônio
  on Brazilian national literature, 106–7, 157
  and cultural production, 183
  on *Dom Casmurro*, 226
  on Machado's exploration of social order, 106–7, 111
  on Machado's narrative innovations, 160
candomblé, 33, 143, 257 n. 15, 264 n. 11
cannibalism, cultural, 184
Canudos, 177–78
capital punishment, 54–55
capitalism, industrial, combined with colonial absolutism, 24
capitalist society, Brazil as, 108
capoeira, 33, 53, 143, 257 n. 18, 258 n. 12
Cardoso, Fernando Henriques, 259 n. 13, 260 n. 4
Carioca, 59, 258 n. 13

Carne (Flesh) (Ribeiro), 172
Carneiro, Maria Luiza Tucci, 16
carnival celebrations, 33, 261 n. 1
Carvalho, Estevão Leitão de, 259 n. 10
Carvalho, José, 110
Carvalho e Melo, Sebastião José de. *See* Pombal, Sebastião José de Carvalho e Melo, Marquês de
Casa da Misericárdia (House of Charity), 255–56 n. 1
"Case of the Whipping Stick, The" ("O caso da vara") (Machado), 85, 86
Castro, Hebe Maria, 20
Catholic Church
  and African Brazilian religion, 33, 249, 257 n. 17
  on Canudos settlement, 177
  high culture provided by, 24
  Machado's views on, 248, 266 n. 7
  on miscegenation and marriage, 12
  in separation of church and state, 249, 257 n. 16
Cavalcanti, Adolfo Bezerra de Menezes, 249–50
Ceará, great drought in, 54
Celso de Assis Figueiredo Júnior, Afonso. *See* Ouro Prêto, Afonso Celso de Assis Figueiredo Júnior, Visconde de
censorship, of theater, 78, 260 n. 1
census, Brazilian
  approach to data collection on race, 147, 148
  on literacy rates, 257 n. 2
  on literary professions, 37
  on racial composition, 26, 27, 150
  on Rio de Janeiro, 26, 27
centralized political systems, 108–9
Chalhoub, Sidney
  on Machado's exploration of social order, 117–19
  on Machado's life, 80–81
  on Machado's narrative innovations, 160
  on slavery in Machado's chronicles, 82, 83–84
characters. *See also* narrators; *specific works*
  African-Brazilian (*see* African Brazilian characters)
  in Impressionism, 204, 207–10, 229–37
  of Machado: duality in, 124–34, 137, 250–51; in first *vs.* second phase novels, 114, 191; in the grotesque, 136–37; historical allusions in names of, 116–17; without identifiable race, 101–2; identity crises of, 105; as Impressionist, 229–37; lack of interracial unions among, 103; mulatto, 102–4;

characters of Machado (*continued*)
　national identity in, 154; as Romantic Realist, 211–12, 217–19; from urban bourgeoisie, 102; white, 102
　in Naturalism, 209–10
　in Realism, 202, 208–10
　in Romantic Realism, 201, 202, 207, 211–12, 217–19
　in Romanticism, 202
　women (*see* women characters)
Chekhov, Anton, 198, 237, 265 n. 6
Chinese immigrants, 257 n. 12
Chrisman, Laura, 180–81
chronicles, of Machado
　humor in, 261 n. 1
　slavery in, 79–80, 81–84, 99
Chrysalids (*Crysálidas*) (Machado), 71
Church. *See* Catholic Church
Cidade do Rio, A (*The City of Rio*) (newspaper), 51, 52, 54
cities. *See* urban areas
citizenship, Constitution on, 159
city planning, 31–32
civil rights movement, U.S., 149
civil service
　Barreto's career in, 57
　Machado's career in, 66, 68–69, 80–81
Clara of the Angels (*Clara dos anjos*) (Barreto), 59
claramente mulato, 27
class. *See* social class
clientelism
　in literary culture, 39
　in Machado's writings, 113–18
　origins and rise of, 84, 110, 111
Cobb, Martha, 137, 138
coercion, in miscegenation, 11–12, 14
coffee economy, 34, 60
Cole, Nicki Lisa, 139
colonial Brazil, 10–15
　European immigration to, 10–11
　free coloreds in, 14–15
　gender ratios in, 10–11, 12, 65
　miscegenation in, 11–14, 65
　in national identity, 157
　Native Americans in, 11, 13, 14, 165
　racial composition of, 10, 11, 14
　racial order in: origins of, 3–4, 10–14, 21; shift away from, 35
　titles of nobility in, 21–22, 23–24
colonial United States, racial formation in, 3–4
colonialism
　definition of, 180

　dismantling of, 180–81
　relationship of neocolonialism and postcolonialism to, 180–81
colonization, Eurocentrist view of, 145
color, skin
　in Brazil, 4
　in U.S., 1–2
color-blind antiracism, 150
color-blind racism, 148, 150
"colored people," 1–2
common-law interracial unions, 12–13
Comte, Auguste, 172, 264 n. 12
concubinage, 12, 14
Confederação Abolicionista (Abolitionist Confederation), 52
Conference for the Promotion of Racial Equality, First (2005), 148
Conrad, Joseph, 265 n. 6
consciousness
　in Impressionism, 205, 206, 207
　mestizo, 121, 189
　racial (*see* racial consciousness)
Conservative Party, Brazilian
　Black Guard support for, 53
　ideology of, 118
　social order under, 118
Conservatório Dramático Brasileiro, 78, 260 n. 1
Constitution, of Brazil
　European influence on, 159–60
　on presidential succession, 54
　and purity of blood statutes, 16
　on religion, 257 n. 16
constructive postcolonialism, 188–89
constructive postmodernism, 241–43, 246
Conteçipe, Baron de (João Maurício Wanderly), 18
Cony, Carlos, 163
Cordeiro, Francisca de Basto, 72
Correio da Manhã (*Morning Mail*) (newspaper), 75
cortiços (tenements), 32, 33
Costa, Bonifácio Gomes da, 70
Costa, Christine, 73
Costa, Cláudio Manuel da, 258 n. 9
Costa, Emilia da, 17
Costa, Laura Gomes da, 70, 259 n. 10
Costa, Sara Braga Gomes da, 70
Costigan, Lúcia, 47
costumismo, 196, 197, 265 n. 3
counter-Enlightenment, 240
Cousin Basílio (*O primo Basílio*) (Queiroz), 193–94, 226

Coutinho, Afrânio, 27, 156–57, 197–98, 206
covering, of identity, 120
Crane, Stephen, 265 n. 6
creoles, 22
creolization, 182
Crespo, Gonçalves, 74–75
crioulos, 22
critical hybridity, 121, 182–83, 252
critical mestizaje, 182–83
crônicas. See chronicles
Crown. See Portuguese Crown
Crusade of the West, 256 n. 5
Cruz, Osvaldo Gonçalves, 31
Cruzeiro, O (Southern Cross) (newspaper), 194
cryptomelanism, 27
cult of the primitive, 140–41
cultivated tradition, 42–44
    Alvarenga in, 43–44
    characteristics of, 43
    Machado in, 62, 77
cultural cannibalism, 184
cultural theft, 42
culture
    African Brazilian: African influence on, 22, 166; vernacular (*see* vernacular culture)
    Brazilian: African influence on, 22, 166; development after independence, 157–59; European influence on, 24–33, 157–58; high *vs.* low, 24, 33; Native American contribution to, 163–66; state imposition of national, 25–26
    literary (*see* literary culture)
Cunha, Euclides da, 176–78, 179–80
Cyrus, Stanley, 137

DaMatta, Roberto, 184
dance, in vernacular culture, 142, 185–87. *See also specific types*
Darwinism, 173–74
Daudet, Alphonse, 265 n. 6
Davis, Murray, 139
Day of Multiraciality (Dia do Mestiço), 148
Day of the Caboclo (Dia do Caboclo), 148
Dead Souls (Gogol), 82
death penalty, 54–55
Deceptive Realism of Machado de Assis, The (Gledson), 115
deconstructive postcolonialism, 189
deconstructive postmodernism, 241–43, 246, 266 n. 2
Degler, Carl, 17
Deleuze, Gilles, 266 n. 1

democracy
    racial (*see* racial democracy)
    rural, 51
Demônio familiar (Family Devil) (Alencar), 77–78
Dennis, Jeana, 161
deracination, 120
Derrida, Jacques, 266 n. 1
"desertor das letras, O" (Alvarenga), 43–44
determinism
    in Cunha's account of Canudos, 178
    of Naturalism, 170, 175, 209
developing nations, in cult of the primitive, 140–41
"Devil's Church, The" ("Igreja do diabo") (Machado), 266 n. 7
Dia do Caboclo (Day of the Caboclo), 148
Dia do Mestiço (Day of Multiraciality), 148
Diário do Rio (journal), 102
diary form, novels in, 97, 221
Dias, Antonio Gonçalves, 164, 264 n. 10
Dickens, Charles, 64, 200, 202, 259 n. 4, 265 n. 5
Diop, Cheikh Anta, 144
dis-ease, societal, 7–8, 124
disease control, 31
Dixon, Paul, 225, 266 n. 6
"Does Amalgamation Work in Brazil?" (Thompson), 2
dog, in *Quincas Borba*, 132, 136
Dom Casmurro (Machado)
    agregados in, 115
    dual identities in, 130–31
    exploration of social order in, 116–17, 118–19
    the grotesque in, 136–37
    as Impressionist novel: in characterization, 230–31, 235, 236; in narrative point of view, 221–28; in narrative structure, 219–21
    influence of civil service work on, 81
    intentionalism and, 226–27
    lack of interracial unions in, 103
    patriarchy in, 225, 266 n. 6
    as Realist novel, 190
    slavery in, 95
Dostoyevsky, Fyodor, 156, 200, 265 n. 5
Douglass, Ellen, 263 n. 3
Doumer, Paul, 63
dowries, 255–56 n. 1
doxa, 244
"Dr. Semana" (pseudonym), 260 n. 4
dreams, in *Dom Casmurro*, 231
duality, 124–34
    in human experience, 7–8, 121, 124–25

duality (*continued*)
  in Machado's characters, 124–34, 137; in *Ayres's Memorial*, 133–34; in *Brás Cubas*, 126, 128–30; in *Dom Casmurro*, 130–31; in *Esau e Jacó*, 133; in *The Hand and the Glove*, 127; in *Helena*, 127; in *Iaiá Garcia*, 127–28; postmodern sensibility of, 250–51; in *Quincas Borba*, 131–33; in *Ressurreição*, 127
  in Machado's personal experience, 124, 244
  Machado's views on, 250
  materialist rationalism as source of, 124–25
Duarte, Eduardo, 56, 84, 85
Dutra, Francis, 256 n. 5

Ebony magazine, 2
economy, of Brazil
  in abolition of slavery, 19–20
  coffee, 34, 60
  free coloreds in, 14–15, 20
  libertos in, 30–31
  of Old Republic, 34
  political, 108–12
education
  in colonial era, 14, 15
  of free coloreds, 15
  higher, 39
  of multiracial Brazilians, 14
  public, 38–39
  in Rio de Janeiro, 64, 259 n. 3
éducation sentimentale, L' (*Sentimental Education*) (Flaubert), 199–200
egalitarian integration, 29, 30
egalitarian pluralism, 29, 144, 241
egoism, of Machado's characters, 124–26, 129–31, 137
either/or perspective
  characteristics of, 124
  Machado's critique of, 250, 253
  moderate Afrocentrist views on, 151–52
  postmodernism on, 243–44
Elísio, Filinto, 47
elite, Brazilian
  on African Brazilian religion, 33
  Barreto's criticism of, 58
  on Canudos settlement, 177
  dance and, 185, 186
  European culture and, 24–33
  genealogical histories of, 22, 23, 27
  Indianist movement among, 163–66
  Machado's characters drawn from, 102
  Machado's narrators as device for criticism of, 85, 91–92
  Portuguese Court in Brazil and, 23–24
  power of, 34
  racial insecurity of, 21, 23
  resistance to abolition among, 80–81
  rise of vernacular culture among, 141–42
  in ternary racial order, 21–24
  titles of nobility for, 21–22, 23–24
  urban, 34, 102, 173
elite, Portuguese, visits to Brazil by, 23–24
emancipation, true, *vs.* abolition, 100
Empire of Brazil. *See* Brazil, Empire of
engineering schools, 39
English language, Machado's knowledge of, 64, 263 n. 5
English literature
  Machado's translations of, 64, 259 n. 4, 263 n. 5
  Machado's use of, 64, 160
entrepreneurs, 111
entrudos, 261 n. 1
environment, in Naturalism, 170, 175, 209
epilepsy
  cause and treatment of, 63, 75–76, 258 n. 2
  of Flaubert, 63, 258 n. 1
  of Machado, 63, 66, 75–76, 157, 191
epiphanies, in Impressionism, 208
epistemology
  of Eurocentrism, 145
  of moderate Afrocentrism, 151–52
epithets, 49
equality. *See* racial equality; social equality
Esau and Jacob (*Esau e Jacó*) (Machado)
  dual identities in, 133
  as Impressionist novel: in characterization, 232–33; in narrative point of view, 221–23, 229; in narrative structure, 220
  lack of interracial unions in, 103
  as Realist novel, 190
  slavery in, 95–97, 101
Escola das Belas Artes (School of Fine Arts), 25
escrava Isaura, A (*The Slave Isaura*) (Guimarães), 167–68
Espelho, O (journal), 102
Espírito Santo, 178
essentialism
  in Afrocentrism, 144, 151, 262 n. 9
  postmodernism on, 246
  strategic, 146, 262 n. 4, 262 n. 9
estate, bureaucratic, 108–9
estate-based society, 108–10, 112
Estatuto da Igualdade Racial (Statute of Racial Equality), 149

Estrella, Hairton, 234
ethics. *See* morality
eugenics, 28. *See also* whitening through miscegenation
Eurocentrism
  Afrocentrist response to, 144–46, 150–51
  global impacts of, 145–46
  Machado's response to, 8, 137–38, 152
  origins of, 145
  on universality of literature, 104
  views of, 145–46
Europe
  culture of, influence on Brazilian culture, 24–33, 157–58
  literature of: influence on Brazilian literature, 157–59, 262–63 nn. 2–3; Machado on use of, 158, 159, 183, 192, 246, 263 n. 3
  Modernism in, 60
  racism in, 27
  Romanticism in, 25
European Americans, use of one-drop rule by, 3
European Brazilian(s) (whites). *See also* Portuguese immigrants
  in abolitionist movement, 18–19
  as audience for black literature, 37, 40
  in colonial era: miscegenation by, 11–14, 65; population of, 11; titles of nobility for, 21–22, 23–24
  European *vs.* Brazilian identity of, 23
  literary culture influenced by, 39–40
  in Old Republic, 34, 35
  population of: in Belle Époque, 26–27; in colonial era, 11
  in racial hierarchy, 35
European Brazilian literature, by African Brazilian writers, 42–43
European Brazilian writers
  African Brazilian vernacular used by, 41–42
  on black experience, 41–42
  slave stereotypes used by, 55–56
evolution, human, 150–51
Expressionism, 198, 202–6
extermination, 173, 264 n. 14

Faithful Slave stereotype, 167–68
families. *See also* patriarchal families
  in colonial Brazil: European, 10–11, 12; interracial, 12
  Machado's writings on: agregados in, 112–13, 115; lack of interracial unions in, 103
"Famous Man, A" ("Um homem célebre") (Machado), 184–87

Fanger, Donald, 265 n. 5
Faoro, Raymundo, 90, 99, 107–11, 112, 260 n. 3
Faria, João, 78
farming. *See* agriculture
"Father Against Mother" ("Pai contra mãe") (Machado), 86–90
favelas (shantytowns), 33
feiticeiro (witch doctor), 169, 264 n. 11
female characters. *See* women characters
Fernandes, Florestan, 260 n. 4
Ferrões, Os (*The Bee's Stingers*) (journal), 52
fiction, in tradition of opposition, 57–58. *See also* novels; short stories; *specific writers*
Figueiredo Júnior, Afonso Celso de Assis, 264 n. 16
Filipe II (king of Portugal), 256 n. 4
Filipine Ordinances, 16, 17, 256 n. 4
Fitz, Earl, 192, 197–98
Flaubert, Gustave, 63, 198, 199–200, 226, 258 n. 1
FNB. *See* Frente Negra Brasileira
folk Catholicism, 249
Fonseca, Deodoro da, 25, 54
Fonseca, Godín da, 71
foreign languages, Machado's knowledge of, 64, 259 nn. 4–6, 263 n. 5
Formation of Brazilian Literature (Cândido), 157
Foucault, Michel, 266 n. 1
France
  influence on Brazilian culture, 25
  Naturalism in, 55, 193
  urban infrastructure in, 32, 257 n. 13
Frank, David, 245, 252
Frank, Zephyr, 19, 256 nn. 7–8
free coloreds
  in abolitionist movement, 18–19
  economic roles of, 14–15, 20
  population of, 11, 27
  in Rio de Janeiro, 27
  slaves' relationship with, 15, 18
  upward mobility of, 20
freed slaves. *See* libertos
French Artistic Mission, 25
French language, Machado's knowledge of, 64, 259 nn. 4–5, 263 n. 5
French literature, 160
Frente Negra Brasileira (Brazilian Black Front) (FNB), 146
Freud, Sigmund, 140, 141
Freyre, Gilberto
  on black movement, 147
  on Brazilian national identity, 143
  on Brazilian national literature, 155

Freyre, Gilberto (*continued*)
   on interracial unions in Machado's works, 103
   on Machado's understanding of social reality, 105–6
   on ternary racial order, 10
   on whitening of portraits, 27–28
   and writers on black experience, 41
Fry, Peter, 147
Futurists, 60
Futuro, O (journal), 102

Gallot, Madame, 259 n. 5
Gama, Basílio da, 258 n. 10
Gama, Brás Carneiro Nogueira da Costa e (Conde de Baependi), 249–50
Gama, Luís Gonzaga de Pinto da, 48–51
   in abolitionist movement, 50, 101
   and constructive postcolonialism, 189
   death of, 51
   exploration of human behavior by, 105
   on humanity under slavery, 139
   response to Eurocentric standards, 138
   successors to, 56
   in tradition of opposition, 48–51
   use of term "mulatto" by, 74
García Canclini, Néstor, 187, 188
Garnier (publisher), 69
Gazeta da Tarde (Evening Gazette) (newspaper), 52
Gazeta de Notícias (News Gazette) (newspaper), 52, 54, 67–68, 97, 184, 260 n. 4
Gellner, Ernest, 141, 154
gender ratios, in colonial Brazil, 10–11, 12, 65
genealogical histories, of Brazilian elite, 22, 27
genetic inheritance, of humans, 151
Gennep, Charles-Arnold Kurr van, 123
genocide, laissez-faire, 31, 264 n. 14
Gerardin, Alfred, 259 n. 4, 263 n. 5
German immigrants, 28, 257 n. 2
German language, Machado's knowledge of, 64
Ghostly Matters (Morrison), 124
"*Ghostly Matters*": *Haunting and the Sociological Imagination* (Gordon), 112, 124
Gide, André, 265 n. 8
Ginsberg, Elaine, 261 n. 7
Gledson, John
   on abolitionism, 99
   on *Dom Casmurro*, 225, 226–27
   on Machado as Realist, 197
   on Machado's exploration of social order, 106, 111, 112, 115–17, 246
   on Machado's mulatto identity, 124
   on Machado's narrative innovations, 160
   on Machado's response to Eurocentrism, 138
   on Machado's skepticism, 247
Gliddon, George, 27
goats, 49
Gobineau, Arthur de, 27
Godoi, Rodrigo, 79
Goffman, Irving, 119, 261 n. 7
Gogol, Nikolai, 82, 202, 265 n. 5
Gomes, Eugênio, 78
Gomes, Heloísa, 138–39
Goncourt, Edmund de, 203
Goncourt, Jules de, 203
Gonzaga, Tomás António, 258 n. 9
"Good Morning!" ("Bons Dias!") (Machado), 82
Gordon, Avery, 112, 124, 251
Graden, Dale, 18, 48
Gramsci, Antonio, 35
Graziela (dog), 259 n. 5
Greek language, Machado's knowledge of, 64
Greek literature, Machado's quotations from, 64
Griswold, Wendy, 40
"Grito de Ipiranga," 159, 263 n. 4
grotesque, the
   definition of, 135–36
   Machado's use of, 8, 135–39, 245
group identity
   in black movement of Brazil, 146–49
   Eurocentrism in formation of, 146
   one-drop rule in formation of, 149
   strategic essentialism and, 146
group pluralism, 146, 147
Guarda Negra (Black Guard), 53
Guatimozim, 264 n. 9
Guattari, Félix, 266 n. 1
Guimarães, Bernardo, 167–68
Guimarães, Hélio de Seixas, 37–38
gypsies, 16

Haabás, 78
habanera, 142, 185, 262 n. 3
Haberly, David
   on abolitionism, 167, 169, 174–75
   on conflict between individual morality and public ambition, 8
   on *Dom Casmurro*, 131
   on lack of African Brazilian characters in Brazilian literature, 166
   on laissez-faire genocide, 264 n. 14
   on Machado's mulatto identity, 7, 73, 121, 124
   on Machado's response to Eurocentrism, 138
   on Naturalism, 173, 175, 176

on Romanticism, 174
Haiti, slave uprising of 1799 in, 261 n. 5
Hand and the Glove, The (A mão e a luva) (Machado)
  dual identities in, 127
  earnings from, 69
  the grotesque in, 136
  lack of interracial unions in, 103
  marriage in, 113
  as Romantic novel, 190
  as Romantic Realist novel: in characterization, 217–19; in narrative point of view, 216–17; in narrative structure, 212, 213
  "tragic mulatto" theme in, 103–4
Hansen, João, 251, 252
Harlem Renaissance, 141
Hartshorne, Charles, 266 n. 3
Hauser, Arnold, 266 n. 5
Haussmann, Georges-Eugène, 32, 257 n. 13
Hawthorne, Nathaniel, 265 n. 5
health, of Machado, 63, 66, 75–76, 191
Hegel, Georg, 238, 266 n. 3
Heidegger, Martin, 238, 266 n. 3
Helena (Machado)
  dual identities in, 127
  exploration of social order in, 117–18
  indications of Machado's transformation in, 191
  influence of civil service work on, 81
  lack of interracial unions in, 103
  as Romantic novel, 190
  as Romantic Realist novel: in characterization, 217–19; in narrative structure, 212, 213–14
  slavery in, 89
  "tragic mulatto" theme in, 103–4
Henriques, João, 56–57
heredity, in Naturalism, 170, 175, 176, 209
Hesse, Herman, 265 n. 8
heterogeneity, multitemporal, 188
hierarchies. *See* racial hierarchy; social hierarchy
higher education, opportunities for, 39
historical allusions, in Machado's novels, 116–17
Holanda Ferreira, Aurélio Buarque de, 155
homosexuality, in Naturalism, 171–72
Hugo, Victor, 167, 199
human nature
  as basis of societal problems, 105–6, 124–25
  vs. human behavior, 105
  Machado's exploration of, 85, 105–6, 190
Humanism
  in *Brás Cubas*, 129
  in *Quincas Borba*, 103, 129, 132, 229

humanity
  of African Brazilians, 139, 170, 175
  African origins of, 150–51
  critics on Machado's dark view of, 155–57
  of Native Americans, 164
humor
  Machado on need for, 261 n. 1
  Machado's use of, 138–39; as brasilidade, 160; in first vs. second phase novels, 190; purposes of, 8, 138–39
  in tradition of opposition, 48
  in vernacular tradition, 45, 46
Hutcheon, Linda, 263 n. 3
Huysmans, Joris-Karl, 265 n. 8
hybrid degeneracy
  in Aranha's writings, 179
  Machado's views on, 176, 180
hybridity, 181–89
  and binarism, 187
  critical, 121, 182–83, 252
  definitions of, 182, 187
  hypocritical, 182–83
  Machado's use of, 187–89
  origins of concept, 182
  in postcolonialism, 181–89
  in postmodernism, 243
hybridization, racial, U.S. fears of, 104
hypocritical hybridity, 182–83
hypodescent. *See* one-drop rule of hypodescent

Iaiá Garcia (Machado)
  dual identities in, 127–28
  exploration of social order in, 118
  as first phase novel, 192, 265 n. 1
  indications of Machado's transformation in, 191, 192
  influence of civil service work on, 81
  lack of interracial unions in, 103
  as Romantic novel, 190, 192
  as Romantic Realist novel: in characterization, 217–19; in narrative structure, 212, 214–15
  slavery in, 89–91
Ianni, Octavio, 138, 140, 261 n. 4
Iberian Peninsula, Crusade of the West in, 256 n. 5
Iberians, in purity of blood statutes, 16
IBGE. *See* Brazilian Institute of Geography and Statistics
"ideal do crítico, O" (Machado), 38
ideational paradigm
  cycle of, 239, 240, 243
  in postmodernism, 239, 243

identity
　of European Brazilians, 23
　group (see group identity)
　racial (see racial identity)
　schism between internal and external (see duality)
identity crises, in Machado's characters, 105
illness, of Machado, 63, 66, 75–76, 191
immigration
　of African Americans to Brazil, 28–30
　of Europeans to Brazil: in Belle Époque, 28; in colonial era, 10–11; whitening through, 28
Immoral Slave stereotype, 168–70
immorality. See morality
Imperial College of Dom Pedro II, 25
Impressionism, artistic, 204–5
Impressionism, literary
　aesthetic of, 202–10; characterization in, 204, 207–10; evolution of, 198–99; narrative point of view in, 206–7; narrative structure in, 206–7; objectivism and subjectivism in, 198–99, 203–6; setting in, 207
　Machado's writings as, 9, 192, 219–37, 252; characterization in, 229–37; narrative point of view in, 221–29; narrative structure in, 219–21
　Realism-Naturalism's relationship to, 198, 199, 202–4, 208
income, average Brazilian, 259 n. 8
Inconfidência Mineira (Minas Gerais Conspiracy), 43, 258 n. 9
independence of Brazil (1822), 13, 157–59, 263 n. 4
Indianist movement, 163–66, 264 nn. 9–10
indigenism, 141, 142
industrial capitalism, 24
industrialization, 34, 60
inegalitarian integration, 29, 30, 35, 119, 144, 182, 183
inegalitarian pluralism, 29, 31, 35, 144, 182
Inês da Silva, Maria
　Machado accused of abandoning, 68, 71
　in Machado's education, 71, 259 nn. 5–6
　marriage of, 66, 71
infrastructure, urban, improvements to, 31–32
Innes, Catherine, 42
integration
　egalitarian, 29, 30
　inegalitarian, 29, 30, 35, 119, 144, 182, 183
intellectuals
　in cult of the primitive, 140–41
　education and careers of, 39
　social status of, 39–40

　on whitening through miscegenation, 123, 176
intelligentsia. See also intellectuals
　African Brazilian entry into, 34, 36
　social status of, 39
intentionalism, 160, 226–27
international relations, in Old Republic, 31
interracial families, in colonial Brazil, 12
interracial marriage. See also miscegenation
　in Brazil: in colonial era, 12–13, 65; Machado's avoidance of topic, 103; prevalence of, after abolition, 65–66
　in U.S.: one-drop rule for children of, 2–3; proscription on, 12
Introduction to Machado de Assis (Barreto Filho), 156
ironic detachment, Machado's use of, 87, 114, 160
irony
　in Impressionism, 209–10
　Machado's use of, 8, 135–39; in Brás Cubas, 91–94; regarding clientelism, 115; in Esaú e Jacó, 96; in first vs. second phase novels, 190, 192; the grotesque combined with, 136–37; in Iaiá Garcia, 192; postmodern sensibility in, 245; in Quincas Borba, 132; regarding slavery, 87, 91–94, 96, 138–39
Isabel (princess of Brazil), 51, 53, 69
Isfahani-Hammond, Alexandra, 42
Italian immigrants, 257 n. 12
Italian language, Machado's knowledge of, 64

Jackson, Richard, 137, 138
James, Henry, 237, 265 n. 6
James, William, 266 n. 3
Japanese immigrants, 257 n. 12
jealousy, 237
Jequitinhonho, Francisco Gomes Brandão, Visconde de, 72
Jesuits, 16–17, 24, 164
Jesus, Antónia de, 45
Jews, in purity of blood statutes, 16
Jim Crow segregation
　dismantling of, 149
　institutionalization of, 3
João VI (king of Portugal), 23, 24–25
"João das Regras" (pseudonym), 260 n. 4
Jobim, José, 78–79
Jornal da Tarde (Evening Journal), 64, 263 n. 5
José I (king of Portugal), 13
Journal das Famílias, 249
journalism
　Barreto's work in, 57

Barreto's writings on, 57, 59
careers for writers and intellectuals in, 39
Machado's work in, 39, 69, 73
Patrocínio's work in, 52, 54
upward mobility through, 73
journals, African Brazilian, racial consciousness in, 36
Joyce, James, 206, 208, 265 n. 8
Juderías, Julián, 259 n. 7
judicial system, Brazilian. *See* legal system
Jung, Carl Gustav, 141

Kafka, Franz, 265 n. 8
Kamel, Ali, 147
Kant, Immanuel, 238
Kardec, Allan (Hippolyte Léon Denizard Rivail), 248
Kardecism, 248–49, 257 n. 15
Karenga, Maulana, 144
Kellogg, Robert, 265 n. 5
Kipling, Rudyard, 265 n. 8
Kristal, Efraín, 111, 113, 154–55

labor force, Brazilian
  colonial, 11, 14–15
  libertos in, 30–31
  Machado's civil service work on, 80–81
  mulattoes in, 14–15
  Old Republic, 34
  racial composition of, 11, 14
Lacerda, Cesar de, 78–79
laissez-faire genocide, 31, 264 n. 14
Lamarck, Jean-Baptiste, 28
land distribution, to freed slaves, 51, 99
landscape, Brazilian, 162–63
Lapouge, Georges Vacher de, 27
Laranjeiras section of Rio, 68
Latin American Cultural Studies, 6–7
Latin language, Machado's knowledge of, 64, 259 n. 6
Law no. 3353 (1888). *See* Lei Áurea
Law of September 28, 1871. *See* Lei do Ventre Livre
law schools, 39
Lawrence, D. H., 265 n. 8
Lebanese immigrants, 257 n. 12
legal system
  Brazilian (*see also specific laws*): abolitionist movement in, 50; African Brazilian religion in, 33, 257 n. 16; antimultiracial racism in, 149; European influence on, 159–60; marriage in, 13; purity of blood in, 16

U.S., one-drop rule in, 3
Lei Áurea (Golden Law) of 1888, 51, 53, 184
Lei do Ventre Livre (Law of the Free Womb) of 1871
  abolitionist movement on, 50
  effectiveness of, 50, 80
  effects on social order, 117, 118
  Machado's work with, 80–81
  Paraguayan War in passage of, 18
Lei dos Sexagenários (Sexagenarian Law) of 1885, 80, 82
leisure, as status symbol, 111
"Lélio" (pseudonym), 260 n. 4
"Lereno melancólico" (Barbosa), 46
Lesser, Jeffrey, 257 n. 12
Lessing, Gotthold, 105
liberalism
  in Brazilian legal system, 159–60
  in Brazilian social order, 24, 111–12
libertos (freed slaves)
  in Black Guard, 53
  challenges facing, 30–31
  economic roles of, 30–31
  land distribution to, 51, 99
  Republican Party plans for, 53
  slave ownership by, 19
libraries, 64
Lima, Luiz Costa, 110, 178, 233
liminality
  definition of, 123
  Machado's experience of, 9, 123, 238
Lipsitz, George, 151
literacy rates, 37, 257 n. 2
literary aesthetic
  of African Brazilians, evolution of, 36
  Brazilian, creation of, 159
  of Machado, 5, 155, 191–93
literary canon
  European, 41
  European Brazilian, 42, 43
literary culture
  of Brazil, 36–42; clientele system and, 39; educational system and, 38–39; European Brazilian influence on, 39–40; European influence on, 158, 262 n. 2; impartiality in, 38; literacy rates and, 37; Machado's criticism of, 38; in national identity, 153–54; national independence in, 157–59; Naturalism in, rise of, 55, 170; racial consciousness in, 36–37, 40–42; readership and, 37–38
  of Europe, Brazil influenced by, 158, 262 n. 2

literary professionals, number of, 37. *See also* journalism; writers
literary whiteness, 43
Locock, Sir Charles, 258 n. 2
Longfellow, Henry Wadsworth, 64
López, Francisco Solano, 256 n. 6
love
  and jealousy, 237
  in Machado's characters: rarity of, 134, 137; selfless love *vs.* self-love, 126–27, 134, 250
  same-sex, in Naturalism, 171–72
Lucas, Fábio, 225
Luisa (queen consort of Portugal), 17
Lula da Silva, Luiz Inácio, 259 n. 13
Lund, Joshua, 181–82
lundu, 45, 185, 262 n. 3
Lyotard, Jean-François, 247, 266 n. 1

Macedo, Joaquim Manuel de, 169–70
Machado de Assis (Meyer), 156
Machado de Assis (Pereira), 155
Machado de Assis, Joaquim Maria
  in Barreto's writings, 59
  career of: in civil service, 66, 68–69, 80–81; in journalism, 39, 69, 73
  death of, 67, 70, 74, 75–76, 247–48, 259 n. 10
  life of, 62–76; baptism, 70; black friendships in, 71–72; discovery of documents on, 5, 70–71; education, 64; finances, 66, 67, 68–70; gaps in account of, 4–5; illness, 63, 66, 75–76, 191; marriage, 62–63, 66–67, 72; parents, 5, 65–66, 68, 70–73; psychological struggles in, 156–57; residences, 68, 69, 70, 259 n. 9; spirituality in, 247–50
  on literacy rates, 37
  photographs of, 63, 72, 73, 259 n. 11
  racial identity of: Afrocentrist views on, 152; debate over, 4–5; as descendant of African slaves, 62, 70; documentation of, 5, 70; Machado's perception of, 4, 7, 72–74, 120–24, 253; Machado's veiling of, 7–8, 119, 120; marginality in, 121–22; in physical appearance, 72–73; *vs.* racelessness, 7, 119–21; society's perception of, 73–75
  racial indifference of, critics' accusations of, 4, 67–68, 71–72, 77
  writings of, 77–100 (*see also specific genres, themes, and works*): aesthetic of, 5, 155, 191; audience of (*see* audience); in cultivated tradition, 62, 77; discovery of new facts about, 77–78; earliest, 66; evolution in complexity of, 38, 128, 191; history of criticism on, 4–6; innovations in, 91–92, 115, 116, 160–61, 192–93, 195–96; lack of autobiographical detail in, 72, 124; lack of racial consciousness in, 62, 77; legacy of, 155; number of, 191; phases of, 5, 91, 114, 190–93, 195–96; under pseudonyms, 81–83, 194, 260 n. 4; as representative Brazilian author, 154–57, 160; rise in reputation of, 66; selling of rights to, 69; subtext of, 8, 135–39; universality as aim of, 8, 103, 104–5, 119, 161–63, 246–47; use of term "mulatto" in, 74, 77; voice of (*see* narrators)
Machado de Assis, Public Servant (Magalhães Júnior), 80
Machado de Assis: Fiction and History (Gledson), 115
Machado de Assis: Historian (Chalhoub), 80, 117
"Machado de Assis: Novelist of the Second Reign" (Pereira), 106, 157
Machado de Assis: The Development of His Narrative Works (Woll), 190
Machado de Assis: The Enigma of Perspective (Bosi), 125
Machado de Assis: The Novel with People (Passos), 125
Machado de Assis: The Pyramid and the Trapezoid (Faoro), 107, 109, 260 n. 3
Maciel, Antônio Vicente Mendes (Antônio Conselheiro), 177, 264 n. 15
Maciel, Yv Scarlett, 259 n. 4, 263 n. 5
MacNicoll, Murray, 195
macumba, 33, 257 n. 15
Madame Bovary (Flaubert), 199–200, 226
Mãe (Mother) (Alencar), 77–78
Magalhães, Domingos José Gonçalves de, 164
Magalhães Júnior, Raimundo, 68, 71, 72, 77, 80–81
magazines, women readers of, 37
Maggie, Yvonne, 147
Mahin, Luisa, 48–49
malandro, 107, 260 n. 2
Malês Revolt of 1835, 48, 258 n. 11
Malinoff, Jane, 47
"Malvólio" (pseudonym), 81, 260 n. 4
Mamede, Condessa de São, 69
mamelucos
  vs. caboclos, 256 n. 2
  in colonial era, 13, 14
  in interracial marriages, 13
"Manassés" (pseudonym), 81
Manaus, multiracial movement in, 147–48
"Manifesto antropófago" (Andrade), 184

Mann, Thomas, 237, 265 n. 6
Mannerism, 266 n. 5
Mansfield, Katherine, 265 n. 6
Mansions and the Shanties, The (Freyre), 10
Manuel I (king of Portugal), 256 n. 4
Manueline Ordinances, 16, 256 n. 4
manumissions, 51, 82, 99
mão e a luva, A (Machado). See *Hand and the Glove, The*
marginality, racial, Machado's experience of, 121–22
"Mariana" (Machado), 81, 84–85
Marinetti, Filippo, 60
Marotti, Giorgio, 82, 92, 93, 96, 97, 175, 260 n. 5
marriage
    adultery in, 224–26
    Catholic Church on, 12
    common-law, 12–13
    cost of entering into, 13, 255 n. 1
    interracial (*see* interracial marriage)
    of Machado, 62–63, 66–67, 72
    in Machado's novels, 103, 113
Martins, Heitor, 47
Martins, Luciana, 23, 24
Marx, Karl, 266 n. 3
Marxist theory, 108, 111
Mascarenhas, Manuel de Assis, 72
masquerading as white, 119–20
Massa, Jean-Michel, 64, 73, 78
master class
    Machado's writings on changes to, 117–19
    resistance to freedom for slaves, 80–81
Master on the Periphery of Capitalism, A (Schwarz), 113–14
Masters and the Slaves, The (Freyre), 10
masturbation, and epilepsy, 258 n. 2
materialist rationalism
    in *Quincas Borba*, 132, 229
    in schism between internal and external self, 124–25
Mathews, Thomas, 27
matriarchy, 266 n. 6
maxixe, origins of, 142, 185–87, 262 n. 3
McPhail, Mark, 245, 252
medical schools, 39
medieval era, cosmology of, 239, 240, 266 n. 5
Melville, Herman, 138–39, 265 n. 5
Memoirs of a Police Sergeant (Almeida), 106–7, 260 n. 1
Memórias póstumas de Brás Cubas (Machado). See *Posthumous Memoirs of Brás Cubas*
memory, in dual identities, 125

Mendonça, Francisco Maria de Sousa Furtado de, 50
Mendonça, Lúcio de, 180, 258 n. 12
Menezes, José Ferreira de, 71
merchants, free coloreds as, 15
meritocracy, in Old Republic, 34, 35
Merquior, José, 106, 110–11, 159, 197–98
mestiços
    Machado as, 4
    vs. mulatos, 4
    multiracial movement on right to identify as, 148
    vs. pardo, as term on census, 27, 148
mestizaje, 182, 187
    critical, 182–83
    radical, 121
mestizo consciousness, 121, 189
meta-mulatto, 7, 120–21, 253
metanarrative, 241, 242, 247
Meyer, Augusto, 156
middling wealth holders, 19, 20, 256 n. 8
military orders, purity of blood in, 256 n. 5
militia, civilian, mulattoes in, 15, 20
Mill, John Stuart, 111
Mills, Charles, 257 n. 9
mimesis, 197, 239–40, 252
Minas Gerais Conspiracy (Inconfidência Mineira), 43, 258 n. 9
minstrels, in vernacular tradition, 44–45
"Mirror, The" ("O espelho") (Machado), 125
"mirror of nature" worldview, 239–40
miscegenation, in Brazil. *See also* interracial marriage
    in abolitionist literature, 169–70
    attitudes toward, 11–12, 65, 104
    in colonial era, 11–14, 65
    fictional characters created to discourage, 104
    Indianist movement and, 165–66
    by Native Americans, 11, 13, 14, 22, 165–66, 264 n. 10
    novels confronting, 176–80
    in origins of ternary racial order, 4, 11–14, 21
    pervasiveness of, 4, 12, 174
    vs. U.S., 104
    whitening through (*see* whitening)
Misplaced Ideas (Schwarz), 159
Mistérios sociais (*Social Mysteries*) (Lacerda), 78–79
mixed mentalities, 243–44, 266 n. 5
MNU. *See* Movimento Negro Unificado
moderate Afrocentrism, 150–52

Modernism
    Barreto's role in, 60–61
    Black, 141
    Brazilian, 262 n. 2
    hybridity in, 182
    indigenism in, 142
    Latin American *vs.* Western European, 60
    Machado's writings classified as, 198
    neocolonialism and postcolonialism in, 183–84
    paradigm of, 239
    vs. postmodernism, 240–42
modernity
    crisis of, 240
    deconstruction of, 242
    definitions of, 60
    of Machado's narrative voice, 116
    postmodernism's critique of, 240–43
modinhas, 45, 47
Moehn, Frederick, 183–84
moleque, 91, 96, 260 n. 7
Monasterio, Leonardo Monteiro, 259 n. 8
mongrelization
    vs. hybridity, 182
    Machado's views on, 176, 180
    U.S. views on, 104
monological paradigm, 244
Montaigne, Michel de, 156
Monteiro, Ivan, 234
Monteiro, João Carlos, 51–52
Monteiro, Pedro Meira, 183
Moors, 16
morality
    in abolitionist literature, 168–70
    in Impressionism, 208–10
    individual, conflict between public ambition and, 8, 124–34
    of Machado's characters, 126–27, 218
    in Naturalism, 170–72, 175
    in Romantic Realism, 202, 218
Morrison, Toni, 124
Morton, Samuel George, 27
Motta Coqueiro ou a pena de morte (Motta Coqueiro or the Death Penalty) (Patrocínio), 54–55
Movimento Negro Unificado (MNU), 146
Movimento Pardo-Mestiço. *See* multiracial movement
mulato claro, 27
mulatto(es)
    all Brazilians as, 21, 27
    in black movement, 146–50
    in colonial Brazil, economic roles of, 14–15
    connotations of term, 74
    in Cunha's account of Canudos, 178
    definitions of, 2, 74, 255 n. 1
    discrimination against, 62
    divide between African Brazilians and, 35, 53
    epithets used for, 49
    escape hatch for, 17–18, 35
    as free coloreds, 14–15
    Machado accused of indifference to, 67–68, 71–72
    Machado as: critics on, 4–5; society's perception of, 73–75; veiling of, 7–8, 119, 120
    as Machado's characters, 102–4
    Machado's use of term, 74, 77
    vs. mestiços, 4
    Naturalist view of, 175–76
    in Old Republic, 34, 35
    origins of term, 74, 259 n. 14
    population of, in Belle Époque, 26–27
    in purity of blood statutes, 16, 17
    in racial hierarchy, 35, 58
    social status of, 35, 73
    in ternary racial order, 4
    "tragic," theme of, 103–4
    upward mobility of, 20–21, 34, 35, 73, 103–4
    in U.S. *vs.* Brazil, 2
    use of term, 74, 255 n. 1
    views on blacks, 35
    with white status, 17, 73–74, 259 n. 13
    writers (*see* African Brazilian writers)
Mulatto, The (O mulato) (Azevedo), 102–3, 170–71, 196
mulatto escape hatch, 17–18, 35
Müller, Lauro Severiano, 32
multiracial individuals. *See also* mestiços; mulatto(es); pardos
    all Brazilians as, 21, 27
    black movement on identity of, 148–49, 150
    in Cunha's account of Canudos, 178
    Indianist movement and, 165–66
    liminality experienced by, 123–24
    one-drop rule in racial identity of, 2–3
    as slaves, 14
    statistical category used for, 149
    use of term, 255 n. 1
multiracial movement
    in Brazil, 147–50
    in U.S., 255 n. 2
multiraciality, novels confronting, 176–80
multiracialphobia, 149
multitemporal heterogeneity, 188
Municipal Councils, 12

music, of vernacular culture, 142, 185–87

Nabuco, Joaquim
    on African Brazilians in abolitionist movement, 50
    and Aranha's admission to Brazilian Academy of Letters, 180
    Machado's letters to, 247–48
    on racial identity of Machado, 74, 75, 119
    racism of, 122–23
Nagel, James, 265 n. 6
Napoleon, 23
narrative point of view. *See* point of view
narrative structure
    in Impressionism, 206–7, 219–21
    in Naturalism, 207
    in Realism, 201, 207
    in Realism-Naturalism, 200, 206, 207
    in Romantic Realism, 200–201, 211–15
    in Romanticism, 201
narrators and narrative voices, of Machado. *See also* characters
    audience's shared viewpoint with, 114, 136–37
    vs. author's voice, 83
    black experience in, 137–38
    in chronicles, 83–84
    as device for criticism of elite, 85, 91–92
    duality in (*see* duality)
    in first vs. second phase novels, 114–15, 190, 195
    as Impressionist, 219–29
    ironic detachment of, 87, 114
    postmodern sensibility in, 245
    as precursor of modern novel, 116
    as Romantic Realist, 211–17
    unreliability of, 114–16, 195, 222, 223, 224
Nascimento, Abdias do, 30, 41
Nascimento, Gizêldo, 102
National Archives, 70, 80
National Conference for the Promotion of Racial Equality, First (2005), 148
national culture. *See* culture
national history, in Romanticism, 25–26
national identity, Brazilian, 153–89
    abolitionist literature and, 166–70
    colonialism in, 157
    European influence on, 24–26
    evolution of, 36, 142–43, 157–58
    hybridity in, 181–89
    Indianism in, 163–66
    literary culture in, 153–54
    Machado's preoccupation with, 154, 161
    modernist vision for, 142

    Naturalism in, 170–76
    neocolonialism and postcolonialism in, 180–89
    schism between old and new, 153
    slaves in, 166
national instinct, 9, 162, 246
national literature, Brazilian, 153–63
    of Alencar (José de), 112, 155, 157–58
    of Cândido, 106
    debate over Machado's place in, 154–63
    European influence on, 157–59, 262–63 nn. 2–3
    Machado's influence on, 155
    Naturalism's influence on, 170–76
    universal appeal of, 161–63
"national race," 28
nationalism
    anticolonial, 181, 246
    Black, 144, 150
    Neo-Romantic, 179
Native Americans
    cannibalism and, 184
    in colonial Brazil: death of, 14, 165; miscegenation by, 11, 13, 14, 22, 165–66, 264 n. 10; population of, 11; treatment of, 165
    end of slavery for, 164
    in genealogical histories of elite, 22
    in Indianist movement, 163–66
    in indigenism, 142
    languages of, 163–64
    in Modernist movement, 183–84
    in multiracial movement, 148
    as national symbol, 163–66
    population of, 11, 165
    in purity of blood statutes, 16
    Romantic idealization of, 163–66
    as slaves, 17, 164
natural selection, 173–74
Naturalism, 170–76
    abolition in, 174–76
    African Brazilians in, 170
    characteristics of, 170
    characterization in, 209–10
    and Darwinism, 173–74
    French, 55, 193
    Machado's experimentation with, 195
    Machado's parody of, 235
    narrative point of view in, 210
    narrative structure of, 207
    Native Americans in, 163
    novels of, 55–56, 170–73
    vs. positivism, 172–73

rise of, in Brazil, 55, 170–71
scientific racism in, 170
slave characters in, 55–56, 171–72
stereotypes in, 55–56, 163
naturalization, of immigrants, 28
nature, Eurocentrist view of, 145
Nazareth, Ernesto, 186
Nazzari, Muriel, 12
neck rings, 86
Needell, Jeffrey, 24, 25, 32, 33, 118
Negritude
　Machado's relationship to, 140, 144
　origins of, 140–41
　as strategic essentialism, 262 n. 9
"Negro," as skin color, 1–2
negros
　African Brazilian writers as, in tradition of opposition, 48
　black movement's use of term, 147
　evolution of term, 20
　Machado as, 4
　as racial *vs.* color term, 147
　as statistical category, 149
neocolonialism, 180–83
　hybridity and, 182
　Machado's avoidance of, 183
　Machado's place in, 180
　relationship to colonialism, 180–81
Neo-Romantic nationalism, 179
Neo-Romanticism, 198, 202–6
neo-subjectivism, 198, 204, 205
Neto, Coelho, 52, 71
New Christians, 16
"New Generation, The" ("A nova geração") (Machado), 195, 262 n. 1
Nietzsche, Friedrich, 238, 266 n. 3
nihilism, in postmodernism, 241
nobility, titles of, 21–22, 23–24, 110
Noble Slave stereotype, 167–68, 169
Notes from Underground (Dostoyevsky), 156
"Notice on the Present State of Brazilian Letters" ("Notícia da atual literatura brasileira") (Machado), 158, 161–62
Nott, Josiah, 27
Nova Arcadia literary society, 45, 47
Novais, Adelaide Xavier de, 66, 70
Novais, Antonio Luís Pimental de, 66–67
Novais, Carolina Augusta Xavier de
　in *Ayres's Memorial*, 265 n. 1
　correspondence with Machado, 72
　death of, 67, 70, 76, 248
　family of, 66–67, 70

during illnesses of Machado, 191
influence on Machado, 66, 67
marriage to Machado, 62–63, 66–67, 72
residences of, 68, 69, 259 n. 9
Novais, Custódia Emília Xavier de, 67
Novais, Faustino Xavier de, 66, 67
novels, by Machado. *See also specific works*
　audience of (*see* audience)
　characters of (*see* characters)
　dual identities in, 125–34
　evolution in complexity of, 38, 128
　exploration of social order in, 106–19
　historical allusions in, 116–17
　influence of civil service work on, 81
　lack of interracial marriage in, 103
　phases of, 5, 91, 114, 190–93, 195–96
　Rio de Janeiro as setting for, 162–63
　slavery in, 89–100, 101
　sophistication of, 9, 106, 135, 191, 197–98
Nunes, Maria, 228

obedience, of slaves, 89
obituary, of Machado, 75
objective reality
　Machado's views on, 251–52
　in Modernism, 239
　in postmodernism, 240–42
objectivism
　in Impressionism, 198–99, 203–6
　Machado's criticism of excessive, 153
　Machado's efforts to blend subjectivism and, 9, 191–92, 197–98, 211
　in Romantic Realism, 198–201, 210
　subjective, 203
Obra completa (Machado de Assis), 258 n. 3
Oc. See Obra completa
Old Christians, 15
Old Republic of Brazil. *See* Brazil, Old Republic of
Oliveira, João Alfredo Correio de, 51, 53
Oliver Twist (Dickens), 64, 259 n. 4, 263 n. 5
Omi, Michael, 6, 35
On Behalf of the Appeal of the Name (Baptista), 160
one-drop rule of hypodescent, in U.S.
　and black movement in Brazil, 147, 149
　definition of, 2–3
　group identity created by, 149
　vs. other countries, 3, 17
　and passing as white, 120, 261 n. 7
　rise and institutionalization of, 3
opposition, tradition of, 42–43, 48–61

Barreto in, 56–61
characteristics of, 43
Gama (Luís) in, 48–51
Patrocínio in, 51–56
oppression. *See* racial oppression
Order and Progress (Freyre), 10
"Order and Progress" slogan, 170, 172, 177, 251, 264 n. 12
organizations. *See* African Brazilian organizations
"Other"
   assumptions about race of, 102
   Eurocentrist view of, 145, 146
   in Machado's narrative voice, 85
Ouro Prêto, Afonso Celso de Assis Figueiredo Júnior, Visconde de, 56–57
"Outline of Machado de Assis, An" ("Esquema de Machado de Assis") (Cândido), 106
Ouvidor, 163, 263 n. 8

"Pacotilha" (Poorly Made Product) (Gama), 49
Paiva, Manuel de Oliveira, 264 n. 13
Papéis avulsos (Machado), 249
Paraguay, 256 n. 6
Paraguayan War (1864–70), 18, 117, 256 n. 6
pardos (multiracial individuals)
   black movement on use of term, 147
   as color *vs.* racial term, 147, 148
   evolution of term, 20
   Machado as, 4
   vs. mestiço, as term on census, 27, 148
   population of, 27, 149
   pretos classified as, 73
   in ternary racial order, 4
Paris, infrastructure of, 32, 257 n. 13
Park, Robert E., 121
Parks, Rosa, 1
parliament, Brazilian, debates over slavery in, 80–81
Parnassian classicism, 60
parody, Machado's use of, 8, 137–38
   in *Brás Cubas*, 135, 234–35
   European literature and, 263 n. 3
   postmodern sensibility in, 245
Pascal, Blaise, 156
passing, as white, 120, 261 nn. 7–9
Passos, Francisco Pereira, 32
Passos, José Luiz, 111, 113, 125–26, 154–55
paternalism, 113
patriarchal families
   agregados in, 39, 112–13, 115
   in *Dom Casmurro*, 225, 266 n. 6
patrimonialism, 108–9

Patrocínio, José Carlos do, 51–56
   in abolitionist movement, 52–56, 101
   Black Guard under, 53
   death of, 54
   in exile, 53–54
   family of, 51–52
   journalism career of, 52, 54
   Machado criticized by, 67
   novels of, 54–56
   in tradition of opposition, 51–56
patronage. *See* clientelism
Peçanha, Nilo, 35, 257 n. 1
Pedro Espanhol (Peter Spain) (Patrocínio), 54
Pedro I (emperor of Brazil), 25, 118, 263 n. 4, 264 n. 9
Pedro II (emperor of Brazil)
   coup overthrowing (1889), 25
   in Gama's poetry, 49
   imposition of national culture by, 25
   in Indianist movement, 166
   Lei Áurea signed by, 51
   Machado as civil servant under, 68
   Machado's writings set in reign of, 115, 116
   in Regency period, 118
Peirce, Charles, 266 n. 3
Peixoto, Floriano Viera, 53–54
Pelinca, Luís Ferreira Nobre, 52
Pena, Afonso, 257 n. 1
Penal Code of 1890, 33
Pereira, Astrojildo, 106, 157, 162
Pereira, Leonardo, 78
Pereira, Lúcia Miguel, 155–56, 157, 172
personhood, complex, 251
pessimism, of Machado, 5, 154, 156–57, 190
phenotype
   of European Brazilians, 23, 27
   of Machado, 72–73
   racial traits in, 151
Philosophy of Machado de Assis, The (Coutinho), 156
photographs
   and Impressionism, 204–5
   of Machado, 63, 72, 73, 259 n. 11
   Patrocínio's use of, 54
physical appearance. *See* phenotype
Pitiful Slave stereotype, 167–68
Piza, Daniel, 162, 191
plague, 31
planter aristocracy. *See* elite
plays
   censorship of, 78, 260 n. 1
   Machado's reviews of, 77–79

pluralism
  egalitarian, 29, 144, 241
  group, 146, 147
  inegalitarian, 29, 31, 35, 144, 182
Poe, Edgar Allen, 64
poetry
  in cultivated tradition, 43–44
  by Machado, 81 (*see also specific works*)
  in tradition of opposition, 48–51
  in vernacular tradition, 45–48
point of view, narrative
  in Impressionism, 206–7, 221–29
  in Machado's writings, 215–17, 221–29
  in Naturalism, 210
  in Realism, 210
  in Realism-Naturalism, 210, 215
  in Romantic Realism, 200–201, 215–17
  in Romanticism, 215
polemics, Machado's avoidance of, 8, 102–3
"Policarpo" (pseudonym), 260 n. 4
political economy, of Brazil, 108–12
political mobilization
  of African Americans, 149
  of African Brazilians: after abolition, 53, 146; in twentieth century, 146–49
politics
  African Brazilians in, 35, 257 n. 1
  centralized systems of, 108–9
  and Naturalism, 172–73
  in racial order, 6
polka, 184–85, 187, 262 n. 3
Pombal, Sebastião José de Carvalho e Melo, Marquês de, 13, 16, 44, 256 n. 3, 258 n. 10
populations, erosion of boundaries between, 151
Portugal
  Brazil under (*see* colonial Brazil)
  Brazilian independence from (1822), 13, 157–59, 263 n. 4
  end of slavery in, 256 n. 3
  Napoleon's invasion of (1807), 23
  nobility in, 21–22, 23
  purity of blood statutes in, 15–16, 256 n. 5
Portuguese Court, transfer to Brazil (1808), 22–24
Portuguese Crown
  and immigration of women, 10–11
  on miscegenation, 12, 13
  on slavery, 13, 256 n. 3
  titles of nobility under, 22, 23
Portuguese immigrants
  difficulty of recruiting, 11
  gender ratios of, 10–11, 12, 65
  vs. immigrants from other countries, 257 n. 12
  miscegenation by, 11–14, 65
  number of, 11
  in origins of ternary racial order, 10–14, 21
  titles of nobility for, 21–22, 23–24
Portuguese language, as official language of Brazil, 164
positivism, 172, 264 n. 12
postcolonialism, 180–89
  constructive *vs.* deconstructive, 188–89
  definition of, 181
  hybridity in, 181–89
  Machado's place in, 181, 187–88
  relationship to colonialism, 180–81
Posthumous Memoirs of the Brás Cubas, The (*Memórias póstumas de Brás Cubas*) (Machado)
  dual identities in, 126, 128–30
  exploration of human nature in, 105
  exploration of social order in, 107, 113–14, 118–19
  as first novel of second phase, 114, 190–91, 193, 195–96
  the grotesque in, 136
  as Impressionist novel: in characterization, 230, 234–36; in narrative point of view, 221–23, 227–28; in narrative structure, 219–21
  influence of civil service work on, 81
  irony in, 91–94
  lack of interracial unions in, 103
  Machado's illness and, 191
  Machado's views of humanity in, 156, 157
  narrative voice of, 114
  parody in, 135, 234–35
  as Realist novel, 190
  reception of, 196
  Romantic elements of, 195
  serial publication of, 157, 190
  slavery in, 91–94, 101
  sophistication of literary technique in, 135
postmodernism, 238–53
  ambiguity of term, 240
  both/neither perspective in, 238
  constructive, 241–43, 246
  deconstructive, 241–43, 246, 266 n. 2
  features of, 238–39, 240–42
  goals of, 242
  Machado's place in, 244–53
  origins of, 238–42
Prado Júnior, Caio, 108
prejudice, racial. *See* racism

Premodernism, 60
president(s), of Brazil
    African Brazilian ancestry of, 35, 257 n. 1
    Constitution on succession of, 54
    first, 54
press
    African Brazilian, 36
    mulatto, 20–21
Preto-Rodas, Richard, 40–41, 44
pretos (blacks). *See also* African Brazilian(s)
    black movement on use of term, 147
    classified as pardos, 73
    as color *vs.* racial term, 147
    evolution of term, 20
    population of, 27, 149–50
    in Portuguese military orders, 256 n. 5
    in ternary racial order, 4
priesthood, purity of blood in, 16–17
Primeiras trovas burlescas (First Burlesque Ballads)
    (Gama), 49
primitive, cult of the, 140–41
primitivism, in Cunha's account of Canudos, 178
printing press, 24
Proença Filho, Domício, 225
progress. *See also* "Order and Progress" slogan
    African Brazilian religion and, 33
    postmodernism on, 239
    whitening as, 28
Proust, Marcel, 198, 237, 265 n. 6
pseudonyms, Machado's writings under, 81–83,
    194, 260 n. 4
psychological development, in Impressionist
    novels, 219–21
psychological struggles, in life of Machado,
    156–57
public education, 38–39
public health, 31, 257 n. 16
public sphere, clientele system in, 39
purity of blood statutes, 15–17, 256 n. 5. *See also*
    racial "purity"
pyramid, 109–10

"quadroon," 72
Queiroz, José Maria Eça de
    adultery in works of, 226
    Cousin Basílio (O primo Basílio), 193–94, 226
    Machado's criticism of, 191, 196, 265 n. 2
    Realism-Naturalism of, 193–94, 197, 265 n. 2
"Quem sou eu?" (Who Am I?) (Gama), 49
quilombo settlements, 14
Quincas Borba (Machado)
    dual identities in, 131–33
    the grotesque in, 136
    Humanism in, 111, 129, 132, 229
    as Impressionist novel: in characterization,
        233–34; in narrative point of view, 221–23,
        228–29; in narrative structure, 220
    lack of interracial unions in, 103
    Realism-Naturalism in, 228–29, 233–34
    as Realist novel, 190
    reincarnation in, 249
    slavery in, 94–95
quotas, racial, 149
quotations, Machado's use of, 64

Rabelo, Laurindo, 71
Raça Brazil magazine, 259 n. 11
race
    "national," 28
    postcolonial views on concept of, 188–89
    vs. social class, as social signifier, 20
    transcending of, 188–89
racelessness
    Machado's search for sense of, 7, 119–21
    objective of, 120
    vs. passing, 120
racial altruism
    in manumissions, 82, 99
    in ternary racial order, 10
racial composition
    in Belle Époque, 26–27
    in colonial era, 10, 11, 14
racial consciousness
    in African Brazilian literature, 36–37, 40–42
    vs. class consciousness, 20
    in European Brazilian literature, 41–42
    in Machado's writings: chronicles, 79–80,
        81–84; in civil service work, 80–81; critics
        on lack of, 62, 77; poetry, 81; theatrical
        reviews, 77–79
racial contract, 21, 257 n. 9
racial democracy, Brazil as
    challenges to idea, 146–47, 261 n. 4
    inegalitarian integration in, 30
    mulatto escape hatch and, 35
    origins of reputation, 2, 4, 143–44
    whitening through miscegenation and, 30,
        143–44
racial discrimination. *See* racism
racial equality
    black movement on, 146–50
    debate over policies on, 149
    debate over reality of, 146–47
    in marriage, 12

racial equality (*continued*)
   postcolonial views of, 188–89
racial formation theory
   colonialism in, 3–4
   definition of, 6
   on Machado's writings, 6
racial hierarchy
   Afrocentrist views of, 144, 150–52
   black movement on, 146–47, 150
   Eurocentrist views of, 145–46
   Indianist views of, 165–66
   in Old Republic, 35
   postcolonial views of, 188–89
racial hybridization, U.S. fears of, 104
racial identity. *See also specific types*
   in Afrocentrism, 144
   ambiguity and duality in (*see* ambiguity; duality)
   colonialism in formation of, 3–4
   of Machado (*see under* Machado de Assis, Joaquim Maria)
   of multiracial individuals, 2–3
   vs. racelessness, 119–21
   in racial formation theory, 6
   skin color in, 1–2
   in social order (*see* binary racial order; ternary racial order)
   "virtual" *vs.* "actual," 119, 120, 122
racial insecurity, of Brazilian elite, 21, 23
racial marginality, Machado's experience of, 121–22
racial oppression
   as artistic inspiration, 103
   in cultivated tradition, 43
   in Machado's writings, 103
   in tradition of opposition, 43, 48
racial order. *See also* binary racial order; ternary racial order
   definition of, 6
   state role in, 6
racial prejudice. *See* racism
racial projects, definition of, 6
racial "purity"
   evolution of requirements for, 15–16
   exceptions made in, 16–17
   and miscegenation, 3
   through one-drop rule, 3
racial quotas, 149
racial segregation
   dismantling of, 149
   institutionalization of, 3
racial transcendence, 189

racial whitening. *See* whitening
racism
   and abolitionist literature, 166–70, 175–76
   antimultiracial, 149
   Barreto's writings on, 57–59
   color-blind, 148, 150
   Eurocentrist origins of, 145–46
   in Europe, 27
   internalized, 58
   Machado's writings on, 77–78, 84
   against mulattoes, 62
   in purity of blood statutes, 16
   scientific (*see* scientific racism)
   in urban residential patterns, 32–33, 257 n. 14
radical Afrocentrism, 144, 150, 151
radical mestizaje, 121
Ramirez, Manuel, 122
rationalism. *See* materialist rationalism
Ravesco, Cristóvão Vieira, 16, 17
readers. *See* audience
Real Gabinete Português de Leitura (Royal Portuguese Library), 64
Realism
   characterization in, 202, 208–10
   failure of, in Brazil, 174
   Impressionism's relationship to, 204
   Machado's experimentation with, 192, 195, 197, 219
   Machado's writings classified as, 5, 9, 195, 197
   narrative point of view in, 210
   narrative structure of, 201, 207
   Romantic (*see* Romantic Realism)
Realism-Naturalism. *See also* objectivism
   Barreto's rejection of, 60
   costumismo and, 265 n. 3
   first Brazilian novel of, 196
   the grotesque and, 136
   Impressionism's relationship to, 198, 199, 202–4, 208
   Machado's efforts to blend Romanticism and, 9, 197–98, 211
   Machado's views on, 176, 194–97, 252
   Machado's writings classified as, 5, 9, 190, 192, 197–98
   narrative point of view in, 210, 215
   narrative structure of, 200, 206, 207
   parody and, 135
   of Queiroz, 193–94, 197, 265 n. 2
   in *Quincas Borba*, 228–29, 233–34
   rise of, 193, 195, 196

setting in, 201
reality
   in Impressionist literature, 222
   Machado's views on, 251–52
   in Modernism, 239
   in postmodernism, 240–42
   of racial equality, debate over, 146–47
   social, Machado as disconnected from, 105–6
Rebouças, André, 51
Recordações do escrivão Isaías Caminha (Memoirs of the Notary Public Isaías Caminha) (Barreto), 59
Reforma, A (newspaper), 57
Reformation, paradigm of, 239, 240
Regency governments (1831–40), 25, 118, 261 n. 5
regionalism, of Machado, 156
Regionalist movement, 263 n. 2
Rego, José Lins do, 155
reincarnation, 248, 249
Reis, Roberto, 112, 138, 157
relativity, in postmodernism, 241, 266 n. 2
Relics of the Old House (Relíquias da casa velha) (Machado), 69
religion(s). *See also specific types*
   African Brazilian, 33, 249
   freedom of, 257 n. 16
   Machado's views on, 247–50, 266 n. 7
   in separation of church and state, 249, 257 n. 16
religious orders, purity of blood in, 16–17, 256 n. 5
Renaissance, paradigm of, 239, 240
Renfrow, Daniel, 261 n. 7
representation paradigm, 239
Republic of Brazil. *See* Brazil, Old Republic of
Republican Party, Brazilian
   on Canudos settlement, 177
   plans for freed slaves, 53
   on slaves, 50–51
Republicanism, and Naturalism, 173
residential patterns, in urban areas, 32–33, 257 n. 14
Resurrection (Ressurreição) (Machado), 89
   dual identities in, 127
   the grotesque in, 136
   lack of interracial unions in, 103
   as Romantic novel, 190
   as Romantic Realist novel: in characterization, 217–19; in narrative structure, 212–13
retirantes, Os (Refugees of the Drought) (Patrocínio), 54
"Retrato de Lucinda" (Barbosa), 46

Revista Brasileira, 190
Ribeiro, Júlio, 172, 175
Ricardo, Cassiano, 155
Richardson, Dorothy, 265 n. 6
Riedel, Dirce, 197–98
Rio Branco, Baron do, 31
Rio de Janeiro (city)
   African Brazilian religion in, 257 n. 17
   Belle Époque in, 26–27, 58
   capoeira gangs in, 258 n. 12
   as colonial city *vs.* metropolitan capital, 24–25, 26
   educational system in, 64, 259 n. 3
   European culture in, 24–25, 26–27, 58
   gender ratios in colonial, 65
   infrastructure improvements in, 31–32
   inhabitants of, as Carioca, 59, 258 n. 13
   interracial marriage in, prevalence of, 65–66
   Laranjeiras section of, 68
   literacy in, 37
   literary professionals in, 37, 38
   Machado's life in, 68, 70
   modernization of, 24–25, 26
   population of, 26–27
   Portuguese Court in, 23, 24
   public health in, 31
   racial composition of, 26–27
   residential patterns in, 32–33
   São Cristovão section of, 68
   São João Batista cemetery in, 67
   as setting for Machado's novels, 162–63
   slaves in, 26
   upward mobility through slave ownership in, 19, 20, 256 n. 7
   vernacular culture in, 142
Rio de Janeiro (province), racial composition of, 26
Rio Grande do Sul, gender ratios in colonial, 10–11
Risério, António, 147
Rivail, Hippolyte Léon Denizard (Allan Kardec), 248
Rodrigues, Raimundo Nina, 176
Rodrigues Alves, Francisco de Paula, 26, 31–32
Romanization, of Catholic Church, 249
Romantic Realism
   aesthetic of, 198–202; characterization in, 201, 202, 207; evolution of, 198–99; narrative point of view in, 200–201; narrative structure in, 200–201, 207; objectivism and subjectivism in, 198–201, 210; setting in, 201–2

Romantic Realism (*continued*)
  Machado's writings as, 9, 191–92, 211–19, 252; characterization in, 217–19; narrative point of view in, 215–17; narrative structure of, 211–15
Romanticism. *See also* subjectivism
  abolitionist literature as part of, 174
  characterization in, 202
  costumismo and, 265 n. 3
  decline of, 174
  European, 25
  in Indianist movement, 163–66
  Machado's criticism of, 161, 163, 196, 197, 252
  Machado's efforts to blend Realism-Naturalism and, 9, 197–98, 211
  Machado's experimentation with, 192, 195, 197, 219
  Machado's parody of, 234
  Machado's writings classified as, 5, 9, 190, 192
  narrative point of view in, 215
  narrative structure of, 201
  national history in, 25–26
  Neo-Romanticism, 198, 202–6
  in Patrocínio's novels, 55
  setting in, 201
  Social, 167, 174
Romero, Sílvio
  on Machado in Brazilian national literature, 154–55, 156, 157, 262 n. 1
  on Machado's understanding of social reality, 105–6
  on Naturalist novels, 172
  in rise of Realism-Naturalism, 195
Rosa, Francisco Otaviano de Almeida, 71
Rosaldo, Renato, 182
Rua do Ouvidor, 163, 263 n. 8
runaway slaves, in Machado's writings, 86–89
rural democracy program, 51
Russell-Wood, Anthony, 16

Salgueiro, Maria, 86
Salvador
  African Brazilian religion in, 257 n. 17
  purity of blood statutes in, 16
  residential patterns in, 257 n. 14
samba, 33, 142, 143, 185, 186
same-sex love, in Naturalism, 171–72
Santa Catarina, gender ratios in colonial, 10–11
Santiago, Silviano, 55, 183, 187, 226
Santo, Justina Maria do Espírito, 52
Santos, Hermetério José dos, 67–68, 71
São Cristóvão section of Rio, 68

São João Batista cemetery, 67
São Paulo
  African Brazilian religion in, 257 n. 17
  Modernism in, 60–61, 262 n. 2
  residential patterns in, 33
São Paulo School, 260 n. 4
Sarmento, Silveira, 259 n. 6
Sartre, Jean-Paul, 262 n. 9
Sayers, Raymond, 44, 62–63, 85, 139
Schiele, Jerome, 144
Scholes, Robert, 265 n. 5
School of Fine Arts (Escola das Belas Artes), 25
Schopenhauer, Arthur, 156
Schultz, Kirsten, 24
Schwartz, Stuart, 22
Schwarz, Roberto
  on *Brás Cubas*, 91–92, 113–14
  on Brazilian nationalism, 159
  and cultural production, 183
  on *Dom Casmurro*, 225
  on Machado's exploration of social order, 106, 111–15, 117
  on Machado's narrative innovations, 91–92, 160
science
  Eurocentrist view of, 145
  Naturalist literature as type of, 170
  postmodern view of, 238–39, 266 n. 2
scientific method, 145
scientific racism
  Afrocentrism on, 144
  Machado's views on, 176, 180
  in Naturalism, 170
  and whitening through miscegenation, 28, 179
Scott, James, 35, 138
"Second Life, The" ("A segunda vida") (Machado), 249
segregation. *See* racial segregation
Seigel, Micol, 186
seigniorial class, 112
self
  Brazilian, 246
  postmodern understanding of, 250–51
  schism between internal and external (*see* duality)
selfcraft, 123
self-identification, of race, 3
self-interest, in ternary racial order, 10
self-love, *vs.* selfless love, in Machado's characters, 126–27, 134, 250
semana, A (Machado), 261 n. 1

semifeudal society, Brazil as, 108
Senna, Marta de, 224
sensate paradigm
    cycle of, 239, 240, 243
    in postmodernism, 239, 243
separation of church and state, 249, 257 n. 16
Sereno, Renzo, 27
sertões, Os (The Backlands) (Cunha), 176–78, 179–80
setting
    in Impressionism, 207
    Rio de Janeiro as, for Machado's novels, 162–63
    in Romantic Realism, 201–2
sexist stereotypes, 168
sexual abuse, of women slaves, 168
sexuality
    of African Brazilian characters: in abolitionist literature, 169–70; in Naturalism, 171–72, 175, 176; in Patrocínio's writings, 55
    in Realism-Naturalism, 193–94
Shakespeare, William, 64
shamanism, 169, 264 n. 11
Shohat, Ella, 181, 182
short stories, by Machado. *See also specific works*
    African Brazilian characters in, 84–89
    exploration of human nature in, 85
    influence of civil service work on, 81
    as Modernist, 198
    religion in, 249
Silva, Carolina Pereira da, 69
Silva Xavier, Joaquim José da (Tiradentes), 258 n. 9
Silveira, Joaquim Alberto de Sousa da, 70
skepticism, of Machado, 154, 156, 247
Skidmore, Thomas, 27, 28, 30, 36
skilled trades, free coloreds in, 15
skin color
    in Brazil, 4
    in U.S., 1–2
slave trade
    Atlantic, end of (1850), 19, 22
    within Brazil, 18
slave uprisings, 15, 48, 258 n. 11, 261 n. 5
slavery
    in Constitution, 159–60
    end of (*see* abolition)
    Eurocentrism in origins of, 146
    Machado's writings on, 79–100; in chronicles, 79–80, 81–84, 99; in civil service work, 80–81; irony in, 87, 91–94, 96, 138–39; in novels, 89–100, 101; in poetry, 81;
    postmodern sensibility in, 244–45; rarity of, 84, 101; in short stories, 81, 84–89; in theatrical reviews, 77–79
    in Naturalism, 55–56, 171–72
    opponents of (*see* abolitionist movement)
    parliamentary debates over, 80–81
    Patrocínio's writings on, 54–55
    in social order, 113–14, 117
    in upward mobility, 19–20, 256 n. 7
slaves
    African-born *vs.* Brazilian-born, 22
    as characters (*see* characters)
    Crown policies on, 13, 256 n. 3
    free coloreds' relationship with, 15, 18
    freed (*see* libertos)
    Machado accused of indifference to, 67–68
    Machado as descendant of, 62, 70
    multiracial individuals as, 14
    in national identity, 166
    Native Americans as, 17, 164
    population of, 11, 14, 22, 26
    in Rio de Janeiro, 26
    runaway, 86–89
    in ternary racial order, 22
smallpox, 31
Smith, Adam, 111
soccer, 58
social analyses, of Machado's writings, 5–6
social class, in Brazil. *See also* bourgeoisie; elite
    in colonial era, 4, 12, 13, 23–24
    and marriage, 12, 13
    in Old Republic, 34
    pyramid structure of, 109–10
    vs. race, as social signifier, 20
social construction
    in postmodernism, 240–41
    of race, 6, 17 (*see also* racial formation theory)
social contract, 257 n. 9
Social Darwinism, 173–74
social equality, in marriage, 12
social hierarchy, in colonial era, 4, 23–24
social mobility. *See* upward mobility
social order
    liberalism in, 24, 111–12
    Machado's exploration of, 110–19; in *Brás Cubas*, 107, 113–14, 118–19; collapse of traditional, 110–11, 112; in *Dom Casmurro*, 116–17, 118–19; in *Helena*, 117–18; in *Iaiá Garcia*, 118; through narrative voices, 114–16; as primary objective, 116–17; review of literature on, 106–19; slavery in, 113–14, 117

social order (*continued*)
  pyramid structure of social classes in, 109–10
  race in (*see* binary racial order; ternary racial order)
Social Realism, 61
social reality, Machado as disconnected from, 105–6
social reforms, needed with abolition, 51, 79–82, 174–75, 260 n. 2
Social Romanticism, 167, 174
social scientists, on racial inequality, 146–47
social status, of African Brazilian writers, 39–40, 73
societal dis-ease, 7–8, 124
societal problems, human nature as basis of, 105–6, 124–25
society
  Brazilian, capitalist *vs.* semifeudal origins of, 108
  Eurocentrist view of, 145
Society of Jesus. *See* Jesuits
Sodré, Nelson Werneck, 172
Sorokin, Pitirim, 140, 145, 152, 199, 210, 239, 243, 266 n. 5
"Sortimento de gorras para a gente do grande tom" (An Assortment of Hats of the People of Great Tone) (Gama), 49
soul, Brazilian, 162
Sousa, Antônio Gonçalves Teixeira e, 71
Sousa, José de Vasconcellos e, 45
Spanish immigrants, 257 n. 12
Spanish language, Machado's knowledge of, 64
Spencer, Herbert, 173–74
Spiritism, 248–50
Spiritualism, 248
spirituality, Machado on, 247–50
Spivak, Gayatri Chakravorty, 146, 262 n. 4
Stam, Robert, 181–82
state
  in racial order, 6
  separation of church and, 249, 257 n. 16
statistical categories, black and multiracial individuals combined in, 149. *See also* census
Statute of Racial Equality. *See* Estatuto da Igualdade Racial
stereotypes, of African Brazilians
  in abolitionist literature, 55, 163, 166–70
  in Naturalism, 170, 171
  sexist, 168
  in tradition of opposition, 55–56
  in vernacular tradition, 46–47
Sterne, Laurence, 160, 195

stigma, in social identity, 119–20, 261 n. 7
Stonequist, Everett, 121
Stowe, Harriet Beecher, 78, 168
Stowell, Peter, 203, 265 n. 6
strategic antiessentialism, 151–52, 262 n. 9
strategic essentialism, 146, 262 n. 4, 262 n. 9
Streeter, Mark, 78–79
subjective objectivism, 203
subjective reality
  Machado's views on, 251–52
  in Modernism, 239
  in postmodernism, 240–42
subjectivism
  in Impressionism, 198–99, 203–6
  Machado's criticism of excessive, 153
  Machado's efforts to blend objectivism and, 9, 191–92, 197–98, 211
  neo-subjectivism, 198, 204, 205
  in Romantic Realism, 198–201, 210
subject-object duality, 8, 124–26, 135. *See also* duality
submission, of slaves, 89
subtext, of Machado's writings. *See also* irony
  the grotesque in, 8, 135–39
  humor in, 8, 138–39
  parody in, 8, 135, 137–38
success, public, conflict between individual morality and, 8, 124–34
sugar economy, 34
Surrealism, 206, 262 n. 2
Süssekind, Flora, 46, 172
Svevo, Italo, 265 n. 6
Symbolism, 198, 202–6, 232
syncretism, 182, 187
synecdoche, 207, 230, 234, 236
Sypher, Wylie, 266 n. 5
Syrian immigrants, 257 n. 12

tango, 142, 185, 262 n. 3
Teatro Experimental do Negro (Black Experimental Theater) (TEN), 146
Teilhard de Chardin, Pierre, 198–99
ternary racial order
  in Brazil, 10–33; abolition of slavery in, 18–21, 30–31; in Belle Époque, 26–27; challenges to, 4; elite in, 21–26; European influence on, 24–33; miscegenation in, 4, 11–14, 21; origins of, 3–4, 10–14, 21; pluralist and integrationist dynamics of, 29, 30; purity of blood statutes in, 15–17; whitening ideology in, 28–30
  in U.S., movement toward, 255 n. 2

terreiros, 33, 257 n. 17
Thackeray, William, 199
thaumaturgy, 249
theater. *See also* plays
    Black Experimental Theater, 146
    Brazilian Theater Conservatory, 78, 260 n. 1
    dance in, 186
theatrical reviews, by Machado, 77–79
third eye, 190, 264–65
Thompson, Era Bell, 2
Three Sad Races (Haberly), 7
time, in Impressionist literature, 219–22
tin masks, 86
Tiradentes (Joaquim José da Silva Xavier), 258 n. 9
To the Winner Go the Potatoes (Schwarz), 106, 111, 114, 115
Tolstoy, Leo, 226
Torres, Élcio, 259 n. 11
Torres, Rafael Pérez, 182
Tosta, Antonio, 245
tradition of opposition. *See* opposition, tradition of
"tragic mulatto" theme, 103–4
trapeze, 260 n. 3
trapezoid, 109–10, 260 n. 3
Tribuna Liberal, A (Liberal Tribune) (newspaper), 56
tricksterism, 107, 260 n. 2
Triple Alliance, 256 n. 6. *See also* Paraguayan War
Trípoli, Mailde, 102
Tristram Shandy (Sterne), 160
Trochim, Michael, 53
truth
    in Impressionism, 208
    Machado's views on, 251–52
    in Modernism, 239
    in postmodernism, 240, 241, 266 n. 2
truth-illusion theme, in Impressionism, 208
Tupí language, 164
Tupinambá (Tupí) people, 184
Turner, Victor, 123
Twain, Mark, 138–39

ufanismo, 179, 264 n. 16
Umbanda, 257 n. 15
Uncle Tom's Cabin (Stowe), 78, 168
United Black Movement, 146
United States. *See also* one-drop rule
    binary racial order in, 3–4, 255 n. 2
    cult of the primitive in, 141
    end of slavery in, 79
    interracial marriage in, 2–3, 12
    racial segregation in, 3, 149
    whitening through miscegenation in, 104
universality
    of Brazilian literature, 161–63
    Machado's search for, 8, 103, 104–5, 119, 161–63, 246–47
    in postmodernism, 241, 266 n. 2
upward mobility
    of African Brazilian writers, 73
    of African Brazilians after abolition, 30–31
    of free coloreds, 20
    of Machado's characters, 102, 103–4
    of mulattoes, 20–21, 34, 35, 73, 103–4
    in Old Republic, 34, 35, 73
    through slave ownership, 19–20, 256 n. 7
    through wealth, 110
urban areas
    expansion of, 34, 60–61
    infrastructure improvements in, 31–32
    Modernism in, 60–61
    in Old Republic, 31–32, 34
    residential patterns in, 32–33, 257 n. 14
    as setting for Romantic Realism, 201–2
urban bourgeoisie. *See also* elite
    Machado's characters drawn from, 102
    race of, 34, 102
    rise to dominance, 34
Uricoechea, Fernando, 110
Uruguay, in Paraguayan War, 256 n. 6

Vaccine Revolt of 1904, 31
Vargas, Getúlio, 143
Various Stories (Várias histórias) (Machado), 69, 184
Vasconcellos, Luís de, 45
"Verba testamentária" (Machado), 85
Veríssimo, José, 74, 155, 172
vernacular, African Brazilian
    Barreto's ambivalence toward, 58
    white *vs.* black writers' use of, 41–42
vernacular culture, African Brazilian
    dance in, 142, 185–87
    repression of, 32–33
    rise of, 141–43
vernacular tradition, of African Brazilian writers, 42–43, 44–48
Viana Filho, Luiz, 71
Vida e morte de M. J. Gonzaga de Sá (The Life and Death of M. J. Gonzaga de Sá) (Barreto), 59
"Vidros quebrados" (Machado), 84
Vieira, António, 16–17

violence
	in abolitionist literature, 168–70
	in Black Guard, 53
	by capoeira gangs, 53, 258 n. 12
	epilepsy associated with, 63
	in miscegenation, 11–12
	in Naturalism, 170, 175
Violent Slave stereotype, 168–70
"Virginius" (Machado), 84
"Visit from Alcibíades, A" ("Uma visita de Alcibíades") (Machado), 249
vítimas-algozes, As (The Victim Executioners) (Macedo), 169–70

Wacquant, Loïc, 147
Waizbort, Leopoldo, 109
waltz, 185
Wanderly, João Maurício (Baron de Contegipe), 18
Wasserman, Renata, 87, 95, 99, 110–11
Weber, Max, 108–9, 110
Week of Modern Art (1922), 262 n. 2
white. *See also* white status; whiteness
	masquerading as, 119–20
	passing as, 120, 261 nn. 7–9
white Brazilians. *See* brancos; European Brazilian(s)
white domination, in Brazil
	after abolition, shift away from, 34–35
	in colonial era, 10–14, 35
white guilt
	in abolitionist literature, 169
	in Naturalism, 56, 175
	in Romanticism, 174
white hegemony, in Brazil, 35
"white" literature, by African Brazilian writers, 42–43
"White Negritude," 42
white status
	African Brazilians with, 35
	of Machado, 73–75
	mulattoes with, 17, 73–74, 259 n. 13
	and racelessness, 119–21
white supremacy
	Afrocentrist response to, 144
	Eurocentrist origins of, 145–46
Whitehead, Alfred North, 266 n. 3
whiteness
	Afrocentrist views of, 144, 150–52
	in Brazil: black movement on contraction of, 147; continuum of, 4, 73; and passing, 261 n. 9; social advancement associated with, 35; social construction of, 17; ternary racial order of, 4
	Eurocentrist views of, 145–46
	literary, 43
	in U.S.: binary racial order of, 3–4; in one-drop rule, 2–3
whitening through immigration, 28
whitening through miscegenation
	abolitionist supporters of, 123
	European Brazilian supporters of, 36
	government support for, 143–44
	in hybridity, 183
	novels confronting, 176–80
	origins of, 28
	in scientific racism, 28, 179
	in ternary racial order, 28–30
	in U.S. *vs.* Brazil, 104
Wilber, Ken, 241
Wilcken, Patrick, 23
Wilde, Oscar, 265 n. 8
Williams, Patrick, 180–81
Winant, Howard, 6, 35
Wisnik, José, 184–85, 186, 187
witch doctors, 169, 264 n. 11
Wolff, Maria, 195
Woll, Dieter, 190, 191, 198
women
	Brazilian: dowries of, 255–56 n. 1; literacy rates of, 37
	European, in colonial Brazil, 10–11, 12, 65
women characters
	African Brazilian, in Machado's writings, 84–85
	mulatto, as tragic, 104
	slave, in abolitionist literature, 167–70
Woolf, Virginia, 206, 265 n. 6
World War I, origins of Negritude after, 140–41
writers. *See also* African Brazilian writers; European Brazilian writers; *specific writers*
	book sales and, 38
	careers of, 39
	education of, 39
	social status of, 39–40, 73
	upward mobility of, 73

yellow fever, 31
Yoshino, Kenji, 119–20
Young, Robert, 182

Zola, Émile, 193, 196, 197, 199, 200

Made in the USA
Middletown, DE
30 May 2020